MW01014174

ON SEAS
CONTESTED

ON SEAS CONTESTED

The Seven Great Navies of the Second World War

Edited by Vincent P. O'Hara,
W. David Dickson, and Richard Worth

NAVAL INSTITUTE PRESS
Annapolis, Maryland

Naval Institute Press
291 Wood Road
Annapolis, MD 21402

Library of Congress Cataloging-in-Publication Data
On seas contested : the seven great navies of the Second World War / edited by
Vincent P. O'Hara, W. David Dickson, and Richard Worth.
    p. cm.
  Includes bibliographical references and index.
  ISBN 978-1-59114-646-9 (acid-free paper) 1. World War, 1939–1945—Naval
operations. 2. Navies—History—20th century. 3. Naval history, Modern—20th
century. I. O'Hara, Vincent P., 1951– II. Dickson, W. David, 1938–
III. Worth, Richard, 1961–
  D770.O5 2010
  940.54'59—dc22

                                                  2010015566

Printed in the United States of America on acid-free paper

15 14 13 12 11 10   9 8 7 6 5 4 3 2
First printing

Book layout and composition: Alcorn Publication Design

Contents

Illustrations

Tables

Charts

Maps

Acknowledgments

On *Seas Contested* incubated for several years before beginning its slow journey toward realization. Any project with a team of three editors, eight major authors, and four contributing authors—representing an international stew of authorities—faces dangers of the "too many cooks" variety. This project, however, has led a charmed life. Courtesy and respect have been the rule. Deadlines have been cheerfully met, suggestions graciously accepted, and sacrifices willingly made in conforming to this book's structure and length requirements; this is especially noteworthy because every author had a lot more to say. Thus, first and above all else, the editors thank the authors for signing aboard and staying the course.

Special thanks go to Tom Cutler of the Naval Institute Press for believing in this project. John Jordan, Trent Hone, and Enrico Cernuschi went beyond their normal duties and provided photographs and reviews of other chapters. Friends and associates of the editors, including Mark Bailey, David Chessum, Akio Oka, Jon Parshall, and Andrew Smith, have provided input. Thanks go to Matthew Jones for his comments on the Japanese order of battle. Vincent P. O'Hara Sr. searched for photographs. The editors acknowledge the different talents each brought to this project and extend a special thank you to their families for their own contributions to this work and their patience for those times when the man of the house was off *On Seas Contested* rather than with them.

Introduction

From 1939 to 1945, history's greatest naval war raged on, above, and below every ocean and major sea. It involved thousands of vessels, tens of thousands of aircraft, and millions of men and women. It fostered technological advances, such as radar and guided weaponry, and sired revolutionary developments in naval warfare, such as carrier task forces and self-sustaining, transoceanic armadas.

Seven great navies dominated this war: the German Kriegsmarine, the Italian Regia Marina, and the Japanese Teikoku Kaigun squared off against the United States Navy, Great Britain's Royal Navy, and the Soviet Voenno-morskoi Flot. Occupying a unique position was France's Marine Nationale—first an Allied force, then an independent one, and finally Allied once again.

This naval war has generated an enormous body of literature: battles and campaigns have been described and dissected; biographies, memoirs, technical works, and specialized histories abound. However, within this literature there exist several deeply rooted problems. The first is a tendency by many authors to focus on the superficial similarities among the navies, such as warship designs, weaponry, and command structures, and to disregard their profound differences in tradition, doctrine, and national objectives. The second problem is the existence of a subtle bias permeating much of the analysis, a flaw to which the English-language readership has been especially exposed. The Anglo-American fleets were the war's largest and most successful, and many of their former officers, such as Stephen Roskill, Samuel E. Morison, and Donald McIntyre, dominated the first generation of World War II naval historians. They wrote from the perspective of their own traditions and doctrine and quite naturally scrutinized the conduct of their foes by these criteria. Representing the victorious side, the authority of their judgments has gone largely unquestioned and their heirs have tended to follow the same path of shoehorning all navies into the Anglo-American mold. Because information about the training, doctrine, structure, and goals of World War II's great navies lies buried in specialized works, unavailable in many cases to those who cannot read Japanese, German, Russian, Italian, or French, this bias has been self-perpetuating.

On Seas Contested is an international collaboration by historians fluent in their source languages who examine how each navy was organized, how it trained, how it expected to operate, and how it fought relative to its own unique doctrine and objectives. Each chapter follows a parallel structure, delivering a point-by-point evaluation of one of the war's seven major fleets to let readers quickly find, cross-reference, and compare information. The result is a valuable reference and a new vision of the naval war. The chapters cover the following topics:

I. Backstory
   A. History
   B. Mission (includes prewar plans and wartime adjustments)

II. Organization
   A. Command Structure
      1. Administration (includes appropriations)
      2. Personnel (officers/enlisted; includes demographics and training)
      3. Intelligence
   B. Doctrine
      1. Surface Warfare
      2. Aviation
      3. Antisubmarine
      4. Submarine
      5. Amphibious Operations
      6. Trade Protection
      7. Communications

III. Materiel
   A. Ships (includes order of battle)
   B. Aviation
      1. Ship-based
      2. Shore-based
   C. Weapon systems
      1. Gunnery (surface/air, includes fire control and radar)
      2. Torpedoes
      3. Antisubmarine Warfare
      4. Mines

    D. Infrastructure
        1. Logistics
        2. Bases
        3. Industry

IV. Recapitulation
    A. Wartime Evolution
    B. Summary and Assessment

On Seas Contested follows several conventions. Rather than wrestle the metric-measurement navies into the imperial system used by the U.S. Navy and the Royal Navy (or vice versa), this work does not adhere to one system or the other; appendix III provides a conversion table. All miles are nautical miles. Non-English terms are used sparingly, and ranks are expressed in English; appendix II gives a comparative table of ranks. The book is lightly footnoted, and a select bibliography lists the more important works consulted by the authors as well as additional references in English on various topics. Readers can access more complete references at the website www.onseascontested.com.

Editors
Vincent P. O'Hara, of Chula Vista, California, specializes in naval operations. His most recent book is *Struggle for the Middle Sea: Great Navies at War in the Mediterranean Theater, 1940–1945* (Naval Institute Press, 2009). W. David Dickson of Hernando, Mississippi, is an authority on naval doctrine. He is the author of *The Battle of the Philippine Sea* (Ian Allen, 1975). Richard Worth of Bolivar, Missouri, focuses on warship design and is the author of *Fleets of World War II* (Da Capo, 2001), *In the Shadow of the Battleship* (Nimble, 2008), and *Raising the Red Banner* (Spellmount: 2008).

Contributing Authors
Chapter 1, "France: The Marine Nationale," is authored by John Jordan of Portsmouth, England, an expert on the Marine Nationale, editor of the respected annual journal *Warship*, and coauthor of *French Battleships 1922–1956* (Naval Institute Press, 2009).

Chapter 2, "Germany: The Kriegsmarine," is authored by a team headed by Dr. Peter Schenk, of Berlin, a member of the Gröner Group and author of *Invasion of England: The Planning of Operation Sealion* (Conway Maritime Press, 1990) and *Kampf um die Ägäis: Die Kriegsmarine in griechischen Gewässern 1941–1945* (Mittler, 2000). He is assisted by Karsten Klein, Dr. Axel Niestlé, Dieter Thomaier, and Berndt R. Wenzel.

Chapter 3, "Great Britain: The Royal Navy," is from David Wragg of Edinburgh, Scotland, who has written more than twenty books including *The Royal Navy Handbook 1939–1945* (Sutton, 2005) and *The Fleet Air Arm Handbook 1939–45* (Sutton, 2001).

Chapter 4, "Italy: The Regia Marina," is a collaboration by Enrico Cernuschi of Pavia, Italy, author of a dozen books including *Fecero tutti il loro dovere* (Supplemento della Rivista Marittima, 2006), and Vincent P. O'Hara.

Chapter 5, "Japan: The Teikoku Kaigun," is by Mark Peattie of Stanford, California, author of *Kaigun* (Naval Institute Press, 1994) and *Sunburst: The Rise of Japanese Naval Airpower 1909–1941* (Naval Institute Press, 2002).

Chapter 6, "USA: The United States Navy," is the work of Trent Hone of Arlington, Virginia, coauthor of *Battle Line: The United States Navy 1919–1939* (Naval Institute Press, 2006) and author of several articles on the U.S. Navy's doctrinal development.

Chapter 7, "USSR: The Voenno-morskoi Flot SSSR," is authored by Stephen McLaughlin of Richmond, California, author of *Russian and Soviet Battleships* (Naval Institute Press, 2003) and a regular contributor to the annual *Warship*.

chapter one

France: The Marine Nationale

I. BACKSTORY

A. HISTORY

Traditionally France was the dominant mainland power of continental Europe. Its principal maritime opponent until the beginning of the twentieth century was Great Britain. Like Britain, France had become a world power through the acquisition of a vast overseas empire, but the French navy (latterly known as the Marine Nationale but still often referred to as "La Royale") lived in the shadow of Britain's Royal Navy, even during those periods when French armies held sway over the continent. Failure to dominate the seas thwarted broader French political ambitions.

There were periods when the Marine Nationale attempted to contest British maritime supremacy ship for ship, but in the latter half of the nineteenth century policy shifted toward a two-tier strategy: the defense of the French coasts and the prevention of blockade on the one hand, and the construction of powerful long-range cruisers which could disrupt British commerce on the high seas on the other hand. This asymmetric strategy is closely associated with the thinking of Admiral Hyacinthe Aube and a group of admirals known as the Jeune École (young school). Aube and his associates were of the view that squadrons of British battleships attempting to blockade French ports could best be countered by employing large numbers of cheap surface ships and submersibles (*la poussière navale*—literally, "naval dust") armed with torpedoes, which would operate close to their base ports under the cover of powerful batteries of coast defense guns.

These ideas became irresistible for economic reasons during the 1880s and 1890s, when the British Royal Navy of the late Victorian period became a force capable of defeating the fleets of any two of the continental powers at sea. With the Entente Cordiale of 1904, Britain became a potential ally against a newly resurgent Germany, and the Marine Nationale again began to harbor ambitions of maritime domination exercised by a conventional fleet of modern battleships. However, those ambitions were now limited to the Mediterranean, which Britain was increasingly happy to abandon to French hegemony to enable her own fleet to be concentrated in the North Sea against the German Hochseeflotte (High Seas Fleet). From 1900 onward France began to invest heavily in infrastructure in the Mediterranean, creating a base at Bizerte (Tunisia), which it envisaged would rival Toulon in size and capacity—it would be referred to by some as '*le Toulon africain*'—and which would enable France to dominate not only the western Mediterranean basin but the central and eastern Mediterranean too, while at the same time ensuring the security of sea lines of communication with her colonies in North Africa and the Middle East. The Marine Nationale followed the construction of six powerful turbine-powered "semidreadnoughts" of the *Danton* class (1906–1911) with its first dreadnoughts, the four-ship *Courbet* class laid down in 1910–1911. These were closely followed by three similar ships of the *Bretagne* class, and the Navy Act (Statut Naval) of 1912 stipulated a fleet of no fewer than twenty-eight modern battleships to be completed by 1920, together with ten scout cruisers and fifty-two oceangoing destroyers.

All this came to a halt when war broke out in August 1914. Early reverses on land led all military and industrial efforts to be refocused on the army. Work in the west coast dockyards and shipyards was restricted to the completion of those ships already launched, and the Mediterranean yards were fully occupied with the maintenance and repairs of the large French fleet operating there.

In 1918 France's naval infrastructure was in such a poor state that it was impossible to contemplate a new naval program before 1921–1922. In the interim, studies were carried out for a new generation of cruisers, flotilla craft, and submarines, and serious consideration was given to completing the battleships of the *Normandie* class launched 1914–1916 to revised plans. While these studies were under way, the Washington Conference (November 1921–February 1922) intervened. The French negotiators, who had been instructed to push for 350,000 tons with a fallback position of 280,000 tons, which would have given parity with Japan, were shocked to be offered only 175,000 tons of capital ship tonnage and parity with Italy. However, in a meeting of the Conseil de la Défense Nationale on 28 December it was proposed that France should opt for a purely defensive fleet, and it was suggested that for the not-unreasonable sum of 500 million francs per year, 330,000 tons of light surface ships and 90,000 tons of submarines could be built over a period of ten years. These views were accepted, and the two-year 1922 naval program was fixed at three 8,000-ton cruisers (*Duguay-Trouin* class), six ships of a new 2,400-ton superdestroyer type (the *contre-torpilleurs* of the *Jaguar* class), twelve large 1,500-ton fleet torpedo boats (*Bourrasque* class), six 1,150-ton patrol submarines (*Requin* class), and twelve 600-ton coastal defense submarines.

Italy was now seen as France's main rival for influence in the Mediterranean, and the naval programs of both countries proceeded in parallel throughout the 1920s, with a similar focus on 10,000-ton treaty cruisers, fast flotilla craft, and submarines, with the French maintaining a slight edge on numbers of ships laid down. This changed when in 1928 the German Republic laid down the first of three *Panzerschiffe* armed with 28-cm guns. The Marine Nationale again seriously contemplated building new battleships to counter the German ships, which led to the laying down of *Dunkerque* and her near-sister *Strasbourg* during the early 1930s. By the mid-1930s France faced a possible naval war on two fronts, against Germany and Italy, and the construction of flotilla craft and submarines was virtually halted in favor of a new program of 35,000-ton battleships. Only one of these had been launched by September 1939, when the Marine Nationale was compelled to focus building efforts on those ships that could be completed within two years; many other ships authorized in 1938 would be canceled.

D. MISSION
The key missions of the Marine Nationale were essentially defensive: to protect the coastline, ports, and harbors of metropolitan France; to secure the integrity of the colonies ("*la France d'outre-mer*"); and to protect the sea lines of communication between France and her overseas empire. Unlike the British and the Americans, the French never envisaged sending an expeditionary fleet to dominate waters far from home. All the key French naval bases were protected by powerful shore batteries, and an unusual parallel command structure meant that there were naval forces composed of torpedo boats, coastal submarines, and land-based aircraft specifically assigned to each of the five *régions maritimes* (maritime regions) for coastal defense under the command of a senior admiral whose headquarters were ashore. These were not only independent of the seagoing forces, which were generally organized as *escadres* (squadrons) under a senior admiral directly responsible at an operational level to the Admiral of the Fleet but were generally funded from a separate budget under the title *défense des côtes* (coast defense).[1]

Following the Treaty of Versailles, which neutralized the German navy, and then the Washington Conference, Italy became France's primary political and military rival and the western Mediterranean the most likely theater of operations. The cruisers and *contre-torpilleurs* laid down during the 1920s were intended to contest these seas; they were fast, lightly protected, and hard-hitting with long-range torpedoes complementing their medium-caliber guns. They could intervene against Italian forces attempting to cut lines of

PHOTO 1.1. The French battle line followed by the aircraft carrier *Béarn*, taken in the late 1930s. (John Jordan collection)

communication with French North Africa, and they could be used aggressively against Italy's own lines of communication in the central Mediterranean. The slow, elderly battle squadron, escorted by a new generation of fleet torpedo boats, served essentially as a back-up force on which the light forces could fall back for support if hard-pressed. The French, like their Italian counterparts, had reservations about the ability of these ships to operate in narrow seas dominated by increasingly capable land-based aircraft.

The rearmament of Germany, beginning with the laying down in 1928 of the first of three *Panzerschiffe*, led to a new type of ship and to a major change both in strategy and the pattern of deployments. The fast battleships *Dunkerque* and *Strasbourg* and the second generation of *contre-torpilleurs* were intended to form hunting groups to protect French shipping in the Atlantic from German surface raiders. The result was the formation of the elite Force de Raid at Brest.

The French naval situation, which had deteriorated significantly with the threat of a war on two fronts, was considerably eased by the revival of the Anglo-French entente in the two years immediately preceding the Second World War. The British took on responsibility for the North Atlantic and the eastern Mediterranean while the French had primary responsibility for the western Mediterranean and the waters off West Africa. The French provided support in the North Atlantic while British forces operated with the French in a composite antiraider force known as "Force X" out of Dakar.

When it appeared that Italy might enter the war in the early summer of 1940, a French squadron was dispatched to operate in the eastern Mediterranean under British command, and the Force de Raid moved to Mers el-Kebir in French North Africa.

When the French armies in Belgium and northern France collapsed in May–June 1940, the navy was experienced and undefeated, and eager to get to grips with the Italian Regia Marina. Italy's late entry into the war frustrated the strategy of the Marine Nationale, which never had the opportunity to carry out the primary missions for which its ships had been designed.

II. ORGANIZATION

A. COMMAND STRUCTURE
1. Administration
The French command structure had a well-conceived framework that was considerably refined during the 1930s. It was in the form of a pyramid, at the top of which was a minister for national defense, who was responsible for drawing up national objectives and putting the means for achieving those objectives at the disposal of the commanders in chief of the respective branches of the armed forces. The minister was seconded by a military chief of the General Staff for National Defense, an executive body comprising the ministers and the senior officers of the armed services charged with coordinating studies for the strategic preparation for war and for drawing up plans for operations and mobilization. There was also a purely military advisory body, the Conseil Supérieur de la Défense Nationale (CSDN), and a war committee (Comité de Guerre).

The next tier comprised the general staffs for each of the services; each service had its own advisory body, or Conseil Supérieur, at this level. The chief of the Naval General Staff (NGS) was Admiral François Darlan, who was an *ex officio* member of the CSDN and the war committee. In 1939, after Darlan had—in accordance with notoriously rigid British protocol—found himself "behind a column and a Chinese admiral" at the coronation of King George VI, Darlan created for himself the rank of Admiral of the Fleet and the position of commander in chief of the French Maritime Forces, which effectively gave him the necessary seniority to engage with the British First Sea Lord, Admiral Dudley Pound, and a greater degree of power and influence than Pound within his own country. As commander in chief of the French Maritime Forces, Darlan now exercised direct command over the commanders in chief of the operational theaters, the seagoing forces, and the naval commanding officers outside the *régions maritimes*.

Darlan's personal staff comprised Vice Admiral Maurice Le Luc and two captains, and he delegated his powers as chief of the NGS to Vice Admiral François Michelier, who was directly responsible to the navy minister. During the late 1930s a new naval command center was built outside Paris at Maintenon (near Chartres). Known as the Amirauté Française, it was generally considered a model of organization; it enjoyed excellent communications with the fleet and the regional naval headquarters and was divided internally into three main departments: intelligence, operations, and special services. It served to increase Darlan's autonomy from the other services until June 1940, when the Amirauté was evacuated to Vichy via Bordeaux. Darlan's power and influence then became incontestable when he agreed to become "number three" in Marshal Henri Pétain's newly formed national government.

In 1939 France and French North Africa were divided into five administrative sectors known as *régions maritimes* (maritime regions), each of which was commanded by a senior admiral known as the *préfet maritime*, and who was directly responsible to the navy minister:

- 1st Maritime Region: HQ Dunkerque
- 2nd Maritime Region: HQ Brest
- 3rd Maritime Region: HQ Toulon
- 4th Maritime Region: HQ Bizerte
- 5th Maritime Region: HQ Lorient

Each *préfet maritime* was responsible for coastal defense in his sector and had under his command local naval forces including torpedo boats, coastal submarines, harbor defense units, coast defense artillery and antiaircraft batteries, naval land-based aircraft for reconnaissance, bombing and torpedo attack, and fighters/bombers placed at the navy's disposition by the air force.

When war broke out in September 1939, shore-based theater commanders were appointed to oversee naval operations in the three key operational areas: the 5th Maritime Region was combined with the 2nd under Admiral West, and the 3rd and 4th regions were combined under Admiral South. Additional theater commanders were subsequently appointed to cover the South Atlantic and the West Indies. These commands were as follows:

- North (North Sea and Channel): Vice Admiral Raoul Castex, HQ Dunkerque
- West (North Atlantic): Vice Admiral Jean de Laborde, HQ Brest
- South (Mediterranean): Vice Admiral Jean-Pierre Estéva, HQ Toulon, then Bizerte
- South Atlantic: Vice Admiral Emmanuel Ollive, HQ Casablanca

- Western Atlantic: Vice Admiral Georges Robert, HQ High Commission French Antilles

The commander in chief of the Forces Navales d'Extrême-Orient (FNEO–Far East), Vice Admiral Jean Decoux, was also the theater commander.

The principal seagoing forces at the outbreak of war were the Atlantic Fleet based at Brest and the Mediterranean Fleet based at Toulon, Oran, and Bizerte. The Flotte de l'Atlantique (Atlantic Fleet), commanded by Squadron Vice Admiral Marcel Gensoul, initially comprised the 1st Squadron (Force de Raid): the two modern battleships *Dunkerque* and *Strasbourg*, a division of light cruisers, and three divisions of the latest *contre-torpilleurs*. The Flotte de la Méditerranée (Mediterranean Fleet) comprised three squadrons: the 2nd, commanded by Squadron Vice Admiral Ollive and based at Toulon, comprised the three older battleships and their fleet torpedo boat escorts; the 3rd comprised two divisions of 10,000-ton cruisers, and three divisions of *contretorpilleurs* and was likewise based at Toulon. In the build-up to the war, a second fast squadron (4th Escadre) was formed at Bizerte with a light cruiser division and three divisions of *contre-torpilleurs* with a view to threatening Italian sea lines of communication with North Africa. Placed under the command of Rear-Admiral André Marquis this grouping was known as the *Forces Légères d'Attaque* (light attack forces). All the submarines except *Surcouf* (under direct command of Darlan) and most of the older fleet torpedo boats were assigned to the *régions maritimes*.

In the seven years leading up to war, the navy's budget increased by 35 percent. Budget estimates for 1933–1939 are provided in table 1.1.

TABLE 1.1 **Budgetary Estimates for the Marine Nationale 1933–1939**

Year	Amount (million FF[a])	Percentage change
1933	4,085	
1934	4,657	+14
1935	4,386	−6
1936	3,574	−18.5
1937	4,460	+25
1938	5,713	+28
1939	5,500	−4

Note: Between 1929 and 1939 the total budget for the armed services amounted to 105,000 million FF. The distribution between the individual services was as follows: Armée de Terre, 52%; Armée de l'Air, 27%; Marine, 21%.

[a] Exchange rate 1937: 100 million FF = £0.8 million / US$3.9 million.

Sources: Espagnac du Ravay, *Vingt ans de politique navale* (1919–39) (Grenoble: B. Arthaud, 1941).

2. Personnel

French naval officers belonged to one of two branches, each of which had its own training procedures and ranking system. The *officiers de la marine* (also known as the Grand Corps) were selected for their leadership qualities and prepared for command, first as heads of the various departments on board ship, and ultimately as captains of ships or senior staff officers; their training was initially multidisciplinary, with specialization after the first four years. The *ingénieurs-mécaniciens* were the future engineering officers; one-third were selected by competition, the other two-thirds on the basis of their technical qualifications.

Officiers de la marine trained at the prestigious École Navale, which from 1935 was housed in an impressive new building at Brest with a colonnaded facade of white stone 180 m long. After two years of formal studies at the École Navale the officer cadets were sent on a ten-month world cruise (October to July each year) aboard the purpose-built training cruiser *Jeanne d'Arc*. Completed in 1931, displacing 8,000 tons, and armed with eight 155-mm guns in twin turrets, *Jeanne d'Arc* could accommodate up to 156 midshipmen. The trainee officers were then posted to a foreign station in the Far East, the Indian Ocean, or West/North Africa for a year before attending one of six specialist schools: Gunnery Officer, Communications, Torpedo, Submarine Navigation (all at Toulon), Officer of Marines (at Lorient), or Naval Aviation (at Versailles, then at Avord and Hourtin). The duration of the courses at these schools was generally three to five months, after which the trainees were accorded the rank of lieutenant and assigned to ships.

Access to the higher ranks was via a one-year course at the naval war college in Paris. Promotion to lieutenant commander was normally at age thirty-eight to forty; an officer of this rank might command a torpedo boat or a submarine, or be appointed to an admiral's staff. A strong performance at this level might lead to promotion to commander at forty-six to fifty years of age and to command of a light cruiser, while officers selected for promotion to captain might command a heavy cruiser or capital ship. From the 118 captains, 32 would be selected for promotion to rear admiral; eighteen months of sea command was a minimum requirement for promotion to this rank. Of these 32, 16 would rise to the rank of vice admiral, the highest rank available. A rear admiral might command a cruiser division or destroyer flotilla, or become the senior admiral ashore outside the five maritime regions; a vice admiral would command a squadron or an operational theater—in which case he would generally be designated *vice-amiral d'escadre* and have a fourth star on his flag—or become *préfet maritime* for one of the five regions.

Prospective engineering officers attended the École d'Application du Génie Maritime in Paris. On completion of their studies, they would, like their

counterparts at the École Navale, embark on the *Jeanne d'Arc* for a world training cruise. They would subsequently be assigned as junior engineering officers
to larger surface ships. Following promotion they would then be appointed as
head of the engineering department of smaller warships or submarines. At age
forty, the engineering officer would normally be promoted to *ingénieur principal*
(equivalent to lieutenant commander rank) and would become chief engineer
on a major ship such as a cruiser or battleship. Further promotion would lead
to shore appointments in supervisory, training, or inspection capacities.

Other ranks first received general training and were then assigned to one
of a dozen specialist schools serving the different branches, such as gunnery,
torpedo, or communications, most of which were located at Brest or Toulon.
Recruitment to the navy relied heavily on the traditional maritime regions,
particularly Brittany, where fishing continued to be a major industry. These
men were hardy, committed seamen with a natural sense of the demanding
nature of their environment. Unfortunately for the Marine Nationale, the
massive expansion of the active fleet during the late 1930s came at a time of
much-improved pay and conditions for workers in the dockyards and industries ashore, and a shortfall in recruitment had to be compensated for by large-
scale mobilization in 1939. Following the Armistice of June 1940, reservists,
who accounted for up to one-third of the crews in some ships, expected an
immediate discharge. Many were anxious to be reunited with wives and families now living in the occupied zone, from whom they were receiving no let-
ters. Potentially mutinous behavior aboard the older battleships was quashed
at Mers el-Kebir in June 1940, but the problem would reemerge in early July at
Dakar, where many crossed the gangways with their kitbags, leaving the crews
of some ships too depleted to sail.

3. Intelligence

The French naval intelligence service was known during the 1930s as EMG/2
(État-Major/Deuxième Bureau) and became FMF/2 (Forces Maritimes
Françaises/Deuxième Bureau) on the outbreak of war. It was centralized at
Maintenon, which had excellent communications both with the fleet and with
naval command centers ashore but was also represented in foreign embassies,
where naval personnel were tasked with the gathering of intelligence from
local sources. The Deuxième Bureau had acquired a high reputation for cryp-
toanalysis during the First World War and prior to the Second World War had
acquired manuals for the German army's Enigma cipher system. However, tactical intelligence appears to have relied heavily on shipboard and shore-based
reconnaissance, and radio-direction finding (RDF) techniques were likewise
generally focused on ships at sea rather than at land sites. This aspect of operations was less well developed than in the United Kingdom.

After the Armistice of 1940 the Deuxième Bureau was disbanded and replaced by a *centre d'information gouvernemental* (CIG) under Darlan. The new service was overtly tasked with rooting out communist sympathizers and resistance factions but was also secretly engaged in counterespionage operations.

During 1942 the Free French government created its own intelligence service, the Bureau Central de Renseignements et d'Action (BCRA). This organization was subsequently reformed under various different names as a result of ongoing internal political maneuvering

The focus on political as opposed to military intelligence operations after the fall of France was to have major repercussions for the navy. Shipborne and land-based reconnaissance aircraft were plentiful and of modern design, and their naval crews were well trained for operations over the water. However, the signals intelligence which would have "cued in" reconnaissance aircraft before contact was often lacking, and the French were twice surprised by hostile forces at Mers el-Kebir in June 1940, then at Dakar in September 1940, and again at Casablanca in November 1942.

B. DOCTRINE
1. Surface Warfare
With the rapid buildup of the German navy following Hitler's renunciation of the Treaty of Versailles, the surface warfare doctrine of the Marine Nationale was subjected to a major revision during the mid-1930s to take account of the two very different major operational theaters: the North Atlantic and the Mediterranean. In the North Atlantic the main threat was posed by German surface raiders—there was as yet no U-boat fleet worthy of consideration, although the German signature to the League of Nations protocol prohibiting unrestricted warfare against merchant shipping did little to allay French fears for the longer term. The Atlantic Squadron (later Fleet) was built around the two new fast battleships *Dunkerque* and *Strasbourg*, three modern light cruisers, and eight of the latest *contre-torpilleurs* of the *Mogador* and *Le Fantasque* classes, which were tasked with scouting for the new battleships and designed with North Atlantic operations in mind. The battleships and light cruisers were each designed to operate three modern Loire 130 reconnaissance floatplanes, which would enable a hunting group formed from the elite Force de Raid to locate its prey. The 330-mm guns of the battleships had a 35-degree angle of elevation and a maximum range of 41,700 m, and were all mounted forward to enable the ships to engage effectively in a stern chase.

The relatively confined waters of the western and central Mediterranean required different ships and different tactics. Operations were expected to be of short duration, comprising fleeting engagements characterized by high-speed maneuvers: raids on enemy shipping and coasts, and interventions to prevent similar raids by enemy forces. The design of the ships built for these purposes during the 1920s and 1930s emphasized high performance (in particular speed and gun power) at the expense of range and endurance. At the center of these forces were the 10,000-ton cruisers and the modern light cruisers, operating in three-ship divisions. The powerful *contre-torpilleurs*, most of which were armed with 138-mm guns, were intended for operations on the flank. When operating in support of the fleet, their principal task was to penetrate the outer screen of an enemy force and transmit information on its composition, heading, and so forth while at the same time providing an impenetrable screen for friendly cruiser and battle divisions. Like the cruiser divisions, the *contre-torpilleurs* operated in tactical divisions of three ships and by 1939 were equipped with shells containing colored dye that enabled each ship to spot its own fall of shot.

With the commissioning of *Dunkerque* and *Strasbourg* during the late 1930s the older battle division, comprising the three *Bretagne*-class ships, transferred from the Atlantic to the Mediterranean. Although slow and outdated, they provided a strong core on which the light forces could fall back if hard-pressed. The *Bretagnes* were to be replaced by fast modern 35,000-ton units from 1940, and a new generation of fleet torpedo boats to accompany them was already on the stocks. Had it been completed, the new battle fleet would undoubtedly have played a much more dynamic and focal role in French surface warfare tactics in the Mediterranean.

2. Aviation

The French were entitled to 60,000 tons of carrier construction under the terms of the Washington Treaty and originally intended to build up to this level. One of the incomplete battleships of the *Normandie* class, *Béarn*, was duly converted into a forty-plane carrier with a function similar to that of contemporary British carriers. Operating in conjunction with the battle fleet, she was to provide fighters for fleet air defense, two- or three-seat aircraft for reconnaissance and spotting, and a torpedo attack capability to slow the enemy fleet and bring it to battle. Additional purpose-built ships of 18,000–20,000 tons were projected, but these failed to materialize, first for budgetary reasons and then because of the formation of the Air Ministry in 1928, which acquired almost total control of naval air assets. The carrier also lost favor as a fleet unit with the advent of more capable land-based aircraft during the 1930s, and there were influential officers in the Marine Nationale who came to believe that carrier operations in the western Mediterranean were no longer feasible, and that carriers were useful only for projecting air power into the more open expanses of the North Atlantic.

By the late 1930s, the *Béarn* was seriously in need of replacement, and although modernized in 1935 and redeployed to Brest, she was too slow to operate with the new fast battleships. The first of two modern 18,000-ton fleet carriers was laid down in 1938 at St. Nazaire, and a new generation of monoplane fighter and bomber aircraft was ordered, some from the United States. *Béarn's* air squadrons were disembarked and were in the process of being reequipped in 1939 when war broke out. The newly equipped air squadrons remained ashore; they almost certainly would have operated from *Béarn* only for deck trials and work-up before being embarked in the new carrier *Joffre* in 1942.

As a cheaper alternative to the fully fledged carrier, the French developed the concept of the *transport d'aviation*, a 10,000-ton mobile seaplane base capable of transporting and operating squadrons of large seaplanes armed with torpedoes handled by cranes and launched from the surface and smaller reconnaissance floatplanes and float fighters launched by catapult. Although regarded as successful in her primary role, *Commandant Teste* was considered too slow and too vulnerable to operate with the fleet, and only a single unit was completed. In December 1939 her air group was redeployed ashore, and the ship was used as an aircraft transport between France and North Africa.

The navy regained control of naval aviation in 1936. Besides embarked aircraft, the navy operated large numbers of reconnaissance aircraft from its own shore bases, and new torpedo strike aircraft became available from mid-1939.

3. Antisubmarine

In the early years following the First World War, the Marine Nationale accorded antisubmarine (A/S) warfare the same degree of priority as did the British Royal Navy. In 1918, 136 A/S depth-charge throwers (DCT) were purchased from Thornycroft, and programs were begun to develop effective underwater sensors. The flotilla craft of the 1922 naval program all had space provided for retractable ultrasonic detection devices and their associated consoles, and were designed to accommodate stern-launched 200-kg depth charges, four DCTs, and Italian Ginocchio towed antisubmarine torpedoes. To accommodate the latter and their associated handling gear on the quarter-deck, the depth charges were carried in two stern tunnels and launched using a continuous chain mechanism at the rate of one every six seconds. These early units of the *Jaguar* and *Bourrasque* classes and their immediate successors carried twelve depth charges in the two tunnels, together with eight and four reloads, respectively, in a below-decks magazine aft. Later *contre-torpilleurs* had sixteen in the tunnels with eight reloads.

Doctrine stipulated that the ship turn toward the last known position of the submarine contact and release four 200-kg depth charges set to a depth of 50 m. In theory this created a "killing ground" 240 m long and 60 m wide; this band could be widened if depth charge throwers were also used. For the second pass, the depth setting was to be 100 m. Sufficient charges were provided for between four and six passes, depending on the size of the ship.

Two factors undermined these ambitious plans. All of the early interwar flotilla craft suffered from topweight and stability problems. Plans to fit four Thornycroft DCTs were quickly abandoned; some ships received two, but most had only the deck reinforcements necessary for wartime installation. The Ginocchio torpedoes and their handling gear also generated additional top weight, and technical problems with these devices meant that their development was suspended in 1933.

The other even more important factor was the failure to develop a successful underwater sensor. From the late 1920s to 1939 the French experimented with a variety of ultrasonic "pingers" and passive hydrophone arrays without ever producing a sensor that could reliably detect a submarine while the ship was under way. In 1939 some fleet torpedo boats were fitted with the French-developed SS 1 ultrasonic device, for which two torpedoes had to be landed as compensation. Installation in other ships was suspended in March 1940 when the SS 1 proved ineffectual. Fortunately a technology exchange with Britain during 1939 resulted in access to the infinitely more capable British Asdic in return for French shell colorant technology. Sixteen sets were ordered in May 1939, and delivery began in August; a further fifty sets were ordered in October. In French service the device was known as Alpha, but the slow rate of delivery (initially two per month) and the extensive modifications that had to be carried out by the dockyards meant that no ships were reequipped before the Armistice.

At the same time, first 50 and then 150 of the latest Thornycroft DCTs were ordered for installation on auxiliaries and the older flotilla craft. The fleet torpedo boats of the *Bourrasque* and *L'Adroit* classes were each to have received two of these DCTs and their associated ready-use racks in place of the after gun mounting. However, as with Asdic, not all of the orders were fulfilled and few ships were modified prior to June 1940.

4. Submarine

The French showed an early commitment to the submersible torpedo boat, which they considered ideally suited to harbor defense and for use against surface ships in confined waters. However, from the plethora of experimental designs, not a single successful production boat emerged, and in the aftermath of the First World War, the Comission d'Etudes Pratiques des Sous-Marins (CEPSM) conducted a thorough evaluation of existing types and future requirements, which included a study of the German U-boats that had made such a profound impression in 1917–1918. The first fruits of this study were a large oceangoing patrol submarine modeled on the German Ms Type and a 600-tonne coastal defense submarine based on the German UB-III. The 600-tonne type spawned successors of the 630-tonne and *Amirauté* types, all of which were funded under the *défense des côtes* budget, and a series of small minelayers. The patrol submarines of the *Requin* class would be succeeded by a fast fleet submarine, the 1,500-tonne type, intended to scout for the battle fleet and to attack enemy warships. The two lead boats had a maximum speed on the surface of only seventeen knots, but in later units this was increased to nineteen to twenty knots.

The coastal submarines were grouped in divisions of four, and the divisions distributed among the four major Régions Maritimes, including North Africa. They were to be deployed in adjacent, non-overlapping patrol areas off the ports and harbors of those regions outside the protective minefields and antisubmarine nets. In this role they constituted the outer layer of a fixed static defense. Their minelaying counterparts were intended for offensive minelaying in the Mediterranean's shallow waters.

The fleet submarines of the 1,500-tonne type, which were likewise grouped in divisions of four, were intended to operate in support of the seagoing surface forces, scouting for them and searching for the opportunity to make attacks on the enemy fleet. As the British and the Americans had found with their own attempts at a fleet submarine, communications between the submarines and friendly surface units were problematic, and station keeping for submarines running on the surface in close proximity to the fleet was potentially hazardous. While seventeen to twenty knots was in theory adequate for maneuvering close to a battle fleet with a cruising speed of only fourteen or fifteen knots, the advent of the fast battleship during the 1930s made such combined operations unlikely. The 1,500-tonne boats were therefore used as conventional patrol submarines during the Second World War.

The French subscribed to the League of Nations protocol restricting the employment of submarines against merchant shipping, and the single French cruiser submarine, the 3,300-ton *Surcouf*, was designed to conform with international law; she had additional accommodation for forty prisoners.

5. Amphibious Operations

The French had a colonial empire that covered the globe and had an extensive network of overseas bases. It was envisaged that local colonial forces would be reinforced in an emergency by troops carried by liners requisitioned for the purpose, or by warships. The Marine Nationale operated a number of "colonial sloops," heavily armed to give fire support to the troops ashore and with accommodation for a large detachment of *fusiliers marins*, equivalent to the Royal Navy's marines, which would be used to stiffen the resistance of the colonial troops to any hostile attack.

Amphibious operations were relatively undeveloped, and there were no specialized amphibious craft as in other navies. Troops were generally disembarked at pierheads and jetties, or sent ashore in boats. The only attempted opposed landing was at Dakar by the Free French forces, and the troops were embarked either in sloops (*fusiliers marins*) or in converted troopships (regular army). The landing failed due to lack of suitable equipment and doctrine.

6. Trade Protection

In the buildup to war in 1939 it was agreed with the Royal Navy that the Marine Nationale would have primary responsibility for the English Channel, the waters between West Africa and the Cape Verde Islands, and the western Mediterranean. Cargo vessels and troopships generally sailed in convoys of half a dozen ships, with a close escort of older destroyers, torpedo boats, or sloops. All of these types were found to lack the endurance necessary for escort work, particularly if evasive measures such as zigzagging were employed, and the light torpedo boats, which had been designed for coastal defense, had poor antisubmarine warfare (ASW) capabilities.

Had Italy entered the conflict earlier, the convoys in the western Mediterranean would have been supported by fast groupings of cruisers and *contre-torpilleurs*, which would have intervened if the convoys were attacked by the fast light forces of the enemy.

7. Communications

In wartime, ships at sea were expected to maintain radio silence where possible to minimize the possibility of disclosing their position to the enemy. Divisions were maneuvered using the traditional technique of hoisting signal flags, and instructions were transmitted within visual range using signal projectors. Embarked aircraft radioed sighting information to the launch ship, whereas shore-based reconnaissance planes reported to a headquarters ashore, which maintained an overall tactical plot and retransmitted relevant data to the sea-based commander's flagship.

In the event of the breakdown of fire control aboard one ship of a division, range data could be transmitted from the other ships via concentration dials as in the Royal Navy. These were removed from 1940 as VHF (very high frequency) short-range radio became more widely available.

III. MATERIEL

A. SHIPS

In 1939 all that remained of the fleet that served in the Great War were the three "super-dreadnoughts" of the *Bretagne* class, which had been partially modernized and were still regarded as first-line units, and the two older battleships of the *Courbet* class, now used only for training. From 1922 onward, under the driving force of Navy minister Georges Leygues, a completely new fleet of modern surface ships and submarines had been constructed that, on paper at least, could rival any in Europe. The major units are outlined in table 1.2.

TABLE 1.2 Major Units on 3 September 1939

	Units as of 3 Sep 1939	Units building	Units authorized
Battleships	5	3	1
Aircraft carriers	1	1	1
Heavy cruisers	7		
Light cruisers	12	1	2
Contre-torpilleurs	32		4
Fleet torpedo boats	26	6	6
Light torpedo boats	12	4	10
Colonial sloops	7	2	1
Cruiser submarine	1		
Fleet/patrol submarines	39	3	2
Coastal submarines[a]	40	8	12

[a] Includes minelaying submarines.

The *Bretagne* class had been extensively modernized during the 1920s: the elevation of their main guns had been increased and director control provided for the main and secondary batteries; they also received high-angle (HA) guns to provide antiair (AA) capability, and their coal-fired boilers were replaced by modern oil-fired units. However, there was a limit to what could be done with such a dated design; by 1939 standards, the *Bretagne* class was slow and had inadequate horizontal protection against plunging shells.

The recently completed *Dunkerque* and *Strasbourg* were very different ships. Inspired by the early British interwar designs, they mounted their eight 330-mm guns in two quadruple turrets forward, and their "all-or-nothing" protection scheme featured a relatively short citadel protected by heavy armor: there were an armored belt 225-mm thick (increased to 280-mm in *Strasbourg*) and a 115–125-mm main armored deck backed up by a 40-mm "splinter deck" beneath. Designed to hunt down the German *Panzerschiffe*, they were as fast as the British battle cruisers, with a top speed of 29.5 knots. However, their dual-purpose secondary battery of 130-mm (5.1-inch) guns in quadruple and twin mountings was not a success; training and elevation speeds were too slow to be effective against modern aircraft, and the 130-mm shell was too light to stop a destroyer.

The new 35,000-ton battleships of the *Richelieu* class were enlarged *Dunkerques*, with 380-mm guns and heavier armor. They were initially to have had a dual-purpose secondary battery of fifteen 152-mm (6-inch) guns in triple turrets, but while the first ship was fitting out it was decided to substitute twelve 100-mm HA guns in twin mountings for the two amidships 152-mm turrets. Maximum speed was thirty-two knots, making them even faster than the latest Italian battleships of the *Littorio* class. *Richelieu* was nearing completion when she was compelled to flee to Dakar in June 1940; her sister *Jean Bart* was still some twelve months away from completion when she too sailed for North Africa, remaining at Casablanca until August 1945. Construction of a third ship, *Clemenceau*, was abandoned.

The first cruisers built for the Marine Nationale during the interwar period were the three units of the *Duguay-Trouin* class. They were fast, modern ships of 8,000 tons armed with eight 155-mm guns in twin, power-operated turrets, but they were virtually unprotected. When the Washington Treaty established the upper limit for cruisers at 10,000 tons with 8-inch guns, the French opted initially for an enlarged *Duguay-Trouin* armed with eight 8-inch guns in twin turrets. Like their predecessors, the two ships of the *Duquesne* class were fast (thirty-four knots designed) but virtually unarmored, relying for their survival on tight compartmentalization with only light splinter protection for their magazines and turrets. They were followed by a series of four "treaty" cruisers of the *Suffren* type, each of which had improved protection at the expense of two knots in speed. The last of France's treaty cruisers, *Algérie*, was of a radically different design and was much more heavily protected, with a 110-mm armored belt and an 80-mm armored deck. She also carried a much more powerful dual-purpose secondary battery of twelve 100-mm guns in twin mountings.

Although France failed to ratify the London Treaty of 1930, the next class of cruisers closely followed its provisions. The six ships of the 7,600-ton *La Galissonnière* class were armed with nine 152-mm guns in triple turrets, and protection was almost on a par with *Algérie*. They proved very successful and were to have been followed by three improved ships of the *De Grasse* class, only the first of which had been laid down by the outbreak of war. The French also completed two minelaying cruisers during the early 1930s: the *Pluton* and the *Émile Bertin*, and a purpose-built training cruiser, the *Jeanne d'Arc*.

The surface warship type with which the Marine Nationale came to be most closely associated during the interwar period was the *contre-torpilleur*. In essence, the *contre-torpilleurs* were large, powerfully armed but lightly built

PHOTO 1.2. *L'Indomptable*, one of the *Le Malin* class of *contre-torpilleurs*, launched in 1933 and scuttled nine years later at Toulon. The *contre-torpilleurs* saw extensive service during the war, fighting the Germans, Italians, British, and Americans. (The Boris Lemachko Collection)

superdestroyers. Operating in homogeneous three-ship divisions, their missions were to screen and scout for the battle fleet, to protect France's sea lines of communication in the western Mediterranean, and to attack those of Italy in the central Mediterranean. The first six ships of the *Jaguar* class were armed with five 130-mm guns in single open mountings and six 550-mm (21.7-inch) torpedo tubes in two triple centerline mountings; in later units the 130-mm was replaced by progressively improved models of the heavier 138.6-mm (5.45-inch) gun, and the number of torpedo tubes was increased to nine. The *contre-torpilleurs* were characterized by their high speed: the *Jaguars* were designed for 35.5 knots, the *Le Fantasques* for thirty-seven knots. These speeds were much exceeded on trials, with *Le Terrible* attaining almost forty-three knots; even in fully loaded wartime condition, a three-ship division could comfortably maintain thirty-four knots in favorable sea conditions.

Thirty *contre-torpilleurs* of the above types were completed between 1927 and 1936. The last of the *contre-torpilleurs*, the *Mogador* and *Volta*, were designed to operate with *Dunkerque* and *Strasbourg* in the broader swells of the Atlantic. Although they were larger than their predecessors and more robustly built, their twin power-operated 138-mm mountings never worked properly despite repeated modifications to their reloading systems. Four slightly modified ships of the class had been authorized 1938–1939 but were cancelled before work could begin.

The third type of surface ship in the 1922 program was a destroyer (*torpilleur d'escadre*—literally, "fleet torpedo boat") intended to accompany the battle fleet. Influenced by the British Modified "W" class of 1918, the design featured the heaviest guns of any contemporary destroyer. In fact, the armament was only one gun short of that of the contemporary *contre-torpilleurs* of the *Jaguar* class. Twelve ships of the *Bourrasque* class were followed by fourteen of the *L'Adroit* class. Most failed to make their modest designed speed of thirty-three knots, endurance was poor, and they suffered from topweight problems. At the beginning of the Second World War, they disembarked two of their six torpedoes and lost the no. 4 gun as compensation for additional depth charge throwers.

When the Marine Nationale embarked on the construction of fast battleships, it became clear that the fleet torpedo boats designed during the 1920s were too slow to accompany them, and a new high-speed design modeled on the latest *contre-torpilleurs* was adopted. The *Le Hardi* class were armed with six 130-mm guns in twin mountings and seven 550-mm torpedo tubes; they had a designed speed of thirty-seven knots, which was exceeded on trials. Eleven ships had been laid down by the outbreak of war, and an additional five authorized. Only the lead ship had run trials by the time of the Armistice, but six others were rushed to completion and entered service during 1940–1941.

In September 1939 the French submarine fleet was one of the largest in the world and was considered by many in the Marine Nationale to be its most powerful and influential arm. Nine oceangoing boats of the *Requin* class were followed by thirty fleet submarines of the 1,500-tonne type, with progressive technical improvements to each subgroup; the last six units (*Agosta* subgroup) were capable of twenty knots on the surface. The twelve coastal submarines of the 600-tonne type were followed by sixteen boats of an improved 630-tonne type, then by six boats built to a standardized Service Technique des Constructions Navales (STCN) design.[2] In parallel with the coastal boats, a class of six coastal minelayers (*Saphir* class), armed with thirty-two Hautter-Sarlé HS4 mines in vertical external tubes, was built at the rate of one per year. All of these designs featured trainable twin, triple, and even quadruple external torpedo tubes, which made possible large torpedo salvos and considerable flexibility in firing angles; most carried a mix of the powerful, long-range 550-mm torpedo and a smaller 400-mm torpedo for use against escorts and targets of opportunity.

The submarine cruiser *Surcouf* was authorized under the 1926 program and was to have been the first of six units intended for the protection of French sea communications in distant waters and for commerce raiding. Armed with 203-mm (8-inch) guns in a rotating twin turret and equipped with a light reconnaissance aircraft carried in a watertight hangar, *Surcouf* was one of the technological wonders of her age; in service, she proved conceptually defective and technically unreliable.

The new generation of French submarines authorized from 1934 comprised two types: a large 1,800-ton fleet boat with a surface speed of twenty-two knots (*Roland-Morillot* class), and an enlarged coastal type capable of seagoing patrol (*Aurore* class). There was also to be a coastal minelayer of an improved *Saphir* type. None of these submarines was commissioned before the outbreak of war, and only *Aurore* was completed before the Armistice of June 1940.

In September 1939 the main surface forces of the Marine Nationale were organized as follows:

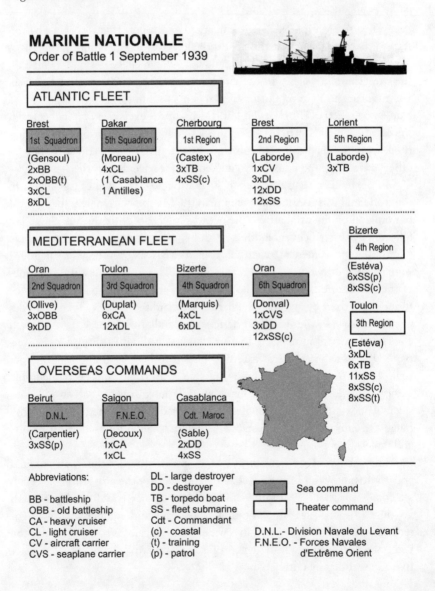

MARINE NATIONALE
Order of Battle 1 September 1939

ATLANTIC FLEET

Brest	Dakar	Cherbourg	Brest	Lorient
1st Squadron	5th Squadron	1st Region	2nd Region	5th Region
(Gensoul)	(Moreau)	(Castex)	(Laborde)	(Laborde)
2xBB	4xCL	3xTB	1xCV	3xTB
2xOBB(t)	(1 Casablanca	4xSS(c)	3xDL	
3xCL	1 Antilles)		12xDD	
8xDL			12xSS	

MEDITERRANEAN FLEET

Oran	Toulon	Bizerte	Oran	Bizerte
				4th Region
2nd Squadron	3rd Squadron	4th Squadron	6th Squadron	(Estéva)
(Ollive)	(Duplat)	(Marquis)	(Donval)	6xSS(p)
3xOBB	6xCA	4xCL	1xCVS	8xSS(c)
9xDD	12xDL	6xDL	3xDD	
			12xSS(c)	Toulon
				3th Region
				(Estéva)
				3xDL
				6xTB
				11xSS
				8xSS(c)
				8xSS(t)

OVERSEAS COMMANDS

Beirut	Saigon	Casablanca
D.N.L.	F.N.E.O.	Cdt. Maroc
(Carpentier)	(Decoux)	(Sable)
3xSS(p)	1xCA	2xDD
	1xCL	4xSS

Abbreviations:

	DL - large destroyer	
	DD - destroyer	▨ Sea command
BB - battleship	TB - torpedo boat	
OBB - old battleship	SS - fleet submarine	☐ Theater command
CA - heavy cruiser	Cdt - Commandant	
CL - light cruiser	(c) - coastal	D.N.L.- Division Navale du Levant
CV - aircraft carrier	(t) - training	F.N.E.O. - Forces Navales
CVS - seaplane carrier	(p) - patrol	d'Extrême Orient

B. AVIATION

1. Ship-based

The Marine Nationale's solitary carrier, *Béarn*, was of limited military value in 1939; she was considered too vulnerable to operate against modern Italian land-based aircraft in the Mediterranean and too slow to operate with the Force de Raid in the North Atlantic. Her air groups were disembarked the day after war broke out, and during early 1940 she was used first to train Navy pilots in the Mediterranean and then as a transport for gold and aircraft between France and Canada. Her two nine-plane fighter squadrons (AC1/2) were still equipped with the obsolescent Dewoitine 376 high-wing monoplane and were assigned to shore bases at Calais and Hyères.[3] The two attack squadrons (AB1/2) were being reequipped with American Vought 156F and Loire-Nieuport 401 dive bombers, respectively, and following landing trials in early 1940 these too were based ashore ready for the completion of the new carrier *Joffre*, the construction of which was abandoned in June 1940.

Shortly before the outbreak of war, the air group of the aviation transport *Commandant Teste* was embarked and she was dispatched to Oran as part of the newly formed 6e Escadre, which was tasked with cooperating with the British at Gibraltar in the western Mediterranean. However, of her two embarked squadrons, HB1, with the new and impressive Laté 298 float torpedo-bomber, would be based on Arzew, and the surveillance squadron HS1, with six Loire 130s, followed shortly afterward.

2. Shore-based

In 1936 the Marine Nationale regained control of its shore-based naval air-craft from the Air Ministry. The shore-based *aéronavale* squadrons were pre-dominantly of two types: long-range maritime patrol (designation "E") and surveillance ("S"). There were also two squadrons of torpedo-bomber sea-planes ("B") at Berre in the south of France.

The land-based squadrons generally comprised six aircraft and were dis-tributed among the five maritime regions, this attribution being part of the squadron designation for surveillance aircraft (1S2 = the second surveillance squadron of the 1st Maritime Region). The standard allocation was a single patrol squadron and two squadrons of surveillance aircraft to each region. The 4th Maritime Region, which covered the whole of French North Africa, had three patrol squadrons, and the 3rd Maritime Region, which was responsible for the narrow waters between France and Italy in the western Mediterranean, had six surveillance squadrons, one of which was based in Corsica. There were also small detachments of patrol/surveillance aircraft in French West Africa, the West Indies, and the Pacific islands.

During the late 1930s the Marine Nationale invested heavily in surveillance and patrol aircraft. Some 125 of the excellent Loire 130 seaplanes were built, and as these were made available to battleships and cruisers, the older but equally useful GL 812 models were transferred to the shore-based squadrons. Older types such as the CAMS 37 and 55 models were more vulnerable to modern fighters, as were the large seaplanes used for long-range patrol.

C. WEAPON SYSTEMS
1. Gunnery
French heavy guns, which had many component parts, continued to be manufactured using a mix of traditional and modern technology. Upward-opening screw breechblocks were a French innovation. In the lighter guns, the German-pattern sliding breech was adopted from the late 1920s, resulting in a much higher rate of fire than for earlier models. Muzzle velocities in the turret-mounted guns tended to be high for a given shell weight; however, the French were not as ambitious as the Italians in this respect, and most destroyer and AA guns had a relatively low muzzle velocity.[4]

French gun mountings varied considerably in design. They were usually powered electrically; later installations had remote power control for training and elevation, but the remote power control systems developed were not successful in service, and they were often switched off or even removed. For the new generation of battleships, quadruple turrets were favored for both the main and secondary batteries largely because of the economies they provided in weight of armor and centerline space. Vulnerability to damage was reduced by dividing each quadruple turret into two independent gun houses with a central 40- or 45-mm bulkhead of special steel. Quadruple turrets were less successful in the antiaircraft role, which favored lightweight gun mountings with high training and elevation speeds.

The complexity of the replenishment and loading mechanisms adopted for many of the turret-mounted guns was a major issue in some designs. The Marine Nationale opted for dual-purpose quadruple 130-mm and triple 152-mm guns for the new generation of battleships, but both of these weapons proved difficult to load at high angles of elevation (due in part to underpowered rammers), and there were frequent breakdowns and jams. Even worse were the 138.6-mm twin gun mountings of the *Mogadors*, the loading mechanisms of which had originally been designed for 130-mm guns firing fixed ammunition. Designed for a firing cycle of ten rounds per gun per minute, they attained only three or four rounds per gun per minute on trials; even after two years of extensive modification, the twin mounting delivered only the same amount of ordnance as the single gun of the *Le Fantasque* class.

PHOTO 1.3. *Le Fantasque* during the war, showing her twin 37-mm model 1933 antiaircraft guns. (John Jordan collection)

The 90-mm and 100-mm HA guns employed for the secondary batteries of the cruisers were much more successful and proved robust and reliable;
they subsequently displaced the two amidships 152-mm dual-purpose mountings on *Richelieu* and *Jean Bart*. However, the 37-mm light AA weapons (single Mle 1925 and twin Mle 1933) had too slow a rate of fire to be effective
against modern aircraft, and the 13.2-mm Hotchkiss machine gun (in twin
and quad mountings) was too lightweight to do serious damage and lacked
sufficient range. New, more advanced 37-mm and 25-mm models were under

development when war broke out in 1939, but the former never entered production and the latter became widely available only in 1942.

French shell (armor-piercing [AP] only for the big guns, semi-armor-piercing and high explosive for the medium-caliber guns) was generally well designed, and by 1939 shells with dye bags inside the ballistic cap were coming into service, enabling ships operating in divisions of three to identify their shell splashes by color—generally white/yellow, red, and green. A design fault in the base of the early 380-mm AP shells, which were intended to accommodate canisters of toxic gas, resulted in premature detonation of the shell in three of the four guns in turret II of *Richelieu* at Dakar in September 1940, wrecking the guns. This problem was subsequently resolved by strengthening the base of the shell. Because of a shortage of charges, SD19 propellant intended for *Dunkerque* and *Strasbourg* was remanufactured for *Richelieu* at Dakar, but the only problem resulting from this was a reduction in muzzle velocity beyond what had been anticipated.

A problem experienced with the large- and medium-caliber guns in quadruple turrets was dispersion caused by gun blast interference. This was only really resolved postwar, when delay coils were fitted to the outer guns.

The French battleships and cruisers laid down before 1914 had been designed to fight at relatively short battle ranges. Modern coincidence rangefinders were purchased from the British company Barr & Stroud during the early part of the war, but the fire-control systems necessary for long-range fire were not developed, and in 1918 the Marine Nationale found itself lagging some way behind the Royal Navy in this respect. *Bretagne* trialed a British Vickers fire-control director from 1920, and this led to the development of a model of French design and manufacture by St. Chamond-Granat. This was subsequently fitted in all of the older battleships and was the basis of the systems that equipped the battleships of the new generation.

French industry also made considerable progress in the development of optical rangefinders during the 1920s. SOM (Société d'Optique et de Méchanique de Haute Précision) produced coincidence rangefinders with three- or four-meter bases for the new generation of flotilla craft, and by the mid-1930s OPL (Optique de Précision Levallois-Perret) had developed an extensive range of stereoscopic rangefinders. The new battleships had 12-m (14-m in the *Richelieu* class) and 8-m OPL rangefinders for their main armament and 6-m and 5-m OPL rangefinders (8-m and 6-m in the *Richelieu* class) for their secondary guns. The latest *contre-torpilleurs* of the *Le Fantasque* and *Mogador* classes had 5-m and 4-m models.

The French were aware of British developments in radar through their close contacts 1939–1940, but it was the spring of 1942 before surveillance radars of indigenous design and manufacture (*détecteur électro-magnétique*, or

DEM) were installed in major units. In *Strasbourg*, which received the proto-type model, four small rectangular antennae were fitted atop the main yards projecting at 45 degrees from the tower; the starboard forward and port after antennae were for transmission, the opposite pair for reception. Trials were cut short by events, but early tests indicated a detection range against aircraft of 50 km with a bearing accuracy of ±1 degree and a range accuracy of ±50 m under favorable conditions.

2. Torpedoes

The standard French torpedo of the Great War was a 450-mm model using wet-heater propulsion; it had a warhead of 144 kg and a range of only 3,000 m at thirty knots. Following the end of the conflict, the French immediately embarked on the design of larger, more powerful 550-mm torpedoes capable of being fired at long range. The Model 1919D, 8.2-m long with a 238/250-kg picric acid war-head, had a range of 6,000 m at thirty-five knots and 14,000 m at twenty-five knots. Its much-improved successor, the Model 1923DT, which had an alcohol-fueled four-cylinder radial engine, was 8.6 m long with a 308-kg TNT warhead, and had a range of 9,000 m at thirty-nine knots and 13,000 m at thirty-five knots. This latter model would be carried by all the French flotilla craft built between the wars.

The standard submarine torpedo between the wars was the 550-mm Mle 1924V, which was developed simultaneously with the Mle 1923DT and had the same propulsion system but at 6.6 m was shorter and optimized for speed rather than long range: the early variants had a range of 3,000 m at forty-four knots, 7,000 m at thirty-five knots; in later variants range was increased. During the late 1920s a smaller torpedo with an advanced propulsion system using alcohol injection, the 400-mm Mle 1926V, entered service. Carried in conjunction with the 550-mm, it was intended for small escorts and targets of opportunity. With a TNT warhead of 144 kg, the 400-mm Mle 1926V had a range of 1,400 m at forty-four knots (in later variants range was increased first to 1,800 m, then to 2,000 m). A Mle 1926W variant was developed for motor torpedo boats, and a Mle 1926DA model for air drop.

3. Antisubmarine Warfare

The standard French depth charge was the Guiraud Mle 1922, which had a 200-kg TNT charge. On the *contre-torpilleurs* and the fleet torpedo boats depth charges were stowed in rows of six or eight in twin tunnels located beneath the quarterdeck, and discharged via square stern apertures using a continuous chain mechanism driven by electric motors. Depth settings were 30, 50, 75, or 100 m, with 50 m and 100 m being the most commonly used. The heavy depth charges were sometimes complemented in wartime by lightweight 35-kg depth charges carried in racks on the quarterdeck and discharged manually; these were also fitted in cruisers and light patrol craft.

To create a broader depth charge pattern, depth charge throwers (DCT) were used, and although many of these were not installed in peacetime due to topweight problems, they were again embarked in 1939–1940. There were two models: a British Thornycroft 240-mm model dating from 1918, and the lighter French 120-mm Mle 1928. Both launched depth charges with a 100-kg charge, the British model to a distance of 60 m, the Mle 1928 to a distance of 250 m. The Mle 1928 could launch two depth charges per minute, and there was an adjacent rack with a single reload; additional depth charges were stowed in a below-decks magazine aft.

During the late 1920s the Marine Nationale experimented with two models of the Italian Ginocchio towed antisubmarine torpedo: a medium type weighing 62 kg that was towed at a depth of 15–37 m; and a heavier type weighing 75.5 kg with a maximum towing depth of 53 m; both types had a 30-kg warhead. Trials with the torpedoes were unsuccessful and, although revived 1939–1940, the Ginocchio was never fitted operationally.

There was provision for ultrasonic submarine detection apparatus on all the French interwar flotilla craft and cruisers, but although many systems were developed and tested, none was successful. The only homegrown model to enter service was the SS 1, which was fitted to a number of fleet torpedo boats in 1939–1940. It too was a failure, and the Marine Nationale was compelled to purchase the British Asdic 128; in French service it became "Alpha," but few models were delivered prior to June 1940, and none was fitted by the time of the Armistice.

4. Mines

There were two main types of mine designed to be laid by surface ships: the Hautter-Sarlé H5 and the Bréguet B4; both were traditional moored contact mines. The Hautter-Sarlé H5, which entered service in 1928, had an overall weight of 1,160 kg and a 220-kg TNT charge. The cruiser minelayer *Pluton* was designed to carry 220 (250 max.) on four upper-deck rails, each 192-m long; the mines were launched over the stern via angled ramps using continuous chains powered by electric motors. The HS4 mine carried by the minelaying submarines of the *Saphir* class was similar; 32 were stowed externally in 16 vertical tubes located in the outer casing on either side of the conning tower. A project to develop mines launched from the torpedo tubes of submarines was abandoned in 1938.

The Bréguet B4 mine was considerably smaller, being only half the weight with an 80-kg TNT charge. It was designed for the later *contre-torpilleurs*, which entered service from 1933 and could carry twenty B4 mines on each of their

25-m twin Decauville tracks. The tracks comprised a fixed after section capable of accommodating five mines and removable sections that took some six hours to assemble; in wartime they were stowed in a below-decks magazine. The mine-laying cruiser *Émile Bertin* was fitted with similar tracks 50 m in length, capable of accommodating eighty-four B4 mines. Unlike her predecessor *Pluton*, *Émile Bertin* was a cruiser first and a minelayer second, and the weight of the mines had to be compensated for by disembarking her catapult and aircraft.

D. INFRASTRUCTURE

1. Logistics

Oil firing was adopted for destroyers from about 1909, but coal firing was retained for the battleships laid down 1910–1914. After the Great War it became clear that oil was the future; all the ships designed from 1918 had oil-fired boilers, and some coal-fired boilers on the older battleships were replaced. However, this had serious implications for stocks. In 1926 there was sufficient storage ashore for only 100,000 tons of fuel oil and 17,000 tons of diesel fuel. In the same year it was decided that these figures were to be increased to 1,500,000 tons and 140,000 tons, respectively—equivalent to nine months' consumption. Because of fears of coastal or aerial bombardment, fuel tanks were to be located underground. The period 1926–1929 also saw the laying down of four purpose-built oilers (the navy's first), each of 8,600-tons, to be used for the importation of oil during peacetime and for replenishment in time of war.

By January 1939 there were reserves of 1,100,000 tons of fuel oil and 90,000 tons of diesel, and an additional 1,745,000 tons of tank capacity (including 105,000 tons for diesel) had been authorized. These figures included substantial stocks overseas to support deployments: at Casablanca (North Africa), Dakar (West Africa), Diego Suarez (Indian Ocean), Saigon (Far East), and Fort de France (West Indies). Ten new tankers were also ordered 1936–1939; only three of these would enter service prior to the Armistice.

2. Bases

The main bases in metropolitan France were at Brest (headquarters of the Atlantic Fleet) and Toulon (Mediterranean Fleet). Both had extensive maintenance facilities, including 250-m graving docks capable of accommodating the largest modern battleships. The other major fleet base was at Bizerte in Tunisia, which could not only accommodate a fleet of ships but also had a well-developed naval dockyard at Ferryville capable of major repairs to all types of ship; the No. 2 Dock was 254 m by 40.6 m. There were important bases and naval dockyards at Cherbourg (North Sea/Channel areas) and at Lorient (Atlantic coast).

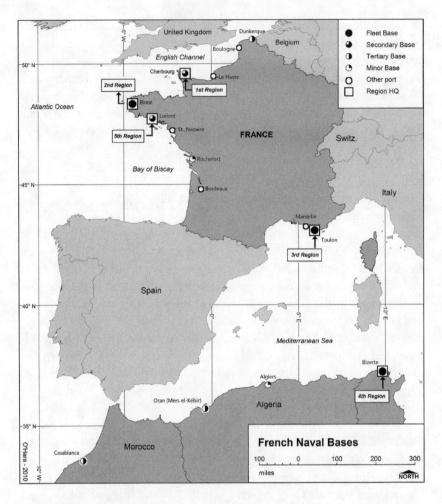

With Italy increasingly seen as France's potential enemy in a Mediterranean conflict, the Marine Nationale feared that both Toulon and Bizerte would
be vulnerable to air attack and in 1934 decided to undertake the construction
of a new naval base capable of accommodating the Mediterranean Fleet at
Mers el-Kebir, west of Oran (Algeria). Work began in 1936: there was to be a
major anchorage sheltered by a 2,000-m jetty, new coast defense guns for the
existing forts, underground command bunkers, batteries of medium and light
AA guns, piers, quays and dry docks, fuel tanks, and munitions stocks. However, little of this was in place by July 1940, when major elements of the French
Atlantic Fleet were attacked by the British; only a 900-m stretch of the main
jetty had been completed, and communications with Oran were rudimentary.

The French overseas bases, especially those in North and West Africa,
were strategically important but had limited facilities for maintenance. This

would become a serious problem after June 1940 when major units of the Atlantic Fleet took refuge there. Dakar had only a small graving dock, and Casablanca had a floating dock capable of accommodating only flotilla craft and submarines.

An important element in the *défense des côtes* strategy was the provision of batteries of large- and medium-caliber coast defense guns, generally sited on headlands commanding the harbor approaches, for all major fleet bases and anchorages. During the Great War, many of the original guns were dismantled and repatriated to bolster the Western Front, but during the 1920s and 1930s, considerable sums were spent on rebuilding the fortifications and providing them with guns removed from the prewar battleships and cruisers. Each of the major batteries, generally comprising between two and four guns, was provided with a battery command post equipped with a 5-m armored rangefinder and a fire control computer, a Bréguet 150-cm searchlight projector for night firing, and in some cases an acoustic aircraft detection system called a *mur d'écoute* (sound mirror). Of particular note were the powerful batteries at Cape Cépet (Toulon) and at Bizerte comprising 340-mm guns from the uncompleted battleships of the *Normandie* class in twin armored turrets, the 240-mm guns in twin armored turrets at Dakar, and the 240-mm and 194-mm batteries in open mountings at Mers el-Kebir/Oran and Casablanca. Passes and harbor entrances were defended by batteries of 100-mm and 75-mm guns.

3. Industry

France's industrial infrastructure suffered badly in the First World War, and considerable rebuilding was necessary before it was again in a position to furnish the navy with the steel, propulsion machinery, and other equipment it required. The ambitious naval programs of the 1920s had the effect of reviving the dockyards and private industry, but they also stretched them beyond their capacity, and by the late 1920s the backlog of construction due largely to the late delivery of components led to a one-year postponement of orders for the ships in the 1928 estimates. Ships were often completed without key items of equipment such as fire-control directors. Industrial problems and social unrest in the mid-1930s resulted in further delays, and the fleet submarines authorized in 1930 took eight years to complete.

The naval dockyards had the key role in the design and construction of surface warships and submarines. Brest laid down the lead unit of virtually every class of interwar cruiser, completing six out of the seven 10,000-ton treaty cruisers and two of the three *Duguay-Trouins*. Brest also built both the lead ships of the *Dunkerque* and *Richelieu* classes, despite not having a building dock sufficiently large to accommodate the full length of the hulls (*Dunkerque* was "launched" minus her bow, *Richelieu* minus her bow and stern). Lorient, with its revolutionary undercover building hall, the Forme Lanester (completed 1922), also built cruisers and was the lead yard for the *contre-torpilleurs*; Cherbourg was the lead yard for the larger submarines. Follow-on units were generally ordered from the private shipyards. *Strasbourg* and *Jean Bart* were built by Penhoët–A. C. Loire at Saint Nazaire, the latter in a purpose-built facility with parallel building and fitting-out docks allowing the completed hull to be floated sideways from one to the other. Light cruisers and destroyers were built at private shipyards such as A. C. Loire, A. C. Bretagne, A. C. de France, F. C. de la Gironde, and F. C. de la Méditerranée at La Seyne (opposite the naval dockyard at Toulon).

The orders for the early coastal submarines of the 600-tonne and 630-tonne types were placed in batches with traditional private submarine builders such as Augustin-Normand, Schneider, and Dubigeon, who produced competing designs to broad STCN requirements. There were some benefits from competitive design, but the lack of standardization of equipment and spares proved to be a major operational drawback, and later coastal submarines were built by the same companies to a standard STCN design.

Major items of equipment such as guns, machinery, and torpedoes were designed and tested in-house. Indret (near Nantes) was responsible for the development of boilers and turbine machinery, Guérigny for the manufacture of anchors, chains, and special steels; Saint-Tropez for the manufacture of torpedoes; and Ruelle for the design and manufacture of guns, shells, and charges. Gun mountings and fire-control systems, conversely, were often designed by private industry. Saint-Chamond was prominent in the design of the large quadruple mountings for the new generation of battleships, and of fully enclosed gun mountings for smaller ships; Saint-Chamond also combined with Granat, who supplied the transmitting systems for the guns in all warships, to produce the first director systems of French design. SOM and OPL produced the new generation of coincidence and stereoscopic rangefinders.

IV. RECAPITULATION

A. WARTIME EVOLUTION

The main problem that the Marine Nationale faced in September 1939 was that the war that broke out in Europe did not follow the course that had been anticipated. This was also a problem faced by other major navies such as that of Britain and the United States. However, British and U.S. maritime forces had been developed primarily for long-range operations and were therefore more inherently flexible in terms of the theaters in which they could be effectively employed. In contrast, the Marine Nationale, which did not subscribe to Mahanian "sea control" doctrine, had prepared for two distinct types of naval warfare in two very different maritime theaters: on the one hand, security operations in the open waters of the North Atlantic, where the primary threat was posed by German commerce raiders, and on the other, fleet-on-fleet action against Italy in the narrow waters of the Mediterranean.

Operations against the German commerce raiders proceeded broadly according to plan. The Force de Raid was divided into two: *Dunkerque*, the light cruisers, and half of the *contre-torpilleurs* operated in the North Atlantic, often alongside ships of the Royal Navy, to block incursions via the Denmark Strait by the German *Panzerschiffe* and the fast battleships *Scharnhorst* and *Gneisenau*; *Strasbourg* and the remaining *contre-torpilleurs* were deployed to Dakar, where they operated in conjunction with the British carrier *Hermes* as Force X to hunt German surface raiders in the South Atlantic.

However, Italy failed to enter the war as expected; as a result, the French Mediterranean Fleet and its ships never had the opportunity to show off their undoubted capabilities in the maritime environment for which they had been designed. The modern heavy cruisers based at Toulon were rotated in pairs through Force X (subsequently Force Y) at Dakar, taking some of the Mediterranean Fleet *contre-torpilleurs* with them. Other units were deployed to ports in northern Britain for the Norway operation of April 1940. However, the bulk of the fleet was retained in Mediterranean waters to cover the anticipated Italian declaration of war. When this finally happened on 10 June 1940, it came too late for the Marine Nationale to affect the overall military situation. Heavy cruisers and *contre-torpilleurs* raided Genoa and Vado on the night of 13–14 June, but this was the only operation of note against the Italians before the Armistice was signed on 22 June.

June and July were difficult months for the Marine Nationale. Under the terms of the Armistice (Article 8), the entire fleet was to be demobilized and disarmed in French metropolitan ports under German and Italian supervision. Following negotiations, the Germans and Italians made concessions: the French would be permitted to demobilize a substantial part of the fleet in North African ports, the remaining units returning to unoccupied Toulon; no ships would be required to return to ports in occupied France. Demobilization was already proceeding, reservists were preparing to disembark, coast defense guns were being dismantled, and submarine torpedo warheads deactivated when the Marine Nationale had to face a threat from an unexpected quarter: the Royal Navy. Prime Minister Winston Churchill was unwilling to accept Admiral Darlan's assurances that no French ship would be handed over intact to the Germans. French warships that had taken refuge in the United Kingdom were to be seized by force, and aggressive action was to be taken against those units of the French fleet outside metropolitan France, with the modern battleships the primary targets.

The powerful squadron under Vice Admiral René Godfroy at Alexandria was subsequently immobilized under the guns of the British Mediterranean Fleet. On 3 July the French Atlantic Fleet at Mers el-Kebir, which included *Dunkerque*, *Strasbourg*, and two of the older battleships, was given the ultimatum of sailing with the British Force H or being sunk. After prolonged and somewhat fraught negotiations—which were not helped by the precarious state of communications between the commander in chief on the spot, Vice Admiral Marcel Gensoul, and the French high command—the three battleships of the British squadron opened fire, sinking the older battleship *Bretagne* and disabling *Dunkerque* and *Provence* within ten minutes; *Strasbourg* and five of the six *contre-torpilleurs* escaped to Toulon. Four days later *Richelieu* was disabled at Dakar by a torpedo dropped by a Swordfish aircraft from HMS *Hermes*.

These unprovoked aggressions by the British gave Darlan a lever to use against the draconian provisions of the Armistice. The French persuaded the Germans and Italians of the wisdom of mobilizing a substantial proportion of the major warships in Toulon to defend Southern France and the African colonies against the threat of attack from their former Allies. In September a grouping of modern warships comprising three light cruisers and three *contre-torpilleurs* designated Force Y was dispatched to West Africa to counter Gaullist influence. These ships served to bolster the local forces at Dakar when in late September General Charles de Gaulle, accompanied by a powerful British squadron, attempted unsuccessfully to rally Senegal to the Free French cause.

From late 1940 until November 1942 the active part of the fleet at Toulon, now designated the Forces de Haute Mer (FHM) under the command of Admiral Jean de Laborde, comprised the flagship *Strasbourg*, two heavy and two light cruisers, and six or more *contre-torpilleurs*. Two training sorties were permitted every month, and the Marine Nationale took the opportunity of rotating the modern cruisers and *contre-torpilleurs* between full commission and refit/maintenance (*gardiennage d'Armistice*). Despite the German occupation of northern France, where most of the French defense industry was located, light AA guns including the twin 37-mm Mle 1933, the single Hotchkiss 25-mm Mle 1939 G, and the Browning 13.2-mm MG were now becoming available in larger numbers, and the opportunity was taken to upgrade ships during refit. The British Asdic sets delivered before the Armistice were also finally installed, and from the spring of 1942 radar (DEM) of French design and manufacture was fitted to some of the major units.

The situation for the ships stationed in North and West Africa was less favorable. Refit and maintenance facilities were poor, and equipment upgrades were limited to the mounting of additional light AA weapons transported by freighter from metropolitan France. Fuel and munitions stocks had to be conserved for use in the event of an Allied aggression, so training at sea was minimal and was confined to local waters.

The uneasy peace that followed the abortive assault on Dakar was broken by only two actions involving the navy, both of which aimed to stop further encroachments on the French overseas empire. In November 1940 Thailand attempted to take advantage of French weakness in Europe by invading French Indochina. On 9 December a temporary grouping was formed with the local naval forces comprising the cruiser *Lamotte-Piquet*, two modern colonial sloops, and two elderly sloops. The French ships launched a preemptive strike against the Thai Navy at Koh-Chang on 17 January 1941, disabling Thai forces there and sinking several vessels without loss. During June and July 1941 the navy was also actively involved in the defense of Syria, which had been invaded by British forces. Although the outcome of the conflict was never in doubt, the local naval forces—comprising the *contre-torpilleurs Guépard* and *Valmy* and three elderly submarines (reinforcements included the *contre-torpilleurs Chevalier Paul* [sunk in transit] and *Vauquelin*)—conducted hit and run raids on superior British forces before being withdrawn to Toulon.

November 1942 was the next crisis point for the Marine Nationale. The Allied Operation Torch landings at Casablanca, Oran, and Algiers beginning 8 November met with a spirited resistance from the light surface forces and submarines based there, but the French were heavily outnumbered and outgunned; virtually all their warships were sunk or disabled and they suffered heavy loss of life. On 27 November, fearing that the remainder of the French fleet would defect to the Allies, the Germans attempted to seize the ships at Toulon. However, the French, true to their promises two years earlier, scuttled the ships as the German panzers entered the dockyard. Four submarines escaped, of which three would continue the fight alongside the Allies. The battleships *Strasbourg*, *Dunkerque* (still under repair), and *Provence*, the four modern heavy cruisers, three modern light cruisers, and a host of flotilla craft and submarines were rendered unserviceable by opening their seacocks and by detonating explosive charges in their guns and machinery spaces; some of the larger ships burned for days.

The only elements of the fleet that were "liberated" by the Allies were the squadron impounded in June 1940 at Alexandria, the incomplete *Jean Bart* at Casablanca, and the *Richelieu* and Force Y at Dakar, plus a handful of submarines. These ships would now form the basis of the Free French Naval Forces (FNFL). However, the ships at Alexandria were quickly assessed as being too old to be of military value, and the completion of *Jean Bart*, which had been heavily damaged by 16-inch shellfire during the U.S. Navy's

PHOTO 1.4. The French battleship *Strasbourg* at Toulon outlined by the smoke from the mass scuttling of the French fleet. (John Jordan collection)

assault on Casablanca, was adjudged too difficult to be accomplished in a U.S. Navy yard.

The only ships deemed worthy of modernization by the U.S. Navy were *Richelieu*, the modern light cruisers and *contre-torpilleurs* of Force Y at Dakar, and the minelaying cruiser *Émile Bertin* in the French West Indies. One by one, these ships were taken in hand at U.S. naval dockyards on the East Coast, stripped of their light AA and aviation facilities, and fitted with a substantial modern AA battery comprising quad/twin 40-mm Bofors and single 20-mm Oerlikons and radar. The cruisers and the *contre-torpilleurs* went on to serve in the Mediterranean theater, where they performed valuable service; *Émile Bertin* would lead the Allied naval forces into a newly liberated Toulon on 13 September 1944. *Richelieu* would serve in the Indian Ocean with the British Eastern Fleet.

With the liberation of French North Africa in November 1942, the FNFL, which had previously experienced severe manning difficulties—in large part as a consequence of the aggressive British actions of July 1940—were now able to undergo a major expansion, and both the British and the Americans provided new warships, mainly antisubmarine escorts and subchasers. The Marine Nationale of 1945 was very different from the force that began the war, comprising a heterogeneous collection of vessels equipped with the latest radars, sonars and weaponry; however, because of its diverse origins it would become increasingly difficult to maintain and operate.

B. SUMMARY AND ASSESSMENT

In 1939 the Marine Nationale had a large fleet of impressive ships of modern design manned by well-trained officers and men. Morale was high, well-developed command structures were in place, and the French were confident of giving a good account of themselves against both the German and Italian navies. This confidence was increased by the revival of the Anglo-French Alliance, which had French warships fighting alongside what was still widely regarded as the premier navy in the world. The high regard in which the French fleet was held by all the combatants in 1939–1940 is evidenced by the determination of the British not to let it fall into enemy hands in June 1940 and the equal determination of Hitler and Mussolini to keep it out of the hands of the British.

In June 1940 the fleet became the most important political card the new French national government at Vichy possessed. Unlike the army and air force, it was largely intact and, as a result of the negotiations that followed the signing of the Armistice, was based at Toulon in the unoccupied zone and in French North Africa. France was now a neutral country and the fleet, although its activities were regulated and circumscribed by the Italo-German Armistice Commission, would be called upon at regular intervals between June 1940 and November 1942 to hold together her overseas empire and to protect it against the opportunist aggression of other powers. The successes at Dakar in September 1940, at Koh-Chang in January 1941, and off Beirut in June–July 1941 served to reinforce morale in an otherwise dark period of the navy's history.

The major surface warships built by the French between the wars were powerful and generally well designed. Although the protection system of the *Dunkerques* proved no match for the 15-inch guns of the British battleships at Oran, this was unsurprising given that armor thickness was intended to be proof only against the 28-cm shells of the German *Panzerschiffe*. The battleships of the *Richelieu* class are generally regarded as among the best ships of their generation: fast, well armed, and well protected.

It is a similar story with cruiser design. The fast but fragile 10,000-ton ships of the *Tourville* class were followed by the elegant and better-protected *Suffrens*, and the last ship, the *Algérie*, is generally regarded as the best of the "treaty" designs.[5] The light cruisers that followed were particularly successful ships; the three that survived the war served until the end of the 1950s. And the *contre-torpilleurs*, unique to the Marine Nationale, were much admired abroad for their combination of hitting power and high speed.

Considerable sums had been invested in France's large submarine fleet. On paper the twenty-nine fleet submarines of the 1,500-tonne type—one had been lost in 1932—were as good as any in the world, capable of high sustained speed on the surface and equipped with a useful payload of heavyweight

Photo 1.5. The French battleship *Richelieu* passes under the East River's Manhattan Bridge heading for dry dock at a New Jersey port. Note the missing gun in B turret. The main rangefinder had to be removed so she would fit under the bridge and is sitting on her forecastle. (U.S. Naval Institute Photo Archives)

torpedoes. They were complemented by a large fleet of coastal boats that were relatively fast, maneuverable, and packed a considerable punch for their size.

Despite the power and prestige of the French fleet, there were some serious weaknesses that became apparent only after the outbreak of war. The fleet was well equipped and well prepared for surface warfare in the western and central Mediterranean, but when the expected conflict with Italy failed to

materialize and ships were diverted to other theaters, they were often found
to be lacking in the necessary qualities. The commissions that reported on
the failings of French warships and submarines following the Great War all
concurred that robustness and reliability had suffered in the relentless pursuit
of improved technical performance. These lessons were initially applied but
were quickly forgotten as the 1920s progressed. The light forces intended for
high-speed combat in the western Mediterranean were designed for optimal
theoretical performance: the guns for ever-higher rates of fire, the ships for
higher and higher speeds; both proved sustainable only in the calmest of seas.
The introduction of lightweight construction materials such as duralumin
served to reduce topweight and improve stability but at the expense of hull
and superstructure strength; the ships that operated in the hostile waters of
the Atlantic during the winter of 1939–1940 frequently suffered weather damage. Moreover, although the design of gun mountings and high-pressure steam
machinery was often innovative and based on sound engineering design principles, French manufacturers did not always succeed in meeting the high specifications, and defective manufacture was often an even more serious problem
than was overambitious design. The twin gun mountings of the *Mogador* class
are one prominent example, the turbine problems of the *Le Fantasque* class—
the subject of an official enquiry during the mid-1930s—another.

Flotilla craft designed primarily for combat in the western Mediterranean
were not required to operate far from their bases. When deployed to the North
Atlantic, these ships were found to lack the necessary endurance for convoy
and patrol work. Not only was fuel capacity insufficient but the French turbines were not economical at cruising speed, largely due to the high consumption of auxiliary machinery. Prewar endurance trials had not been run
in realistic conditions, and in calculating the distances ships were expected
to cover in escorting merchantmen between metropolitan France and North
Africa, little account was taken of the possible need to zigzag or to pursue a
submarine contact. Ships that had been expected to be capable of three thousand miles at cruise speed before the war had this figure downgraded to little
more than half that figure. The *contre-torpilleur Léopard*, seized by the British
in June 1940 and subsequently employed as a convoy escort, had two of her
boilers removed to provide the necessary bunkerage.

The performance of France's large submarine force was disappointing. The
coastal submarines deployed to patrol areas in the North Sea during the early
months of the war achieved nothing. In the 1,500-tonne fleet boats, there
was still inadequate attention to habitability, and they never attained their
designed patrol endurance of thirty days. There was insufficient ventilation in
the early boats, supplies of bottled oxygen were inadequate, and fresh stores
were provided for the equivalent of two and a half days (a defect corrected by

the installation of additional refrigeration during later refits). Wartime experience was to reveal that insufficient attention had been given to protecting the submarines against the shocks likely to be experienced during depth charging. There were problems with watertight hatches and battery integrity; electrically operated systems such as lighting circuits and the external torpedo mountings frequently failed because switchboards and control systems were not seated on flexible mountings.

When in 1943 the latest French battleships, cruisers, and *contre-torpilleurs* were taken in hand for modernization and refurbishment in the United States, the nature of the works performed on them tells its own story. The main task was to strip out the existing light AA weapons, which were relatively ineffectual, and to replace them with a modern battery of quad and twin 40-mm Bofors linked by a centralized fire control system; the Bofors were supplemented by large numbers of single 20-mm Oerlikon guns, which were bolted on wherever space could be found. As with British warships of the period, space and weight aboard *Richelieu* and the cruisers were found by removing the elaborate aviation facilities, which included hangars, catapults, and cranes, and most of the ships' boats; the cruisers also lost their heavy mainmast—a measure which saved weight and cleared AA arcs. The latest U.S.-model radars—albeit the "small-ship" SF surface and SA air surveillance models—were also fitted, although the U.S. Navy refused to agree to the transfer of modern fire-control radars to the French navy, considering this equipment "too sensitive."

Propulsion and auxiliary machinery was extensively overhauled and refurbished. Aboard *Richelieu* the original electrical cabling, much of which was defective, was stripped out and replaced, and new switchboards were fitted; a new AC circuit with converters had to be provided for the 40-mm Bofors mountings, and new radio transmitters and receivers were installed.

When these modernizations were complete, the surviving French surface ships could operate with the various Allied task forces on an equal basis. However, the failure of the French to anticipate the fast-evolving nature of naval warfare, and in particular their failure to appreciate the importance of aircraft carriers and embarked naval aviation, meant that their surviving naval forces were unbalanced; they could fight alongside the Allies but they were no longer capable of operating independently. The first priority of the postwar Marine Nationale would be the acquisition of carriers and carrier aircraft from Britain and the United States; the second would be the development of French naval aircraft to be embarked in purpose-built carriers of French design. Conventional surface units would be tasked primarily as carrier escorts, as was already the case with the U.S. Navy and the British Royal Navy.

chapter two

Germany: The Kriegsmarine

I. BACKSTORY

A. HISTORY

The modern German navy was always part of a continental-minded military power. It developed after 1848 in two wars against Denmark from a short-lived German democratic fleet, a Prussian fleet, and a North German Federal precursor. It was eventually established during the 1870–1871 war against France upon the foundation of the German Empire under Emperor Wilhelm I. In this war the weak German naval forces could not effectively contest the French blockade of their North Sea and Baltic ports but did manage to protect the coasts.

Emperor Wilhelm II promoted a strong navy to advance Germany's overseas and European interests. He found in Alfred Tirpitz an energetic manager to build up his navy. Tirpitz advocated a fleet that would surpass that of the French and threaten the British. His "risk" theory held that a fleet large enough to cripple the Royal Navy in battle could give Germany freedom of action on the seas and keep Britain out of a future continental war.

Tirpitz's theory failed in practice. The British, who held a 3:2 superiority over the German High Sea Fleet, entered the First World War and proceeded to frustrate German hopes for an early battle near their own ports by maintaining a distant blockade. The emperor had hoped for an agreement with Britain after a quick victory over France, but this did not materialize. The only major confrontation between the British and German battle fleets at Jutland in 1916 was indecisive. The German commerce war against British supply lines in the Atlantic had some effect, but the unrestricted sinking of merchant ships by submarines provoked the United States to enter the war on the side of the Allies in 1917. The ensuing German defeat led to the breakup of the German Empire and the scuttling of the German High Seas Fleet at Scapa Flow in 1919.

The Treaty of Versailles reduced the new German Reichsmarine to a coast defense force of eight pre-dreadnought battleships, eight old cruisers, and minor warships. It limited personnel to 15,000 men, and aircraft and submarines were completely forbidden.

B. MISSION

The wish to avoid a new confrontation with Britain dominated planning in the 1920s and early 1930s. Poland and France were regarded as possible opponents. In the 1932 Geneva disarmament conference, Germany called for equality for all League of Nation members and for the removal of treaty restrictions, but France's security concerns blocked any compromise. Germany subsequently left the conference and withdrew from the League of Nations the next year. A separate German–British treaty was signed on 18 June 1935 limiting the German fleet to 35 percent of British tonnage along with 45 and later 100 percent of submarine tonnage.

A setback in the Anglo-German accord remained the limitation on submarines. Opinion within the German navy toward submarine warfare was split. Reflecting the tradition of the Imperial Navy, Admiral Erich Raeder, the navy's commander in chief, considered battleships the center of any fleet, and most of his staff thought the same. They believed that submarines could be neutralized by developments in antisubmarine warfare and would likely play a minor role in any future war. The other school of thought, led by Captain Karl Dönitz, considered the submarine the best weapon for a minor navy such as Germany's.

A war against France and Russia was held possible in 1936 and submarines were developed accordingly: a 250-ton type for coastal waters, a 500-ton type for the Mediterranean, and a 750-tonner for the ocean. The possible use of aircraft carriers together with cruisers in the Atlantic was discussed, but Hitler discounted the carriers as being vulnerable "gas boxes." Instead, the navy planned to use armed merchant cruisers, as in World War I. Nonetheless, two 20,000-ton (actually, 23,000-ton) aircraft carriers were laid down to exploit the treaty's opportunities.

The political climate changed in 1938 with the Czechoslovakian crisis. Although the feared war loomed on the horizon, Hitler still considered a conflict with Britain unlikely before 1944–1945. In the meantime the German navy was to expand considerably. He wished to have Germany's two newest and largest battleships, *Bismarck* and *Tirpitz*, ready in early 1940 and wanted to commission six even larger superbattleships as soon thereafter as possible. The scheme of the so-called Z-Plan emerged. Of the two options discussed— battle cruisers of a smaller type but in a greater number or superbattleships— Hitler and the navy's leaders chose the latter. In addition to the battleships, the Z-Plan called for three battle cruisers and sixteen light cruisers. All new ships were to have diesel engines or at least mixed propulsion for greater range. Submarines were still regarded as strategically unimportant.

In a strategic concept for a possible war with Britain dated 25 October 1938, the inferior German navy's main task was the destruction of enemy shipping. This would be impossible to accomplish from only the German North Sea ports and bases in northern Norway or along France's Atlantic coast were regarded as vital. The naval staff saw battleships as a means for cruiser warfare or at least as a necessary backup to a cruiser force.

A naval study from early 1939 identified the occupation of western Russia as a German war aim and specified an offensive mine barrage in the Gulf of Finland in the war's beginning to hem in the Soviet navy. A war game conducted about that time underlined the prevailing strategic thoughts—an offensive campaign against British maritime traffic and the protection of Germany's own Baltic and North Sea traffic with Scandinavia—to guarantee the import of vital iron ore from Sweden. In the Mediterranean, Italy was to maintain ties with North Africa. Naval staff doubted Rome's ability to weaken the British bastions of Suez and Gibraltar and recommended a German operation to take these positions. Planners regarded a war before 1943 as unsafe but were more optimistic about outcomes after that date with the Z-Plan production coming on line.

II. ORGANIZATION

A. COMMAND STRUCTURE

1. Administration

In 1928 Admiral Raeder became the German navy's commander in chief. His staff was the Naval High Command—Oberkommando der Kriegsmarine (OKM), and from 1933 he reported directly to Adolf Hitler who became supreme commander of the Armed Forces—in 1938. OKM was on an equal level of command with the army high command (OKH) and the high command of the air force (OKL), with all three coordinated by Oberbefehlshaber der Wehrmacht (OKW).

The naval staff, headed from 1938 by Admiral Otto Schniewind, was called the Seekriegsleitung. Prewar the operations department was led by Rear Admiral Kurt Fricke, who replaced Schniewind as chief of naval staff in June 1941. Eight more departments covered other aspects of naval administration. The navy created Marinegruppenkommando Ost in 1938 to cover operational needs in the Baltic and Marinegruppenkommando West in 1939 for the North Sea and Atlantic. After the occupation of Norway, Marinegruppenkommando Nord became Marinegruppenkommando Nord.

Two territorial commands administered the North Sea coast (Marinestation Nordsee) and the Baltic coast (Marinestation Ostsee). Additional commands were added after the conquest of Norway, France, Greece, and the Ukraine. These included Admiral Norway, France, Black Sea, Aegean, and Adriatic, which reported either to the Marinegruppe Kommando or directly to the Seekriegsleitung. The Fleet Commander, overseeing forces afloat, reported to one of the Marinegruppe Kommandos depending on the fleet's area of operations. Commander U-boats, reported directly to Seekriegsleitung, as did the small Danube Flotilla.

2. Personnel

In 1935 Germany reintroduced universal conscription and fixed military service at three years. In 1939 before the outbreak of war the Kriegsmarine's personnel strength was 50,000; conscription raised it to 404,000 in May 1941, and there were approximately 800,000 enlisted men in July 1944.

Draftees entered service as *Matrose* (deck rating) and were trained to different functions at Kiel, Eckernförde, Stralsund, Sassnitz, Wilhelmshaven, Leer, Wesermünde Brake, and Glückstadt in so-called *Schiffstammabteilungen* (naval manning depots). Noncommissioned officers were educated in schools at Kiel-Friedrichsort, Wesermünde, and Plön and started their different specialized careers as *Maat*.

The training for naval line officers lasted three years. The first five months were spent in a *Schiffstammabteilung* at Stralsund with infantry drill. After four months on a sail training ship they became cadets, and after eight and a half months' education on training vessels such as *Emden*, *Schlesien*, or *Schleswig Holstein*, they were promoted to *Fähnrich zur See* (midshipman). After a vacation and seven months at the naval academy at Mürwik, they received five more months of weapon training. In the last six months they trained on board ship and graduated as *Leutnant zur See* (ensign). Engineer officers, weapon officers, and administration officers underwent similar programs. The Kriegsmarine could draft many reserve officers and men who had prior naval service. Many merchant marine officers also received abbreviated instruction.

The main naval academy was, from 1910, in a massive brick building at Flensburg-Mürwick, but during the war, facilities at Schleswig, Heiligenhafen, Husum, and Heiligendamm were also used.

In addition to numerous shore facilities, the Kriegsmarine maintained school flotillas to train recruits and officers. There were school flotillas for minesweepers and motor torpedo boats but the submarine school flotillas were by far the most numerous. The 21st and 22nd flotillas at Pillau and Gotenhafen, respectively, used the small Type II submarines, whereas the 23rd and 24th flotillas at Danzig and Memel had Type VII boats. The 25th and 26th flotillas at Libau and Pillau were nicknamed the "shooting flotillas" because new boats with their raw crews trained on a fixed schedule, launching sixty to seventy torpedoes per boat under all conditions—surfaced, submerged, in daytime, and at night. After this training, the 27th Flotilla at Gotenhafen provided tactical training in a ten-day "convoy battle" with cargo ships and auxiliaries acting as targets and torpedo recovery boats playing the role of escorts. A lamp replaced the warhead on the training torpedoes so the target ships could observe "hits." Every submarine had a training officer, and up to two boats within a training course could be "flunked."

3. Intelligence

The Kriegsmarine's intelligence service was a department of the Seekriegsleitung called Marinenachrichendienst. The office designated Funkaufkläung (radio intelligence) had separate branches for radio interception and interpretation (B-Dienst) and deciphering radio signals, xB-Dienst. The latter had 1,100 men and women, 949 of them used for deciphering. They were assisted by Hollerith computers.

Although the French and British codes were changed at the beginning of the war, xB-Dienst was soon able to decipher some of the British and all of the French signals. At one point the British changed their codes up to four times a month. The Germans were generally able to break the code after about five days. Depending on the code being broken, the Germans could read up to a quarter of the British radio traffic. They could also read the British and Allied Merchant Ship (BAMS) code, which provided valuable information during the Battle of the Atlantic's early phases. In February 1942, B-Dienst broke into the code used for communication with many of the Atlantic convoys, but a change of code in March 1943 blinded them. At the end of 1943, after the British began to change their cipher daily, the xB-Dienst was no longer able to penetrate British codes. After the sinking of the Canadian destroyer *Athabaskan* in April 1944, drifting code documents were recovered that improved the German position, but the war ended before a break could be achieved. Until April 1942 several U.S. Navy codes could be broken. This ceased with newly introduced codes. Russian codes were easier to penetrate. For operations involving the larger vessels, groups of B-Dienst specialists served aboard to provide firsthand information and disrupt enemy signals.

With respect to its own codes, Germany introduced the Schlüssel C coding machine in 1926, followed in 1934 by Schlüssel M, called Enigma. Berlin was very confident that this machine rendered its codes completely secure. The sinking of all supply ships in the Atlantic after the *Bismarck* operation in the summer of 1941 led the U-boat command to introduce a new code machine, the Enigma M4 in February 1942. The British broke the Luftwaffe code in spring 1940 and the naval code in spring 1941 but were unable to read codes produced by the M4 until the end of 1942.

B. DOCTRINE
1. Surface Warfare
Although, in the aftermath of the First World War, Germany was reduced to the size of a minor navy, tactical training still followed the traditional idea of a fleet encounter between lines of battleships. The heavy guns were to open up in a fast series of rounds, a so-called fork. The first round was only to warm up the guns and was not spotted. The following rounds were shot very quickly with small variations in the actual measured range. At greater ranges three salvos were in the air before the first reached the target area. Most often one of the salvos would straddle, which meant that its shells would splash in front of and beyond the target, and shooting at the identified range would start. To get quicker results, the battery was often split in two and alternated fire. It was also considered easier to spot the fall of shot from four splashes rather than eight.

The traditional idea of torpedo boat attacks at night or from the battle line's unengaged side predominated before the war. In an effort to improve nocturnal torpedo boat attacks, the Marinenachrichtendienst, or signals service, developed a radar in cooperation with the GEMA Company in 1934. This radar operated on the 50-cm wavelength and could detect vessels up to 10 km away. A pre-war doctrine called for shore-based radar stations to guide torpedo boats to their targets. This concept worked well on the night of 23 October 1943 when a British cruiser and six destroyers tried to intercept a German convoy off the French channel coast. Five radar-directed torpedo boats surprised them and torpedoed and sank the cruiser *Charybdis* and one destroyer without loss to themselves.

2. Aviation
At the end of the First World War, the Kaiserliche Marine possessed 1,478 planes distributed between thirty-two seaplane stations along the North Sea, English Channel, Baltic, Black Sea, and Mediterranean as well as seventeen airports. The Treaty of Versailles prohibited German air forces. In spite of this, the army and navy trained pilots and developed aircraft. The Reichsmarine used civilian organizations like "Aerosport GmbH" at Warnemünde as a disguised naval air force. In 1925 the navy established a civil aircraft company, Severa, and in 1926 purchased the aircraft factory Caspar–Werke AG at Lübeck-Travemünde, which was later developed as the trial base for seaplanes. From 1933, however, when the NSDAP party took power and Hermann Göring became the minister of air, the still camouflaged Luftwaffe assumed the development of all military aviation, which frustrated the navy because

it believed it could do a better job meeting its specific needs than an independent service could. The Luftwaffe established squadrons at Warnemünde, Kiel-Holtenau, and List/Sylt. Shortly after it was officially founded in March 1935, it ordered 153 planes for naval cooperation, and by 1936 there were eight naval reconnaissance, multipurpose, and fighter squadrons.

In 1934 the navy commenced development of a 450-mm aerial torpedo based on a Norwegian type called the F5. Because of a lack of coordination between the Kriegsmarine and Luftwaffe, this torpedo proved unsatisfactory. After some improvements the new LT5a performed better but production, which began at the end of 1940, climbed very slowly. The navy purchased Italian aerial torpedoes called the F5W and F5i. In 1942 a blockade-runner brought seventy Japanese aerial torpedoes to Germany. However, their performance was inferior to the F5W and they were relegated to use on motor torpedo boats (MTBs). From the end of 1941 the Luftwaffe took over the development and production of aerial torpedoes. The resulting weapon, the LTF5b, proved satisfactory. During the war, fifty-eight merchant vessels displacing 333,135 GRT (gross registered tons) were sunk by German aerial torpedoes, and eighteen ships totaling 146,673 GRT were damaged.

3. Antisubmarine

The minor role played by antisubmarine forces during World War I, when German surface ships sank only two submarines (by gunfire), failed to establish an antisubmarine warfare tradition in the German navy. Given the restrictions of the Versailles Treaty, the ban of U-boats, and the concentration on surface warfare, antisubmarine warfare was considered unimportant in the postwar period and was possibly influenced by British propaganda claims for the great efficiency of the Asdic underwater detection system introduced during the 1920s. Moreover, specialization in antisubmarine warfare was unlikely to advance an officer's career.

During the Kriegsmarine's peacetime expansion, the requirements of fleet operations occupied the small number of destroyers and torpedo boats, and they were ill equipped for the antisubmarine role. No purpose-built antisubmarine vessels were commissioned before the war. For the 1938 naval training exercise, a temporary *Unterseeboots-Jagd* (UJ, subchaser) flotilla was formed at Flensburg by modifying fishing vessels. Based on the experiences gained in the exercise, two UJ-flotillas were temporarily established in July–August 1939. Each flotilla consisted of eight modern fishing vessels, each displacing about a thousand tons. The intended return to their private owners was cancelled when war broke out one month later and the Kriegsmarine entered the war with sixteen auxiliary subchasers in commission.

Once war commenced, Germany's sea-lanes were largely restricted to coastal waters along controlled territory with overseas trade quickly blocked by Allied navies. Standing combat instructions designated Germany's few capital ships for independent raider operations in distant waters without close anti-submarine escort. Thus, German antisubmarine efforts were initially reduced to escorting warships and coastal convoys close to bases and along the coast-line. Contingency plans in the event of war foresaw the conversion of civil-ian fishing trawlers and whalers into military ships for the antisubmarine role. However, many of these small, slow vessels carried inadequate antisubmarine equipment to prevent attacks. To compensate for the lack of ships and trained personnel, the Kriegsmarine deployed extensive mine barrages along the coastal shipping lanes. Moreover, apart from the mines, shallow water often kept enemy submarines out of these areas.

To meet the demand for personnel, an antisubmarine school, the UAS (U-Boot-Abwehr-Schule), was established at Neustadt on 25 September 1939. In November 1939 it moved to Gotenhafen and finally in July 1943 to Bergen, Norway, with a detachment at Hatvik, Norway. Using captured for-eign submarines as target vessels, surface combat units were trained in antisub-marine techniques as far as operational needs allowed.

Throughout the war, German antisubmarine vessels were organized in flotillas of up to ten ships, which were normally allocated to regional navy commands. Initially, the focus was on German waters with 12th UJ-flotilla operating in the North Sea and 17th UJ-flotilla in the Baltic Sea. The 11th UJ-flotilla was formed by eight trawlers at the end of September 1939, and a formation of ten small whalers reinforced the 12th UJ-flotilla in November. Following the occupation of Denmark and Norway and the defeat of France in 1940, the operational area widened greatly. The limited number of antisub-marine vessels was frequently shifted between the various theaters according to need. Changes in the deployment policy for Allied submarines and the start of the German campaign against the Soviet Union in summer 1941 effectively limited the operational areas to the Eastern Baltic Sea, the Norwegian coast, and the Bay of Biscay. In May 1941 a new 14th UJ-flotilla was established, which was eventually based along the French west coast.

To secure the supply lines from Greece to the German garrison on Crete, the 21st UJ-flotilla was formed at Piraeus, Greece, in December 1941, using a variety of locally available ships. In December 1942, following the occupation of Vichy France, Germany established the 22nd UJ-flotilla using converted French fishing trawlers. This flotilla helped escort traffic to North Africa and started operations along the Italian west coast two months later. Similarly, the 1st UJ-flotilla was built up in the Black Sea in May 1943 to escort traffic along the German controlled coasts. This flotilla consisted of former military

PHOTO 2.1. One of many: V 1309, a German patrol boat, former trawler *Kapitän Stemmer*, in the British Channel in 1943 or 1944. (Peter Schenk collection)

transport ships of the KT class. Despite the often poor condition of the ships available to these flotillas, they achieved some remarkable results against Allied submarines until the end of 1943.

Following the Italian armistice, captured corvettes of the *Gabbiano* class were used to strengthen the 22nd UJ-flotilla and create the 2nd UJ-flotilla in the Adriatic. Although these corvettes were well-designed antisubmarine warfare (ASW) ships, the deteriorating German position in the Mediterranean compromised antisubmarine operations during 1944–1945. Only in the Black Sea, where the 1st Flotilla was augmented by the 3rd and 23rd UJ-flotillas formed in April–May 1944 from small wooden-built fishing boats, did success against Soviet submarines continue into 1944. With the loss of the German positions on the Balkan Peninsula in the second half of 1944, German naval operations in the Black Sea and the Aegean Sea ceased and existing flotillas were disbanded.

The navy heavily mined the Gulf of Finland in 1941 to prevent Soviet submarines from entering the central Baltic Sea, which was vital for its supply lanes and training grounds. When the Soviet navy continued its submarine campaign in these waters during 1942 despite suffering severe losses, the navy effectively blocked the western exit of the Gulf of Finland with a net barrier in early 1943. Only after Finland signed an armistice with the Soviet Union in September 1944 did Russian submarines enter the central Baltic. To counter the new threat, the 1st and 3rd UJ-flotillas were re-created at the end of October 1944 using fishing boats and former air force sea rescue motor launches. These vessels, however, proved completely inadequate for their role. Despite numerous operations and reasonable success against German traffic, the Soviet navy lost only a single boat, rammed by a German torpedo boat in the final phase of the Baltic submarine war.

Due to losses and insufficient construction, the nominal strength of all named flotillas never exceeded fifty ships during the war. With the operational strength usually well below that figure, only important convoys and large merchant vessel or warships were escorted by subchasers while smaller vessels were routed independently or escorted by minesweepers and smaller patrol vessels. In 1941 a contract for twenty-five war subchasers (Kriegs-U-Jäger), displacing 830 tons standard, was assigned to five building yards. Representing the only purpose-built class of ASW vessels constructed for the German navy during World War II, the first of its class was commissioned on 11 March 1943. A total of nineteen were commissioned during the war with the rest still incomplete in May 1945. The coal-burning vessels carried six depth charge throwers (DCT) and 120 charges but were much slower than similar Allied designs like the British Flower-class corvettes. None sank an Allied submarine.

The lack of adequate ASW vessels, trained personnel, and offensive combat tactics was reflected by the small number of submarine sinkings by naval and air force units in all theaters of combat. Out of the ninety-four Allied submarines lost, surface ships sank only twenty-five (see table 2.1). Designated antisubmarine vessels accounted for 80 percent of these with the rest coming from torpedo boats, minesweepers, and other small units. In the absence of a naval air force command, the Luftwaffe never committed to ASW. Consequently, aircraft were not a serious threat to Allied submarines. Defensive mine barrages proved to be a most effective submarine-killer, especially in the Baltic, the Black Sea, and along the Norwegian coast. However, apart from the Mediterranean, where the operational situation favored the use of submarines, German shipping losses to submarine attack remained small throughout the war. Allied submarine operations never impaired the vital transport of iron ore from Scandinavian ports or the supply of the German garrison in Norway and the Arctic theater.

4. Submarine

At the outbreak of war, German U-boats were a vital part of the commerce doctrine envisaged as the Kriegsmarine's main offensive role. While enemy warships were considered targets of opportunity, doctrine designated merchant vessels as the U-boat's prime targets.

TABLE 2.1 Allied Submarines Sunk by German Antisubmarine Operations during World War II

Sunk by	1939	1940	1941	1942	1943	1944	1945	Grand Total
Surface ship	0	6	2	5	9	2	1	25
U-boat	0	3	2	1	1	0	0	7
Aircraft	0	3	1	3	0	0	0	7
Mine	0	5	17	13	14	6	0	55
Total by year	0	17	22	22	24	8	1	94

The concept underlying Germany's doctrine of tonnage warfare was quite simple: to reduce enemy shipping below the minimum level required to sustain short- or medium-term economic survivability by sinking more tonnage than was replaced by new construction or through other means. The strategy's main flaw was the lack of reliable statistics and insight into Britain's economic situation. While the German naval staff over the years produced steadily rising target figures required for achieving victory in tonnage warfare, actual successes at sea never approached these targets. When this was realized at the beginning of 1943, and with Germany by then pressed into a defensive role on almost all fronts, the tonnage warfare concept was amended by introducing the concept of supply warfare. This aimed to reduce the material flow, especially from the United States, toward Allied forces poised to attack the German position on the European mainland.

Correctly expecting the Royal Navy to introduce convoys upon the outbreak of war, Dönitz developed the nighttime surface group or wolf pack attack tactic in 1935. Based on lessons from the last years of World War I, this tactic was designed to overcome the problems associated with locating a convoy and to offset the expected concentration of escorts. Advantages in radio communications during the interwar period enabled a U-boat group to be led by a commander embarked on one of the boats or by a central shore command. Control of individual boats usually ended when a boat contacted the enemy. Thereafter, the boat's commanding officer enjoyed full freedom of maneuver.

5. Amphibious Operations

The German navy conducted one major amphibious operation in the First World War. The landing on the Russian island of Ösel in the Baltic in 1917, protected by a large contingent of the High Sea Fleet, was well prepared and a complete success. The transport ships were unloaded by barges and unpropelled landing boats, which were pulled by wire lines through the surf.

Little was done to advance amphibious doctrine or capabilities between the wars. The Norwegian landings were accomplished without special equipment, relying on surprise and the country's weak defenses for success. With the unexpectedly quick defeat of France, preparations for an invasion of Britain commenced. In only three months, the Kriegsmarine improvised a landing fleet of 2,000 converted river barges and 170 transport ships. This effort included the development of a tank landing craft, the *Marinefährprahm* (ferry lighter) driven by three truck engines, which could lift three medium tanks. Some 720 were built during the war.

Although Germany's improvised amphibious fleet was never tested on Britain's shores, the Kriegsmarine proved adept at conducting landings. Although flotillas of Greek caïques and small steamers carrying troops against Crete in May 1941 fell afoul of British naval forces tipped off to their presence by signal intelligence, operations against the Soviet Union were more successful. Using *Marinefährprahm* (MFP) barges along with small army and Luftwaffe landing craft, German forces captured the large Baltic islands of Ösel, Moon, and Dagö in September 1941. German forces leapfrogged the Kerch Strait from the Crimea into the North Caucasian area in 1942 using MFPs, Siebel ferries (another type of invasion barge consisting of a pair of steel pontoons), and army landing craft. In 1943 in the Aegean, German forces overcame British naval superiority and made a number of highly successful landings, including opposed assaults against the islands of Kos in October and Leros in November. In the Adriatic in 1943, the navy ferried battalion-sized forces against the Dalmatian islands occupied by partisan forces after Italy changed sides. There was also an unsuccessful landing on the Finnish island of Suursaari in 1944. These operations were all distinguished by effective navy-army–air force cooperation. The Aegean operations even included paratroop drops.

German forces likewise conducted successful amphibious evacuations including Sicily in August 1943 and Sardinia and Corsica in September–October 1943. In late 1943 the navy withdrew 450,000 German and Axis troops back across the Kerch Strait. The crossing of the river Schelde in Belgium and the Lyngenfjord in northern Norway were also conducted using landing craft.

6. Trade Protection

Except for a few blockade-runners, the Kriegsmarine could not maintain its Atlantic trade routes against the British blockade. However, small convoys, generally escorted by minesweepers, or armed trawlers traversed the coastal waters of German-held Europe, and the Kriegsmarine successfully protected the decisive iron ore trade from Narvik and Lulea, Sweden. The Narvik route was especially important in winter when the Baltic froze. Minefields protected the route along the Norwegian coast, and it was only in 1944 that British air attacks were able to inflict major losses on the convoys. Mine and net barrages laid in the war's opening days effectively sealed the entrances to the Baltic. In 1941 a mine barrage across the Gulf of Finland blocked in the Russian fleet. In the summer of 1942 some Russian submarines penetrated the barrage and sank several German and Swedish cargo ships. In response, a 60-km-long antisubmarine net was laid in the spring of 1943, which was renewed after the spring 1944 thaw, effectively sealing the gulf until the autumn of 1944.

The Allied blockade against German shipping quickly dried up the import of raw materials and other goods from overseas countries, and by early 1941, Germany's available stocks of strategic raw materials, especially natural rubber, had drastically declined. The persistence of the British defense as well as German preparations for the Russian campaign compelled Germany to find new ways to import more materials to maintain war production. Soon Berlin's interest turned entirely to its Axis partner, Japan. Up to mid-1942 eleven German and Italian ships lying idle in Far Eastern ports since the outbreak of war ran the blockade and reached Bordeaux from Japan with 74,960 tons of urgently needed raw material, half of it rubber. Three ships were sunk and one turned back. Due to increased Allied surveillance of the main shipping routes, only four of thirteen ships carrying 29,600 tons reached Bordeaux in the following 1942–1943 blockade-runner season. Blockade running using merchant vessels was abandoned in January 1944 after only one of five ships sailing in the 1943–1944 season arrived. Submarines offered the only alternative to maintain the flow of the most urgently needed raw materials from the Far East. However, repeated attempts in 1944–1945 were frustrated by Allied antisubmarine operations. Only four German and one Japanese submarine, carrying a mere 611 tons of material, completed the trip to Europe, with two more still en route at the time of Germany's capitulation.

7. Communications

From 1927 the Kriegsmarine maintained modern long- and shortwave transmitters at Kiel that could communicate with ships around the world. A special long-wave transmitter was built at Kalbe for submarines. Even submerged submarines could receive its signals. The ships were provided with standardized transmitters and receivers for long- and shortwave. For smaller units and planes, a 40–70 watt radio set from Telefunken worked very well. An ultrashortwave radio was introduced for short-range voice communications.

III. MATERIEL

A. SHIPS

After the defeat in the First World War, the Treaty of Versailles limited the strength of the new Reichsmarine in numbers and in the displacement of new construction:

Battleships	6 + 2 reserve	10,000 tons maximum
Cruisers	6 + 2 reserve	6,000 tons
Destroyers	12 + 4 reserve	800 tons
Torpedo boats	12 + 4 reserve	200 tons

The construction or acquisition of submarines and aircraft was forbidden.

The Reichsmarine could equip itself with only a handful of very old Kaiserliche Marine ships including eight pre-dreadnoughts of the *Braunschweig* and *Deutschland* classes launched between 1902 and 1906, eight old cruisers launched between 1899 and 1903, and thirty-two pre–Great War torpedo boats. Due to treaty limitations on the number of personnel, only a few of these ships could be manned at any one time—for example, no more than four of the pre-dreadnoughts were ever simultaneously active.

The construction of the first replacement vessel, the cruiser *Emden*, started in 1921 and took almost four years due to political and financial reasons. She combined a mixture of proven and innovative elements. The hull lines resembled those of the last of the Kaiserliche Marine cruisers whereas the structure was almost all welded, the first large ship worldwide to be so constructed.

In 1925 *Möwe*, the first replacement destroyer, was laid down. A real destroyer design on 800 tons appeared impossible; consequently, she and her eleven follow-ups were classified as torpedo boats. The hulls of these boats were also partly welded.

In 1926 the next cruiser replacement program started. This consisted of the three K-class vessels followed by *Leipzig* and *Nürnberg* (ordered and laid down in 1933). These cruisers had an adequate main armament of three triple turrets with 15-cm guns but suffered from light construction, and their high length-to-beam ratio affected stability.

The battleship category presented the most difficult replacement dilemma. Since a battleship design of 10,000 tons was impossible, difficult discussions took place over eight years regarding a range of ideas from a heavily armed monitor to a cruiser-like ship. The remarkable result was the *Deutschland* class, classified according to the terms of the Treaty of Versailles as a *Panzerschiff* (armored ship). On a 10,000-ton standard displacement (actual standard displacement ranged from 10,600 tons for *Deutschland* to 12,340 tons for *Admiral Graf Spee*), these vessels carried six 280-mm guns, giving them firepower

PHOTO 2.2. The German *Panzerschiff Deutschland* running trials in Kiel Bay on 19 January 1933. The training ship *Bremse*, built in part as a test ship for the propulsion plant used in this class, is behind. (Peter Schenk collection)

superior to the "Treaty" cruisers of other navies, which were limited to 8-inch guns. Their newly developed diesel propulsion gave them a speed of twenty-eight knots—faster than most existing battleships—and enabled them to sail 10,000 nautical miles at twenty knots. They were ideal for commerce warfare and well suited for missions in home waters. Soon the term "pocket battleship" (partly ironic, partly respectful) was coined to describe them.

In the meantime, many of the old ships found their way to the breaker's yard. Some others were modernized or reconstructed for different duties and saw service during the Second World War.

Two months before *Deutschland* was commissioned, Hitler came to power. At first the new government's direct influence on the Reichsmarine's building program was not obvious. But behind the scenes considerable enhancements were made to the *Panzerschiff* design. The next two ships were laid down early in 1934 to an official displacement of 18,000 tons. Since only the defensive characteristics were improved, discussions continued. Finally, in mid-1934, construction was halted and these ships were again laid down in May and June 1935 to an even larger design, emerging as the battleships *Scharnhorst* and *Gneisenau*. This convoluted development produced handsome but compromised vessels.

At this time Hitler renounced the Treaty of Versailles and entered into the Anglo-German Naval Agreement three months later. This allowed Germany to build a fleet 35 percent of the British navy's strength. The 35 percent limit was valid for each category except the submarines, where the parties agreed upon a 45 percent (later up to 100 percent) limit. Germany's building program was designed around these levels.

At the end of 1938 a new shipbuilding program on a massive scale was being discussed (see table 2.2). Hitler approved this program (called the "Z-Plan") in January 1939 and terminated the Anglo-German Naval Agreement in April 1939. Only a few of the new Z-Plan ships were laid down and, after the outbreak of war, they were broken up on the slip, including aircraft carrier B and light cruisers M and N (see table 2.3).

Some general technological aspects of the shipbuilding program deserve mention. High-tensile steel St 52 was extensively used for hulls. In certain areas, homogeneous armor was used as structural material, especially the new developed types *Wotan hart* and *Wotan weich*. These were chromium-nickel-molybdenum steel alloys with a much higher tensile strength than their predecessors. Welding was extensively employed on smaller units to save top weight. The development of suitable diesel engines took some time, and the required power was not available for the new battleships and cruisers. Only the battleships of the planned but never built "H" class would have received diesel engines. In the meantime, great hopes were placed on a high-pressure steam system. But this ultimately resulted in fragile and uneconomic power plants. Only later installations showed satisfactory reliability.

The most powerful machinery belonged to the aircraft carrier *Graf Zeppelin*. Although almost completed, this ship never saw service.

Scharnhorst and *Gneisenau* were enlargements of the *Panzerschiff* concept. The main fault of these relatively large ships was their insufficiently powerful main armament. An exchange of the three 280-mm triple turrets to three 380-mm twin turrets was planned. Only *Gneisenau* started reconstruction; this commenced while she was under repair from a bomb hit in 1942, but the project was eventually abandoned.

The follow-up battleships, *Bismarck* and *Tirpitz*, were excellent warships and comparable to modern battleships in other navies. They were well armed with a main battery of four 380-mm twin turrets, and their protection was at a high standard.

The *Panzerschiff* proved a useful type for the Kriegsmarine. Their very long range made them ideal for oceanic operations. In contrast, the high-pressure steam system used by the heavy cruisers proved unreliable and suffered from limited range. Machinery problems also hampered the destroyers and new tor-

TABLE 2.2 Germany's Naval Construction Program, Orders up to the End of 1938

	Orders Up to the End of 1938
Aircraft carriers	2
Battleships	2[a]
Heavy cruisers	5
Light cruisers	6[b]
Destroyers	30
Torpedo boats	30
Escorts	10
Submarines	98[c]
Motor Torpedo Boats	35

[a] In addition to *Scharnhorst* and *Gneisenau*.

[b] Of a special type ordered in 1938.

[c] 2 Type I, 32 Type II, 42 Type VII, 22 Type IX.

TABLE 2.3 Major Warships as of 1 September 1939 and Wartime Additions

Ship	1 Sep 1939	Wartime Additions
Battleships	2	2
Panzerschiffe	3	0
Heavy cruisers	1	2
Light cruisers	6	0
Destroyers	21	19
Torpedo boats	11	36
Escorts	10	0
Submarines	57	1,110

pedo boats. Another problem was the unsatisfactory seaworthiness of these ships although some improvements would be achieved during the war.

Eventually, Germany's main instrument of naval power proved to be the submarine. With 659 built, the Type VII C boat was the most numerous. It carried five torpedo tubes and up to fourteen torpedoes on a surface displacement of 760 tons. The 141 Type IX C boats conducted oceanic operations. They had six torpedo tubes and carried up to twenty-five torpedoes at a surface displacement of 1,120 tons. The Walter U-boats performed in trials only; the revolutionary Type XXI (118 completed) and XXIII (60 completed) boats saw only sporadic service in the war's last days.

In addition, the Kriegsmarine deployed a great number of smaller warships, amphibious vessels, and auxiliaries. These vessels played an important role in the navy's war effort.

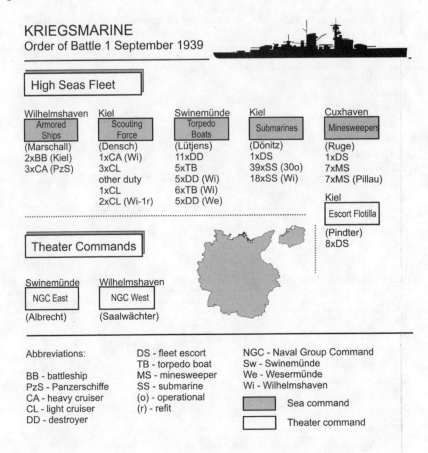

KRIEGSMARINE
Order of Battle 1 September 1939

High Seas Fleet

Wilhelmshaven	Kiel	Swinemünde	Kiel	Cuxhaven
Armored Ships	Scouting Force	Torpedo Boats	Submarines	Minesweepers
(Marschall)	(Densch)	(Lütjens)	(Dönitz)	(Ruge)
2xBB (Kiel)	1xCA (Wi)	11xDD	1xDS	1xDS
3xCA (PzS)	3xCL	5xTB	39xSS (30o)	7xMS
	other duty	5xDD (Wi)	18xSS (Wi)	7xMS (Pillau)
	1xCL	6xTB (Wi)		
	2xCL (Wi-1r)	5xDD (We)		Kiel
				Escort Flotilla
				(Pindter)
				8xDS

Theater Commands

Swinemünde	Wilhelmshaven
NGC East	NGC West
(Albrecht)	(Saalwächter)

Abbreviations:

DS - fleet escort
TB - torpedo boat
MS - minesweeper
SS - submarine
(o) - operational
(r) - refit

BB - battleship
PzS - Panzerschiffe
CA - heavy cruiser
CL - light cruiser
DD - destroyer

NGC - Naval Group Command
Sw - Swinemünde
We - Wesermünde
Wi - Wilhelmshaven

☐ Sea command
☐ Theater command

B. AVIATION

1. Ship-based

In 1939 the Kriegsmarine had two squadrons with Ar196 and He60 in Bord-fliegerstaffel 1/196 and 5/196 for use aboard battleships, cruisers, and armed merchant cruisers. For the projected aircraft carriers, a carrier group (Träger-gruppe) II/186 was established at Kiel-Holtenau with three squadrons 4th/186 (Ju87C) at Stolp and at Brüsterort 5th/186 and 6th/186 (Bf109T). They were trained for catapult takeoffs and engaging arrestor wires to land. The Ju87s helped sink the Polish destroyer *Wicher* and minelayer *Gryf* at Gdynia. Soon after, the group was dissolved as the completion of the carrier was postponed.

2. Shore-based

The shore-based squadrons established by 1939 included Küstenfliegergruppe (KG) 106 with 1st/106 (He115) and 2nd/106 (Do18) at Norderney and 3rd/106 (He59) at Borkum; KG 406 with 1st/406 (He60), 2nd/406 (Do18), and 3rd/406 (He59) at List/Sylt; KG 306 with 1st/306 (He60) and 2nd/306

(Do18) at Dievenow; KG 706 with 2nd/706 (Do18) and 1st/706 (He60) at Kamp; and KG 506 with 1st/506 (He60) and 3rd/506 (He59) at Pillau, 2nd/506 (Do18) at Kamp, and 3rd/706 (He59) at Dievenow.

All units reported to the general of the Luftwaffe as commander in chief Kriegsmarine, General Major Hans Ritter. There were Fliegerführer (air command) west at Jever and east at Dievenow. Tactically they were under Kriegsmarine command. The air force and navy constantly bickered over the command of these units, and the air force generally prevailed. When KGs 106, 606, and 806 got new land-based planes (He111 and Do17Z), the Luftwaffe obtained command and used them for their own purposes. The Kriegsmarine retained only floatplanes and flying boats for reconnaissance, rescue, and escort duties.

Nevertheless, a long-range bomber group, I/KG 40 came under navy command in January 1941. It was operated by the Fliegerführer Atlantic under Luftflotte (air fleet) 3 and flew reconnaissance and bombing missions for Naval Group West and especially for commander U-boats. The planes were four-engined FW200, Ju290 (radar equipped since mid-1943), the new long-range bomber He177 Greif, and some Do217 E-5s. However, KG 40's deployment requirements were never met and the group did not achieve the desired results. Another unit frequently used over the sea was KG 100 equipped with Do217 E-5s and later with the He177. From 1943 both units deployed the Henschel Hs 293A radio-controlled missile and the unpropelled FX 1400, also called the "Fritz X." The radio-controlled bomb's first kill was the British sloop *Egret* on 27 August 1943 in the Bay of Biscay. On the same mission, a destroyer and a sloop were damaged. KG 100's most famous kill with the "Fritz X" was the Italian battleship *Roma* on 9 September 1943. Using these weapons, groups II and III of KG 100 accounted for eight merchant ships of 68,000 GRT, ten destroyers, one landing ship tank (LST), two landing craft, tanks (LCTs), and one hospital ship sunk. They damaged two battleships, three light cruisers, twelve destroyers, and twenty-seven merchantmen.

During the war, Germany used roughly five hundred Hs 293s and "Fritz Xs" and observed about a hundred hits. The ratio would have been higher with better-trained operators.

For operations over the Baltic Sea, a Fliegerführer Baltic was created under Luftflotte 1. It contained KG 806 (Ju88); Seeaufklärungsgruppe (SG) (He114, He60, Ar95), 1st/Fliegergruppe 196 (Ar196); and KG 506 (Ju88). This formation was dissolved in October 1941 and only one squadron of seaplanes, 1st/Fliegergruppe 127, remained in Estonia under Luftflotte 1.

After the Battle of Britain, Luftflotte 5 in Norway deployed seaplane squadrons at Stavanger, Trondheim, Tromsö, and Kirkenes. From spring 1942, when operations against the Allied convoys to Murmansk became important,

Luftflotte 5 received KG 30 (bombers) and 26 (torpedo planes), but after the Allied November 1942 landings in North Africa, these two units relocated to the Mediterranean. The seaplanes were reorganized in 1943 and formed into SG 130 and 131 with BV138 three-engined and BV222 long-range flying boats. Luftflotte 5 had Ju87s for short-range missions as well as Ju88, Ju188, He115, and He111s. The latter four types were used mainly for torpedo missions.

In December 1940, Luftflotte 2's X.Fliegerkorps deployed in Italy, and from April 1941 the 7th Seenotstaffel (rescue) and the SG 126 (reconnaissance) operated over the Aegean. Upon reaching the Black Sea, Luftflotte 4 was given SG 125 with 1st and 3rd /125 squadrons containing twenty-five planes from the Baltic. They were first based at the Crimean Peninsula but redeployed to Constanta, Romania, in May 1944. The commander, chief of aviation Crimean, later chief of aviation Black Sea, also had the 8.Seenotstaffel and a squadron of minesweeper planes.

The number of planes of the naval air arm never exceeded two hundred, some 5 percent of Luftwaffe strength.

C. WEAPON SYSTEMS
1. Gunnery
Surface. Some years before the First World War, the German navy took the necessary steps to achieve good long-range gunnery results employing rangefinders. The excellent shooting of the German battle cruisers and battleships at Jutland is well known. Nevertheless, during some of the battle's phases, the Germans did not fire due to an absence of central fire control. After the battle, the development of such equipment was considered imperative. However, not all ideas could be developed and tested before the war ended.

The Reichsmarine tried some improvements on fire control starting in 1921. A more extensive test program with newly developed equipment was started in 1927 on the old battleship *Schlesien*.

Also in this period the first new guns were developed. Many more followed in the 1930s. The design was an improvement of a well-tried formula. German heavy guns were built up from shrunk-on tubes and had a wedge breech. The main propellant was contained in a brass case. The shells were much improved. Streamlining increased impact velocities. Krupp was the main manufacturer for the larger guns, and Rheinmetall made the smaller ones. See appendix I for a listing of major naval guns.

In the area of fire control, creativity was strongly emphasized; therefore, improvements could be made on almost every new ship. A drawback of this policy was that it resulted in a variety of equipment.

The most advanced fire-control set was the surface gun director (*Seeziel-Feuerleitanlage*) C.35. The main components were a target transmitter, an

PHOTO 2.3. The German Type IXB submarine *U-124* preparing her 105-mm gun in 1941. (Peter Schenk collection)

angle resolver, a gyro platform, a speed sensor, rangefinders, and a fire-control computer. The rangefinders were stereoscopic instruments from Zeiss with different base lengths (the rangefinders of the main fire-control stations and in the turrets B, C, and D on *Bismarck* were 10.5-m instruments).

The first operational radar to be embarked was the FuMO 22 (Seetakt) from GEMA installed on the *Admiral Graf Spee* early in 1938. Subsequently all major warships carried radar. Nonetheless, the Kriegsmarine was slow in adopting radar and in training officers in its use. A special branch for officers was not established until the end of 1941 when a school was also opened at De Haan near Ostend, Belgium. Instructions were only provided at the end of 1943.

Operationally, radar was used for detection. In 1943, *Scharnhorst* and possibly *Admiral Scheer* conducted gunnery trials using radar to spot the fall of shot. *Scharnhorst* was equipped with FuMO 26 (Seetakt) at that time. The accuracy of FuMO 26 is reported as ± 70 m in range and ± 0.25° (which corresponds to ± 65 m at a range of 15,000 m) in direction. The results were reported as good. The cruiser *Nürnberg* achieved excellent results during a test firing against the target ship *Hessen* in December 1944.

Bismarck used her radar's search function in her night action against British destroyers, as did *Lützow* during the 1942 action against convoy JW51B. However, although she had the means for radar-assisted gunnery, *Scharnhorst* did not use radar at all in her last battle fought in December 1943 in the belief that this would disclose her location. This omission proved fatal.

Antiaircraft. Some Kaiserliche Marine battleships were equipped with antiaircraft guns. The 88-mm S.K.L/45 was the basis for the further development in the 1920s and 1930s. Barrel and breech followed similar guidelines as the low-angle guns. Differences were in the rate of fire and the mountings. The AA gun mountings were preferably triaxial.

The navy went through a lengthy and never completely successful process to achieve a satisfactory high-angle fire-control system. It went to war with gyro-stabilized AA control stations; the last two versions, SL6 and SL8, were fitted with spherical armored hoods over 4-m stabilized rangefinders. The SL6 was direct-stabilized with large gyros and heavy balancing weights. The later SL8, in contrast, used small gyros with control loops. Due to the unchanged outer structure, ballast replaced the balancing weights. A technical authority of the Kriegsmarine criticized this before World War II and presented a more modern solution, but his proposal was not acted upon until 1942. Most likely this AA control station (Flakleitgerät M42), now with radar, was fitted as a prototype on *Emden* at the end of the war.

Details of *Bismarck*'s AA system can serve as an example of the problems in this field. *Bismarck* had different types of 105-mm AA gun mounts (Type C.33 and C.37) for the forward and aft batteries. These mounts had different training and elevating rates, which the fire-control system could not compensate for. This meant that targets on one broadside could not be engaged by all guns under one director. Tests with the SL8 AA control stations (there were only two of the planned four on board) were unsatisfactory. The test team made some suggestion for improvements. But they also stated that a complete correction of the flaws could be achieved only with a reconstruction. The condition of *Bismarck*'s AA fire-control system during Operation Rheinübung was insufficient and may have been one of the reasons for the aerial torpedo hit that ultimately doomed her.

2. Torpedoes

The Kriegsmarine introduced two basic dual-purpose 533-mm torpedo models for use on U-boats and surface vessels, both measuring 7.163 m in length and carrying a 280-kg explosive charge. They were developed in the early 1930s, and the first were delivered to the navy in 1934. The air-driven model T-I (or Type G7a) had a top speed of forty-four knots for a running distance of some 6,000 m but could be dialed down to thirty knots and 12,500-m running distance. The design was plagued by engine defects and a tendency to run deep.

The propulsion problems were not rectified until 1939, but depth-keeping failures continued well into 1940.

The battery-driven electric torpedo model T-II (or Type G7e) was more reliable and much cheaper to produce than the Type G7a. Originally intended for use on U-boats, it was capable of only thirty knots at maximum for a running distance of 5,000 m. The electric battery required maintenance every three to four days. Running virtually invisible without the telltale stream of bubbles to alert ships, it eventually became the standard U-boat weapon and was also used by surface ships.

At the start of the war about fifteen hundred of the two models were available for combat use with about the same number in production. Both models were equipped with the standard combined impact/magnetic proximity detonator. High hopes had been placed on the new magnetic detonator, which was to explode below the target to break its keel. However, in the first months of the war numerous malfunctions in frontline use took place, which climaxed during the Norwegian campaign in April–May 1940, when U-boats lost a number of opportunities to score hits upon British capital ships. During a subsequent court-martial of high-ranking officers in the relevant torpedo departments, it was found that the torpedoes and pistols had been declared ready for operational use despite insufficient testing. Faced with the impossibility of improving the design on a short term, the Kriegsmarine had no alternative but to return to the old impact exploder, which, after some improvements up through summer 1940, became the standard German torpedo pistol for the next two years.

Only at the end of 1942 did an improved model of a combined impact/magnetic detonator became ready for frontline service. The Type G7e torpedo fitted with this pistol received the model designation T-III. At the same time, a newly designed spring apparatus guidance system (FAT) allowed the torpedo to run patterns, which theoretically increased the probability of hitting the target under increasingly difficult combat conditions. To improve the performance of the G7e torpedo in the FAT mode, its battery was enlarged in 1943, allowing it to run 7,500 m at thirty knots. This design became known as model T-IIIa. In February 1944 the more sophisticated LUT guidance system was introduced. It allowed torpedoes to follow a spiral pattern independent of the target angle at the time of launching.

In parallel, the Kriegsmarine had worked since 1935 on the development of an acoustic homing torpedo based on the design of the air-driven G7a and for use by U-boats against fast-running warships. In 1940 the focus was shifted to targets running at medium speed, which allowed the use of the G7e design. Following frontline tests with U-boats in February–March 1943 with the prototype T-IV code-named "Falke," the new model T-V "Zaunkönig" was

introduced in August 1943. High hopes for a renewal of the U-boat offensive in the Atlantic following the temporary withdrawal in May of the same
year remained unfulfilled despite a number of successful shots. Postwar evaluation proved that only 15 percent of all T-V torpedoes fired by U-boats during the war actually hit the target. Successful Allied countermeasures, such
as simple towed mechanical noisemakers, and existing design flaws prevented
a higher success rate. The T-V was later also adapted for use by surface vessels, especially by *schnellboot*, or S-boats. At the end of the war the improved
T-XI model (Zaunkönig II) was ready for use on U-boats, but hostilities ended
before any could be used.

Numerous other passive and active torpedo homing and steering designs
were projected or tested, but none became operational. The same applies to
large-scale experiments with new propulsion systems using hydrogen perox-
ide or closed-cycle motors. Many of these developments pioneered postwar
designs in Allied navies.

Exact figures on the total German torpedo production during the war are
not available, but it appears that more than 50,000 torpedoes of all types were
built. Of these, more than 13,000 were fired in anger by the end of November
1944 with U-boats accounting for about two-thirds of the total.

3. Antisubmarine Warfare

A great deal of work in the field of underwater acoustics was preformed using
passive sets. One such set was called GHG (*Gruppenhorchgerät*) and consisted
of two rows (one per each side) of Rochelle salt receivers in the forward part
of a ship. The bearing of an incoming sound wave was detected by the process-
ing of the signal delays in a compensator. All U-boats and most surface warships were equipped with GHG. An advanced version was fitted in the heavy
cruiser *Prinz Eugen*. This set consisted of two rows with sixty Rochelle salt
hydrophones at each side, arranged in an elliptical array on her bows. Before
the battle of the Denmark Strait *Prinz Eugen*'s GHG tracked the *Hood* well
over the horizon.

First steps toward the development of an efficient underwater detection
system began in 1933, using a French Langevin set with piezo-electric transducers aboard the experimental vessel *Grille* and the Finnish submarine *CV
707* as target ship during her builder's trials in the eastern Baltic. However, the
Germans were unaware of the poor conditions for sound propagation in this
brackish, heavily layered body of water, and trials proved unsuccessful until
shifted to the North Sea.

During the following years work concentrated on the development of an
active acoustic location device, designated S-Gerät (*Sondergerät*), using mag-
netostrictive transducers. Following the manufactor of ten experimental sets

in 1937, an additional nineteen were delivered to the navy during the summer of 1939. Of these, thirteen sets were installed on various vessels and the rest allocated to training establishments ashore. Antisubmarine fire-control systems were nonexistent at that time. At the start of the war, there existed almost no practical experience on their use, and the training of operators was in its infancy. Hydrophone or passive listening gear still formed the backbone of underwater location technique. By the summer of 1940 just ninety-one S-Gerät sets for installation on surface vessels were completed. Concentrating on the basic design features, production of a simplified version (Mob-S-Gerät) was started, of which almost fifteen hundred sets were delivered by the end of 1942 and installed on various classes of vessels.

4. Mines

German anchored mines were improvements upon turn-of-the-century weapons, the most common types being EMC and EMD. The EMG was developed for areas with a great tidal range such as the English Channel. The mine was loosely anchored and suspended from a small float. Special antisubmarine mines were the UMA, UMB, and UMC types. Usually they had upper and lower antennas to detonate the mine if a submarine passed over or under the mine itself. This did not always lead to the submarine's destruction if she was too far away.

A magnetic fuze for mines was developed in 1929. Called the BIK, it used the deviation of the Earth's magnetic field caused by a nearby steel ship and had at first to be adjusted to the local magnetic field by hand. A later type introduced in 1940, the SE-BIK, was self-adjusting. It was used for aircraft mines (LMA, LMF), which were dropped with a parachute, and for submarine mines (TMA, TMB, TMC), which were discharged through the torpedo tubes. Most were ground mines with a depth up to 40 m with a heavy explosive load of 300 to 935 kg, but TMA was anchored. By the end of the war, ground mines were provided with combined acoustic, magnetic, and pressure fuzes.

Germany used 223,000 mines in the Second World War compared to 263,376 British, 54,457 Italian, and 40,000 Russian mines. The British lost 281 warships and 296 merchant vessels on German minefields. The Kriegsmarine used mine destruction vessels (*Sperrbrecher*) with strong electric magnets against magnetic mines. There were enough large merchant vessels idle to permit such use.

D. INFRASTRUCTURE

1. Logistics

From 1933 Germany began to expand oil production by increasing exploration and introducing synthetic production from coal (distillation or hydration). Nevertheless, the Kriegsmarine had difficulties meeting its demand for heavy fuel oil from hydration as this method mainly produced light oils (gasoline). In 1936 German oil production covered only 12 percent of the Kriegsmarine's diesel requirement and 31 percent of its fuel oil demands. By 1938 production met 22 percent of the diesel and 22 percent of the fuel oil requirements. According to agreements with the Kriegsmarine, the Deutsche Erdöl AG (DEA) began to build oil distillation plants from which the navy could meet 25 percent of its fuel oil requirements during the war. Another 50 percent could be covered by tar oil from hard coal mined in the Ruhr and Silesia.

Because of these production limitations, the Kriegsmarine started to import and store oil in so-called Ölhäfen, large, underground oil depots, and in other depots during the prewar years. The construction of Ölhäfen started in northern Germany in 1937. By the time of their planned completion in 1943, they were intended to have a capacity (by volume) of 10 million metric tons, but by 1939 only a capacity of 1 million tons had been completed.

When the war started, the Kriegsmarine's fuel situation was good because of its foresight and stockpiling: the 770,000 metric tons of diesel that had been accumulated were expected to last thirty-nine months (given an expected monthly consumption of 20,000 tons), and 450,000 metric tons of fuel oil were projected to last for more than three months (given an expected monthly consumption of 137,000 tons). These estimations proved too high because there were fewer new ships commissioned and less activity than expected in the war's first six months. Oil stocks captured in the Netherlands and northern France offset the Kriegsmarine's own consumptions and its deliveries to the army. Therefore, until the summer of 1941, there were no shortages.

With the beginning of the campaign against the Soviet Union in June 1941, oil reserves began falling, and the drop accelerated with deliveries to the Italian navy, which began at the end of 1941. From September 1941 until August 1943, Italy received 425,000 tons of fuel oil from Kriegsmarine stocks, an amount that equaled more than a quarter of the Kriegsmarine's own consumption during that period (1,600,000 tons). Moreover, the extended area of operations—from the Atlantic coast at the Franco-Spanish border up to Norway's North Cape—proved troublesome and the long distances between the bases and ports affected the accumulation and distribution of supplies. Because all bases had to have a certain minimum stock of oil, supplies often were not at the place where they actually were needed and problems occurred more frequently. From the summer of 1941 river barges had to transport oil in the western areas because all tanker wagons had been withdrawn to the east. This increased transport time by a factor of two or three, which reduced flexibility and availability. After 1941 shortages of fuel restricted the navy's operations. From the beginning of 1942 there were less than 200,000 tons of fuel oil, and from the summer of 1942 there were less than 100,000 tons of diesel, which was the minimum reserve for each.

In the context of logistics, the decommissioning of the heavy units that Hitler ordered at the beginning of 1943 had a special significance because their activity depended upon the availability of oil. The Kriegsmarine tried to become more oil independent by building and commissioning coal-fired ships. The Type 1940 minesweepers, which from 1942 assumed many tasks usually performed by larger units, were the Kriegsmarine's best-known coal-fired ships.

The fuel situation improved at the end of 1943 (see table 2.4). After Rome sought an armistice with the Allies, there was no longer a need to deliver oil to Italy, and fleet consumption dropped because the Kriegsmarine's larger warships undertook fewer missions. Production of synthetics provided 7,500 tons oil a month in 1944 compared to only 1,500 tons in 1942. When the oil fields in Romania, which had covered 45 percent of the requirements, were lost in 1944, the situation deteriorated again. Fuel reserves and distribution influenced operational planning during the entire war.

For the replenishment of ships at sea, so called *Troßschiffe* (supply ships) were deployed. The Kriegsmarine had tested their use during the Spanish Civil War. However, a building program started in the mid-1930s was not complete at the beginning of the war. One of these purpose-built supply ships was the *Altmark*, which became famous through its association with *Admiral Graf Spee*. In February 1940 a party from the British destroyer *Cossack* boarded her in Norwegian waters.

In addition to these purpose-built supply ships, suitable civilian ships were used for supply services. After the sinking of *Bismarck*, the Allies destroyed the German system of floating supply stations by capturing these vessels. For the replenishment of submarines, special types of supply U-boats (*Milchkühe*) were introduced. But after breaking the German codes, the Allies learned their rendezvous points, attacked the supply boats, and destroyed this system as well.

2. Bases

The Kriegsmarine's main German bases were Wilhelmshaven for the North Sea and Kiel for the Baltic. At the height of the German expansion, the Kriegsmarine needed to guard more than 18,000 km of coastline. To cover the needs of its ships and vessels, different kinds of bases were established in Germany and the occupied countries:

Kriegsmarine-Werften were fully equipped ship building and repair yards (first-level bases).

TABLE 2.4 Fuel and Diesel Oil Reserves of the Kriegsmarine

	Fuel oil (1,000 m³)	Diesel oil (1,000 m³)
October 1939	437	747
January 1940	364	728
April 1940	332	640
July 1940	328	440
October 1940	312	328
January 1941	564	296
April 1941	456	172
July 1941	408	108
October 1941	396	124
January 1942	300	136
April 1942	115	142
July 1942	135	73
October 1942	174	62
January 1943	117	80
April 1943	144	86
July 1943	139	91
October 1943	171	107
January 1944	220	126
April 1944	233	121
July 1944	279	86
October 1944	359	57

Kriegsmarine-Arsenale were efficient and large equipment stores (second-level bases).

Marineausrüstungs- und Reparaturbetriebe (MAUREB) were local naval equipment and repair stores (third-level bases).

Marineausrüstungs- und Versorgungsstellen were local naval equipment and supply stores (fourth-level bases).

Marineausrüstungsstellen (MAST) were local naval equipment stores (fifth-level bases).

The Kriegsmarine had its own naval yards in Wilhelmshaven and Kiel. During the war several more naval yards were established in the occupied countries. The need to transfer personnel from German yards to these new yards slowed work in Germany.

To protect U-boats from air attacks, large submarine bunkers were built along France's Atlantic coast at Brest, Lorient, St. Nazaire, La Pallice, and Bordeaux starting in 1941. In Norway, bunkers were constructed in Bergen and Trondheim. In Germany, Helgoland, Hamburg, and Kiel received bunkers. Unfinished bunkers included two at Bremen, two at Marseille, and two at Salamis in Greece. For MTBs (S-boats) and motor minesweepers (R-boats),

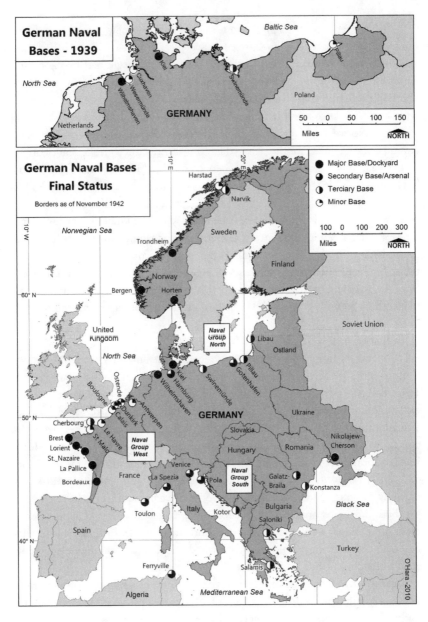

bunkers were built along the Channel coast at Cherbourg, Le Havre, Boulogne, Ijmuiden, and Rotterdam; one at Den Helder remained unfinished.

After 1918 Germany retained only a few coastal batteries: Wangeroog, Borkum, Norderney, Sylt, and Schillig on the North Sea coast, and only Pillau on the Baltic coast. Helgoland and the western Baltic coast could not be armed because of treaty restrictions. This changed after 1933.

The occupation of much of Western Europe made new demands on Germany's coastal defenses. The Kattegat was protected by two 380-mm batteries at Kristiansand, Norway, and Hanstholm, Denmark. Narvik had two 406-mm batteries originally intended for battleship H. In the last phase of the war, two 280-mm triple turrets from the damaged *Gneisenau* were placed near Trondheim and Bergen. A large number of medium batteries guarded the coastal shipping along the Norwegian coast. The heaviest fortification was built in autumn 1940 around Calais, France, for the planned landing in England with six heavy batteries from 240 mm to 406 mm. Most of them came from German bases. The Channel Islands were also heavily armed. The biggest battery there was *Mirus* with four 305-mm guns from the Russian battleship *General Alexeiev*. The French Biscay bases were protected by one heavy battery each and a number of medium batteries. Brest got a 280-mm battery; Lorient, two 203-mm twin turrets from the unfinished cruiser *Seydlitz*; St. Nazaire, four 240-mm railway guns in two positions; and La Rochelle, two more 240-mm guns. In the Mediterranean and Black Sea, only medium batteries were used, with two exceptions: Constanta, Romania, with a 280-mm battery, and Chersonnes (Sevastopol), a 203-mm battery.

3. Industry

As demands for iron and steel were higher than the amounts available, a continuous shortage of these materials hampered production from the summer of 1936. For this reason, the Wehrmacht's focus was on weapons while insufficient ammunition was produced and infrastructure was built reluctantly. The Kriegsmarine was the armed service least affected by this situation because it could always use the long building times of its ships to trump attempts to reduce its allocations. Thanks to preparations, sometimes clandestine, made since the end of the First World War, the Kriegsmarine was able to launch a full-scale building program in 1935 despite a seventeen-year hiatus. Nevertheless the gap between plans and feasibility soon widened, especially since yards, barracks, and depots were affected by iron and steel quotas. In spite of this, the Kriegsmarine was the only one of the armed services to accumulate sufficient stocks of ammunition.

During the first years of the war, the building program could be carried out more or less according to plan, but by the beginning of 1942 resources had to be shifted to army production because of the demands of the Russian campaign. For example, the Kriegsmarine declared a requirement for 300,000 tons of iron for the first quarter of 1942 but was granted only 157,000 tons. To secure the U-boat program, the building of surface units had to be reduced. Repairs took priority over new construction.

From mid-1943 the German war industry had to cope with steadily climbing requirements and growing Allied air attacks. But thanks to an improved organization under the supervision of Minister of Armament Albert Speer and with millions of slave workers from the occupied countries, industry succeeded in meeting the armed forces' needs. In 1943 industry started to construct vessels such as U-boats and minesweepers in sections that could be delivered from inland factories to seaside assembly yards. In the last stage of the war the increasing bombing took its toll; in the beginning of 1945 the coal and fuel supply broke down and work in the yards stopped.

In all, some forty German yards built for the Kriegsmarine during the war. Many more inland yards and factories were engaged in the building of ship sections or components. Furthermore, more than thirty yards in occupied or allied countries—France, Netherlands, Belgium, Italy, Greece, Denmark, Norway, Rumania, and Bulgaria—worked on German warships. Even Swedish yards constructed motor fishing vessels for the Kriegsmarine.

IV. RECAPITULATION

A. WARTIME EVOLUTION

The war developed slowly after the fall of Poland; Hitler hoped for a negotiated settlement of the conflict, but after Britain and France rejected Hitler's October 1939 peace offer, Germany gradually introduced submarine warfare and declared a war zone around Britain. The *Panzerschiffe Deutschland* and *Admiral Graf Spee*, which were already at sea, were ordered to start operations. The efforts to build a battle fleet had compromised submarine construction, and talks to gain bases in neutral countries were initiated to increase the efficiency of the limited U-boat force. Italy refused because of British pressure, and Spain only allowed secret replenishment in her coastal waters. The best offer came from Russia for a base near Murmansk.

A first successful campaign, one that was surprising effectively even to the Seekriegsleitung, was the offensive use of magnetic ground mines in British waters, even though limited production and lack of Luftwaffe cooperation compromised the results. After a successful sortie by *Scharnhorst* and *Gneisenau* against the British blockade in the North Atlantic, the loss of *Admiral Graf Spee* in the South Atlantic was a severe setback for the Kriegsmarine and clearly showed the limited potential of cruiser warfare against a hopelessly superior enemy.

The Kriegsmarine kept a watchful eye on Scandinavia from the beginning of the war. The import of iron ore from northern Sweden, which could only be shipped from Norway when the Baltic was iced over, was threatened; Scandinavia also offered favorable base locations in the North Atlantic. At first the neutrality of these countries was regarded favorably, but after receiving

hints of a planned Allied intervention during the November 1939–March 1940
Russo-Finnish war, Raeder convinced Hitler of the need to invade Denmark
and Norway. This invasion, under the code name Operation Weserübung,
succeeded but at staggering cost to the navy—one heavy cruiser, two light
cruisers, ten destroyers, and a torpedo boat were sunk and the *Panzerschiff*
Lützow (ex-*Deutschland*) was heavily damaged. The Kriegsmarine had originally intended to send her on an Atlantic operation and had included *Lützow*
in Weserübung only because of pressure from OKW.

In an operation against the Allied supply routes to Norway, the battleships *Scharnhorst* and *Gneisenau* sank the British aircraft carrier *Glorious* but
were both damaged by torpedo hits. This displeased Raeder, and he dismissed
the fleet commander who had led the sortie, Admiral Wilhelm Marschall.

The occupation of France seemed to offer another opportunity to end
the war, but London refused an agreement. The obvious next step was an
invasion of Britain. Hitler decided to commence preparations, but the armed
forces did not act in concert. The Luftwaffe believed it could bomb Britain
into submission, but this effort failed. Then the army and navy became entan-
gled in a lengthy dispute over the size of the bridgehead. The Kriegsmarine
believed it would be possible to secure with minefields only a small passage
in the Channel narrows, but the army requested an additional landing zone
in Brighton Bay for a larger lodgment. A compromise was achieved too late.
The decision to cancel this risky operation was understandable. With hindsight, however, it may have been Germany's only chance to win the war.

By the end of July 1940 it became clear to Raeder that Hitler was considering war with Russia the following summer to acquire resources and secure
Germany's position, even if the United States entered the conflict. Raeder
realized that this would leave the Kriegsmarine to continue the war with
Britain largely alone. However, with new bases in France and Norway, conditions had significantly improved. The first convoy battles opened the Battle
of the Atlantic's initial phase. Operations against British shipping by the battleships, the *Panzerschiff Admiral Scheer* and the cruiser *Admiral Hipper* in the
Atlantic and Indian Oceans were also successful.

When Italy joined Germany in June 1940 the Seekriegsleitung developed
new ideas: Italy needed help to dislodge the British from the Mediterranean,
and Spanish support would be required to take Gibraltar. Cooperation with
France was also thought necessary to secure Italy's positions in North Africa.
These ideas, however, did not meet with Hitler's approval. He deemed the
Mediterranean a secondary theater and opposed cooperation with France.

The Italian navy saw its main task as protecting traffic to Libya and dis-
regarded German requests to take Malta and Crete in September 1940 as a

precautionary measure. Rome's offer to send submarines to the Atlantic was readily accepted and resulted in successful operations.

The *Bismarck* operation marked the climax of Atlantic operations by cruisers and battleships. The original plan was to have all four battleships and the cruisers in the Atlantic, assisted later by the aircraft carrier *Graf Zeppelin*, to attack convoys even those escorted by battleships. However, the completion of *Graf Zeppelin* was suspended in 1940 in favor of the submarine program. *Gneisenau* and *Scharnhorst* were not ready to go after their successful March 1941 sortie and Raeder did not want to wait for *Tirpitz*, which would not be ready before the summer of 1941. Thus, only the cruiser *Prinz Eugen* accompanied *Bismarck*. Both decisions proved fatal to the operation. The lack of an aircraft carrier was especially decisive. The Kriegsmarine regarded carriers as unimportant until they proved their value in the war, by which time it was too late. Despite her brilliant victory over *Hood*, luck ran out for *Bismarck* when a torpedo dropped by a plane from *Ark Royal* jammed her rudders.

Bismarck's foray signaled the end of Atlantic operations by the battleships and cruisers. The utility of Brest as a battleship base faded when air attacks there damaged *Gneisenau* and *Scharnhorst*. A further setback was the British destruction of the Atlantic supply tanker network. This forced the cancelation of planned operations by *Lützow* and *Admiral Scheer* in the autumn of 1941. Following Hitler's urgent desire to protect northern Norway from a feared British landing, Raeder reluctantly agreed to withdraw the heavy ships from Brest. The February 1942 "Channel Dash," the breakthrough of *Scharnhorst*, *Gneisenau*, and *Prinz Eugen* from Brest to Germany succeeded beyond expectation, but Germany thus relinquished its ability to conduct the Atlantic war with heavy ships.

Raeder tried in vain to dissuade Hitler from attacking the Soviet Union. Confronted with the final order, the Kriegsmarine contributed only the necessary measures like the mining of the Gulf of Finland to bottle up the Soviet fleet. No suggestions were made to ease the campaign with sea transport. After Russian resistance unexpectedly stiffened in the later summer, a well-organized supply line along the Baltic coast would have provided valuable support to the army's assault. However, a small scale of sea power had to be established in the Black Sea to support the Romanian navy in the escort of shipping along the conquered coast. Small units like S- and R-boats, small submarines, and MFPs were brought via the Elbe River to Dresden, transported overland to the Danube, and shipped down to the Black Sea. Several MFPs sailed through the Bosporus Strait, painted in civilian colors. In a similar way, light units were transferred from the French Channel coast on the Seine, transported by land to the Rhône, and down to the Mediterranean for the North African campaign.

Photo 2.4. To reach the Mediterranean and Black Sea, Germany had to transport by land small ships like MTBs, motor minesweepers, minisubmarines, barges, and landing craft. Here the MFP *F 411*, her ramp missing, makes her way through France from the river Seine to the Rhone in 1943. (Peter Schenk collection)

U-boats made the best use of the new bases on the French Atlantic coast. They had intensively trained in pack tactics during the prewar period, culminating in a full-scale war game under Atlantic conditions in September–October 1938 in the Bay of Biscay. In a May 1939 memorandum Dönitz demanded three hundred frontline boats to achieve decisive results against British commerce in the event of war. However, at the start of hostilities four months later, a mere fifty-seven boats were in commission. Of these, only twenty-four boats of the I, VII, and IX classes capable of operating west of Britain were ready for frontline use.

Although a large U-boat building program was implemented in October 1939, the first large boats did not become available for operations until some fifteen months later (see table 2.5). Until then, U-boat losses and the withdrawal of operational units to train new personnel kept the number of frontline oceangoing boats small. Hence, group operations did not materialize until the summer of 1940, apart from a few ill-fated attempts in the previous months. However, following the defeat of France, the new bases on the Biscay coast changed the situation greatly. By then, even small U-boat groups operating along the western approaches to Britain achieved great success. U-boat pack tactics with surface night attacks rendered British Asdic practically useless. With hydrophones ineffective in the vicinity of a convoy, visual observation offered the only means of detecting a surfaced U-boat at night, but their low silhouettes made this nearly impossible. Without assistance from radar, which was not yet commonly available, the convoy escorts, insufficient in number and often too slow to pursue a surfaced U-boat at high speed, were virtually helpless against nocturnal pack attacks.

The medium-sized Type VIIC boat eventually became the North Atlantic workhorse in anticonvoy operations. The larger, long-range Type IX boats usually operated independently in waters along the American and African coasts. From summer 1943 several of these boats deployed in the Indian Ocean, using bases in the Japanese occupied Dutch East Indies. The appearance of special supply U-boats in spring 1942 greatly enhanced the use of German boats by extending their endurance in operational areas. However, beginning in the second half of 1941, the diversion of significant parts of the U-boat force to secondary theaters like the Mediterranean and the Arctic upon Hitler's or the naval high command's direct orders offset these positive developments.

The successful U-boat campaign in the Atlantic until the summer of 1941 and again during operations off the North and Central American coast in the first half of 1942 prevented U-boat Command from correcting the obvious technical and tactical limitations with existing U-boat types. Lulled into security and inactivity by exaggerated sinking figures, both U-boat Command and the naval construction office feared that the introduction of new designs and types would interfere with the momentum gained by the U-boat construction program.

Allied advances in detection technology, especially the use of radar and direction-finding sets, and improvements in ASW weaponry carried by ships and aircraft made existing U-boat types increasingly vulnerable in the following years. Combined with the continuous extension of air support to convoys, by mid-1942 the productive operational area for U-boat groups was reduced to the central North Atlantic, known as the "Black Gap" area. When escort carriers finally closed this gap in May 1943, pack tactics with the available U-boat types came to an abrupt end, despite the fact that Dönitz could muster a record 236 frontline boats at the beginning of this month. The existing U-boat types were now technologically outdated and suffered grievous losses. This quickly resulted in a shortage of experienced officers and men badly needed to man new boats completing in home yards.

Manning the large number of U-boats with experienced personnel was always a serious problem. From January 1944, even commanding officers hastily drawn from other service branches lacked U-boat experience. Undoubtedly, this increasing lack of combat savvy in the U-boat arm contributed to the horrific loss figures in the submarine campaign's final two years.

Belatedly, a radical change of opinion toward novel designs and propulsion systems took place at higher command levels during the summer of 1943. This

TABLE 2.5 Nominal and Operational Strength of the German U-boat Arm during World War II

	German U-boat Arm							
	Newly Commissioned		Recommissioned after repair	Total Commissioned		Available at start of month	In frontline use, total	In frontline use, %
Month	German	Foreign			Losses			
Sep 1939	1	1		2	2	57	48	84
Oct 1939	0			0	5	57	43	75
Nov 1939	2			2	1	52	34	65
Dec 1939	3			3	1	53	35	66
Jan 1940	1			1	2	55	34	62
Feb 1940	1			1	5	54	41	76
Mar 1940	2			2	4	50	39	78
Apr 1940	3			3	4	48	41	85
May 1940	3			3	1	47	31	66
Jun 1940	3			3	1	49	28	57
Jul 1940	3		2	5	2	51	27	53
Aug 1940	5			5	2	54	25	46
Sep 1940	7			7	1	57	22	39
Oct 1940	7			7	1	63	25	40
Nov 1940	6	3		9	2	69	21	30
Dec 1940	9			9	0	76	21	28
Jan 1941	10	1	1	12	0	85	20	24
Feb 1941	9			9	0	97	22	23
Mar 1941	11			11	5	106	30	28
Apr 1941	14			14	2	112	29	26
May 1941	19			19	1	124	32	26
Jun 1941	14	1		15	4	142	38	27
Jul 1941	19			19	1	153	57	37
Aug 1941	19			19	4	171	66	39
Sep 1941	15			15	2	186	72	39
Oct 1941	24			24	3	199	77	39
Nov 1941	23	2		25	5	220	81	37
Dec 1941	22			22	10	240	85	35
Jan 1942	15			15	4	252	89	35
Feb 1942	16			16	2	263	101	38
Mar 1942	18			18	7	277	111	40
Apr 1942	17			17	5	288	119	41
May 1942	20		1	21	3	300	124	41
Jun 1942	21			21	3	318	127	40
Jul 1942	21			21	12	336	139	41
Aug 1942	21			21	13	345	149	43
Sep 1942	19			19	11	353	172	49
Oct 1942	23		2	25	16	361	195	54
Nov 1942	23	1		24	14	370	206	56
Dec 1942	23		1	24	5	380	204	54
Jan 1943	21	1		22	7	399	215	54
Feb 1943	21			21	18	414	221	53
Mar 1943	27			27	15	417	227	54
Apr 1943	18			18	18	429	233	54
May 1943	26		3	29	44	429	236	55
Jun 1943	24		1	25	16	414	213	51

Table 2.5 German U-boat Arm (*cont.*)

Month	Newly Commissioned		Recommissioned after repair	Total Commissioned	Losses	Available at start of month	In frontline use, total	In frontline use, %
	German	Foreign						
Jul 1943	22			22	38	423	207	49
Aug 1943	17		1	18	25	407	173	43
Sep 1943	21		7	28	13	400	165	41
Oct 1943	25	5	6	36	30	415	174	42
Nov 1943	25			25	20	421	164	39
Dec 1943	28			28	9	426	163	38
Jan 1944	20			20	14	445	171	38
Feb 1944	19		1	20	23	451	169	37
Mar 1944	23			23	25	448	166	37
Apr 1944	23		1	24	23	446	163	37
May 1944	19		1	20	23	447	161	36
Jun 1944	11			11	30	444	180	41
Jul 1944	14			14	26	425	178	42
Aug 1944	15		4	19	40	413	156	38
Sep 1944	20		1	21	22	392	143	36
Oct 1944	16		1	17	15	391	132	34
Nov 1944	21			21	11	393	131	33
Dec 1944	28			28	14	403	135	33
Jan 1945	37			37	14	417	139	33
Feb 1945	18			18	29	440	150	34
Mar 1945	26		1	27	40	429	146	34
Apr 1945	8			8	56	416	147	35
May 1945	1			1	15	368	145	39

led to the development of true submarines capable of high underwater speeds in a remarkably short period; but even with innovative construction methods, the new type XXI and XXIII U-boats could not be produced in time to reverse the tactical situation. The introduction of snorkel equipment in early 1944 enabled the old U-boats to travel or charge batteries using diesel engines while submerged at periscope depth, which drastically reduced the effectiveness of ASW aircraft. To tie down Allied antisubmarine forces, U-boat command continued operations in the North Atlantic and the European shelf areas until the end of the war but was never able to regain the initiative or interfere with Allied intentions despite severe losses.

S-boats were developed as a means for the Kriegsmarine to contest superior sea power in coastal waters using hit-and-run tactics. Nearly a hundred tons bigger than their British counterparts during the first years of the war and equipped with diesels rather than the more sensitive British gasoline engines, S-boats operated effectively in the Channel and the British east coast. They were most effective during the war's first two years and in 1940 sank three destroyers and twenty-six merchant and auxiliary vessels displacing 49,985 GRT. In 1941 they accounted for one destroyer and twenty-nine merchant vessels of 63,081 GRT in the same area. Twelve more merchant vessels displacing 50,396 GRT sank on their mines. In 1942 in the Channel and North Sea, they sank two destroyers, one motor gunboat (MGB), one minelayer (ML), and nineteen merchant ships displacing 33,049 GRT; five more with 14,667 GRT were lost to their mines. In 1943 their kills in the area consisted of one destroyer escort, five patrol boats, one LCT, and seven merchant ships totaling 17,979 GRT; and in 1944 they sank a destroyer, two destroyer escorts, four LSTs, three LCTs, one MGB, three patrol boats, two tugs, and eleven merchant vessels of 18,004 GRT. They achieved less in the Mediterranean, where they sank with torpedoes or mines three destroyers, two destroyer escorts, one MTB, one ML, and two patrol boats. The operations in northern Norway, the Baltic, and the Black Sea were not very successful either. Seventy-seven S-boats survived the war, and 147 were lost.

The remaining heavy units were transferred to northern Norway to protect Narvik and to act against Murmansk convoys. The battlefleet had shrunk to two units after *Gneisenau* received a bomb hit into the forward powder magazine at Kiel before she could be sent to Norway. She was never repaired. A first sortie by *Tirpitz* with destroyers against convoy PQ12 in March 1942 was unsuccessful as she did not find the enemy, but she escaped an attack by torpedo planes undamaged. In the next operation against PQ17 in July 1942, *Tirpitz*, *Admiral Hipper*, and *Admiral Scheer* were recalled after being sighted. However, the British command panicked and scattered the convoy, allowing aircraft and U-boats to inflict heavy losses.

For the next battle in December 1942, the cruisers *Admiral Hipper* and *Lützow* and their escorting destroyers were used to attack convoy JB57b. The action was fought in very low visibility. *Admiral Hipper* was damaged and *Lützow* was ordered to retreat just as she started to attack the convoy because of instructions to avoid risk. Hitler had put high hopes on the operation and was deeply disappointed by the outcome. He ordered the immediate decommissioning of the battleships and cruisers. Admiral Raeder resigned and Admiral Dönitz was appointed as his successor.

Dönitz was clever enough to gain Hitler's reluctant consent to keep the heavy ships commissioned a few weeks later. He argued that it was still possible to operate against Arctic convoys by being more aggressive and accepting some risk. But a year later, in December 1943, after *Scharnhorst* sortied to attack a convoy, she was sunk by *Duke of York*, cruisers, and destroyers. She had run a high risk. Heavy ship operations were over for the Kriegsmarine. *Tirpitz* stayed in Norway until she was sunk by air attack in November 1944; the cruisers were used as training ships in the Baltic. They lent fire support to the retreating German army before being sunk by air attacks in the last days of the war. Only *Prinz Eugen*, *Nürnberg*, and *Leipzig* survived.

PHOTO 2.5. Scene on board the German battleship *Tirpitz* as she lay exerting sea power while camouflaged in Norway. (U.S. Naval Institute Photo Archives)

The navy's last great operation was the epic transportation of one and a half million civilians and half a million soldiers from East Prussia to the west. It was the greatest maritime evacuation in history.

B. SUMMARY AND ASSESSMENT

The Kriegsmarine entered war unprepared and helplessly inferior to the British and French navies. In spite of that, it began the struggle actively—unlike the Hochseeflotte in the First World War. In the war's first years Admiral Raeder laid more emphasis on capital ships, and he resigned when this strategy ended. Admiral Dönitz pushed the submarine war but did not receive Hitler's full support. The leaders of the Kriegsmarine never realized that Hitler's aims were continental. He wanted Russia and her resources. In his concept, the Kriegsmarine only served to keep Britain at bay.

Under these circumstances, the Kriegsmarine performed comparatively well. With its weak means, it sank about as many ships as it lost (see tables 2.6 and 2.7).

TABLE 2.6 Allied Losses Caused by German Forces

Type	Surface ships	Submarines	Aircraft	Mines or coast artillery
Battleships	1	2	2	0
Carriers	1	4	0	0
Cruisers[b]	5	7	11	1
Destroyer types	18	83	75	54
Mine warfare ships	2	6	10	10

TABLE 2.7 German Losses Caused by Allied Forces

Type	Surface ships	Submarines	Aircraft	Mines or coast artillery
Battleships[a]	2	0	1	1
Cruisers[b]	1	1	8	1
Destroyers	18	0	6	2
TBs/Escorts	23	3	44	6
Mine warfare ships	18	5	47	11

[a] German battleships include an old one by mine or coast artillery.
[b] Allied cruisers sunk include two coast defense by surface ships and one monitor by aircraft. German cruisers include an old one by surface ships, an old one by aircraft, and two gunboats by aircraft.

A look at the merchant war against Britain shows that the submarines were the main threat (see table 2.8). U-boats conducted more than 3,400 combat patrols during the war and 648 were lost at sea in frontline operations. In comparison, Allied merchant ships made more than 300,000 successful Atlantic voyages and 100,000 more in British coastal waters.

The problems with U-boat warfare had many causes: The German submarine campaign arose from Germany's limited options for waging war against Britain in 1939. The military failed to topple Britain's homeland position by air attack or invasion, and the excellent results achieved in the initial submarine actions led to overoptimistic expectations. U-boats were an effective weapon as long as their technical and tactical superiority was unimpaired by Allied tactics and countermeasures (radar, direction finding, escort carriers, and so forth). The U-boat building program was trapped between the demand for high production figures and the need for technical improvements. The numerical inferiority of the German U-boat arm compared with Allied ASW forces increased greatly toward the end of war. Even at the height of the U-boat campaign in May 1943, only 236 boats with approximately twelve thousand men were available for frontline service, equaling the personnel strength of a single army division. Expectations of victory under these circumstances were

TABLE 2.8 Allied Merchant Ships Sunk in World War II

Agent of Loss	Number	GRT
Submarines	2,828	14,687,231
Aircraft	820	2,889,883
Mines	534	1,406,037
Surface vessels	104	498,447
Armed merchant cruisers	133	829,644
Motor torpedo boats	99	229,676
Scuttlings, prizes, unknown	632	1,029,352
Total	5,150	21,570,270
Accidents, collisions	1,600	3,000,000

unrealistic. The U-boat campaign lacked substantial cooperation from other services in the Wehrmacht, especially the Luftwaffe. The notorious German limitations in personnel and resources reduced chances for victory in a lengthy campaign to starve out Britain, which was based mainly on wishful thinking in naval staff circles, not on reliable economic and logistic analysis of the enemy situation. The operational staff of U-boat Command, which consisted of former U-boat officers promoted to staff positions, lacked external scientific advice and the operational research skills needed to improve combat effectiveness and tactics.

Quick numerical expansion of the U-boat arm during 1941–1942 and the high casualty rate thereafter resulted in a constant decline in combat experience and professional skill on the part of the U-boat crews, which negatively affected operational efficiency and loss rate. In the end, the Kriegsmarine lost a war it had not wanted and fought until the end in a hopelessly inferior situation.

chapter three

Great Britain: The Royal Navy

I. BACKSTORY

A. HISTORY

British naval power has its roots in Anglo-Saxon times but came into its own in the successful wars against the Spanish and the Dutch in the sixteenth and seventeenth centuries. During the Napoleonic Wars, the Royal Navy reached the peak of supremacy under its most revered admiral, Horatio Nelson. Nelson's triumph at Trafalgar over the combined French and Spanish fleets remains synonymous with decisive victory even today.

The Royal Navy ushered in the modern era during the Crimean War when the first steam-powered ships of the line entered service. The rifling of cannon improved accuracy and the explosive shell that followed proved devastating against wooden hulls, prompting the introduction of armor plating. In 1870 the Royal Navy was the first to purchase the self-propelled torpedo. The turret ship *Devastation* entered service in 1873, giving Britain its first major warship without sails. The enormous *Inflexible* of 1881, with four 16-inch muzzle-loaded guns and a speed of fifteen knots, was the largest warship of its day. By 1900 the Royal Navy had its first submarines.

In 1906 the battleship *Dreadnought* revolutionized naval warfare and became the model for subsequent capital ship designs with her turbine propulsion and all-big-gun weaponry. But this radical escalation from previous standards had serious ramifications. British policy had held that the Royal Navy should match the size of any two combined foreign fleets, the so-called Two-Power Standard, but with all major navies inspired to acquire their own dreadnoughts, the Royal Navy instantly forfeited its numerical advantage in top-quality ships, and the British found themselves in a naval construction race with a newly expanding German fleet.

This rivalry set the stage for the First World War, an event the Royal Navy found distinctly unsatisfying. The navy's vast battleship fleet failed to fulfill the public's expectation of a decisive victory to match Trafalgar while the threat of starvation presented by German submarines presented challenges its admirals had failed to anticipate prewar.

World War I saw other unexpected innovations. Seaplanes rapidly evolved in capability to operate from shore and from specialized seagoing tenders. *Furious*, a cruiser conversion fitted with a short flying-off deck, launched a carrier-borne attack on the Zeppelin sheds at Tondern in August 1918. Soon after, *Argus*, a converted liner, became the world's first flush-deck aircraft carrier. These accomplishments, however, came after the Royal Navy had lost command of its air service with the creation of the Royal Air Force on 1 April 1918, a move that would stunt Britain's naval aviation for twenty years.

Peacetime brought additional challenges. The Washington Treaty of 1922 dictated a "One-Power Standard" for the Royal Navy, now nominally equal to the United States Navy with a total battleship tonnage of 525,000 tons. For the 1930 London Treaty, Britain sacrificed its stated cruiser requirements. Six years later, the British signed another London Treaty to limit the weaponry permitted on new battleships to 14-inch guns. The Royal Navy, its supremacy clearly waning, had additional disadvantages attached to its carrier force. Although the navy finally regained command of the Fleet Air Arm, this could not instantly erase the consequences of the twenty-year divorce, and the carriers themselves were generally older and less capable than those operating with the Japanese and American fleets. Nevertheless, September 1939 found the Royal Navy anticipating the outbreak of war and still believing itself the world's premier fleet.

B. MISSION

In 1939 no navy had a spread of responsibilities like the Royal Navy's, with the need to maintain fleets in the Mediterranean and the Atlantic as well as a worldwide presence. The primary mission was the historic one of protecting trade. Densely populated, the United Kingdom could grow only half the food it needed, and while it had ample supplies of coal, it had insignificant quantities of home-produced oil. Most British iron ore had a sulfur content too high to produce good quality steel, so iron ore had to be imported, along with most other raw materials.

The second mission was to protect the United Kingdom, the Empire, and the dominions—Australia, Canada, New Zealand, and South Africa (political entities that differed from the colonies because they were self-governing)—from invasion by a foreign power. In this mission the British were assisted by the independent but closely affiliated royal navies of Canada and Australia, the Royal Indian Navy, and the New Zealand and South African naval services. These forces are described later. Between the wars, London promised

PHOTO 3.1. Maintaining the Empire. The heavy cruiser *Cornwall* and the carrier *Hermes* on the China Station in 1935. (NARA 80-G449064)

Australia and New Zealand that, in the event of war with Japan, a strong fleet would be sent east to protect them. This pledge did not take into account the possibility of war in Europe.

As war with Germany grew increasingly likely, a third mission emerged. The navy collaborated with the French fleet while also supporting the lines of communication across the English Channel for the troops of the British Expeditionary Force, which began moving to France the day after war was declared.

II. ORGANIZATION

A. COMMAND STRUCTURE

By 1939 the Royal Navy had endured a number of reorganizations. The Grand Fleet of the First World War had become first the Atlantic Fleet and, later, the Home Fleet. The Inskip Award of 1937 had returned naval aviation from the Royal Air Force (RAF) to the Admiralty, which formally took control of the Fleet Air Arm in May 1939 although the RAF retained shore-based maritime-reconnaissance and search and rescue.

In 1939 the Royal Navy was organized into the following commands:

The Home Fleet, the largest administrative formation with its main bases at Portsmouth, Devonport (near Plymouth), and the Nore, more usually known as Chatham.
The Mediterranean Fleet, with bases at Malta, Gibraltar, and Alexandria
The China Station, at Hong Kong
The East Indies Station centered at Singapore
The American Station, at Bermuda
The African Station, based at Simonstown, South Africa
The West Indies Station based on Jamaica

Under wartime pressures, new North Atlantic and South Atlantic Commands were created. There were also six home commands: Orkney and Shetland, Rosyth, Nore, Dover, Portsmouth, and the Western Approaches (initially at Plymouth, soon moved to Liverpool). The China Station became the British Eastern Fleet on 2 December 1941, with its own commander in chief. After the fall of Singapore and the Japanese attacks on Ceylon, the British Eastern Fleet moved its headquarters to British East Africa. Operations in the Indian Ocean were supported by a secret refueling base at Addu Atoll.

In 1939 the Mediterranean Fleet had Malta with its extensive dockyard facilities as its main base with secondary bases at Alexandria in Egypt and at Gibraltar. In June 1940, with the Mediterranean cut in two by Italy's declaration of war and France's surrender, the Mediterranean Fleet was effectively confined to the eastern Mediterranean. The Admiralty created Force H under Vice Admiral Sir James Somerville and based it at Gibraltar to operate in both the western Mediterranean and the Atlantic. Although Force H was officially a squadron, it was in reality a small but balanced fleet with an aircraft carrier, a battleship and battle cruiser, cruisers, and destroyers.

1. Administration

A key feature distinguishing the Royal Navy from the British Army and the Royal Air Force was that the Admiralty was not simply the power that directed the Royal Navy; it was also an operational headquarters. While the navy did have local commanders with substantial delegated authority, usually designated as flag officers (holding the rank of rear admiral and above), there would often be a commander in chief over and above any flag officers. As an example, the Mediterranean Fleet had a commander in chief with subordinate flag officers for cruisers, destroyers, and aircraft carriers while Force H based on Gibraltar had a flag officer and enjoyed considerable autonomy, moving between the Atlantic and the western Mediterranean as the strategic position required. As the war developed, not only was there a commander in chief for the Home Fleet but one for the Western Approaches as well.

As an operational and an administrative headquarters, the Admiralty could send orders to commanding officers aboard ships over the heads of their local commanders, as justified by developments in naval intelligence. Indeed, the withholding of information by the Admiralty had contributed to the disappointing outcome of the Battle of Jutland in 1916, and that lesson had been learned. The Admiralty included an Operational Intelligence Centre (OIC), and this was to prove especially successful in countering the U-boat threat.

The Admiralty dated from the reign of Henry VIII and, long before the Second World War, was controlled by the Board of Admiralty. The First Lord of the Admiralty was a political post and a member of the cabinet; at the outbreak of war, Winston Churchill held this position. The naval officers on the board were led by the First Sea Lord, who was also the chief of the naval staff. The other sea lords were the Second Sea Lord, responsible for personnel; the Third Sea Lord or controller of the navy, responsible for shipbuilding and repair, including the naval dockyards; the Fourth Sea Lord, responsible for victualling, supplies, and the naval hospitals; and the most recent addition to the group, the Fifth Sea Lord, in charge of naval aviation.

The First Sea Lord was supported by the vice chief of the naval staff, who had wide-ranging responsibilities including intelligence, planning, communications, hydrography, and navigation. The First Sea Lord was also supported by three assistant chiefs of the naval staff, otherwise known as ACNS, who had responsibility for home, foreign, and trade matters. In addition to these individual roles, each ACNS would also look after local defense, operations, training, gunnery, and minesweeping.

The Western Approaches Command exemplified how this structure worked. Tasked with the battle of the Atlantic and the convoys, it came under the direct responsibility of the ACNS Trade. The Admiralty trade division planned routes for the convoys, working with the submarine tracking room at the Admiralty, itself part of the Naval Intelligence Division. The allocation of merchant ships to convoys was the responsibility of the Naval Control Service, which had a presence in each merchant port. Escort vessels were organized into groups under the control of Western Approaches.

Within the fleets, major warships of similar types were organized into squadrons, each of which could have two or more ships. Smaller warships such as destroyers, minesweepers, and submarines were formed into flotillas, again with varying numbers of ships, although destroyer flotillas ideally consisted of nine vessels. A destroyer flotilla would be subdivided into two divisions. Within forces, the squadron and flotilla distinction was often dropped, so that Force K, for example, when first established on Malta consisted simply of two cruisers and two destroyers. A submarine flotilla often operated independently and could have any number of craft while submarine commanders usually had considerable delegated authority—with none of the centralized direction that characterized the German U-boat fleet. Later, the Admiralty became heavily involved in combined operations, and when the time came, this organization took over amphibious ships and landing craft.

With no separate ministry for defense but three separate services ministries (Admiralty, War Office, and Air), appropriations during the war were based on overall defense requirements rather than on a service-by-service basis. A good example arose when Churchill wrote to the Chancellor of the Exchequer demanding that a sum of £20 million per year be allocated to improving pay and allowances for service personnel, with priority being given to the lowest paid and those who were married. There was no distinction between the individual services.

In the last year of peace, the total amount allocated for defense was £254 million. The navy estimates in the decade 1930 to 1939 averaged £63.5 million a year, with £78.1 in 1937, £93.7 in 1938, and £69.4 million in 1939.[1]

2. Personnel

In June 1939 the Royal Navy and Royal Marines had 129,000 men, of whom just fewer than 10,000 were officers. The 12,400 officers and men of the Royal Marines had a number of shipboard roles, including security and the band service, but on cruisers and battleships they also manned the X turret. The Fleet Air Arm included a significant number of marine pilots and some observers.

To achieve maximum strength in wartime, the navy could recall recently retired officers and ratings as well as two categories of reserves, the Royal Naval Reserve (RNR) and the Royal Naval Volunteer Reserve (RNVR), which between them provided another 73,000 officers and men in 1939. The RNR consisted mainly of people drawn from the merchant navy, who often had outstanding navigation and ship-handling skills, although there were other branches, notably marine engineering. The RNVR, which consisted of people from all walks of life, underwent massive wartime expansion—to 48,000 officers and 5,000 ratings—because most wartime recruits went into the RNVR. Many RNVR personnel rose to command corvettes, minesweepers, and destroyers; others commanded Fleet Air Arm squadrons.

By mid-1944, the Royal Navy had reached its peak strength of 863,500, including 73,500 of the Women's Royal Naval Service (WRNS, also known as "Wrens"). Many of the lower deck personnel in wartime were conscripts called up under the National Service Acts for "hostilities only." Frequently, when merchant shipping was taken up from trade, the ships' companies were signed up under special articles so that they became part of the navy and subject to naval discipline, with temporary naval ranks, although they retained certain merchant navy terms of service, such as danger money for working in a war zone.

The Royal Navy's wartime casualties amounted to 50,758 killed with another 820 missing and presumed dead, and 14,663 wounded. The WRNS lost 102 killed and 22 wounded, mainly in air raids.

In peacetime, regular officers entered the service as early as age thirteen, spending four years at the Royal Naval College at Dartmouth, which operated as a fee-paying school. Those who had attended other schools joined at age seventeen or eighteen and spent a term at Dartmouth. In both cases, after graduating from Dartmouth, they would serve eighteen months as midshipmen. Despite the cap badge, midshipmen were not regarded as officers in the full sense, being addressed as "mister" and not joining their seniors in the wardroom, the naval term for the officers' mess, instead being confined to the gunroom mess. In peacetime, a midshipman who wanted to fly would undergo most of his training with the RAF, with the Royal Navy providing catapult training so he could fly ship-launched seaplanes and amphibians. The two-year training program for pilots and observers was compressed into ten months after war broke out.

Though commissioning from the ranks—or, in naval parlance, the lower deck—became significant during and after the Second World War, this had been a rarity in the prewar Navy. To obtain a sufficient number of experienced officers for the rapid wartime expansion, many senior ratings, normally chief petty officers, were commissioned under the "upper yardman scheme."

With war looming, a "special entry scheme" at Dartmouth was introduced. In September 1942, the college was bombed and it was evacuated to Eaton Hall, Cheshire, until the end of the war. It was already clear, even before the bombing, that extra training facilities would be needed. In 1939 the government requisitioned Hove Marina and nearby Lancing College and commissioned them as HMS King Alfred. The reservists' college later relocated to Exbury House near Southampton before the Normandy landings in 1944. During the war years, 22,508 RNVR officers graduated from King Alfred.

Nevertheless, by 1942 it was apparent that King Alfred alone could not meet the demand for officers, and methods of selecting suitable lower deck candidates were improved. A trial scheme at HMS Glendower, a seaman new-entry training establishment at Pwllheli in North Wales, showed promise and was soon extended to the seamen training establishments at HMS Collingwood, Ganges, Raleigh, and Royal Arthur. Engineering candidates were found at the stokers' school at HMS Duke, communications specialists at HMS Excalibur, and naval airmen at HMS Gosling.

The peacetime practice of naval officers becoming midshipmen before undertaking aircrew training also changed under wartime conditions. The reduced ten-month program produced naval airmen who were not strictly speaking "sailors who could fly" but were instead "fliers who went to sea." An air branch was formed to accommodate both the RNVR pilots and RAF personnel who had volunteered to transfer to the Royal Navy when it regained control of its aviation. Aspiring pilots and observers were given basic training at HMS St. Vincent, a stone frigate at Gosport, before being sent to start their basic flying training, initially with the RAF. As the RAF struggled to cope with its own expanded needs, many received training with the U.S. Navy (USN) at Pensacola, returning to the Royal Navy for the final stages. They were not commissioned until flying training was completed but started operational conversion courses as naval officers. With a few exceptions, naval pilots and observers were all commissioned.

In the prewar Royal Navy, personnel could join either as adults or, more usually, as boys. They were sent to one of the training establishments at HMS Ganges near Ipswich, St. Vincent at Gosport, or Caledonia on the Clyde. Ganges itself was still being developed, and a new school block opened just before the outbreak of war. Under the pressure of wartime needs, the Admiralty decided in spring 1940 to use the establishment for training adult ratings, including many wartime "hostilities only" (HO) personnel, and for the duration it lost its role as a boys' training establishment. At first, an entry of 264 HO ratings arrived while Ganges was still home to fifteen hundred boys, but in May six hundred boys were transferred to the Isle of Man where they were joined by evacuees from the other two establishments to create a new combined boys' training establishment, St. George, on the site of a former holiday camp. New training establishments had been planned before the war, including Collingwood in Hampshire and Raleigh in Cornwall. Although training of specialists such as wireless telegraph ratings had been conducted at Ganges, this activity was removed to Gloucester, which was commissioned as a satellite of Ganges.

These measures were accompanied in 1940 by a halving of the time allotted to ratings for basic training. By then the Royal Navy had more than 250,000 personnel, demonstrating the pace of wartime expansion. Highnam Court was developed to accommodate up to 3,000 personnel, while Ganges's capacity was expanded to 17,000. From Easter 1940 to October 1945, no fewer than 60,968 HO ratings passed through Ganges. Specialized training such as that for wireless telegraphy followed basic training. One of the new training establishments, Collingwood, started to receive wireless telegraph trainees in June 1940, with 1,000 trainees joining every three weeks for a ten-week course, and a radio direction finding school was added in 1942. Collingwood also trained Wrens.

3. Intelligence

The Admiralty included a Naval Intelligence Division (NID) dating from 1886, although this had been run down considerably between the wars and had lost its team of cryptographers, who transferred to the Secret Intelligence Service (SIS) as the Code and Cypher School at Bletchley Park. The NID was organized in geographical sections and obtained intelligence from a single country or group of countries that provided the planners with information for any future conflict. Initially the naval attachés in British embassies generated many of the reports; after the German occupation of Western Europe, agents or resistance workers in the conquered countries became a principal source of intelligence. Information on Axis merchant shipping came from Lloyds and the Baltic Exchange. The RAF flew photoreconnaissance missions. While the working relationship between the RAF and the Royal Navy was reasonably good, difficulties could arise. For example, despite being tasked by the Admiralty to fly reconnaissance missions over Taranto, the RAF refused to allow a naval officer on Admiral Andrew Cunningham's staff to take the photographs. He had to unofficially "borrow" them overnight to have them copied.

The first moves to prepare for war came with the Ethiopian crisis of 1935. The director of naval intelligence was ordered by the deputy chief of naval staff to prepare an intelligence center so that operational intelligence would be passed to the units at sea and to the RAF without delay. The OIC was put on a war footing shortly before the outbreak of war in Europe. In addition to reports from various sources, the OIC used a network of directional wireless stations that plotted the positions of Axis signals.

Naval intelligence dramatically improved with the capture of German Enigma ciphers from a German weather-reporting trawler and a U-boat in May 1941. These coups enabled Bletchley Park to decipher and translate signals before forwarding them to the NID. In some cases, information reached the OIC within minutes. OIC would assess the intelligence and, after taking precautions to protect the source, pass it on to the operational units concerned.

It was the wartime director of naval intelligence, Rear Admiral John Godfrey, who initiated the Inter-Service Topographical Department, bringing together experts from all three services to collect, collate, and analyze information about ports, coastlines, communications, and other matters in enemy-occupied territory so the information was available for invading forces. NID also included a section designated 17M, which supplied naval information to the Germans through a network of controlled double agents.

B. DOCTRINE

1. Surface Warfare

In many ways, the Royal Navy expected that the Second World War would follow the pattern of the first. Given the size of German surface forces, the navy did not anticipate a major battle such as Jutland with the Kriegsmarine. Conversely, they did expect a fleet action in the Mediterranean with the Italian navy, which had sufficient battleships and cruisers to threaten the combined British Mediterranean Fleet and French Mediterranean Squadron.

British doctrine was to concentrate fire as closely as possible on the target, usually firing salvos but sometimes firing broadsides, in the belief that, if accuracy was spot on, an opponent could be seriously or even fatally damaged. A high rate of fire was also encouraged, and this could be twice the rate of Italian ships, for example.

2. Aviation

The Royal Navy had taken an interest in aviation as early as 1910, and the Royal Naval Air Service played an important role during the First World War. This was almost a "service within a service" and at one time was given responsibility for the air defense of Great Britain, which may have contributed to its undoing because the overlap of duties with the British Army's Royal Flying Corps led to the formation of an autonomous Royal Air Force on 1 April 1918. The new service inherited 2,500 aircraft and 55,000 officers and men from the Royal Navy.

With the benefit of hindsight, it is clear this decision had unfortunate consequences for the navy. Aircrew and maintainers serving shipboard became members of the RAF, coexisting alongside the carrier's general service officers and ratings. The main exceptions to this arrangement were those concerned with seaplanes and flying boats operated from battleships and cruisers, who remained naval aviators, as did a small number sprinkled through the fighter and bomber squadrons. The aircraft embarked in battleships and cruisers provided the reconnaissance and spotter role for the fleet's guns. Aboard the carriers, however, there was a demarcation line between the seafarers and the aviators. This was emphasized to a great extent by the system under which RAF stations in the Mediterranean and Far East included flights that could operate from aircraft carriers visiting those areas. In practical terms, units were under Admiralty control afloat and Air Ministry control ashore.

Following the recommendations of the Balfour Committee of 1923, which examined Royal Navy and RAF cooperation, the Fleet Air Arm (FAA) of the RAF was formed with five squadrons belonging to what was then known as RAF Coastal Area but became Coastal Command in 1936. In 1937, it was proposed that the FAA be handed over to full Admiralty control. Nevertheless, the Admiralty did not formally take over until 24 May 1939. In between parliament authorized the Admiralty to increase FAA personnel by 300 percent. While most of the RAF personnel serving with the FAA returned to other postings within the service, around fifteen hundred transferred to the Royal Navy. One innovation introduced by the RAF that survived the handover was the squadron numbering system, which can be described briefly as being in the 7XX series for noncombatant and support squadrons and the 8XX series for combat squadrons. The RAF has been criticized for neglecting the needs of naval aviation between the wars, but these were periods of acute financial stringency for all of the armed forces, and under the pressures of building up its own strength to meet wartime needs, the RAF's systems were under even greater stress.

The authority for expansion made it seem that the Royal Navy was finally equipping its air arm for war. The reality, though, was different; there were few naval aviators and maintenance personnel, hardly any naval air stations, and no high-performance naval aircraft. The Fairey Swordfish biplane formed the fleet's offensive mainstay, and two aircraft provided defense, the monoplane Blackburn Roc and the biplane Gloster Sea Gladiator. While criticism often centers on obsolescent Royal Navy aircraft, the reconstituted FAA's real problem was that an entire generation of senior officers with aviation experience had been lost with the transfer of so many to the RAF, and even many naval officers believed that high-performance aircraft could not operate from ships. Nevertheless, while many still saw the carrier aircraft as providing a supporting role, others appreciated their offensive potential, and as early as the Ethiopian Crisis plans were prepared for an aerial attack on the Italian fleet at Taranto. Considerable emphasis was placed on the torpedo-bomber, partly due to the lack of high-performance aircraft that could carry bombs large enough to cripple a warship. In any case, experience was to show that all but the largest bombs bounced off armor plating, and torpedoes were far more effective at sinking or crippling warships.

In home waters, the FAA's shore-based aircraft covered convoys from the beginning of the war in Europe until the German surrender on 8 May 1945. At times shore-based FAA squadrons were placed under RAF Coastal Command control to ensure better integration. The FAA complemented the work of the RAF, with the latter using larger twin-engined and four-engined long-range aircraft while the FAA operated over shorter ranges, all that was necessary for the North Sea and English Channel.

The Fleet Air Arm started the Second World War with 232 aircraft and 360 qualified pilots, with another 332 under training. The Royal Navy had seven aircraft carriers, of which four—*Argus*, *Eagle*, *Furious*, and *Hermes*—were officially due to retire but remained in service as war clouds gathered.

This meant that with the first of the *Illustrious*-class carriers still incomplete, the best ships were the converted battle cruisers *Courageous* and *Glorious* and the new *Ark Royal*. None of these three ships survived the first two years of war. The seaplane carrier, *Pegasus*, was mainly used for training aircrew in catapult operations.

There were few Royal Naval Air Stations at the outset. HMS Daedalus at Lee-on-Solent on the Hampshire coast was one of them. Not only was "Lee" convenient for the ships of the fleet based at Portsmouth, it also had a slipway for seaplanes and amphibians. Yeovilton was under construction. The Fleet Air Arm also had lodging facilities at RAF bases.

3. Antisubmarine

British antisubmarine warfare doctrine was based on two concepts, forming merchant shipping into convoys and conducting sweeps of the open seas for enemy submarines. The latter method saw the loss of the aircraft carrier *Courageous* on 17 September 1939 and was quickly dropped as being costly and unproductive. Prewar expectations for Asdic were soon proven too high; nevertheless, the Royal Navy entered the war with an advantage that at one time made senior German naval officers such as Raeder question the value of submarines.

Determined attempts were also made to destroy submarines before they could reach the open sea. The Royal Air Force sent its Bomber Command aircraft on mine-dropping missions, known as "Gardening Operations," and attacked U-boat yards but was hampered at the beginning of the war by the lack of a true long-range heavy bomber. After the fall of France, the Germans built U-boat pens on the French coast that were impregnable until subjected to 12,000-pound "Tall Boy" and 22,000-pound "Grand Slam" bombs.

Convoys were a joint venture between RAF Coastal Command and the Royal Navy. The British and Commonwealth navies as well as "free" forces under Royal Navy command accounted for 514 of the 785 German U-boats sunk, with another 166 credited to the USN and 12 shared between the Royal Navy and USN. RAF Coastal Command accounted for 93.

British escort vessels, destroyers, frigates, sloops, and corvettes carried Asdic which enabled them to home onto a submarine before dropping depth charges. Depth charges were deployed using rails and throwers, which remained a standard system throughout the war, eventually supplemented by the ahead-throwing weapons Squid and Hedgehog.

Swordfish biplanes on antisubmarine warfare (ASW) patrols were eventually fitted with air-surface vessel (ASV) radar, able to pick up a submarine periscope in good conditions. Eventually, maritime-reconnaissance aircraft also received radar. Aircraft maintaining patrols around a convoy would often

direct escort vessels toward the submarine largely because the aircraft escorting the convoy could only carry four depth charges each, due to weight and
their limited number of strong points.

4. Submarine

The Admiralty decided in 1939 that the priority target for the Royal Navy's
submarines would be enemy warships, in part because Britain had sponsored
the London Naval Treaty of 1930, which required submarines to conform to
international law and to avoid sinking noncombatant vessels without fair
warning. In practice this meant that submarines would lurk within individual patrol areas, submerged, waiting for enemy warships to appear. Later, in
1941 in the Mediterranean, they were frequently given roving commissions to
attack anything that appeared a worthy target. The same approach was later
applied in Asian waters.

Because Germany had little in the way of overseas trade, other than the
convoys bringing Swedish iron ore down the coast of Norway when the more
direct route via the Gulf of Bothnia froze in winter, the main theater in which
the Royal Navy's submarines operated was in the Mediterranean. Before the
war, the Admiralty had identified Malta as an ideal base for submarines and
light forces.

Overall, British submarines sank 169 warships, including 35 U-boats, and
493 merchant vessels throughout the war years, but this came at an extremely
high cost, with no less than 77 British submarines sunk, a third of the total
number deployed during the war. While just 1 submarine was lost in the four
months of war in 1939, the losses grew to 24 submarines in 1940, and were
almost as high again in 1942 when 20 boats were lost. A third of all losses
resulted from enemy minefields.

5. Amphibious Operations

The Royal Navy had mixed results with amphibious operations during the
First World War, and the doctrine that would drive the Royal Navy's successes
during the second war had just begun development as war erupted. As early
as 1923, the Admiralty had received the Madden Committee's recommendations, including the suggestion that the Royal Marines provide an amphibious striking force and a mobile force for defending overseas bases. Initially
ignored, these recommendations would form the foundation of the Royal
Marine Commandos after war broke out. However, only when Churchill came
to power was the importance of combined operations stressed, and in July
1940 he set a special directorate to develop the specialized training and equipment required for successful amphibious operations. Fortunately, Admiralty
control of the Royal Marines facilitated this task.

British and Dominion forces conducted two major raids on German bases in occupied territory. The first of these was to destroy the dry dock at St. Nazaire on the night of 27–28 March 1942, which was the only one on the Biscay coast capable of accommodating the German battleship *Tirpitz*. The operation was successful but bloody, with 144 men killed and 288 captured. In the other raid, the Germans detected the assault on the beaches and the harbor at Dieppe on 19 August 1942, and this operation, in part a rehearsal for an invasion of France, was a failure, with many of the mostly Canadian troops taken prisoner.

The first pure British amphibious assault of the war was Operation Ironclad, the invasion of French Madagascar. On 5 May 1942, British forces landed north of Diego Suarez, taking the French by surprise and capturing their objective. Just over thirty ships were involved, including two aircraft carriers and the battleship *Ramillies*.

Most of the invasions that followed were joint Allied ventures. Their success was helped by the advent of landing craft able to land men, vehicles, and tanks efficiently on beaches, and specialized versions were used to suppress enemy defenses with intense rocket fire. The landing ships were far larger. As naval technology developed, these even extended to the landing ship dock, with a floodable stern from which landing craft could be launched.

As the war progressed the British conducted or participated in a series of large-scale assaults against objectives in North Africa, Sicily, Italy, southern France, Normandy, Burma, and Borneo. After the fiasco at the well-defended port at Dieppe, every operation succeeded.

6. Trade Protection

Convoys required protection across the North Atlantic or south across the Bay of Biscay to Gibraltar, where they often divided, with one convoy heading for the Cape of Good Hope and the other into the Mediterranean. There were also convoys in the Indian Ocean and up the Red Sea, and, after Germany invaded the Soviet Union, Iceland often served as a convenient mustering point for convoys to Archangel and Murmansk.

While convoys were not compulsory, only the fastest ships, such as the large ocean liners *Queen Mary* and *Queen Elizabeth*, could safely cross the Atlantic on their own. The fall of France gave the Germans valuable bases on the Atlantic so that their surface ships and the growing number of U-boats no longer had to sail around the north of Scotland to reach their operational areas, while the German conquest of Norway meant that air and submarine attack was a constant hazard for convoys to and from the Soviet Union. The British government had banned British merchant ships from the Mediterranean even before Italy entered the war, and by 1941 the situation was so desperate that supplying the beleaguered island of Malta became all but impossible. British forces in North Africa were supplied by the roundabout means of convoys sailing south to the Cape of Good Hope, and then north through the Indian Ocean, Red Sea, and Suez Canal until they reached Egypt's Mediterranean ports.

The considerable menace posed by Germany's surface ships kept the Royal Navy's Home Fleet heavily occupied, especially in the war's first two years. German motor torpedo boats (MTBs) threatened coastal convoys for the entire war.

To meet the need for mass-producible escorts, the Flower-class corvette was introduced, and later the frigate was reinvented for convoy duty. Escort forces got a boost by the exchange of old U.S. destroyers for the use of British bases in the Caribbean, Newfoundland, and Bermuda.

Fighter protection against German aircraft was another problem. As a stopgap, the naval fighter catapult ships (FCS) and mercantile catapult-armed merchant ships (CAM) went into service carrying a single modified Hawker Hurricane or Fairey Fulmar—a one-shot solution because the fighter could launch but not land, leaving the pilot to hunt for a land base or bail out and hope for rescue. A better solution, merchant aircraft carriers (MAC) operated by merchant personnel were grain carriers and oil tankers converted with a short flight deck suitable for three or four antisubmarine Fairey Swordfish biplanes. The grain carriers, with a rudimentary hangar, could accommodate four aircraft, but the tankers had no hangar and could carry just three. These ships sufficed on the North Atlantic but did not carry enough aircraft for the Arctic convoys or those to the Cape. Fortunately, escort carriers began to appear in large numbers by 1943. The Royal Navy had a small number of British-converted ships, but the United States supplied most. Escort carriers could operate anywhere although even fast and heavily armored fleet carriers were vulnerable in the Mediterranean.

Other steps were taken to improve the security of merchant vessels, so that by March 1941, the Admiralty Defensively Equipped Merchant Ship organization had equipped 3,434 ships with antisubmarine guns and 4,431 British and Allied ships with one or more close-range antiaircraft guns. Initially, naval ratings and army gunners were seconded, but later merchant seamen were trained to take their place.

The statistics for World War II convoys were impressive. During the war years, there were 2,889 escorted trade convoys to and from the United Kingdom, for a total of 85,775 ships. There were another 7,944 coastal convoys comprising 175,608 ships.

PHOTO 3.2. In their struggle against submarines, the British employed some ingenious expedients. Here a Fairey Swordfish takes off from a converted grain carrier operating as merchant aircraft carrier, or MAC. (The Late Lord Kilbracken courtesy of David Wragg)

7. Communications

As an operational headquarters, the Admiralty maintained firm control of most naval operations, with the exception of the submarines, and not only communicated with the naval commander in chief but also with individual ships. Operational commanders varied in their use of communications. Admiral Tom Phillips, in command of *Prince of Wales* and *Repulse*, planned to attack the Japanese invasion fleet off Malaya but maintained strict radio silence, making it impossible for RAF units to provide air cover, and on 10 December 1941, his two capital ships fell victim to Japanese aircraft. By contrast, during the Battle of the North Cape on 26 December 1943, Admiral Sir Bruce Fraser decided that good communication outweighed the benefits of radio silence, and this was a factor in his forces being able to intercept and sink the German battleship *Scharnhorst*.

The Royal Navy adopted the American TBS (Talk Between Ships) radio system. Shipboard signals staffs were also trained in Morse code using Aldis lamps or flags.

III. MATERIEL

A. SHIPS

The battleships included the First World War veterans of the *Queen Elizabeth* class (30,600–31,585 tons [all displacements are standard unless otherwise indicated] and carrying eight 15-inch guns), of which only one, *Warspite*, had been completely modernized before the war, while *Queen Elizabeth* and *Valiant* were in the process of being modernized. The remaining two ships of the class, *Malaya* and *Barham*, had been only partly modernized. The smaller size of *Royal Sovereign*–class ships (29,150 tons, eight 15-inch guns) complicated modernization plans, and although their AA defenses were updated, none enjoyed a major reconstruction. Completed in 1927, *Nelson* and *Rodney* (33,900 tons, nine 16-inch guns) had a broadside of 18,432 pounds compared with the 15,360 pounds of the 15-inch gunned ships. The most modern battleships, the *King George V* class (37,000 tons, ten 14-inch guns), entered service during the war. One remaining ship, *Vanguard* (46,100 tons), marked a return to eight 15-inch guns but was not commissioned until after the war. At one stage, consideration was given to completing her as an aircraft carrier, but this was rejected in mid-July 1942. See table 3.1 for data on the strength of the Royal Navy in 1939 and 1945.

TABLE 3.1 **Strength of Royal Navies of the United Kingdom and the Commonwealth**

Type	1939	Losses	1945[a]
BB/BC	15	5	15
CV	7	5	7
CVL/CVE	0	3	52
Cruisers	58	32	62
DD/DE	178	149	257
DS/DC/DF	41	62	543
Fleet MS	29	39	274
Submarines	71	77	131
MTB/MGBs	18	144	420

[a] Includes on loan and in reserve.
Sources: Stephen Roskill, *The War at Sea 1939–1945* (London: HMSO, 1954), 583–87 and (1961), 436–449.

There were also three battle cruisers. *Hood*, completed in 1920 and for many years the world's largest warship at 42,100 tons, had eight 15-inch guns. The other two ships, *Renown* and *Repulse*, dated from 1916 but had been modernized between the wars; both displaced 32,000 tons and had six 15-inch guns.

Royal Navy
Order of Battle 3 September 1939

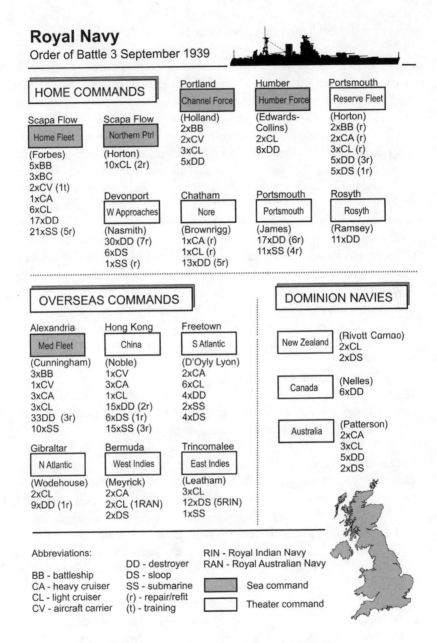

HOME COMMANDS

Scapa Flow
Home Fleet
(Forbes)
5xBB
3xBC
2xCV (1t)
1xCA
6xCL
17xDD
21xSS (5r)

Scapa Flow
Northern Ptrl
(Horton)
10xCL (2r)

Devonport
W Approaches
(Nasmith)
30xDD (7r)
6xDS
1xSS (r)

Portland
Channel Force
(Holland)
2xBB
2xCV
3xCL
5xDD

Chatham
Nore
(Brownrigg)
1xCA (r)
1xCL (r)
13xDD (5r)

Humber
Humber Force
(Edwards-Collins)
2xCL
8xDD

Portsmouth
Portsmouth
(James)
17xDD (6r)
11xSS (4r)

Portsmouth
Reserve Fleet
(Horton)
2xBB (r)
2xCA (r)
3xCL (r)
5xDD (3r)
5xDS (1r)

Rosyth
Rosyth
(Ramsey)
11xDD

OVERSEAS COMMANDS

Alexandria
Med Fleet
(Cunningham)
3xBB
1xCV
3xCA
3xCL
33DD (3r)
10xSS

Hong Kong
China
(Noble)
1xCV
3xCA
1xCL
15xDD (2r)
6xDS (1r)
15xSS (3r)

Freetown
S Atlantic
(D'Oyly Lyon)
2xCA
6xCL
4xDD
2xSS
4xDS

Gibraltar
N Atlantic
(Wodehouse)
2xCL
9xDD (1r)

Bermuda
West Indies
(Meyrick)
2xCA
2xCL (1RAN)
2xDS

Trincomalee
East Indies
(Leatham)
3xCL
12xDS (5RIN)
1xSS

DOMINION NAVIES

New Zealand
(Rivett Carnao)
2xCL
2xDS

Canada
(Nelles)
6xDD

Australia
(Patterson)
2xCA
3xCL
5xDD
2xDS

Abbreviations:

BB - battleship
CA - heavy cruiser
CL - light cruiser
CV - aircraft carrier
DD - destroyer
DS - sloop
SS - submarine
(r) - repair/refit
(t) - training

RIN - Royal Indian Navy
RAN - Royal Australian Navy

Sea command
Theater command

Aircraft carriers included the converted *Courageous*-class battle cruisers: *Furious* (converted in stages starting in 1917), *Courageous* (1928), and *Glorious* (1930). The two later ships displaced around 22,500 tons, and could carry up to forty-eight aircraft compared with thirty-three on *Furious*. Elderly *Argus* (14,000 tons), due to be scrapped when war broke out, could accommodate just fifteen aircraft by 1941. She was hulked as an accommodation ship before the war's end. Another ship that was showing her age was the converted battleship *Eagle* (22,600 tons), which could carry just twenty-two aircraft by 1942, the year that she was sunk. The first carrier to be designed as such from the keel upward was *Hermes* (10,850 tons), able to carry just twelve aircraft by 1939.

The most modern aircraft carrier in the Royal Navy on 3 September 1939 was *Ark Royal*, displacing 22,000 tons and intended to carry up to sixty aircraft in her two hangar decks, but by 1941 this was reduced to fifty-four. The loss of one hangar deck and the addition of an armored flight deck and hangar deck substantially reduced the aircraft capacity of the carriers that followed. Planned to replace the oldest of the carriers, the new *Illustrious* class (23,000 tons, originally designed for up to thirty-three aircraft) was fast and heavily armored; *Illustrious* and *Formidable* were completed in 1940 and *Victorious* in 1941. These were followed by the modified *Illustrious*-class *Indomitable* (fifty-four aircraft on two hangar decks). Finally in 1944, came the *Implacable* class of two ships (23,450 tons, sixty aircraft, and two hangar decks). The previous year had seen a maintenance and support carrier, HMS *Unicorn* (14,750 tons, up to thirty-six aircraft), join the fleet; she performed operationally on one occasion.

By this time, the Royal Navy had started to introduce escort carriers. The first of these, *Audacity* (9,000 tons, eight aircraft), was converted from a German cargo ship in 1941. She was followed in 1942 by a British ship, *Activity*, which was larger at 11,800 tons but still able to carry only ten aircraft.

U.S.-built escort carriers started to appear in 1941 with the *Archer* (10,220 tons, twelve aircraft). Three ships of the *Avenger* class (8,200 tons, fifteen aircraft) arrived in 1942. Then came the *Attacker* class (10,200 tons, twenty aircraft) and the 1943–1944 *Ameer* class (11,420 tons, twenty aircraft). The Royal Navy obtained further escort carriers from British sources, largely because the Admiralty incorrectly believed that the welded hulls of U.S.-supplied vessels would be unsuitable for Arctic waters. The first of these were *Vindex* and *Nairana* of 1943 (14,000 tons, twenty-one aircraft), which were based on a refrigerated cargo ship design. *Campania* (12,450 tons, twenty-one aircraft), similar to *Nairana*, joined the fleet in 1944. She was the first British escort carrier with an Action Information Organization.

Escort carriers displayed their worth during the war years but also their limitations. The fleet needed a capable aircraft carrier that could be built to merchant shipping standards in civilian yards. Thus was born the *Colossus* class (13,190 tons, designed for thirty-seven aircraft), known to the Royal Navy as a light fleet carrier. Five were commissioned before the end of the war but reached the Far East too late to see active service.

PHOTO 3.3. *Ark Royal*, the Royal Navy's most modern carrier in 1939. *Ark Royal* was unusual for having three aircraft elevators, which can be seen clearly here. (The Late S. H. Wragg, courtesy of David Wragg)

The oldest heavy cruisers in service at the outbreak of war were the *Kent* class built in 1927–1928, armed with eight 8-inch guns and displacing 9,750 tons in compliance with the Washington Treaty limits. A slightly modified *London* class was commissioned in 1929. The *Norfolk* class of 1930 was similar. These ships, known collectively as the County classes, were easily identified by a three-smokestack design. The two-ship *York* class of 8,300 tons with just six 8-inch guns and two stacks followed in 1930–1931.

Light cruisers included the *Leander* class of 1933–1935 (7,000 tons, eight 6-inch guns, eight torpedo tubes). The Royal Navy's requirement to have fifty cruisers by the end of 1936 meant a reduction in the next class, the *Arethusa* class (5,220 tons, six 6-inch guns, six torpedo tubes), and the small-cruiser concept recurred in two *Dido* classes (5,600 tons, ten 5.25-inch dual purpose guns, six torpedo tubes). Shortages left some ships with only ten guns or an alternate 4.5-inch battery.

The need to match the powerful 6-inch cruisers appearing in other navies led to the Town series—the *Southamptons* (9,100–9,400 tons, twelve 6-inch guns, six torpedo tubes) and the *Edinburghs* (10,550 tons, twelve 6-inch guns, six torpedo tubes). The *Fiji* class attempted a similar armament on 8,600 tons, though some ships had a 6-inch triple turret removed. Nine guns became standard on the similar *Uganda* and *Swiftsure* classes.

A number of older vessels augmented these ships, of which the most modern was the E class (7,550 tons, seven 6-inch guns, sixteen torpedo tubes).

Three surviving members of the *Raleigh* class, dated from 1914–1916, had undergone considerable modification over the years, with one retaining a 7.5-inch armament and another being used for training, but in 1939 they generally carried six 6-inch guns. The C class (4,180–4,290 tons, five 6-inch guns, eight torpedo tubes in some) also dated from the First World War. Several underwent conversion to an antiaircraft role armed with ten 4-inch high-angle (HA) guns. It had also been decided to convert the 1918–1922 D class (4,850 tons, six 6-inch guns, and twelve torpedo tubes) to antiaircraft cruisers, but only *Delhi* made the switch, armed with American 5-inch guns.

The Royal Navy used fifty-six merchant vessels as armed merchant cruisers, most of which retained their civilian names. These varied enormously in size, speed, and armament but usually carried obsolete 6-inch guns that had been recovered from ships being scrapped. Unlike German armed merchant cruisers, which were purpose-built commerce raiders, the British ships served to escort convoys and were no match for real warships, as demonstrated on 23 November 1939 when the battleships *Scharnhorst* and *Gneisenau* easily dispatched the former P&O liner *Rawalpindi* off Iceland, and on 5 November 1940 when the *Panzerschiff Admiral Scheer* sank *Jervis Bay*.

Destroyers included the First World War V and W classes, which soldiered on, many being converted to antiaircraft vessels or, after the war began, to an escort role. Postwar the mass production of destroyers commenced with the A and B classes of 1929–1930. Almost every year thereafter saw a nine-vessel flotilla competed. The practice was for each class to have a flotilla leader and two divisions of four ships, with the destroyer-leaders usually being larger but in other cases having a turret removed to provide room for the flotilla commander's staff. Destroyer sizes, which had increased during the First World War, continued to grow between the wars so that while V and W classes displaced 1,120 tons, the J class of 1939 displaced 1,690 tons standard. Armament also changed. All destroyers had 21-inch torpedo tubes, but most laid down during the First World War had 4-inch guns and some had the 4.7-inch caliber that would become standard between the wars. Wartime circumstances forced some new ships to revert to 4-inch guns in HA mounts, and 4.5-inch guns made an appearance late in the war. From the B class of 1931 onward, all ships mounted Asdic. At the time, the British shipbuilding industry had a considerable export market, and on the outbreak of war, the Royal Navy seized a batch of H-class destroyers building for Brazil along with a pair of I-class ships intended for Turkey. Fifty ex-USN First World War destroyers were received as the Town class; of these, fifteen eventually went to the Royal Canadian Navy, five spent time with Norwegian crews, and nine passed on to Soviet custody. For Royal Navy service, the ships were modified with deeper bilge keels and ballasting to improve seakeeping.

World War I had shown the value of the Flower-class minesweeping sloops in a variety of tasks, especially escort duties. Postwar, no new sloops were constructed until 1927, when two were ordered incorporating improvements, and small numbers were thereafter ordered in the following years. In 1931 renewed interest in sloops saw the decision to build two new classes: the simple and cheap Halcyon minesweeping class and the improved Grimsby escort class still capable of minesweeping and equipped for duty in the tropics. Under wartime conditions, even the Halcyons operated mostly as escorts, with minesweeping needs being met by new construction and converted fishing vessels.

The Kingfisher class appeared soon after being a coastal ASW sloop, displacing 510 tons and with a speed of twenty knots and a range of 4,050 miles. The improved Guillemot class followed. Both classes, later reclassified as corvettes, were built between 1934 and 1939. At the same time, planning began for a new sloop known as the ocean convoy, without minesweeping gear but with increased armament and antisubmarine abilities. This was a larger vessel than any before, at 1,190 tons, with almost nineteen knots maximum speed and a respectable endurance of 6,400 miles. Construction began with the Bittern class of 1935–1938 and continued with refinements in the Egret, Black Swan, and Sutlej classes, extending to war's end with the modified Black Swan class. As the war progressed, these ships changed from being riveted to having as much as 30 percent of the structure welded, and stabilizers were fitted to both the Black Swan and modified Black Swan classes. Under Lend-Lease, ten U. S. Coast Guard cutters were also transferred to the Royal Navy.

The Royal Navy eventually commissioned about 3,500 trawlers, whalers, drifters, and fishing vessels to perform miscellaneous duties including local patrol and minesweeping, but these were not suitable for antisubmarine work. Something faster was needed, ships that would cope better than destroyers with constant patrolling on the high seas. Four classes were selected: the 950-ton Flower-class corvettes, the 1,060-ton Castle-class corvettes, the 1,370-ton River-class frigates, and the 1,435-ton Loch-class frigates; the Bay class was a related design with AA emphasis. The Captain-class frigates were supplied under Lend-Lease from the USN, which rated them as destroyer escorts (Evarts and Buckley classes). Britain's own escort destroyers of the 1,000-ton Hunt classes, while intended as escorts, more nearly approached destroyer capabilities.

The Royal Navy placed considerable emphasis on minelaying and mine countermeasures. Six large minelayers of the Abdiel class were commissioned between 1940 and 1943. These fast (almost forty knot) vessels displaced 2,640 tons and could carry 150 mines; although equipped with 4-inch guns, they were sometimes referred to as cruisers.

A few Hunt-class minesweepers remained from World War I, and large numbers of new ships were commissioned, including the *Bangor* class (often pressed into escort duty) and the *Algerine* class (large enough for ocean escort, though not the equal of the Flowers). These were augmented by almost 400 motor minesweepers for coastal waters; the Americans supplied 152 others under Lend-Lease, along with 22 larger vessels known as the *Catherine* class.

Among the submarine fleet, some elderly boats of the H and L classes lingered after lengthy service. The wartime classes included:

O classes (1,831–2,038 tons submerged, eight torpedo tubes, a 4-inch gun, 1927–1930), designed for distant patrol with habitability suitable for the tropics, three series, none of which performed as expected.

P class (2,040 tons submerged, eight torpedo tubes, a 4-inch gun, 1930–1931) was successor to the O classes and similarly unsuccessful.

R class (2,030 tons submerged, eight torpedo tubes, a 4-inch gun, 1930–1932), final expression of the O concept.

Thames class (2,700 tons submerged, six torpedo tubes, a 4-inch gun, 1932-35), a larger and faster ocean patrol class, the first British submarines capable of more than twenty knots, intended to keep pace with a battle fleet.

S class (935 tons submerged, six torpedo tubes, a 3-inch HA or 4-inch gun), for work in narrow waters. An initial batch entered service in 1932–1933, followed by more in 1934–1938, then two more sets in wartime as the admiral (submarines) decided that additional submarines were required to operate in the North Sea, for which the U class was too small and the T class too big. Each series incorporated improvements in the light of experience, such as increased diving depth and noise reduction. Later versions had increased fuel provision created by using part of the ballast tanks, with operations in the Far East in mind, for which Freon air-conditioning units were also fitted.

Porpoise-class minelayers (2,157 tons submerged, eight torpedo tubes, a 4-inch gun, fifty mines, 1933–1937). One problem with this class was the time required to flood the mine casing, so diving took longer, but with a special Q-tank fitted, diving time dropped from ninety-two to seventy-four seconds, about the same as for the O class. These submarines also proved their worth as cargo carriers on "Magic Carpet" runs to besieged Malta.

T class (1,595 tons submerged, eight torpedo tubes, a 4-inch gun and two Lewis guns), commissioned in three series from 1938 onward with the first eight operational on the outbreak of war and another eleven under construction. The type was intended to replace the P and R classes in the Far East. The increased use of welding and better steel gave the second batch improved diving depth of 350 feet with the first craft diving to 400 feet safely on trials.

The U and V classes (700 tons submerged, four to six torpedo tubes, a 3-inch or a 12-pounder gun), three series commissioned from 1938 onward, initially as training submarines. Experience in the Mediterranean soon showed the need for small submarines in the clear and relatively shallow waters. Diving depth was 200 feet. Later vessels had superior welded pressure hulls and the two external bow tubes omitted in favor of a deck gun, a modification that also improved seakeeping.

P 611 class (856 tons submerged, 5 torpedo tubes, a 4-inch gun, 1941–1942), four boats built for Turkey, but the British kept two for themselves.

In all of the wartime submarine classes, the general practice was to have one torpedo reload for each internal tube. Under wartime pressure, Oerlikon AA guns were introduced on all except the U class. Stern firing tubes were also added in 1940 and 1941 to the S and T classes, with both having a stern tube and the T having two aft-facing tubes amidships. Air-conditioning was gradually introduced because the dehumidifiers in the T and S classes were inadequate for tropical operations, increasingly important as the Royal Navy moved back into the Far East. Freon air-conditioning allowed patrols of up to forty-five days, sometimes longer.

The Royal Navy came late to the concept of midget submarines, on which the pioneering work, as with human torpedoes, was largely conducted in Italy. After experiments with the one-man Welman, which was effectively a cross between a human torpedo and submarine, the Royal Navy developed the 35-ton X craft, which were deployed against the German battleship *Tirpitz* with considerable success. There were two types, the original X series and the XE series developed for Far Eastern operations. Both types had a four-man crew, one of whom had to be a diver, and carried two large explosive charges that had to be laid under the target. The diver could also add limpet mines to the hull. The midget submarines had to be taken fairly close to the target by a mother ship, ideally a larger submarine, but in the case of the attack on Japanese shipping at Singapore, the XE craft managed an eighty-mile round trip.

MTBs had been used by the Royal Navy during the First World War, but although British builders exported many craft between the wars, the Admiralty placed no new orders until 1935. By 1945, 500 motor gunboats and torpedo boats had seen service, perhaps the most famous being the Fairmile D "dog boats" with firepower provided by two 6-pounders. Fairmile also had great success with motor launches. The dozen Fairmile A launches earned few friends but taught important lessons that led to mass-production of the B-type craft: 388 were built in the United Kingdom, with another 264 in the Dominions, many of them funded locally. Another mass-production success, the Admiralty harbor defense motor launch, resulted in roughly 450 completions. In the Mediterranean, these craft also undertook open-water duties, including escorting convoys off the North African coast.

B. AVIATION
1. Ship-based
The outbreak of war found the Fleet Air Arm with inadequate aircraft. The Fairey Swordfish was outdated. Its successor, the Albacore, yet another biplane, had an engine so troublesome that the Swordfish soldiered on. The Gloster Sea Gladiator fighter was the last biplane fighter built for the RAF. The Fairey Fulmar monoplane fighter looked modern, but its two-man crew made the aircraft heavy and its intended use as a long-range escort for torpedo-bombers meant that its performance was barely adequate for the role it often found itself trying to fill, countering bombers—much less enemy fighters. An oddity was the Blackburn Skua, officially a fighter/dive bomber/reconnaissance, but to those who had to cope with it, "more dive bomber than fighter." All of this was partly because of neglect of the Fleet Air Arm's aircraft procurement needs while under RAF stewardship but also partly because many senior British naval officers believed that aircraft carriers could not safely operate high-performance aircraft.

Many transport types served with the Fleet Air Arm during the war and many of the aircraft used for communications and training duties were not unique to naval use. While FAA aircraft improved as the war progressed, the newcomers were not without their shortcomings. Apart from the Albacore's problems, the Fairey Barracuda was a maintenance nightmare, and although it did useful work in the European theater, it was badly outclassed in the Far East and soon withdrawn. The Hawker Sea Hurricane was an interim measure that lacked folding wings and could not be struck into the hangars of the latest carriers due to their long narrow elevators. The Supermarine Seafire was too delicate for carrier work and lacked range. The Vought Corsair was a tough, fast, fighter-bomber with a good range, but its bouncy landing gear and long nose made for difficult landings.

U.S. aircraft started with the Grumman Wildcat, initially known to the British as the Martlet until American involvement in the war brought about a much-needed standardization of terms. It was followed by the Hellcat and the Corsair, and, in early 1943, the Fleet Air Arm at last obtained a modern bomber and torpedo-bomber with the Grumman Avenger.

Capital ships and cruisers initially operated the Supermarine Walrus amphibian, but they were later replaced by the Supermarine Sea Otter. Both designs were single-engined biplanes but with the Sea Otter having a tractor propeller and the engine mounted in the upper wing whereas the Walrus had a pusher propeller and the engine mounted just below the upper wing. These were slow, lumbering aircraft, useful for search and rescue (SAR) and fleet spotting but not combat.

2. Shore-based

British shore-based maritime aviation was provided by the Royal Air Force's Coastal Command, although the Fleet Air Arm's Swordfish squadrons in particular could, and often did, come under RAF control and took part in offensive actions, often including mine-dropping off ports in Belgium and the Netherlands.

At the outbreak of war in September 1939, Coastal Command aircraft included the Avro Anson. There was also the Vickers Vildebeest biplane. Among the more capable aircraft, a torpedo-bomber version of the Handley Page Hampden was also available, as well as some elderly flying boats. The sole aircraft capable of the duties expected of it was the Short Sunderland, a four-engined long-range maritime-reconnaissance flying boat capable of remaining on patrol for twelve hours or more and heavily armed as well as being able to carry 2,000 pounds of depth charges. The RAF also mounted antishipping strikes, using aircraft such as the Hampden, Bristol Blenheim, and later the fast Beaufighter from the same manufacturer.

As the war progressed, Vickers Wellington medium bombers provided useful service, and these were augmented by American Lend-Lease aircraft such as the Consolidated Catalina flying boat, the B-24 Liberator heavy bomber, the Boeing B-17 Flying Fortress, and the Lockheed Hudson as well as the British Avro Lancaster and Vickers Warwick. ASV radar and the Leigh light, a high-powered spotlight, enhanced efficiency. There was always strong competition between RAF Bomber Command and Coastal Command for the most capable heavy bombers, and the bomber-types in Coastal Command were called upon to make up the numbers for the famous "Thousand Bomber Raids."

Although search and rescue was part of Coastal Command's duties in mid-ocean, in home waters this activity was usually carried out by a unit of RAF Fighter Command, which also deployed air-sea rescue launches. Naval aircraft and fast patrol vessels also helped as needed, but the RAF had a substantial force of fast air-sea rescue launches, with personnel recruited into the service from the Merchant Navy.

C. WEAPON SYSTEMS
1. Gunnery

British battleships ordered or commissioned during the First World War had guns of 15-inch caliber whereas the 1927 vintage *Rodney* and *Nelson* had 16-inchers. However, following the 1936 London Naval Treaty, the most modern battleships to see war service reverted to 14-inch guns. The heaviest cruiser guns were 8-inch while most modern light cruisers had 6-inch although the *Dido* class carried 5.25-inch or even 4.5-inch weapons.

Escort vessels had varying calibers as their main armament. The older destroyers had 4-inch, but 4.7-inch became standard by the end of World War I. The 4-inch caliber made a return in some wartime ships, like the Hunt-, L-, and P-class destroyers, compensating for its lesser hitting power with improved antiaircraft performance. Some late-war destroyers introduced the 4.5-inch gun, with the Battle class featuring dual-purpose mounts. Frigates, sloops, and corvettes carried 4-inch weapons. Submarines carried either a 4- or 3-inch gun, usually mounted forward of the conning tower.

Both Bofors and Oerlikon 20-mm guns were fitted to most warships for antiaircraft protection while the larger ships also received the 2-pound multiple pompom, which many regarded as the best AA defense against low-flying aircraft.

2. Torpedoes

All British torpedoes used thermal propulsion. Initially, contact detonators were used. Later magnetic fuzes were introduced, but these did not always perform well. The Royal Navy fired 7,770 torpedoes during the war, of which 1,627 (21 percent) were judged as certain hits. Submarines launched 5,121 of this total for 1,040 hits, followed by MTBs with 1,328 and aircraft with 609 torpedoes fired and 318 and 167 hits, respectively. Destroyers (606/86) cruisers (94/16), and even battleships (12/0) completed the total.[2]

3. Antisubmarine Warfare

Great Britain produced a variety of depth charges. Those used by aircraft had a preset depth, but shipboard charges could be set to detonate at various depths, the maximum increasing from three hundred to a thousand feet. Depth charges would be dropped in patterns, with three rolled over the rails and two fired by throwers off the port and starboard quarters, attempting to leave a space of between 120 and 180 feet between each depth charge. A depth bracket was also possible combining lighter and quick-sinking heavier depth charges, for example, the Mk VII (about 420 pounds) and the Mk VII Heavy (about 570 pounds). Overall, depth charges accounted for 43 percent of German submarines lost due to enemy action.

One problem was that, as the hunter ran over the target, the Asdic signal was briefly lost, allowing the submarine time to take evasive action. Consequently, forward-firing projectors proved invaluable. The Hedgehog of late 1941 fired up to twenty-four light projectiles. The Squid, used only by the Royal Navy and introduced in 1943, was effectively a mortar firing three 390-pound projectiles that exploded at a set depth giving a triangle with sides of roughly 120 feet. A variation was the Double Squid, which could fire two sets of projectiles set to explode at two different depths, which in theory raised the possibility of destroying a target from just 6 percent with standard depth charges, and 20 percent using Hedgehog up to 50 percent.

Because many U-boats were caught on the surface or because their commanders decided to fight the Swordfish biplanes that were used extensively in the antisubmarine role, many were later fitted with rocket projectiles, mounted four under each lower wing. A single rocket projectile was sufficient to destroy a U-boat, with the pilot diving toward the target at around 20 degrees.

4. Mines

The Royal Navy used mines offensively and defensively during the war, including laying six thousand to deny the Straits of Dover to U-boats. The RAF, using both Coastal Command and Bomber Command aircraft, also made strenuous efforts to drop mines in enemy estuaries, harbors, and inland waterways. The May 1940 effort over the Rhine succeeded in temporarily stopping most of the river traffic between Karlsruhe and Mainz. For the nearer ports of mainland Europe, land-based Royal Navy Swordfish squadrons often served in the mine-dropping role.

Moored contact mines, usually laid by surface vessels, carried 600 pounds of high explosives and were used in coastal waters not exceeding 600 feet in depth. Influence mines (either pressure, acoustic, or magnetic) with around 775 pounds of explosive were usually dropped by parachute from aircraft; by early 1944 this could be done accurately using radar from as high as 15,000 feet, reducing the danger from AA fire.

Despite these activities, the service devoted even more effort to mine countermeasures than to mine laying. By chance, Britain recovered intact a German magnetic mine in the Thames Estuary in November 1939 and by the middle of 1940 had developed a magnetic sweep. The Germans also introduced acoustic mines, which were detonated by the sound of a ship's propellers or machinery; by November 1940, the British had developed an acoustic sweep. Contact mines were swept using paravanes towed by the minesweeper to slice the mine's mooring cable with specially weighted sharp cutters, leaving the mine free to float to the surface and be destroyed by gunfire. In addition to magnetic sweeps, warships and merchantmen alike were fitted with degaussing equipment that eliminated a steel hull's magnetic field while RAF Coastal Command used low-flying aircraft with circular magnetic coils.

Britain and Germany both developed pressure mines but hesitated to use them for fear that an unexploded example might be found and its secrets revealed. When the Germans eventually sowed them off Normandy, they had four hundred available. Inevitably, one was found and dismantled, but no countermeasure could be developed: all the British could do was calculate the maximum speed a ship could move in different depths without detonating the mine.

D. INFRASTRUCTURE
1. Logistics
Despite the pressures exerted on the over-stretched Royal Navy, it rarely suffered the logistics constraints that the Axis navies experienced. The one notable exception was the forces based on Malta, where shortages of ammunition in late 1941 and of fuel in mid-1942 affected naval operations.

The Royal Fleet Auxiliary, a branch of the Merchant Navy that dated from 1905, provided the Royal Navy's fleet train. In peacetime the Royal Navy's supply chain was spread across the world with a network of base ports, refueling stations, and depots. During the war many of these were denied to the Royal Navy, which lost its main Far East bases at Hong Kong and Singapore. Fortunately, as early as 1936 "the increased likelihood of bombing attacks on fixed bases" had caused the Admiralty to consider "the provision of floating and mobile support for the fleet."[3]

During the war, replenishment at sea became well established. The German method of transferring fuel in rubber hoses was adapted after the capture of two of *Bismarck*'s supply vessels. In Pacific operations, the astern method was used with oil pumped over through a flexible bronze hose. It was not until late in the war that the navy adopted the U.S. Navy's abeam technique of fuel replenishment and the heavy jackstay method for transfer of stores.

The number of ships in the Royal Fleet Auxiliary varied, increasing as the war progressed with purpose-built ships and others requisitioned from merchant service. For the Normandy landings, these included many converted trawlers and fuel barges. By August 1945, it totaled ninety-two vessels.

Submarines helped keep Malta in the war by bringing in supplies at a time when convoys could not get through. The *Porpoise*-class minelayers were especially effective in this role, with plenty of cargo space in the mine stowage tunnel and between the casing and the pressure hull, and sometimes one of the batteries would be removed to provide extra room. *Rorqual* on one occasion carried 24 personnel, 147 bags of mail, 2 tons of medical stores, 62 tons of aviation spirit, and 45 tons of kerosene.

PHOTO 3.4. The British escort carrier HMS *Ameer* refuels a Royal Canadian Navy destroyer. (C. S. "Bill" Drake courtesy of David Wragg)

2. Bases

The main naval bases for the Royal Navy in 1939 were the historic ones of Devonport, Portsmouth, and Chatham. Each was more than simply a port and a dockyard; they also included a number of shore stations for training and specialized aspects of the fleet's work. Augmenting these bases were those at Rosyth and Pembroke Dock. During the Second World War, the Royal dockyards laid down more than 30 new ships and carried out more than 97,000 refits.

Devonport was the dockyard area of Plymouth and, during the Second World War, was ideally situated to protect the Western Approaches. This also meant that Devonport was within easy reach of German bombers, so much of its command work was relocated to Liverpool. In the same way, the advantages of Portsmouth, such as proximity to the English Channel, also worked against it since the approaches were easily mined and the dockyard was subject to bombing.

Although for most of British history the threat had come from the south, by the early twentieth century it was clear that a newly united and ambitious Germany posed the biggest danger. Rosyth on the north bank of the Firth of Forth and not too far from Edinburgh was chosen as the base for the future. Rosyth, unlike Chatham, Devonport, and Portsmouth, was not a manning port and did not undertake construction of warships but concentrated instead on refitting and repair work. Many senior officers disliked Rosyth because they considered it too far from the open sea, and the railway bridge across the Firth

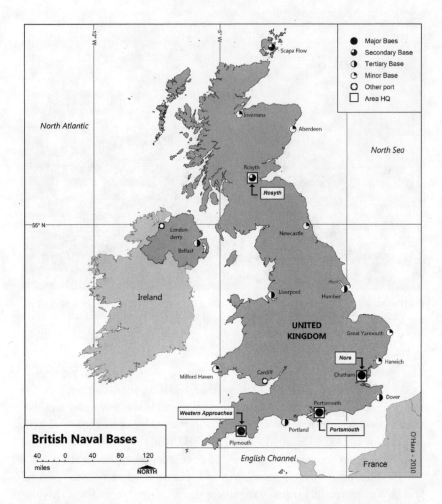

British Naval Bases

Legend:
- ● Major Baes
- ◗ Secondary Base
- ◑ Tertiary Base
- ◔ Minor Base
- ○ Other port
- ▢ Area HQ

Scapa Flow · Inverness · Aberdeen · Rosyth · Newcastle · Londonderry · Belfast · Liverpool · Humber · UNITED KINGDOM · Great Yarmouth · Harwich · Nore · Chatham · Dover · Milford Haven · Cardiff · Portsmouth · Western Approaches · Portland · Portsmouth · Plymouth · North Atlantic · North Sea · Ireland · English Channel · France · 10° W · 5° W · 55° N

40   0   40   80   120
miles   NORTH

O'Hara - 2010

of Forth was seen both as an obstacle to navigation in fog, a frequent problem in the area, and a likely obstruction if the bridge was bombed. Scapa Flow was simply an anchorage without major repair facilities and, as proved, inadequate defenses. Its value was that it offered unrestricted access to both the Atlantic and North Sea. Londonderry became the main operational base for the escorts used on the Atlantic convoys, and was also a naval air station. The main overseas bases for the Royal Navy in 1939 were Gibraltar, Malta, and Singapore. Gibraltar, the only one to remain fully operational throughout the war, provided refit and repair facilities, and its security was enhanced when a runway was built on the site of the racecourse. It was used as a base by Force H and provided access to the Mediterranean and the Atlantic. Had Spain entered the war on the Axis side, Gibraltar would have become untenable, and as it was, Spanish workers were sent home at nightfall to ensure security.

Despite the excellence of Malta's dockyard facilities, heavy Axis air attacks from June 1940 onward made use of the base difficult, although it did sterling work in January 1941 in making emergency repairs to the stricken aircraft carrier *Illustrious*. During the height of the war in the Mediterranean, Malta remained a base for light forces and also for submarines, but between June 1940 and April 1943, the main base for the Mediterranean Fleet was Alexandria in Egypt, although this port lacked adequate maintenance and repair facilities so that badly damaged ships were often sent to the United States for repairs.

Preoccupation with the war in Europe left Singapore neglected, despite promises made to Australia and New Zealand between the wars. After Japanese forces captured Singapore in 1942, other bases became important. However, these, such as Trincomalee in Ceylon, were effectively anchorages rather than main bases, although "Trinco" did have the advantage of nearby airfields for the Fleet Air Arm and the Royal Air Force. Kilindini (near Mombasa in Kenya), Capetown, and Sydney were also used, especially after the creation of the British Pacific Fleet. Addu Atoll, in the Indian Ocean, today known as Gan, was established as a secret refueling facility for the British Eastern Fleet shortly after the outbreak of war and proved invaluable after Japan entered the war.

3. Industry

Despite the country's small size, the United Kingdom has a heavily indented coastline with many ports. During the first half of the twentieth century it had extensive shipbuilding facilities. Before war broke out, heavy engineering firms established the shadow factory system, under which their factories had counterparts duplicating their output, both to increase production and to guarantee against the complete interruption of materiel if the home factory was bombed. The shadow factories became available as, under wartime restrictions, production and the supply of raw materials, labor, and power was limited to those industries contributing toward the war effort. Consumer goods virtually ceased to be produced for home consumption until later in the war when utility models prevailed.

Despite heavy bombing of the shipyards and the major industrial areas of the Midlands, production of major naval vessels rose from 57 in 1939, to 148 in 1940, to 236 in 1941, and leveled there before dropping to 188 in 1944. Naval construction peaked in 1943 with 316,112 tons of naval vessels, 5,398 landing craft, and 1.2 million GRT of merchant ships produced by British yards. Aircraft production in terms of structural weight almost quadrupled between 1940 and 1944.[4]

Many naval vessels were designed to make use of shipyards that would not normally work on warships. Boatyards produced motor torpedo boats and motor gunboats and the big merchant shipyards built the *Colossus*-class aircraft carriers.

Conscription went beyond the requirements of the armed forces; all adults were liable to be conscripted, and the war dictated a focus of labor to relevant industries. Only the young, the elderly, and mothers of young children were exempt. All women over the age of eighteen and under the age of sixty were registered for war work. No combatant nation mobilized its people as thoroughly as the United Kingdom, with 22 percent of the population in the armed forces and 33 percent in industry. The Ministry of Labour maintained a record of all adults capable of work, and a separate Ministry of Supply was created early in the war to coordinate the supply of raw materials to the factories and to coordinate the equipment needs of the armed forces.

IV. RECAPITULATION

A. WARTIME EVOLUTION

The Royal Navy had entered the war believing, as did the government and the other two services, that the Second World War would follow the lines of the First World War, with the British and French armies engaging the Germans in France and Belgium. No one foresaw the French collapse or the invasion of Denmark and Norway, or for that matter, the Netherlands. If there was one expected difference, it was that war would come with Italy, and there was surprise that Italy did not join Germany at the outset but instead waited until June 1940. The possibility of war in the Far East at the same time as war with Germany was not publicly acknowledged until it was too late for effective precautions. It was quite clear that the Royal Navy could only fight one war and would be hard pressed to cope with two theaters, but it was also important that the Dominions were not aware of this, especially when early in the war manpower from Australia and New Zealand was needed in Europe and North Africa.

The First World War had taught the necessity of a convoy system and the need to counter a combination of U-boats and German surface raiders. History did not forecast that the Royal Navy would have to fight on its own against Germany until the United States entered the war or that Germany would, for the first time, possess ports in northern France and along that country's Biscay coast on which to base ships and submarines.

At first, with stretched resources, the Royal Navy had ships operating in small groups, essentially in squadron rather than fleet strength. This was mainly a weakness in the Far East, where during the first few months of the war with Japan, British warships were picked off one or two at a time by the overwhelming might of the Japanese. This was a lesser problem in the Atlantic because the Germans did not at any time send a fleet, let alone a balanced fleet, to sea. It was also a lesser problem in the Mediterranean because both the British Mediterranean Fleet and Force H were in effect balanced fleets.

Even before it had regained control over its own aviation from the RAF, British naval officers recognized the importance of air power. As early as 1935, when Italy invaded Ethiopia, plans were drawn up for a carrier strike against the Italian fleet in its major base of Taranto. Nevertheless, the Royal Navy lacked modern strike aircraft, and this was to continue until the arrival of the Grumman Avenger from the United States. Indeed, before Taranto, much had to be done to improve the launch and recovery of aircraft from carriers; even at this early stage, some U.S. ideas had to be adopted, including the use of the flight deck crash barrier to protect aircraft parked forward from any landing aircraft that missed the arresting wires.

Britain's navy suffered, as did the other two services, from budgetary problems during the interwar depression, made worse by a national strike arising from a longer-running work-stoppage by coal miners. But far worse was the constant interference in naval matters by well-meaning but naïve politicians attempting to reduce the size of warships and their armaments. British defense policy was also hampered by the Ten Year Rule, which maintained that the country would have ten years in which to prepare for war. As it happened, Hitler assumed absolute power in 1933, and the nation went to war in 1939. Financial constraints on rearmament were not eased until 1937.

While the Royal Navy in 1939 was smaller than that of 1914 and no longer had overwhelming superiority over its opponents, it was in many ways better prepared. Many of its senior officers had served in the First World War, and there was far less of the arrogance and reluctance to learn that had made the earlier conflict so costly. Most of the ships were better designed. Inevitably, however, there were mistakes. Antisubmarine sweeps in the pre-Ultra days were a waste of time, and as it turned out, a waste of an aircraft carrier, *Courageous*. Conversely, there were examples of individual courage and flair, which saw the German *U-570* captured intact with the secrets of the Enigma codes. Although the withdrawal from Norway was costly, in two destroyer battles at Narvik and in the sinking of the light cruiser *Königsberg* by shore-based naval aircraft, the Royal Navy performed well. From the start, in the Mediterranean it struggled against a stronger enemy but won most of its battles against the Italian Regia Marina, often at great cost.

The Royal Navy in 1945 was a far better service than it had been in 1939. It had learned how to use naval air power properly. It had learned how to improvise, as with the MAC ships, and innovate, as with antisubmarine devices such as Hedgehog and Squid. It realized the need to provide heavy antiaircraft defenses for its ships to the extent that some late-war and postwar ships were criticized for being over-armed.

U.S. support and involvement helped greatly, at both the national level and local level, where liaison between two rival navies was doubtless helped by the existence of alcohol in the wardrooms of British ships, in contrast to the "dry" U.S. Navy.

B. Summary and Assessment

The Royal Navy was one of the three strongest navies in the world in 1939 and 1940, but it was also the most stretched. It was meant to protect the world's largest empire, but it lacked the resources for this role and the many others that were cast upon it. It was deficient in many areas. It had ignored the development of small fast craft, doubtless because it believed that in wartime, the Germans could be held in France and Belgium, as in the First World War. Its ships had suffered from interwar governments attempting to reduce their size and their armament below even those limitations imposed by the Washington Naval Treaty of 1922. The recommendations of the Madden Committee in the mid-1920s that the Royal Marines be developed into a strong amphibious force had been ignored. In negotiating the Anglo-German treaty of 1935, the future foe was not only allowed a fleet increase to 35 percent of the Royal Navy's total tonnage but also granted 100 percent of its submarine tonnage. Despite Germany's rise, nothing was done to provide adequate base facilities on the east coast of Scotland. The naval base at Rosyth had been closed for much of the interwar period. Having spent the 1920s and 1930s fighting to regain control of its own air power, the Admiralty still lacked not only high-performance aircraft but also its own training system. It was initially dependent upon the Royal Air Force and then the U.S. Navy.

These weaknesses emerged largely from public opinion and the world's economic situation. Successive British governments struggled to balance their budgets, and it was easy to ignore defense spending. The jingoism and lust for battle evident at the start of the First World War had evaporated into war-weariness, the threat of starvation and defeat, and casualties far worse than anyone had expected. After the Armistice, the British public wanted to believe that it had been through the "war to end all wars," and the desire to appease Hitler in 1938 was widely accepted. One survey of public opinion reported, "The leadership which found the prospect of peace in our time in a small piece of paper was a leadership intensely acceptable to a nation which had made up its mind in 1918 not to fight another war if it could possibly be avoided."[5]

Additionally, as in 1914, the man in the street actually believed Britain's armed forces to be stronger and better equipped than they really were. In 1939 the armed forces were rebuilding and recruiting as fast as they could, but it was a race against time. Many of the ships in service still dated from the previous war, and although many had been modernized, others had not. Even the carrier fleet had just one modern vessel.

Conversely, the Royal Navy included many officers at all levels who recognized the problems and were determined to win. They knew that the German Kriegsmarine was no match for their surface fleet, even though the surface raiders posed a threat. They saw that the U-boat posed the real menace to the country's survival. The Admiralty regarded the shortage of flight decks momentous enough to consider converting the ocean liners *Queen Mary* and *Queen Elizabeth*, the world's two largest ships, into aircraft carriers—a move certain to shake public opinion—but ultimately the liners proved even more valuable as troopships.

Although there were still those who refused to recognize either the potential of the airplane or the threat that it posed, or those such as Admiral Phillips who maintained radio silence and lost his battle squadron as result, there were others who took daring challenges and won. The fact that a heavy cruiser and two light cruisers with nothing heavier than 8-inch guns could fight, trap, and eventually see scuttled a German *Panzerschiff* with 11-inch guns in the Battle of the River Plate demonstrated that initiative and courage were not lacking.

To overcome its weaknesses, the Royal Navy needed U.S. support in the form of the Town class destroyers, transferred in return for the use of British bases; in the form of ships and aircraft under Lend-Lease; and in the U.S. Navy escorting convoys to a mid-Atlantic handover point even before the United States entered the war. One can also include the *Wasp*'s two aircraft delivery runs to the beleaguered island of Malta in this. At the same time, the Royal Navy was eventually capable of coping with both Germany and Italy, even without the support of the French fleet. The British also had technology to offer under the less well-known Reverse Lend-Lease that saw developments in radar and Asdic, for example, shared with the United States.

Where the Royal Navy did need to learn was in the Pacific, where the largest naval battles of the Second World War took place. American help in getting British naval aviation into gear was invaluable with improving deck landing and takeoff rates, mounting massed attacks with aircraft from more than one carrier at a time, and with fighter cover. Many British naval aviators admired the Americans but claimed that by the end of the war they were as good as, if not better than, the American aviators! Friendly—and sometimes not-so-friendly—rivalry persists.

It was in the Pacific that many lessons were learned. The commander in chief of the U.S. Navy did not want the British in the Pacific because he considered the Americans capable of finishing the job themselves. Many other officers agreed with him. Many Americans also resented helping a colonial power to regain its territories; after all, were they not liberating people from German and Japanese occupation?

The British, conversely, had scores to settle with Japan, and they did not want their dominions, Australia and New Zealand, to feel that the "Mother Country" had abandoned them. They had ruled in much of the East for a long time, and while they had recognized that some colonies, especially India, would have to be granted independence as soon as possible after the war, they knew that others were not so ready, or even so insistent.

The British Pacific Fleet was the largest and most powerful ever sent to sea by the Royal Navy. It was also the best balanced, and for the first time a serious effort was made to ensure that bases could be made available quickly and the fleet train could provide all of the support needed. They even went so far as to have a ship converted into a floating brewery.

The Royal Navy ended the war with a different balance than it started with: relatively stronger in submarines than in 1939 with a fifth of the service accounted for by naval aviation. The Royal Marines had developed into a flexible amphibious fighting force, and combined operations were placed under the control of a senior Royal Navy officer. Such innovations as Chariot human torpedoes and miniature submarines were sideshows, but the importance of fighting war under the waves and above them, and of amphibious assault, were changes that became permanent.

The irony of it all was that in the early years of the twentieth century, a First Sea Lord, Admiral of the Fleet Sir Jacky Fisher, had forecast that the future of naval warfare lay under the waves and in the air above it. This would be relearned painfully and expensively thirty-five years after he became First Sea Lord.

ADDENDUM: THE OTHER "ROYAL" NAVIES

A. BACKSTORY

Toward the end of the nineteenth century, Great Britain began to press its colonies and dominions to assume a greater role in the Empire's maritime defenses. Naval cooperation had became an imperative with the growing obsolescence of much of the Victorian navy and with the need to build more dreadnoughts and concentrate the Royal Navy in home waters to face a growing German menace. Canada, which had been a self-governing dominion since 1867, established the Naval Service of Canada in 1910, which became the Royal Canadian Navy the next year. Australia obtained dominion status in 1901 and created a commonwealth naval force, the Royal Australian Navy, in 1911. New Zealand established a naval service that became an integral part of the Royal Navy until 1 October 1941, when it became the Royal New Zealand Navy. Although India remained a colony, the Royal Indian Navy was established upon the basis of the Royal Indian Marine in 1934.

These new services played a small role in the First World War and quickly contracted after its conclusion. The Royal Canadian Navy, which had only 366 men in 1922, struggled to define a mission and at first assumed many of the civil duties of the Ministry of Marine and Fisheries. Not until 1931 did Canada receive its first new ships, two destroyers delivered from the United Kingdom. When World War II broke out in Europe, the Canadian navy still had only six destroyers, five small minesweepers, and two training vessels. It numbered 145 officers and 1,674 men. At this time, the Canadian service lacked a clear mission, and the Royal Navy viewed it as an adjunct that would provide support and bases for ships escorting North Atlantic convoys. In fact, it was the urgent need for convoy escorts that gave the Canadian navy its wartime role, sparking a massive expansion so that by August 1945 it had 365 warships and 95,750 personnel.

The Royal Australian Navy functioned as an integral part of the Royal Navy. Only the Australia Station was under Canberra's control, with the Australians responsible for trade protection on the station. After the First World War, a debate developed concerning the "one hemisphere" Royal Navy and its two hemispheres of responsibility. This resolved into the Singapore Strategy: the United Kingdom began construction of a major naval base at Singapore, and, in the event of war with Japan, the Royal Navy's full power would steam eastward (assuming Europe was at peace). The Australians had the role of harassing an advancing Japanese navy prior to the main fleet's arrival at Singapore. Between the wars, the Royal Australian Navy's personnel strength fell to as low as 3,117 men with another 5,446 in the reserves. It took delivery of two new County-class cruisers in 1928, but the depression effectively suspended further expansion until 1934. From the late 1930s, as the threats from Germany and Japan became apparent, fleet modernization accelerated. During World War II, the Australian navy's strength rapidly grew to 39,650 personnel.

New Zealand contributed to a New Zealand division of the Royal Navy. The light cruiser *Chatham* formed the New Zealand division from 1921–1924, when she was replaced by *Dunedin*, which was subsequently joined by her sister, *Diomede*. These two cruisers served until 1936–1937, when they were replaced by *Achilles* and *Leander*. New Zealand's other major naval effort between the wars was its strong support of the Singapore naval base's development, maintaining significant pressure on the British government to complete the base. This pressure was backed by a contribution of £1 million toward the base's cost.

Upon the outbreak of war, the Royal Indian Navy numbered 1,708 men and deployed two modern and three old sloops, a patrol boat, and two auxiliaries all serving in the East Indies command. The Union of South Africa also contributed a small naval service to the empire's defense that included auxiliary minesweepers. In 1942 this service became the South African Naval Force.

B. ORGANIZATION

The dominion navies were organized along British lines; they used British signals and methods and were commanded, in many cases, by British officers seconded from the Royal Navy. As one Canadian history expressed it, "The influence of the Royal Navy permeated every fibre of the younger service."[6] In the case of the Indian navy, three quarters of the officers in 1939 were European.

Canada's equivalent to the British Admiralty was Naval Service Headquarters based in Ottawa. Upon the outbreak of war the Admiralty asked for control of the Royal Canadian Navy's destroyer flotilla. The Canadian cabinet, while reserving the right to protect Canadian interests, authorized full cooperation, retaining control only of warships operating in Canadian waters and permitting ships deployed elsewhere to be controlled by the commander in that particular theater. The small size of Canada's prewar navy acted against effective training, and it operated without the infrastructure needed for a truly autonomous service, with many of its officers being trained by the Royal Navy.

On the outbreak of war, the officers commanding each of the three Australian armed services formed the chiefs of staff committee, echoing the similar organization in London. Nevertheless, unlike their British model, the Australian version dealt mainly with matters such as strategic appraisals and training or support functions since in the operational theaters of war Australian forces were under the command of the respective Allied commanders in chief. Australian commanders in these theaters did have the right of direct appeal to Canberra if they felt that an operation unduly hazarded their forces.

The New Zealand division of the Royal Navy was administered by a naval board consisting of the civilian minister and senior naval staff. Operational command for ships on the New Zealand station was exercised by the New Zealand chief of naval staff, and operational control for ships deployed out of New Zealand waters was transferred to the British Admiralty. New Zealand

naval personnel were trained along Royal Navy lines, and all advanced training was conducted in the United Kingdom. New Zealand's naval forces were
heavily dependent upon personnel (particularly officers) on loan from the
Royal Navy. In September 1939, of the New Zealand Division's strength of 82
officers and 1,257 ratings, only 8 officers and 716 ratings were New Zealand–
born, and all senior appointments were filled by Royal Navy officers on loan.

C. MATERIEL

The dominion navies quite naturally used British ships, aircraft, and weapons. Australia and Canada both developed significant shipbuilding industries, however.

The Royal Canadian Navy was initially built around six destroyers, which
reflected a mission to defend Canada's coasts from enemy fleets seeking lodg-
ments or to raid its ports (see table 3.2). These included the B-class units
Saguenay and *Skeena* and the C-class units *Restigouche, Fraser, Ottawa,* and
St. Laurent. However, driven by the demands of the war, the Canadian navy
rapidly developed into a powerful antisubmarine force with dozens of frigates
and minesweepers and more than a hundred corvettes. The Canadian navy
did not deploy submarines, and only late in the war did Canada commission a
pair of cruisers. With the exception of some transferred American destroyers,
designs were of British origin, even when Canadian-built. Local yards, despite
no previous experience with warships, proved able to build large numbers of
small units quickly and efficiently. Eight Tribal-class destroyers began construction and four were commissioned before war's end. Weaponry was based
on Royal Navy practice. Nevertheless, throughout the war Canada proved
slow in equipping its ships with the most up-to-date weaponry and systems
such as radar.

TABLE 3.2 **Canadian Order of Battle**

Ship Type	1939	1945	Wartime Losses
Escort aircraft carriers	0	2	0
Light cruisers	0	2	0
Destroyers	6	22	6
Frigates	0	67	4
Corvettes	0	120	11
Minesweepers	5	77	4

In 1939 the Royal Australian Navy consisted of two County-class heavy
cruisers, *Australia* and *Canberra*; three modern *Leander*-class light cruisers,
Hobart, Perth, and *Sydney*; the World War I–vintage cruiser *Adelaide*; five
elderly destroyers; and two sloops (see table 3.3). War losses were replaced

by new construction and Royal Navy transfers, which included a heavy cruiser and N-class destroyers. Local shipyards had built light cruisers dur-' ing World War I, but the immense commitment to repairing damage and providing maintenance for Allied units precluded production of anything more demanding than a few Tribal-class destroyers. Australian builders did provide sloops, frigates, and minesweepers as well as a reverse Lend-Lease program of small craft for the U.S. Army and Navy in the Pacific. The peak achievement of Australian construction was the fifty-six locally designed and built *Bathurst*-class minesweepers (later reclassified as corvettes). The war also saw the construction of the large Captain Cook graving dock in Sydney, capable of docking any Allied warship of the era.

TABLE 3.3 Australian Order of Battle

Ship Type	1939	1945	Wartime Losses
Heavy cruisers	2	2	1
Light cruisers	4	2	2
Destroyers	5	10	1
Frigates	0	6	0
Sloops	2	2	1
Corvettes	0	53	1

The principal strength of New Zealand's naval division was its cruisers, the *Leander*-class vessels *Leander* and *Achilles*. It was intended to commission a third *Leander*; however, *Neptune*, with one-fifth of her crew New Zealanders, was lost in the Mediterranean on an Italian minefield on 19 December 1941 before she could transfer. In 1943, following damage sustained fighting alongside the U.S. Navy at the Battle of Kolombangara, *Leander* was returned to the Royal Navy and was replaced by the Colony-class cruiser *Gambia*. In 1941 New Zealand took delivery of three Bird-class antisubmarine minesweeping corvette-style trawlers, *Kiwi*, *Tui*, and *Moa*, which subsequently operated in the Solomons. *Kiwi* and *Moa* sank the Japanese submarine *I-1* in a surface engagement on 29–30 January 1943, and *Tui* was predominantly responsible for sinking *I-17* on 19 August 1943. *Moa* was lost in a Japanese air raid on 7 April 1943. New Zealand also operated several dozen minor vessels during World War II, built to standard British designs. These included the modified Flower-class corvettes, *Arabis* and *Arbutus*, and four Isles-class and thirteen Castle-class minesweeping trawlers.

During the war the Royal Indian Navy added six sloops, three corvettes, seventeen minesweepers, and eighteen locally built minesweeping trawlers to its force. The South African Navy Service ended the war with five frigates and a corvette.

D. RECAPITULATION

The story of the three dominion navies during World War II was one of expansion and increasing capabilities. During World War II the Royal Australian Navy evolved into a significant force. Its main strength lay in trade protection—convoy escort, antiraider, and antisubmarine duties—and in this it achieved notable success. It played an important role in the advance across the Pacific toward Japan and showed itself capable of global reach, with its ships seeing service as far away as the Arctic and the Mediterranean. Closer collaboration with the U.S. Navy after the heavy British losses early in 1942 doubtless did much for the Australians. Nevertheless, it is interesting to note that the ties with the Royal Navy continued after the war, with British warship classes favored until the 1960s, when Australia acquired three *Charles F. Adams*–class guided missile destroyers.

Australian warships saw extensive action in the Mediterranean, the Red Sea, the Indian Ocean, the East Indies, and the Pacific. The cruisers *Perth*, *Sydney*, and *Canberra* and the sloop *Yarra* were all sunk in surface actions, and the destroyer *Vampire* and the minesweeper *Armidale* by air attack. The Japanese accounted for all, save *Sydney*. The loss of *Sydney* with all hands (645 men) to a German disguised raider was the navy's greatest tragedy and accounted for 35 percent of the total lives lost aboard Australian warships.

While anticipating war with Germany and possibly with Italy, the Royal Canadian Navy had to develop from a pitifully small base relying largely on the country's own industrial and manpower resources. There was no attempt to build a balanced fleet. Canadians manned their first carrier (albeit with a British air group) in 1943, and a modern cruiser entered Canadian service the following year. Trade protection remained the overriding concern throughout the war, which effectively meant antisubmarine warfare, centered at first around convoy protection until later in the war when antisubmarine hunting groups could be formed. In the beginning, the lack of infrastructure and the demands of rapid expansion meant that too often personnel went to sea with minimal training, and the Royal Canadian Navy's performance was initially disappointing. At one point, the British pulled most Canadian vessels from active duty for retraining. By late 1942 the Canadian navy was pulling its weight. Canadian forces sank thirty German and three Italian submarines during the war. Canada lost six destroyers (three in accidents, two by submarines, and one in a surface action), eleven corvettes (one by accident, one by mines, one by air attack, and eight by submarines), four frigates by submarines, and four minesweepers (one by accident and three by submarine).

Designed to cooperate with the Royal Navy, the Royal Canadian Navy benefited also from operating alongside the U.S. Navy. Unprecedented growth made it the world's third largest navy—by number of ships—and in control of its own substantial sea area off the country's Atlantic coast.

New Zealand fulfilled its wartime mission of contributing to the empire's worldwide naval forces, its cruisers seeing action in the Atlantic, Mediterranean, Red Sea, Indian Ocean, and Pacific. During the war New Zealand also acquired and operated the light forces necessary for both local defense and operations in the Solomon Islands. In addition, the Kiwis provided a large number of trained personnel to Great Britain, with some seven thousand New Zealanders serving in the Royal Navy and Fleet Air Arm.

The Royal Indian Navy operated in the Indian Ocean and Red Sea. It lost the patrol boat *Pathan* to an Italian submarine and the sloop *Indus* to Japanese aircraft. South Africa did not lose any warships, and one of its frigates, the newly commissioned *Natal*, sank a German U-boat in March 1945 off the coast of Scotland while en route to antisubmarine warfare training.

chapter four

Italy: The Regia Marina

I. BACKSTORY

A. HISTORY

In 1860 the newly unified nation of Italy established the Regia Marina (Royal Navy) on the foundation of Sardinia's navy, a force with a history of successful operations against its traditional foe, the Barbary States. The Sardinian navy had also fought during Italy's wars of unification, and in the 1855–1856 Crimean conflict. Other components incorporated into the Regia Marina up through 1870 included the navies of Naples, Tuscany, the Papal States, and the revolutionary coastal corps of Emilia and Sicily.

This new and imperfectly integrated service faced its first test against the Austrian navy in 1866 and lost the Battle of Lissa, the largest naval action between Trafalgar (1805) and Tsushima (1905). After a few years of political crisis, the Regia Marina adjusted to this setback by eschewing a balanced fleet and building powerful and unusual ships such as the revolutionary *Duilio* (1876), the first battleship to forego sailing rig and armed exclusively with "giant guns," and *Italia* (1880), "forerunner of the battle cruiser" and for several years the world's largest and fastest ship. Along with fast battleships, the navy also built cruisers, torpedo boats, and, later, submarines. "Sacrificed were protection, operating radius and auxiliary ships, in which Italy generally had modest interest."[1]

In Italy's 1911–1912 war against the Ottoman Empire, the navy conducted amphibious landings, supported the army, attacked harbors, raided into the Dardanelles, and swept the Red Sea of Turkish vessels. In a postwar assessment, a U.S. naval officer concluded that the Italian nation had "diligently trained her navy for this degree of efficiency, and the result justified the expense."[2]

Italy's main theater of operations during the First World War was the Adriatic Sea, where the battleships swung at anchor while the smaller units waged a hit-and-run campaign against Austria-Hungary. Cruisers and destroyer-sized units fought twenty-four generally inconclusive surface actions, mostly at night. The navy also conducted more than a hundred shore bombardments. Mines, submarines, and small attack units proved the most effective naval weapons. The Regia Marina won its greatest victory when the motor tor-pedo boat MAS 15 torpedoed and sank the Austro-Hungarian battleship *Szent István* off Premuda Island on 10 June 1918.

Victory in the First World War and the break-up of the Austro-Hungarian Empire shifted Italy's naval priorities. In Rome common opinion held that the peace treaties had reneged on Allied promises made to draw Italy into the war, and the nation considered itself an orphan in the European political and security system. Rivalry with France in North Africa and the Balkans made the Marine Nationale the Regia Marina's most likely future adversary, but Great Britain, because of its control over the vital choke points of Gibraltar and Suez, loomed in the background as a greater threat. As early as 1922, even before Benito Mussolini's march on Rome, the Italian naval attaché in Constantinople warned that "it was necessary, at all costs, to avert the danger of transforming the Mediterranean into an English sea, which would one day present us with the dilemma either of being starved or of following England without reservation."[3]

The 1922 Washington naval treaty sparked an arms race with France. The two nations agreed to accept parity in battleships and cruisers but not destroyers and submarines. Between 1923 and 1933 Italy, seeking fast and expendable warships to gain an advantage in a campaign against France's North African lines of communication, laid down thirty-six light scouts (*esploratori leggeri*, actually flotilla leaders) and destroyers and forty-nine submarines. France countered with forty-six *contre-torpilleurs* and *torpilleurs* (large or "super destroyers" and destroyers) and fifty-five submarines. *Guépard*, France's first 5.5-inch gunned *contre-torpilleur* and Italy's first Condottieri-class cruiser, originally classified as a *grandi esploratori* (large scout), were laid down within days of each other.

The logic of Italy's maritime strategy, and its attendant construction program, changed when war with Great Britain threatened during the 1935 Ethiopian crisis. Given limited resources and an apparent lack of time, the Italian navy continued to construct tested designs such as the Soldati-class destroyers, the *Spica*-class torpedo boats, the 500-series MAS boats, and the 600-series sub-marines. Navy staff knew their limitations, and the continued construction of these early 1930s designs reflected the need to balance the necessary quantity with acceptable—if hardly ideal—quality. At the same time, Italy and France, dismayed by the Nazi regime's rise and confronted by Great Britain's apparent understanding with Germany, highlighted by the 1935 Anglo-German naval

PHOTO 4.1. The Italian light cruiser *Abruzzi* fitting out in 1937. (Enrico Cernuschi collection)

treaty, which unilaterally released Germany from its Versailles Treaty naval limitations, enjoyed an inverse détente until mid-1936.

Although this Latin rapprochement formed a short intermezzo as France once again became a potential adversary during the second half of 1936 with the Front Populaire's rise to power, the Italian navy continued to focus on a confrontation with Britain. To this end, the Regia Marina's staff even developed its own concept of an oceanic fleet designed to project power into the Atlantic and Indian oceans. However, such an ambitious program was beyond Italy's means, and of the new warship types envisioned, only four long-range cruiser submarines of the *Caracciolo* class and three fast and unprotected Capitani Romani–type light cruisers ever materialized.

In 1933 the government acted to modernize the two pre–World War I *Cavour* class dreadnoughts to match the new French battleship *Dunkerque*. Rome authorized two modern battleships of the *Littorio* class the next year while in late 1936 the two *Dorias* were scheduled for reconstruction along the same lines as the *Cavour* to answer France's new *Richelieu* class. Rome recognized that the rebuilds were a pauper's reply to these modern battleships in terms of punch and protection, but Italy lacked the funds and the slips to do anything better until December 1937 when the government authorized two more *Littorios*.

In June 1940 Italy declared war against Great Britain, Europe's greatest naval power. This was not the foe the fleet was designed to fight. Nor was the Regia Marina truly prepared for war, even after nine months' fair warning (which, complicated by the Allied blockade, was used to complete the four battleships *Littorio*, *Vittorio Veneto*, *Doria*, and *Duilio* and warships already on the slip). The government believed and the navy high command hoped that Italy had entered the end stages of a brief and victorious European conflict. No one, except perhaps the foe, anticipated a drawn-out, life-and-death struggle.

B. MISSION

The Regia Marina's mission evolved during the interwar period. From 1919 to 1934, the mission was to exclude the French from the Tyrrhenian and Ionian seas, to preserve communications with Libya and the Dodecanese, to protect traffic with the Black Sea and the Indian Ocean, to impede French shipping in the Western Mediterranean and raid Corsica, and to attack France's oceanic trade with submarines and auxiliary cruisers. The Mahanian vision of the decisive naval battle, which fascinated American, Japanese, and British planners, had little relevance in Italian doctrine as the balance of power in the 1920s and early 1930s saw five (later four) Italian 12-inch-gunned battleships outnumbered by the Marine Nationale's three super dreadnoughts of the *Bretagne* class and three *Courbet*-class 12-inch vessels. The refurbishment of Italy's battle line from four elderly to four rebuilt and four modern units would have opened up new possibilities, but war arrived three years before this force was ready.

Instead, driven by the expectation of a short war, the economic pressure of the Allied naval blockade, and Germany's battlefield successes, Mussolini initiated hostilities with a speech rather than with a series of surprise attacks, as envisioned by the navy's chief of staff, Admiral Domenico Cavagnari, or with a sudden (if risky) descent on Malta. Mussolini's hurry to sit at the peace table as a combatant also meant that insufficient preparation attended Italy's entry into the war except for the recovery, during the last three weeks of peace, of about a half million tons of the Italian merchant fleet that was sailing, as usual, worldwide from Australia to the Americas. Because Italy absolutely relied on maritime trade to sustain its economy, the navy had, since 1931, expected to lose about a third of its mercantile fleet on the first day of a war against Great Britain; in fact, actual losses were a little less than that. The navy, however, did not issue its war plans until 29 May. These established that expendable units such as light forces, submarines, and airplanes would assume the major risks. The fleet's principal tasks were to protect the *madrepatria's* coasts, supply the army in Libya, close the Sicilian Channel, dispute the British presence in the central Mediterranean, and maintain maritime communications with the Balkans and Spain. As the situation evolved and the two *Dulios* returned to service and the two *Littorios* were completed, high command also envisioned the navy fighting a general action under favorable conditions.

Some historians have interpreted an April 1940 memorandum from Cavagnari to Mussolini about the dangers of entering the war without first conducting a surprise attack as an indication that the naval leadership's ulti‑ mate purpose was to preserve the fleet as a postwar bargaining chip. This was never official policy, but Cavagnari, like Germany's and Japan's naval leaders, was painfully aware that Italy could not match the Allies in a war of mate‑ riel. Naval leaders on both sides expected that advances in weapons and fire control had rendered long‑range gunnery deadly, and that just a few minutes of naval combat would lead to crippling losses. Thus, Cavagnari cautioned Mussolini in the same memorandum: "a full‑scale naval battle soon after the opening of hostilities was likely. Losses on both sides would be 'immense.' The Allies, with their superior forces and industrial capacity, could make good their losses. Italy could not."[4]

II. ORGANIZATION

A. COMMAND STRUCTURE

1. Administration

Benito Mussolini concentrated power in his own hands as the of head of gov‑ ernment, the supreme commander of all armed forces, the minister of war, and the minister of the navy and air force. From 1934 the navy's undersecretary and chief of staff was Admiral Cavagnari. He reported directly to Mussolini while the army‑dominated armed forces high command, the *Stato Maggiore Generale* (renamed *Comando Supremo* in May 1941) coordinated the various service commands. After May 1941, following reforms undertaken by its new commander, General Ugo Cavallero, Comando Supremo gained more effec‑ tive control over all the services. Even so, the Regia Marina always retained a large degree of autonomy.

The supreme naval headquarters established shortly before hostilities was called Supermarina. Cavagnari commanded, but, because he was a govern‑ ment member and mainly occupied with strategic, political, and administra‑ tive matters, the supervision of day‑to‑day operations rested in the hands of his deputy, Admiral Odoardo Somigli, a Ciano protégé appointed in August 1939 over Cavagnari's candidate, Admiral Luigi Sansonetti. Supermarina closely managed the subordinate naval commands. This centralization of authority, quite heavy until December 1940 when Admirals Arturo Riccardi and Inigo Campioni replaced Cavagnari and Somigli, affected the navy's performance throughout the war and discouraged tactical commanders from exercising ini‑ tiative and ingenuity.

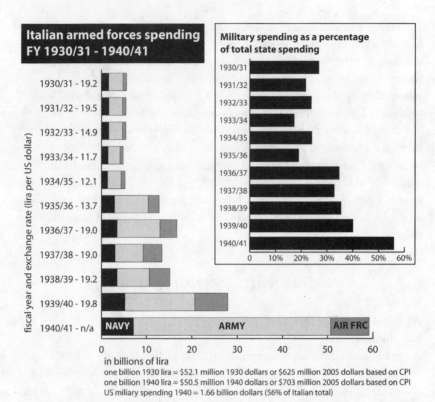

Italian armed forces spending FY 1930/31 - 1940/41

fiscal year and exchange rate (lira per US dollar)

1930/31 - 19.2
1931/32 - 19.5
1932/33 - 14.9
1933/34 - 11.7
1934/35 - 12.1
1935/36 - 13.7
1936/37 - 19.0
1937/38 - 19.0
1938/39 - 19.2
1939/40 - 19.8
1940/41 - n/a

NAVY   ARMY   AIR FRC

0   10   20   30   40   50   60
in billions of lira

Military spending as a percentage of total state spending

1930/31
1931/32
1932/33
1933/34
1934/35
1935/36
1936/37
1937/38
1938/39
1939/40
1940/41

0   10%   20%   30%   40%   50%   60%

one billion 1930 lira = $52.1 million 1930 dollars or $625 million 2005 dollars based on CPI
one billion 1940 lira = $50.5 million 1940 dollars or $703 million 2005 dollars based on CPI
US miliary spending 1940 = 1.66 billion dollars (56% of Italian total)

sources: Sadkovich, *Italian Navy in World War II*, table 1.9; Historical Tables Budget of the United States Government, FY 2005; measuringworth.com

The navy's place in the Fascist pecking order was indicated by the division of military funds, over which Mussolini maintained ultimate control. The navy received a fairly consistent allotment totaling about a quarter of armed forces spending from 1925–1926 through 1935–1936 while the army, which had supported the Fascist movement even before Mussolini's seizure of power, averaged 56 percent. The air force (Mussolini's own pet service) received the balance (18 percent) until 1935.

Once war started, the army received 74 percent of appropriations and the navy's share plummeted to 12 percent. The military's total appropriations rose from 23 billion lire in 1925–1926 to 105 billion in 1940–1941. Just the same, appropriations remained limited. In 1939, even if it had grown rapidly since the 1920s, Italy's gross domestic product (GDP) measured half of Great Britain's and 42 percent of Germany's, yet Italy spent only 10 percent of its GDP on the military compared to Germany's 32 percent. Even democratic Britain spent 50 percent more on the military as a percentage of GDP than Fascist Italy.

2. Personnel

The Regia Marina numbered 4,180 officers and 70,500 ratings prior to mobilization and quickly expanded to 168,800 upon the outbreak of war. In September 1943 the navy had 259,100 men under arms. Of all the Italian armed forces, the Regia Marina enjoyed the highest quality personnel; 53 percent of ratings were volunteers serving a four-year enlistment while draftees served two years. Nonetheless, there existed a large social gap between officers, noncommissioned officers (NCO), and enlisted men. Italy had low literacy rates and life expectancies compared to its northern European neighbors. As one historian noted, "Society's peasant base, relatively small industrial sector and narrowly selective educational system (85,535 university students, of whom only 13.56 percent were studying engineering, out of a total population of just under 44 million in 1939–40) meant a pervasive shortage of technical talent that placed severe limits on the extent to which the Italian armed forces could imagine, commission, operate and maintain complex machinery."[5]

The navy's officers were generally more conservative and monarchical in outlook than were their army or air force peers. The only ex–naval officer high in the Fascist hierarchy was Costanzo Ciano, the father of the more famous foreign minister who married one of Mussolini's daughters. Based on his personal and professional observations, the French admiral and historian Raymond de Belot described the officer corps as "well-informed, well-trained, and competent."[6] However, the navy suffered from a relative shortage of officers "who made up only 5.4 percent of total personnel, as opposed to 7.5 percent in the French Navy and the Royal Navy's 9.2 percent."[7]

At the lower levels, Italian officers proved aggressive and often independent-minded. At higher levels, doctrine required strict adherence to orders. There were occasions when division admirals exercised their judgment, such as when Rear Admiral Pellegrino Matteucci opened fire against his commander's orders during the battle of Cape Spartivento, but such actions were atypical, and independent-minded commanders did not prosper in the Italian system. Vice Admiral Eberhard Weichold, the German navy liaison officer in Rome for most of the war, and commander of Kriegsmarine forces in the Mediterranean from 1941 until 1943, noted that "every decision resting on personal initiative had to be submitted to the officer in charge of the operations."[8] Other factors affecting the higher naval leadership included a well-founded lack of confidence in aerial reconnaissance and support as well as the belief, since November 1941, that British night-fighting doctrine and equipment were superior.

Italian naval personnel generally performed well in combat. The torpedo boats and destroyers completed thousands of wartime missions, and even near the end, fighting supplies through on the notorious Tunisian "Route of

Death," morale never cracked. Admiral Weichold wrote after the war, "the caution shown in high places was not caused by lack of courage among the men."[9] Admiral de Belot endorsed this assessment as early as 1951 and noted that "history . . . will correct the impression of wartime propaganda which attributed the defeats of the Italian Navy to a general lack of fighting spirit."[10] When Italy signed an armistice in September 1943, the navy was the only service that remained intact and effective. The lower decks never revolted or refused to serve as did Austro-Hungarian, German, and Russian sailors during the First World War, British sailors between the wars, and elements of the French navy after the 1940 armistice.

Training of Officers: Naval Academies. Naval officers were long-term professionals. The Accademia Navale di Livorno was established in 1881. Its curriculum stressed mathematics and ballistics, and every graduate was expected to be a sailor first and foremost. The instructional day commenced at 0530 and continued until 2130. Students were allowed just one opportunity to make up a failed exam. In 1940 its enrollment was 697 students (up from 222 in 1934), and it graduated about 150 officers a year who entered service as midshipmen.

Photo 4.2. Italian officer candidates learning the use of a sextant, Leghorn naval academy, 1941. The building to their right is the Marinelettro center where the Italian navy tested its first radar set in October 1939. (Enrico Cernuschi collection)

Training. The Regia Marina's fleet exercises followed the classic big-gun standard prevalent in the major navies during the 1930s and evolved little during the war. Men and officers were taught to rigidly follow detailed procedures designed to cover every conceivable situation. For example, on 22 May 1941 when attacking a British surface force, the torpedo boat *Sagittario* raised the flag "J," meaning "I am launching," because this was the procedure, even though she was a one-ship flotilla and there was no one to read her signal.

Practice shoots were limited until 1939 when gunnery exercises became more frequent (and the results demonstrated that increased drills yielded better accuracy). Lack of antiaircraft ammunition hampered training; in 1942, for example, the machine-gun personnel at the Pola naval school could fire only two magazines (less than four seconds' worth) before being qualified for war.

The Regia Marina's training regimen, however, also had its strong points. In the 1930s, concerned about the largely theoretical threat presented by torpedo aircraft, the fleet practiced defending against torpedo plane attacks, and these exercises prefigured the general success that Italian warships would enjoy avoiding aerial torpedoes during the war.

3. Intelligence

Italian naval intelligence, originally Reparto Informazioni then Servizio Informazione Segreto (SIS) after 1941, had the task of gathering technical and operational naval information while keeping an eye out for political, economic, and military information that might affect the navy. It was organized into four sections: section B intercepted and deciphered enemy radio communications; section D operated intelligence networks in neutral and hostile countries; section C evaluated and distributed information supplied to it by sections B and D; and section E engaged in counterespionage and police work in conjunction with a specialized branch of the Reali Carabinieri.

Between 1940 and 1943, section B deciphered 13.3 percent of British radio traffic—slightly less than the 13.75 percent British code breakers achieved against Italian traffic. These efforts often generated actionable information. In July 1940, for example, the penetration of enemy codes disclosed British intentions leading up to the action off Calabria and that the navy's submarine and fleet codes had been compromised. Sighting reports of Italian submarines and convoys were routinely intercepted, allowing the threatened units to take avoiding action. Intelligence also compromised many British minelaying missions—at least five of the twelve barrages laid by *Manxman* and *Abdiel* in November 1942 through February 1943 were revealed within hours by signal intelligence and left intact so the British would not realize their codes were being read.

B. DOCTRINE

1. Surface Warfare

Going into the war Italy's surface warfare doctrine envisioned an opening long-range gunnery phase with well-spaced salvos to permit observation of the fall of shot. Once the shells had bracketed the target, rapid fire would commence. The intent was to inflict damage at the maximum possible range to weaken the enemy force before the decisive short-range phase. The ability to hit with effective, long-range gunfire proved far more difficult than all navies envisioned prewar, but Italian performance in this area equaled that of any preradar navy.

Although the navy conducted some big-gun night exercises in the 1920s, the high command decided that the battle fleet would fight only day actions. Thus, major warships had almost no night training with their main armament and had inadequate doctrine should circumstances force a night battle, especially against a British enemy that diligently exercised night combat in the 1920s and 1930s. Destroyers and torpedo boats, conversely, practiced an offensive night doctrine that called for ships to operate individually in extended lines of bearing ("rake" formations) with up to four miles between units. Upon sighting a target, the torpedo boats would immediately attack, aiming by eye single tubes at short range, like a hunter sighting and shooting, meanwhile signaling their position to the flotilla. This doctrine did not envision coordinated or mass night torpedo attacks. At the beginning of the war, Italian doctrine for the fleet destroyers specified that no more than two-thirds of a ship's load should be expended in any one attack. This practice arose from training exercises that indicated a second opportunity to fire torpedoes could occur during naval actions. The navy also doubted whether its fleet destroyers would be able to close to effective torpedo range during daylight actions.

The navy continually studied its wartime experiences and updated doctrine to specify the action to be taken under most circumstances. For example, the fleet tactical instructions distributed in January 1942 specified under the subsection, *Combattimento in caccia* (Combat in pursuit), "If the enemy is attempting to disengage at maximum speed, our formations will pursue while always seeking to close range and engage. As our ships' speed is generally superior to that of the enemy's, it should be easy to maintain contact. In every case, it is better that our pursuers divide in two groups, one to port, one to starboard of the enemy's course, in order to prevent him from suddenly turning into a smoke screen."[11]

2. Aviation

The Regia Marina was the largest World War II navy to not operate an aircraft carrier. From 1931 everything that flew, except for reconnaissance floatplanes, operated under Regia Aeronautica (air force) control. Experience gained in the Spanish Civil War heavily affected offensive air force doctrine relating to naval cooperation—including a claimed success against the Republican dreadnought *Jaime I*. By 1939 the Regia Aeronautica had developed horizontal bombing tactics that called for inundating anchored targets with 50-kg and 100-kg bombs because the air force staff considered the chances of getting a hit at sea using larger but less numerous bombs to be almost zero. The air force believed that dive bombing held the best promise for attacking ships under way, but attempts to develop an indigenous, twin-engined dive bomber, the S.85, and its follow-up, the S.86, failed, which forced Italy to purchase and import German Ju87s. These aircraft were not operational until September 1940. Efforts to develop a torpedo bomber likewise fell afoul of air force requirements that called for a plane capable of dropping a torpedo at 500 km/hr and from a height of 300 m—extremely ambitious specifications for the mid-1930s. The air force finally activated torpedo bomber squadrons in July 1940 after the action off Calabria confirmed to all the ineffectiveness of high-altitude bombing and British Swordfish torpedo bombers demonstrated the aerial torpedo's practicality and potential. The deployment of the S.79 in this role improved the Regia Aeronautica's effectiveness as they torpedoed the cruisers *Kent* on 19 September, *Liverpool* on 14 October, and *Glasgow* on 3 December 1940. There were never enough torpedo or dive-bomber squadrons, however, to make a decisive difference.

By September 1943 Italian torpedo bombers had sunk three destroyers; one sloop; one corvette; one landing ship tank (LST); and fifteen freighters and had damaged one battleship; one carrier; six cruisers; one destroyer; one LST; three auxiliary ships; and six freighters. The high-altitude level bombers sank three destroyers, and the dive-bombers sank two destroyers and one Greek torpedo boat.

3. Antisubmarine

During the First World War, Italy conducted antisubmarine warfare with a variety of small coastal craft armed with 47-mm guns, depth charges, and towed torpedoes. By 1918 the navy deployed some three hundred vessels supported by more than a hundred flying boats, seven airships, and a system of defended anchorages. By the eve of the Second World War, Italy's antisubmarine capabilities had regressed. The hydrophone remained the principal means of locating a submarine underwater; the navy lacked a specialized corvette-sized warship and a modern coastal subchaser, much less the swarms of small coastal craft and seaplanes available two decades before.

This situation existed because of a lack of funds, not a lack of vision. After a solitary and expensive 1929 prototype (the aptly named *Albatros*) and four long-range escorts of the *Pegaso* class laid down in 1934, and facing the planned retirement of many of the old torpedo boats and destroyers, Regia Marina staff requested sixty economic, 500-ton corvettes and a division of twelve floatplane-equipped antisubmarine sloops. However, the money was not there. Moreover, the government's belief in a short war encouraged the notion that existing units (which in 1940 totaled thirty-six old destroyers and torpedo boats and two dozen armed merchant cruisers) would suffice, even if they were hardly ideal for the task. Fortunately for the Regia Marina, the modern torpedo boats proved adequate antisubmarine vessels, despite the much different intentions behind their design. With the modern destroyers, they sank three of the twelve British submarines present in the Mediterranean in the war's first weeks.

Nonetheless, by October 1940 it was clear to the navy's leadership that they needed to drastically improve the navy's antisubmarine capabilities. That month the Italian yards received the order for the first twelve (later sixteen) specialized antiair/antisubmarine (AA/ASW) escorts of the *Ciclone* class. On 1 August 1941 an ASW command, Ispettorato Antisom, began operation. This led to plans to construct sixty subchasers and sixty corvettes. The new command also greatly increased the number of personnel trained to use the hydrophones and sonar equipment and began to draft Italy's first modern tactical antisubmarine doctrine.

4. Submarine

In 1940 Italy possessed 115 submarines (84 operational, 29 undergoing repairs, and 2 working-up). Of the subs, 39 were oceangoing while 69 were "Mediterranean" boats. Italy's submarine operations during the First World War were limited to the Adriatic's narrow waters where targets were few. The Regia Marina, moreover, diligently studied the German experience and concluded that antisubmarine forces and new technology had defeated the conventional submarine. Based on this conclusion, Italy explored the concept of a snorkel and later a workable single engine, air-independent submarine during the 1920s and 1930s but failed to develop an effective prototype. Therefore, the Regia Marina relied on numbers.

Italy envisioned its oceanic submarine cruisers operating alone. Their number demonstrated an intention to project power on the high seas and plans existed to construct naval bases on the Indian Ocean in Italian East Africa. However, the advent of war found Italy's oceanic access constricted by choke points at Gibraltar and Aden. Moreover, the Regia Marina's lack of experience in oceanic warfare led to unrealistic training and unsatisfactory technical characteristics. Italy's interwar boats were designed for cruiser tactics and did not compare favorably to the smaller and faster German boats adapted for wolf-pack tactics.

Comando Supremo tasked the submarine force with launching an immediate offensive, and when war began, fifty-five boats lurked in ambush positions or in multiboat patrol lines throughout the Middle Sea. However, the
Allies had stopped all Mediterranean traffic beginning 30 April 1940, and from
23 May in the Red Sea, which left few targets. Italian submarines only sank
one light cruiser, one steamship, and two tankers in the war's first two weeks
and damaged a tanker and a freighter. Moreover, because the British had penetrated some Italian naval codes, the undersea force took a beating, losing by
all causes ten boats in the first weeks. Once the Regia Marina switched codes,
however, losses fell sharply.

Italy generally maintained twenty to twenty-five boats at sea at any given
time until late 1941 when a new doctrine went into effect whereby Supermarina
withheld submarines until it detected a large operation. Mediterranean conditions, unrealistic training, inadequate tactics, a shortage of targets, and British
antisubmarine expertise prevented Italy from realizing significant advantages
from its large submarine force. Most of the successes achieved by Italy's "dol-
phins" came in the Atlantic.

5. Amphibious Operations

Prewar Italian amphibious doctrine was based on the concept of the *coup de
main*. Planners envisioned operations against Corsica, Yugoslavia's Dalmatian
coast, and the Greek Ionian islands. The Regia Marina maintained a flotilla of
semispecialized amphibious units in June 1940 (a prototype and four ships of
about 1,000 tons, which doubled as water carriers) and the San Marco marine
infantry brigade.

After a failed March 1939 assault against Cartagena, Spain, delivered
by two Nationalist merchant vessels adapted as amphibious ships, Italian
staff concluded that many small landing craft would stand a better chance
of success in an opposed landing than a few large ones. In May 1939 they
projected a 20-ton craft capable of landing a 13-ton tank from a forward
ramp. However, the program for a batch of fifty such units was cancelled in
November 1939. Although the army and some young admirals argued that an
assault against Malta in the war's first month was feasible, Cavagnari rejected
the idea believing that such an enterprise would require the battle force—
which at the time consisted of only two rebuilt battleships—to concentrate
in a predictable place and time where it would be exposed to an overwhelming Franco/British counterattack.

In the end, the navy did not undertake any large-scale amphibious operations. On 28 October 1940 bad weather foiled an operation to land the San
Marco Regiment and the Bari Infantry Division on Corfu on the opening day
of the invasion of Greece. There were, however, many small actions including

a successful counterinvasion of Castellorizzo in February 1941, landings on the Dalmatian islands in April and on Greek islands in May 1941 (including Crete), and unopposed landings on Tunisia and Corsica in November 1942.

6. Trade Protection
The Regia Marina maintained a dedicated escort command to protect the sea routes to Spain, France, and the Balkans. Communications with Libya and the Dodecanese were responsibilities of Supermarina. Because the North African and Balkan harbors were generally small with limited facilities, Italy favored small convoys and frequent departures. Torpedo boats and old destroyers performed most routine escort duties, but in special cases fleet destroyers, cruisers, and even battleships would put to sea to shepherd a convoy through. Up until the fall of Greece in April 1941, Supermarina supplied the Dodecanese using submarines and solitary merchant ships, which made six successful voyages between August 1940 and January 1941; the fast sloop *Diana*, when she became available, made two decisive trips in February and March 1941.

7. Communications
The tight control exercised by Supermarina and the officer in tactical command required quick and reliable communications. Italy considered its ship-to-shore links to be reasonably efficient from the beginning, and these improved with war experience. For tactical communications, the Regia Marina introduced in spring 1940 the TPA (*telefono per ammiragli*), equivalent to the American TBS (Talk Between Ships).

At the same time, navy doctrine, sensitive to security requirements, minimized radio traffic. One ongoing problem for nearly the entire war was the lack of direct ship-to-plane radio links (except for the floatplanes catapulted by the cruisers and the battleships). Finally, in August 1943, after about eighteen months of study and experiments, certain ships finally received a fighter-direction capability that was considered efficient and affordable.

8. Special Forces
The Regia Marina was the only navy to enter the Second World War with a coherent special forces doctrine and a specialized unit with the training and weapons to carry it out: Decima Flottiglia MAS (Tenth MTB Flotilla).

The idea of forcing enemy harbors is as old as naval warfare, but in the First World War Italy took the next step of using specialized personnel, tactics, and weapons to penetrate Austro-Hungarian harbors on numerous occasions. The sinking of the dreadnought *Viribus Unitis* by frogmen confirmed that special forces could obtain great results. During the 1935 Ethiopian crisis, the old doctrine crystallized under Admiral Cavagnari's leadership, who, in November 1916, had himself penetrated the main enemy base of Pola with his torpedo boat during a combined operation. In brief, this doctrine called for hand-picked and highly trained personnel and carefully planned operations using hitherto unknown weapons. The first prototypes of new weapons, the SLC for *siluro a lenta corsa* (slow speed torpedo), a manned torpedo called the "pig" for its horrible sailing qualities, and the MT, an explosive motor boat, appeared at this time.

In 1937, while testing a mechanical system to let the SLC pass under a protective boom, an accident revealed that, contrary to medical literature, human beings could breath pure oxygen from their respirators for more than an hour. This discovery, tested over the next two years, opened new opportunities because the Italian frogmen could undertake a longer underwater approach to their target.

Although surprise attacks do not win wars, the Regia Marina's leadership considered a strong blow by their secret weapons a good way to commence hostilities against Great Britain and France. However, the rush to war as well as teething problems experienced by the SLC frustrated this intention. A plan, studied and tested since 1936, to attack Alexandria using a regularly scheduled liner to ram the booms at dawn while four MAS boats, previously launched by that same ship, followed and attacked the enemy battleships and carriers was frustrated in early June 1940 by the elementary British precaution of interdicting Italian vessels entering the harbor. The idea of forcing Malta's highly fortified base with a pair of old and expendable MAS boats was cancelled in late May due to a lack of targets; the contemporary plan to send an old submarine, the *Bausan*, with a party of frogmen armed with compressed air scissors to cut a passage through Alexandria's booms did not materialize either as it was considered too desperate and would jeopardize more realistic SLC attacks once those weapons were combat ready, presumably before the end of the next summer.

Finally, rivalry with the air force also affected use of the commandos. Plans to insert a force on seaplanes existed, but in May 1940 the Regia Aeronautic refused to release the necessary aircraft on the basis that they had a superior plan. This was a surprise low-altitude strike against Gibraltar by twenty S.79s flying out of a Spanish field at Cartagena. The group arrived in Spain on the last day of June, but the raid was cancelled on 4 July, the day after the attack on Mers el-Kébir, when Generalissimo Franco suddenly revoked permission for the raid.

III. MATERIEL

A. SHIPS

Between 1922 and 1939 Italy laid down 126 surface warships displacing more than 600 tons and armed with at least a 100-mm gun, and 108 submarines. By 10 June 1940 the Regia Marina possessed a modern fleet with its World War I holdovers consisting of just four (reconstructed) battleships, two light cruisers, and a collection of second-line destroyers and torpedo boats (see table 4.1).

TABLE 4.1 **Warships Available on the Outbreak of War and Subsequent Additions**

	Post-1922	Pre-1922	Subsequent Additions
Battleships	0	2	2 pre-1922 recommisioned and 3 new construction
Heavy cruisers	7	0	0
Light cruisers	12	2	3 new construction
Destroyers	57	2	5 new construction and 7 captured
Torpedo boats	34	33	16 new construction and 1 recommissioned
Sloops	1	0	1 new construction and 1 captured
Corvettes	1	0	29 new construction and 2 captured
Submarines	115	0	38 new construction and 3 captured

The four old battleships of the *Cavour* and *Doria* classes were extensively reconstructed, having their main batteries rebored from 12-inch to 12.6-inch, losing a turret, adding new secondary batteries, superstructures, machinery, fire control, and some protection. They emerged as useful, twenty-eight-knot ships, although hardly the equal of the French *Dunkerque* class. Their protection proved vulnerable when tested in action; a single 15-inch shell caused *Giulio Cesare* to terminate a surface action, and at Taranto one torpedo sank *Conte di Cavour*. The three commissioned battleships of the *Littorio* class, conversely, were arguably equal to any design in the world with powerful guns, adequate protection, and a good turn of speed.

Italian heavy "treaty" cruisers, like all warships built under the Washington Treaty limitations, were compromises because it was impossible to incorporate high speed, protection, and eight 8-inch guns on a 10,000-ton displacement. The first two ships, *Trento* and *Trieste*, at 500 tons over limit, were fast and well armed. Their belt could not defeat an 8-inch shell outright but was effective against smaller rounds, and they had decent deck protection. They also validated many post–World War I machinery and fire-control solutions adopted by the navy. The *Zara* class, nearly 2,000 tons over treaty limits, had better protection (1,500 tons devoted to armor compared to 888 tons in the earlier class). Moreover, their 8-inch/53 guns represented a major improvement over the *Trento* class's 8-inch/50 weapons.

Italian light cruisers have the reputation of being fast and fragile. One historian went so far as to write: "Most of Italy's light cruisers were foreseeable disasters; they achieved trial speeds in the vicinity of 40 knots in calm seas, but sometimes disintegrated when hit and lacked protection against heavy weather."[12] In fact, the so-called Condottieri classes of six light cruisers were originally designated large scouts: heavily armed, unprotected, and expendable units designed to hit and run. They had little role in the war of attrition Italy ended up having to fight. The subsequent light cruisers of the *Montecuccoli*, *Duca d'Aosta*, and *Abruzzi* classes incorporated progressive improvements, particularly in their protection. *Giuseppe Garibaldi* was among the world's best 6-inch cruisers up through the late 1930s and served in the Italian navy until 1972, after a reconstruction in the 1950s, as Europe's first missile cruiser.

All of Italy's destroyers launched after 1924 had twin mounts that lacked the elevation and fire control to double as antiaircraft weapons. They suffered from poor stability (particularly the thirty-six ships launched up through 1931) and carried only two triple torpedo mounts. They were short-ranged, which limited the fleet's effective intervention zone to an area between Bone in eastern Algeria and Gavdos Island south of Crete. Their antiair armament was good by prewar standards because it was based on the effective Breda 20-mm, while the British relied, until 1942, on their 0.5-inch machine guns and the old, slow-firing, and short-range 40-mm pom-poms, and the French on the 13.2-mm machine gun. By late 1942, however, the Breda was inadequate in the face of growing Allied air power. The last class, the Soldati, saw hard war duty and proved tough and capable fleet units notwithstanding the faults described above.

Italy built thirty-two 600-ton torpedo boats prewar (including two for Sweden). This did not reflect a true commitment to torpedo warfare because these boats carried feeble broadsides of only two small, short-range torpedoes. Instead, they represented an inexpensive class of ships that Rome could construct without regard to treaty limits; as such, they were truly expendable vessels. Although they turned out to be disappointments in their intended role of nighttime interceptors, they proved adequate escorts.

On 10 June 1940 the Supermarina's fleet units were mostly assigned to two formations: the 1st Fleet (*Squadra*) based at Taranto under Vice Admiral Inigo Campioni and the 2nd Fleet under Vice Admiral Vittorio Paladini at La

Photo 4.3. The torpedo boat *Calliope* in 1941. The *Spica*-class torpedo boats were uncomfortable and expendable ships but proved effective escorts. (Enrico Cernuschi collection)

Spezia until late May 1940 and then transferred to Taranto. When both fleets were at sea, Campioni, the senior officer, held command. The two fleets did not train together, except for a few annual exercises.

The navy also maintained various regional commands, called *dipartimenti*, responsible for the interior sea communications and coastal warfare. A special escort command named Comando Difesa Traffico MARICOTRAF, under Vice Admiral Arturo Riccardi, was responsible for the defense of sea lanes with Albania and of the civilian traffic with Spain (and, after the armistice, France

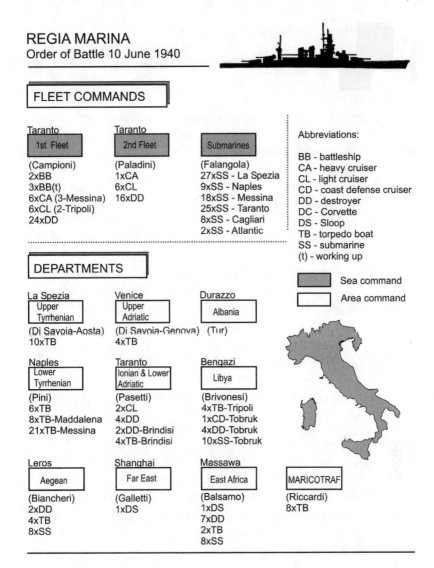

REGIA MARINA
Order of Battle 10 June 1940

FLEET COMMANDS

Taranto
| 1st Fleet |

(Campioni)
2xBB
3xBB(t)
6xCA (3-Messina)
6xCL (2-Tripoli)
24xDD

Taranto
| 2nd Fleet |

(Paladini)
1xCA
6xCL
16xDD

| Submarines |

(Falangola)
27xSS - La Spezia
9xSS - Naples
18xSS - Messina
25xSS - Taranto
8xSS - Cagliari
2xSS - Atlantic

Abbreviations:

BB - battleship
CA - heavy cruiser
CL - light cruiser
CD - coast defense cruiser
DD - destroyer
DC - Corvette
DS - Sloop
TB - torpedo boat
SS - submarine
(t) - working up

▨ Sea command

☐ Area command

DEPARTMENTS

La Spezia
| Upper Tyrrhenian |

(Di Savoia-Aosta)
10xTB

Venice
| Upper Adriatic |

(Di Savoia-Genova)
4xTB

Durazzo
| Albania |

(Tur)

Naples
| Lower Tyrrhenian |

(Pini)
6xTB
8xTB-Maddalena
21xTB-Messina

Taranto
| Ionian & Lower Adriatic |

(Pasetti)
2xCL
4xDD
2xDD-Brindisi
4xTB-Brindisi

Bengazi
| Libya |

(Brivonesi)
4xTB-Tripoli
1xCD-Tobruk
4xDD-Tobruk
10xSS-Tobruk

Leros
| Aegean |

(Biancheri)
2xDD
4xTB
8xSS

Shanghai
| Far East |

(Galletti)
1xDS

Massawa
| East Africa |

(Balsamo)
1xDS
7xDD
2xTB
8xSS

| MARICOTRAF |

(Riccardi)
8xTB

and Tunis). Supermarina considered traffic with Libya and the Dodecanese a strategic matter and the responsibility of the battle force.

B. AVIATION

1. Ship-based

At the start of the war, Italy's ship-based aviation consisted of catapult-launched floatplanes that were used for reconnaissance and spotting. In the autumn of 1942 some Re.2000 fighters aboard the modern battleships gave an extremely limited ship-borne air defense capability, but in the only occasion it was really required, in the battle force's voyage south following the armistice with the Allies, the one fighter catapulted off *Roma* did not have time to climb to altitude before Luftwaffe bombers sank the battleship.

2. Shore-based

In 1923 most of the Regia Marina's considerable aviation assets, along with about one hundred officers and its most air-minded personnel, transferred to the newly established Regia Aeronautica. Air force control over maritime aviation solidified during the following decade until, in 1931, a law decreed that the navy would retain control over only the land-based and catapulted reconnaissance floatplanes and flying boats. An even stricter version of this law followed in 1937. Thus, the Regia Marina went to war with no control over its aviation except for reconnaissance planes that, although flown by air force personnel, at least were under the navy's direct orders. However, there were in June 1940 only twenty-four such *squadriglie* as opposed to the navy's stated requirement for forty-five, and there was no effective increase throughout the conflict.

Not surprisingly, coordination with aerial units controlled by separate commands and subject to different doctrines and priorities was poor. Cooperation at its best consisted of a naval asset requesting air support, which local naval command would forward to Supermarina. Supermarina would alert Superaereo, which would pass the request along to the appropriate local air command for execution. In the dynamic environment of naval warfare, this tortuous process seldom resulted in prompt and effective support.

C. WEAPON SYSTEMS
1. Gunnery

Surface. Italy's high command regarded guns—the bigger the better—as the navy's primary weapon. The accuracy of Italian guns and the quality of the ordnance they used has been much debated. For example, John Campbell, an authority on World War II naval weapons, has commented, "Italian shells of almost all types suffered from over wide manufacturing tolerances, which increased the often high dispersion."[13] This assertion echoes Admiral Angelo Iachino, a fleet commander, who wrote in 1959 that, "[Our guns] had the defect of insufficient precision resulting obviously from excessive longitudinal dispersion of the salvos . . . because our prescribed norms for testing ammunition were less rigorous than those used in foreign navies."[14] However, more recent Italian scholars such as Giuliano Colliva have used contemporary documents and artillery trial results to assert that the accuracy of Italian gunnery was similar to British and superior to French shooting.[15]

The principal difference between Italian and British gunnery was doctrinal. Many British wartime accounts report that Italian salvos seemed excessively dispersed; that is, when the shells fired by a group of guns landed, they were scattered over a large area. The British goal was always to bunch salvos as tightly as possible on the principal that multiple hits might be scored if the aim was on. The Italians favored a deliberate rate of fire while generally the British fired at about twice the Italian rate. The Italian Navy sought high muzzle velocities, which allowed their guns to outrange enemy weapons of identical bore. This, along with the traditionally higher speed of Italian warships, supported the Italian objective of gaining an early advantage in a surface action by outranging the enemy. Italian doctrine stated, "We have every interest in prolonging the shooting at maximum range seeking to hit the enemy before he can hit us, in order to provoke a tactical unbalance of forces that will assure our success in the later close-range phase of the fighting."[16] Also, high muzzle velocities resulted in lower shell trajectories because the angle at which a shell fell from any height was determined by its velocity, and a lower trajectory resulted in a target having a larger danger space, which would offset some loss of accuracy resulting from salvo dispersion, at least at lower ranges. Ultimately, however, the Regia Marina decided that high muzzle velocities had too great an effect on barrel life—they could get only 110–130 rounds from their 15-inch weapon before the barrel liner required replacement, and this led to some reductions.

Fire was controlled with a director system using a fire-control computer. The best rangefinders combined stereoscopic and coincidence instruments in one unit. The modern battleships had 12-m rangefinders while those on the heavy cruisers measured 7.2-m. Italian fire-control systems also included instruments to continuously measure the variation of a target's bearing, which the Italians believed would be a decisive asset.

Naval researchers developed prototype radars as early as October 1939, but because they had been conceived mainly for gunnery and the metric sets then available had an excessive goniometric error, they failed to generate much interest. In 1940, staff asked its small electronic branch to give precedence to the TPA Talk Between Ships system mentioned earlier, believing that radar was futuristic and that the British had not yet developed a naval set. The first Italian radar, a combined search and fire-control set, did not appear shipboard until August 1941—four months after intercepted radio communications persuaded naval staff that the British were employing radar to locate Italian ships from beyond visual range.

Antiaircraft. In the context of the 1930s, the Regia Marina was as conscious as any of the world's major navies of the need to protect its warships from aerial attack. However, it lacked efficient fire control for close-range antiair weapons. Battleships and cruisers had dedicated 90-mm or 100-mm heavy antiaircraft batteries, with the accurate and reliable 100-mm weapon being most common. Italy had tested a 4.7-inch/46 dual-purpose weapon in 1938–1939, but the results were unsatisfactory. Consequently, destroyer main batteries lacked the elevation and fire control needed to serve as effective antiair weapons. The principal close-range antiaircraft weapons were the 37-mm/54 and the 20-mm/65 Breda guns. Both were reliable, although early versions suffered from heavy vibration and required a strong supporting structure.

2. Torpedoes

Italian torpedoes were generally reliable and had working detonators and low wander and malfunctioning values (5 percent and 1 percent, respectively, according to tests conducted in the summer of 1937). Germany imported nearly a thousand Italian aerial torpedoes, and the Japanese copied features of an Italian high-speed version.

The fire-control systems introduced on the destroyers and the modern torpedo boats in 1937 determined solutions using directors in the bridge wings with a calculating apparatus, a rate-of-change-of-bearing instrument (*teleinclinometro cinematico*) in the crow's nest, and binocular sights and tables fitted in each bank of tubes. War experience would show, however, that the night fire-direction systems, which worked based on estimated range and target speeds, were ineffective, and many captains preferred to aim by eye.

At the beginning of the war, Italy had an inventory of 3,660 torpedoes, including 1,689 modern 21-inch weapons, 648 modern, and 1,323 old 17.7-inch torpedoes (see table 4.2). Production was 50 per month but increased to 120 per month by late 1941. Italian torpedoes sank or damaged 216 ships.

TABLE 4.2 Torpedo Expenditures

Year	Fired by navy	Fired by air force	Total fired
1940	546	35	581
1941	1,185	180	1,365
1942	1,600	368	1,968
1943	346	n/a	>346

3. Antisubmarine Warfare

In considering the lessons of the First World War, navy staff concluded that submarines would be a minor threat in any future war. Consequently, the Regia Marina was underprepared for modern antisubmarine warfare in terms of ships, equipment, and doctrine.

The principal antisubmarine weapon was the depth charge, although towed torpedoes remained in use. In the 1930s a pneumatic depth charge thrower with a 100-m range appeared on destroyers and torpedo boats, but in action it proved too hard to reload and was replaced in late 1942 by a weapon with a shorter range and a faster reload cycle. Other refinements included a multiple-launch rack system, called the *scaricabombe Gatteschi*, which appeared in late 1942 on the *Gabbiano*-class corvettes and permitted a saturation attack of up to forty-eight depth charges in a single pass. The later *Gabbianos* were scheduled to carry an automatic 12-inch antisubmarine mortar called the Menon, but none was actually fitted.

By 1939 Italy had developed, after an effort of almost fifteen years, an effective sonar (*ecogoniometro*), but the small capacity of Italy's electronics industry and its priority on consumer products led to the postponement of its production. Thus, in the war's early period, hydrophones, including the almost useless First World War "C" type, provided the major tool for detecting submarines underwater. Auxiliary escort vessels and MAS boats had to rely on the drift-and-listen technique. This required highly trained operators with sensitive ears. Specialized antisubmarine craft consisted of only the *Albatros*, equipped with one of the navy's two echo-detection sets available in June 1940, and the four *Pegaso*-class escort torpedo boats. The navy acquired German sonars in late 1941, and Italian-made sets arrived the next year. However, even as late as September 1943, the Regia Marina possessed only thirty-six Italian and thirty-one German sets. For comparison, Great Britain entered the war with roughly two thousand Asdic.

Italian air force flying boats and floatplanes used a 160-kg depth charge bomb. This weapon damaged, according to Royal Navy sources, five boats and on numerous occasions helped Italian vessels to avoid subsurface threats sighted in the Mediterranean's clear waters. Some sources credit Regia Aeronautica fighters with sinking HMS *Urge* on 29 April 1942 off the Libyan coast, although the official Statement of Losses speculates that she was mined.

Despite their lack of preparation and material deficiencies, Italian antisubmarine forces fought effectively against Great Britain's submarine offensive, accounting for thirty-three of the thirty-eight British submarines lost in the Mediterranean through September 1943 (excluding three boats sunk in Malta's Grand Harbor by Axis bombers). Italian depth charges sank at least twelve British submarines and probably another three; three British boats were rammed, and one was sunk in a surface action with an Italian submarine. Mines accounted for at least eleven.

4. Mines

Mine barriers were fundamental to Italy's strategy of closing the Sicilian Channel to British traffic between Gibraltar and Suez. In June 1940 the navy had an inventory of 25,000 mines, all moored contact types, and it laid 54,457 during the war. The best, the Pignone P.200, had 200 kg of explosives, a mooring cable as long as 820 m (by 1943), and could be deployed in waters as deep as 100 m. Most Italian production was based on World War I technology, however, and Italy, even if it adopted an efficient German acoustic device in 1941, lacked a magnetic mine. Throughout the course of the war, Italian mines sank one cruiser, three destroyers, at least eleven submarines, and twenty-six other vessels. Italy's greatest mine warfare success occurred in December 1941 when a field off Tripoli eviscerated Force K, sinking a cruiser and a destroyer and damaging another two cruisers.

D. INFRASTRUCTURE
1. Logistics
The Italian navy began the war with 2 million tons of fuel oil stockpiled, reduced to 1.7 million when Mussolini ordered Cavagnari to surrender 300,000 tons to industry in June 1940. Operations during the war's first seven months consumed 676,560 tons, and the navy burned another 1,123,148 tons through 1941. By late September 1941 the Regia Marina's fuel supply was dependent on the Italian oil concession in Romania and on German charity.

Italian ships were designed to operate in the Mediterranean and tended to have short ranges and high fuel consumption. For example, the light cruiser *Da Barbiano* could steam 3,800 nautical miles at economical speeds consuming 6.1 tons of oil an hour. In contrast, a British *Leander*-class cruiser could travel 5,730 miles at 3.9 tons/hour. An Italian Soldati-class destroyer had a range of 2,340 miles at 3.0 tons/hour compared to a larger British Tribal-class vessel, which could range 5,700 miles at a rate of 1.4 tons/hour.

The limited endurance of their destroyers defined the battle fleet's radius of action. To the east, the fleet's practical limit was the waters off central Crete, and to the west, operations never extended past Majorca and Bone. Although it practiced underway replenishment in prewar exercises, Italy considered this technique too dangerous under wartime conditions, especially in waters subject to submarine attack, and did not use it operationally.

2. Bases
The Regia Marina had an extensive network of strong naval bases. The principal fleet anchorages, Taranto and La Spezia, could maintain and repair all warship classes. Secondary bases included Naples (with yards capable of repairing up to cruiser-sized warships), La Maddalena in Sardinia, Venice (with a naval arsenal), and Brindisi and Pola on the Adriatic Sea, all of which could receive ships of up to battleship size. Genoa's port was mainly commercial, but it could also receive and repair any class of warship.

Tertiary-level bases included Cagliari in Sardinia, Messina, and Augusta in Sicily, which had harbors that could host cruisers but limited repair facilities.

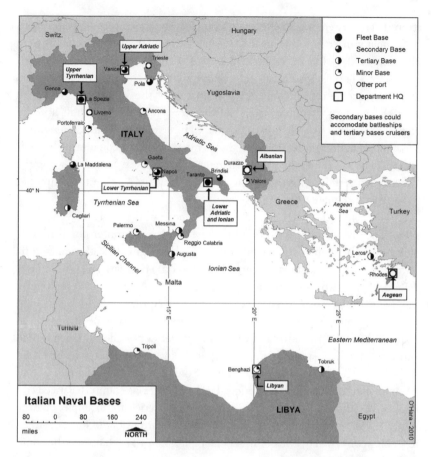

Italian Naval Bases

80 0 80 160 240	
miles	NORTH

Leros in the Aegean Sea and Tripoli and Tobruk in Libya could briefly base cruisers. Massawa, on the Red Sea, had a five-thousand-ton floating dock.

Fuel, water, and ammunition could be supplied at Elba's Portoferraio; Gaeta, Reggio Calabria, and Ancona on the peninsula; Valona in Albania; Sicily's Palermo; Benghazi and Tripoli in Libya; and Kysimaiu in Somalia. Palermo and Ancona also had limited repair facilities in private yards.

Until the Taranto attack in November 1940, harbor defenses were designed to permit warships to swiftly sortie. After the attack, net boxes that reached to the bottom were adopted and deployed in Taranto beginning in March 1941, and at the others harbors as quickly thereafter as materials could be manufactured. After October 1942 harbors also incorporated anti-small-attack-craft defenses.

An important defensive development was a smoke curtain system that, from January 1941, proved able to protect harbors from enemy bombers (La Maddalena was the exception because the wind there was generally too strong). The system was so effective that five army smoke battalions were sent to Germany in 1942 following a Kriegsmarine request. Antiair defenses were also improved, although the general lack of effective fire directors mandated the use of a barrage system. By July 1943 only 23 of the 121 batteries armed with the excellent 90-mm/53 AA gun and 11 of the 31 batteries equipped with the modern 75-mm/46 gun had directors. Italian antiaircraft artillery employed a collection of Italian, German, Hungarian, and French fire directors. Italian fighter protection was always numerically and qualitatively modest (two Fiat Cr.42 biplanes with the navy controlled 1st Squadriglia Riserva Navale at Spezia during the spring of 1943) and able, at best, to interdict reconnaissance flights.

The shore batteries that defended Italian ports were tested on several occasions. The first British operation of the war was a brief cruiser bombardment of Tobruk. The French conducted cruiser bombardments of Vado and Savona on 14 June 1940; British battleships hit Genoa on 9 February 1941, which was defended by a two 15-inch guns, two 7.5-inch guns, and eight 6-inch guns; Valona on 19 December 1940; and Tripoli on 21 April 1941, which had eight 7.5-inch/39 guns. Some ports enjoyed an apparently lavish scale of defense. In 1940 six batteries ringed Massawa with nineteen 4.7-inch and three 6-inch guns. By March 1941 another seven 4.7-inch and four 4-inch guns had been added. Even Kysimaiu and Mogadishu in Somalia each had a battery of four 4.7-inch cannons. However, a serious lack of munitions counterbalanced this impressive infrastructure. The Sicilian coastal batteries, for example, met the Allied invasion with enough ammunition for a quarter hour of fire, according to a court convened by Mussolini's social republic in 1944 that tried the admiral commanding Augusta for treason.

3. Industry

Before the war, Italy had established a worldwide reputation for building innovative warships, constructing vessels for the Soviet Union, Sweden, Japan, Thailand, China, Finland, Argentina, Brazil, Uruguay, Venezuela, Turkey, Iran, Greece, and Romania. The principal yards consisted of the Ansaldo Company in Genoa; Cantieri Navali dell'Adriatico in Trieste, and Odero-Terni-Orlando (OTO) at Leghorn. Other important shipbuilding centers included OTO at La Spezia; Cantieri Navali Riuniti at Riva Trigoso, Palermo, Ancona, Marghera, and Castellammare; the Bacini e Cantieri Navali Partenopei in Naples; and Fiume's Cantieri Navali del Quarnaro.

The problem with Italy's shipbuilding industry was not a lack of infrastructure or skilled labor; it was a shortage of raw materials and power. In 1939, for example, Italy constructed only 135,000 tons of shipping against a theoretical capacity of 300,000 tons. The country produced 2.3 million tons of steel compared to 10 million for Great Britain and 23 million for Germany. Italy was largely or entirely deficient in coal, oil, copper, tin, nickel, manganese, tungsten, chromium, molybdenum, phosphates, potash, and rubber. Other factors that affected Italy's industrial capacity were inefficient work practices and corruption in the delivery of contracts although the navy, under the Cavagnari's harsh rule, was less affected than the other services.

IV. RECAPITULATION

A. WARTIME EVOLUTION

During the parallel war period from June 1940 through the end of the year, the Regia Marina's strategy was based on the premise that the war was practically over and that there was little to gain and much to lose by aggressively risking major assets. British historians generally criticize this policy. One author recently wrote, "The Regia Marina was hampered by its leaders' belief in 'the fleet in being'—the idea that a naval force's very existence had an effect on strategy and sometimes it was better to protect it in harbour than risk it at sea. . . . The Italians might . . . have won a decisive victory had they not been so cautious."[17] There is some truth in this observation, given the way the war developed, but the evolution of the Anglo-German conflict into a life-and-death world war seemed preposterous in mid-1940, and not only in Rome. In terms of the war that Italy's leaders believed they were fighting, seeking a decisive victory at sea made little sense.

Italy's performance in its parallel war was uneven. The Regia Marina kept the Balkan and North African armies supplied and enabled each to undertake offensive operations, although these armies proved woefully incapable of the tasks Mussolini's government assigned them. The navy also tested itself against the British in a fleet action off Calabria and was satisfied with the result. Rome correctly judged that British battleships would no longer venture into the Ionian Sea because the loss of even one without corresponding or greater casualties to the Italian battle fleet could jeopardize the balance of force. Italy was thus able to control the sea-lanes to North Africa and maintain traffic with neutral nations. Theoretically, this gave the army the opportunity to seize the Suez Canal and effectively end the war. The navy calculated that if peace was not forthcoming after such a success, it could, with little risk and high dividends, conduct its long dreamed *guerra sportiva* (sporting war) on the oceans with submarines and auxiliary cruisers.

On the negative side of the balance sheet, the navy discovered that its submarine force was less effective than anticipated; worse, it learned that high-level bombing, which was the only type of attack the air force could initially deliver, was impotent, and that air–sea cooperation would be a critical problem with no easy solution given the Byzantine nature of Italy's Fascist government and military structure. Commando attacks by Decima MAS were foiled in August and September 1940 when their transport submarines were sunk en route to their attack points. A third effort in October failed due to mechanical defects with the SLC-manned torpedoes.

In 1940 the Regia Marina sank eleven Allied submarines, which in turn sank twenty-four Italian ships displacing 58,809 tons—a ratio of 5,346 tons per submarine lost. The Regia Marina lost twenty submarines during this period and sank twenty-eight Allied ships displacing 103,400 tons—a ratio of 5,170 tons per submarine lost.

The British air raid at Taranto on 11 November 1940 damaged three battleships (one never completed repairs) but did little to alter the strategic situation because the Regia Marina still possessed enough battleships to maintain a credible fleet in being and intervene against British movements into the central basin, as it did just two weeks after Taranto in the Battle of Cape Spartivento.

The first period ended with the Italian army's collapse in North Africa and the frustration of Mussolini's Grecian adventure. These twin failures by the poorly organized and led Italian Royal Army created the conditions that caused Germany to intervene in Mussolini's parallel war.

In the winter of 1940–1941 Germany enjoyed boundless opportunities and remained certain of victory. The introduction of limited German ground forces in North Africa and some air forces throughout the theater strengthened the two weakest components of the Italian war machine. The impact of German intervention on the Regia Marina's operations was less benign, however. The British were routinely able to read German air force and railroad Enigma-encrypted code from January 1941. Security leaks facilitated every one of Britain's nighttime interceptions of Italian convoys. Empty German promises of air support contributed to the failure off Cape Matapan, the Regia Marina's largest attempt at an offensive action. Britain's German-created intelligence advantages were reflected in the ratio of losses suffered on the convoy routes before and after Berlin's intervention (see table 4.3).

TABLE 4.3 Italian Shipments to Africa 1940 Compared to 1941

Period	Men Average/Month (lost)	Materiel Average Tons/ Month (lost)
1940	4,140 (70)	42,570 (1,000)
1941	12,000 (1,180)	71,080 (12,080)

Source: Sadkovich, Italian Navy, 343.

In 1941 the British submarine effort taxed Italian antisubmarine forces. In the Mediterranean, British submarines accounted for 212,643 tons of Axis shipping. Italian ASW forces sank ten Allied submarines giving a net ratio of 21,264 tons of shipping sunk per submarine lost. By contrast, Italian submarines sank thirty-seven Allied vessels displacing 175,670 tons, largely in the Atlantic. The Regia Marina lost eighteen boats and achieved an average of 9,760 tons of enemy shipping sunk per boat lost.

By September 1941 the Regia Marina's and Regia Aeronautica's oil reserves were exhausted. For the next two years these services operated hand to mouth, concentrating on supplying the Axis armies in North Africa and the Balkans up through May 1943 and retaining in reserve a powerful one-time strike capacity up through the time of the armistice in September 1943.

By December 1941 British forces were pressing hard, and the Italian navy faced a crisis in the convoy war. However, the Regia Marina's successes during this month in the First Battle of Sirte, in a commando strike by Decima MAS that sank two British battleships in Alexandria and in the crippling of Force K by mines, provided a dramatic turnabout and a tremendous boost to the navy's morale.

For most of 1942 the Axis powers dominated the Mediterranean. They reduced Malta to starvation rations, with the Regia Marina playing its part in several large convoy battles. The navy's leadership had long since abandoned the idea of a short war, but Mussolini and the country's economic establishment harbored hopes that the Germans and Soviets could negotiate a separate peace and, after London had been detached from its unnatural continental ally, the Axis partners could focus on the Mediterranean if the war continued.

In the submarine war, Italian boats sank 344,307 tons of Allied shipping at a cost of 21 boats for an average of 16,396 tons per boat lost. The Allies lost 17 boats and sank 119 vessels in the Mediterranean grossing 294,681 tons for an average of 17,334 tons per boat lost.

The Axis position of superiority abruptly flip-flopped in November 1942 when the Anglo-Americans invaded French North Africa. More than the British victory at El Alamein, this spelled the beginning of the end for Italy. Rather than cut their losses, the Axis poured a new army into Tunisia with the pipe dream of sweeping the Anglo-Americans back to Morocco.

From November 1942 through May 1943 the Regia Marina fought its hardest campaign. Its ability to keep the Axis armies operating in Tunisia for such an extended period, despite Allied air, naval, and intelligence superiority, was a tremendous accomplishment. Battleships and cruisers remained at anchor as destroyers and corvettes burned oil pumped from their bunkers. The fact that the Germans and Italians seized 800,000 tons of French shipping as a consequence of Torch made the task easier. Moreover, by supporting the

Photo 4.4. The heads of government and the navy aboard the light cruiser *Montecuccoli* in June 1942 after the Battle of Pantelleria. Admiral Riccardi, his face hidden, Mussolini, and Admiral da Zara to the far left. (Enrico Cernuschi collection)

position in Africa, the Regia Marina ensured that more than 2 million tons of Allied shipping remained tied up maintaining the Middle and the Far East around the Cape of Good Hope. The ramification of this on the global war is seldom evaluated, but it certainly guaranteed there would be no second front in France in 1943.

By the spring of 1943 the Axis undersea campaign against the Allied sea-lanes in the western Mediterranean had been defeated by the new Allied ASW tactics and weapons. Italian submarines sank 87,793 tons at a cost of twenty-five boats for a mere 3,512 tons per boat lost. In the meantime, Allied boats destroyed 238,443 tons of shipping in Mediterranean waters, losing up to the Italian armistice of 8 September 1943 nine boats for a ratio of 26,493 tons per submarine lost.

The Italian navy and air force collectively sank approximately 1 million tons of Allied and neutral shipping. This was a modest percentage of the 18.87 million tons lost by the Allies up through 31 May 1943. However, the nature of the Mediterranean war and the heavy protection afforded to most targets subject to Italian attack must be considered when counting gross numbers. Moreover, Italy's efforts greatly facilitated Germany's war. For example, the destroyers and escort vessels the Royal Navy had to dispatch to the Mediterranean and the Red Sea from the spring of 1940 enabled the U-boats to enjoy their first "happy time" in the Atlantic.

With the final fall of Tunisia in May 1943, the Regia Marina harbored its strength and continued to convoy vital maritime traffic in the Tyrrhenian, Ionian, Adriatic, and Aegean seas. The battle fleet did not intervene during the Sicilian invasion, principally because these landings occurred beyond its air umbrella and because only two modern battleships were operational at the time to face six enemy battleships and two fleet carriers.

By the time Italy signed an armistice in September 1943, the Regia Marina's surface fleet included six battleships (one a training vessel), eight light cruisers, eighteen destroyers, seventeen modern and fifteen old torpedo boats, and twenty corvettes. Most of these ships went on to fight with the Allies.

B. SUMMARY AND ASSESSMENT

There was a time when the English-language literature was unanimous in its assessment of the Regia Marina's wartime performance—the Italian navy avoided combat, conceded to the British a moral superiority, and was generally an ineffective force. American historian Samuel E. Morison's famous remark was typical. "There was also the Italian fleet to guard against, on paper, but the 'Dago Navy' had long been regarded by British tars as a huge joke."[18] A minority of historians, however, offered other views. One wrote that it is necessary "to appreciate the weakness of Italy, but not to assume that weakness translated into excessive caution or simple cowardice," and that the Italians "preformed well despite their handicaps."[19]

The Regia Marina operated under many handicaps, but so did the navies of Great Britain and its allies. Rather than assess the Regia Marina in terms of the difficulties it faced, it is better to begin an assessment by examining facts.

The first fact is that the Allies inflicted more harm to Italy's navy than they suffered. The Italian navy and air force sank or captured thirty-three large Allied warships and forty-two submarines. Italy lost eighty-three warships and eighty-three submarines in the Mediterranean and Red Seas between 10 June 1940 and 8 September 1943—seventy to the British and their allies and thirteen to the Americans. German forces sank an additional forty-three Allied warships and six submarines in this period. In total the Allies lost seventy-six ships and forty-eight submarines. In terms of warship tonnage, the Italians sank 145,800 tons and the Germans 169,700, for a total of 315,500. The British sank 161,200 tons of Italian surface warships and the Americans 33,900, for a total of 195,100 tons.

The Italians accounted for 43 percent of Allied warship losses and 86 percent of submarine losses. A comparison of the cause of loss shows that German aircraft sank 30 percent of the Allied warships lost while Italian aircraft only accounted for 9 percent. German submarines sank 21 percent compared to 7 percent for Italian submarines. In all other causes, including special forces, surface actions, mine warfare, shore batteries, and capture, Italy accounted for 28 percent of the Allied warships lost compared to 5 percent for the Germans.

Thus, German aircraft and submarines were more successful than their Italian counterparts when it came to sinking Allied surface warships. Italian naval forces sank many more Allied submarines than did German forces. Some of the difference can be explained by opportunity and mission and by the fact that Germany's greater production and resources allowed for a more aggressive strategy. However, these results also indicate that the Italian air force did not develop the weapons and tactics to adequately support its sister service. Had the Regia Marina been able to control its own aerial assets and develop an adequate reconnaissance force and the torpedo-bomber squadrons envisioned in the mid-1930s, Italian aircraft (and warships) would have enjoyed more success at sea.

Italian submarines were not as deadly as German ones. Much of the fault for their lack of success is attributed to design flaws—they were too large and dived too slowly to be effective in the Mediterranean's clear waters, but the hard truth was that the Regia Marina introduced the necessary physical modifications to the boats by late 1940 but improved training and doctrine took another year to show results. Italian submarines were much more effective by 1942, but by the spring of 1943 they faced the same defeat inflicted on the Germans U-boats in the Atlantic.

The Italian navy suffered more damage than the Allies in naval surface combat, but nearly all such damage occurred in night engagements during a few sea denial actions. Sea control, conversely, was exercised by day when the Regia Marina's fighting capacity was at its best and when it won the victories necessary to maintain the sea-lanes to Africa and the Balkans.

The nature of its missions and Italy's national goals required the navy to operate in a largely defensive posture defending convoys in an environment where the Allies enjoyed air supremacy, technological and intelligence advantages, and a superior night fighting doctrine. Italy's government and high command remained acutely aware that the battle fleet's existence was the key to maintaining sea control and were accordingly conservative in their conduct of offensive operations. Nonetheless, the Regia Marina did carry out effective offensive operations, such as its forays against Britain's February, March, June, and August 1942 Malta convoys. While the ratio of damage inflicted in surface engagements in these daylight offensive actions was in Italy's favor, it should be noted that in the most successful action of all, the June 1942 battleship sortie that forced the Vigorous convoy to turn back, the two fleets did not even make contact.

Italy's underwater commandos of Decima MAS pioneered a type of low-cost, high-return naval warfare that was attractive to the Axis powers, which could not afford to trade ships in the face of Anglo-American industrial might. Decima MAS proved more effective than any other navy's special warfare units, accounting for two battleships, a heavy cruiser, and two dozen merchant vessels sunk and others damaged. However, commandos could not establish sea control, and Italy wasted the moment when the unit would have had its greatest impact because it was not ready to strike in the conflict's opening hours.

The true measure of Italy's performance was that the Allies never eliminated the Regia Marina as an effective force as they eliminated the Japanese and German navies. That the Kingdom of Italy sought an armistice instead of fighting to the bitter end helped, but the fact remains that after thirty-nine months of war, Italy still possessed a fleet capable of effective intervention (even if, by the summer of 1943, the odds of such intervention succeeding were very slender) and that when the Ligurian-based battle fleet received the unexpected news of the armistice on 8 September, boilers had already been fired and the fleet was prepared to expend the last of its men and oil on a do-or-die strike against the Salerno landings.

Regardless of the blunders, deceptions, and failures of political courage associated with the Italian armistice, the Regia Marina's continued effectiveness allowed Italy to obtain better terms than did the French in their armistice signed with the Allies on 22 November 1942.

Another factor that emerges from this brief analysis is that the Regia Marina's performance and effectiveness improved as the war progressed, in contrast to the navies of its Axis partners. Italian escorts proved better able to fight off British surface forces in 1942 and 1943 than in 1940 and 1941. In the Mediterranean antisubmarine war, the Italians maintained a constant monthly average of 3.5 Allied boats sunk or damaged against an average of 25 submarines active throughout the period of January 1941 through September 1943, despite British improvements in tactics, training, and weapons. The Regia Marina was likewise more successful interdicting British convoys in the war's latter half. Overall, as the war progressed, the navy gained experience and proved a grimmer and more resolute foe.

Navies do not set national policy; they are instruments of policy. Ultimately, the question is, how well did the Regia Marina accomplish its missions?

In the all-important convoy war, the Regia Marina kept Italy's and Germany's expeditionary armies in Africa and the Balkans supplied, delivering 98 percent of the men and 90 percent of the material loaded in Italian ports despite crippling handicaps such as Ultra, which let the Allies know the composition, sailing date, and route of nearly every African convoy from late

July 1941 to December 1942 when a new submarine cable between Sicily and Tunis secured Italy's communications, although the Germans continued to rely upon messages encyphered with their Enigma system.

The Regia Marina closed the direct passage through the Mediterranean for thirty-six months, almost its entire war, to all but eight fast freighters in three massively protected convoys, Collar, Excess, and Tiger, which ran between November 1940 and May 1941. This forced Great Britain to build and supply an army in Egypt around the Cape of Good Hope rather than the Strait of Gibraltar, a twelve-thousand-mile voyage, nearly four times longer than the direct Mediterranean passage. With the Mediterranean shortcut closed to British shipping, Bombay was nearly a thousand miles closer to Plymouth than Suez. The impact on Britain was devastating. Imports to the Home Islands collapsed in August 1940 from 46.5 million tons to 33 million and never recovered, declining constantly in the following years until leveling off in the spring of 1943 to less than 15 million tons a year.

The Regia Marina's so-called policy of risk avoidance was critical to its mission. By merely existing the fleet protected Italy's inner seas, secured its convoy routes, and maintained the vital blockade of the Sicilian narrows. Only by destroying the fleet in battle could Great Britain hope to secure sea control; the Regia Marina effectively denied the Royal Navy this victory, much to the frustration of Churchill, the Admiralty, and many later-day historians seduced by Mahan and the cult of the decisive naval battle.

By these objective measures, Italy's Regia Marina was an effective force. It suffered its failures and defeats, but it also won its victories and succeeded in the jobs it was tasked to do. Its leadership forged before and during the war a coherent strategy that proved effective in meeting the nation's requirements within the geopolitical constraints under which it operated, given the tools it possessed, and considering the nature and caliber of the opposition it faced.

chapter five

Japan: The Teikoku Kaigun

I. BACKSTORY

A. HISTORY

The history of the Japanese Imperial Navy, 1868–1945, is the story of the navy's transformation from an odd collection of sailing vessels in the early 1880s into the world's third most powerful fleet by the end of World War I. The navy's progress is emblematic of Japan's meteoric rise from feudal isolation in the mid-nineteenth century to one of the world's great powers by 1918.[1]

In the decade 1868 to 1878, the Japanese sailing navy, inadequate even for coastal defense, lacked not only modern warships but also any professional understanding of tactical deployment, any strategic awareness, and any technological and industrial base. Yet a handful of modernizing officials, recognizing the priority of Japanese self-defense, including the establishment of a modern navy, acutely identified the first steps to developing such a force. Although they could not call upon a consistent Japanese maritime tradition, or upon a store of technological expertise, Japan's military and naval circumstances at the time bore several advantages. First, because Japan had no real fighting navy, it was not burdened by a dominant naval establishment resistant to change, nor by a large fleet that rapid shifts in technology could make obsolescent or expensive to replace. On the contrary, confronted with kaleidoscopic changes in world naval affairs, the handful of forward-looking and decisive leaders who came to the forefront of Japanese political and military development in these years was influenced by the Japanese propensity to adopt the latest and most useful practices, even if they came from abroad. These men were surprisingly able to make wise choices and take fresh initiatives in an era of worldwide strategic, tactical, and technological uncertainty.

In the 1880s, when Japan had limited economic resources and Western power was encroaching on East Asia, it was clear to the Japanese leadership that the strategic priority must be the defense of the home islands. For the time being, Japan's navy, such as it was, would depend on foreign technology for its modern warships and on foreign instruction for its tactical and technological training until it could build its own industrial base for naval construction and its own autonomous professionalism.

At this embryonic stage of naval development, Japan was particularly fortunate to have a mentor in Britain, although it kept its options open for any and all foreign assistance and counsel. In 1878 one modern steam frigate and two corvettes were built in British yards and delivered by British crews to Japanese ports. Complementing these new fleet units, a series of British naval advisers and instructors introduced Japan's fledgling officer corps to the latest Western tactical advances and strategic thought.

By the 1880s the navy had taken the first steps in the development of a naval arms industry, including the construction of shipyards at Nagasaki and Yokosuka and the establishment naval arsenals at Tsukiji in Tokyo Bay and Yokosuka south of it. The arsenals, using machinery from Britain, soon began to turn out a few steam vessels of modest size. But for the most part, the navy was still dependent on foreign industry to design and construct its modern fleet. Casting about for the latest advances in naval thinking, the navy came under the influence of the French Jeune Ecole and its emphasis on coast defense, a raiding strategy, and small fast naval units.

Taken together, Japan's material limitations and this latest trend in Japanese naval thinking confirmed the navy's defensive posture in the 1880s. But by the end of that decade, the nation's changed geopolitical concerns sharply altered that outlook. The eastward advance of Russian power across Asia provoked Japanese interests on the continent, particularly on the Korean peninsula where Japanese ambitions confronted Chinese hegemony. This emerging confrontation fueled the support of the government and the public for a force capable of projecting Japanese power into East Asian waters. With the purchase of its three French steel steam-driven cruisers, the navy acquired its first modern warships designed to battle a specific opponent, the Chinese Beiyang Fleet, which included several large warships purchased from Germany.

Simultaneous with the acquisition of its first modern fleet units, the Japanese navy, struggling with its sister service for strategic status, organized itself for combat, constituted itself as an emperor-centered service, established its standing fleets and major base commands, reformed its personnel system, and formulated its first tactical doctrine. These initiatives were in large part due to the vision and ferocious energy of one of the early navy's greatest figures, Admiral Yamamoto Gombei (1852–1933).

On the eve of the nation's 1894–1895 conflict with China, the navy had made great advances in the requirements for modern naval combat. Its largest force, the Combined Fleet, centered on ten first-line warships, all foreign-built. Although it was hastily brought together, its unified command, superior speed, offensive doctrine, and superior armament proved triumphant in the war's several naval engagements, most dramatically in the Battle off the Yalu River, 17 September 1894. Those victories confirmed the lessons the navy had been taught by its British advisers: the tactical superiority of the column over the line abreast, the importance of strict station keeping and the consequent concentration of gunfire, the effectiveness of the torpedo and the quick-firing gun, and the necessity for a homogeneous fleet able to maneuver together. For the navy, its victory over the Beiyang Fleet provided a dazzling argument for its primacy of place in the Japanese armed services.

But victory over imperial China did not bring Japan all the rewards it had hoped for at the beginning of the war. True, it had wrenched from China a large monetary indemnity, the island of Taiwan as Japan's first overseas colonial territory, and the Kwantung Peninsula with its valuable naval base at Port Arthur. But the "Triple Intervention" (by Russia, Germany, and France) forced the retrocession of Kwantung to China, a national mortification that made clear Japan's maritime weakness relative to the West. To deal with this humiliation and to plan for an eventual showdown with Russia, Japan undertook two initiatives. It linked itself by treaty with Britain, the world's greatest naval power, and it set about acquiring sufficient naval strength to confront Russia over the mastery of northeast Asia.

In the process, Japan acquired a battle force of state-of-the-art capital ships, a difficult and risky decision because all navies, trying to find the dominant weapon, the most effective fleet organization, and the most successful tactical system, still labored in a fog of conflicting technological and doctrinal choices. Fortunately for Japan, the nation retained the services of Yamamoto Gombei, whose influence and acumen were greater than his position as chief of the Navy Ministry's Naval Affairs Department. Thanks to his efforts, in 1896, the navy pushed through the Diet an expansion plan that committed the government to a theoretical standard of naval power not unlike Britain's "Two-power Standard." It also represented a conscious effort to match the navy's qualitative strength against all other naval powers because it called for four new British-built battleships, more powerful than anything yet afloat. This emphasis on quality over quantity was to be a fundamental principle in the navy's force structure for the next half century.

The decade 1895–1904 saw Japanese advances across a range of naval technologies, including new explosives, ammunition, and fire control. By its alliance with Britain, Japan not only gained access to stocks of superior Cardiff coal but also neutralized the threat of a potential coalition of hostile powers, such as the one presented in the Triple Intervention. During these years, the Japanese Naval Staff College began to shape a modern yet indigenous tactical doctrine that combined Japanese classical military concepts, the navy's experience in the war with China, and the latest Western innovations. From these different conceptual strands the navy wove together certain lasting principles, including the tactical effectiveness of superior speed, the importance of close-in torpedo attacks pressed home relentlessly, and the necessity of a battle line homogenous in speed and firepower.

Exploiting all these measures on the eve of its war with Russia, Japan had raised itself to fourth among the world's maritime powers. It was, to be sure, still a navy of regional not global reach. Yet in preparing for a conflict with Russia, whose navy was divided into two fleets separated by the world's largest continent, this regional focus was a definite advantage. Furthermore, the missions of the Japanese Combined Fleet under the command of the redoubtable Admiral Tōgō Heihachirō were perfectly clear: the defense of Japan's home waters; the blockade of Russian naval forces in East Asian ports; the escort of a Japanese expeditionary force to the northeast Asian coast; the protection of its maritime communications; and the destruction of any Russian naval force sent from European waters to intervene. In the war that followed, Tōgō's Combined Fleet carried out all these tasks with superb efficiency. They were crowned by Tōgō's annihilating victory over the Russian Baltic Fleet in the Tsushima Straits on 27–28 May 1905.

Yet the impact of the war on world naval thinking is less important for this chapter than the legacies it provided to the evolution of Japanese naval doctrine. Of these, the first was the concept of the decisive fleet engagement fought with big guns, a concept that led to the navy's mantra of "big ships, big guns." The second legacy of the Battle of Tsushima was the conclusion that a strategy of attrition was the best means of overcoming enemy numerical superiority prior to the decisive battle. Third, the Japanese navy believed that priority must be given to superior quality over quantity in warship design and construction. Last, there was a resurgent emphasis in Japanese tactical thinking on torpedo warfare, less because of any startling results achieved by torpedoes during the war than for the fact that torpedoes seemed to recall the tactics of ancient Japanese land warfare—the thrust of small groups of warriors against the heart of the enemy. But for the navy leadership, the chief legacy of the war was the primacy of the capital ship in destroying the enemy fleet. While this was a concept shared by other navies, for the Japanese it had a special and, it turned out, fatal import. This was because the eventual appearance of submarines and aircraft fundamentally crippled the dominance of the capital ship and the big gun. But beyond even this, the most harmful legacy of the

Russo-Japanese War for the Japanese navy was the conviction by Japan's naval leadership that battle at sea was not only the essence of naval war but that it was *the* determinant of the whole outcome of a war.

In the decade and a half that followed Japan's complete victory at Tsushima, several unexpected challenges confronted the nation and the navy. The first of these was that the spreading naval arms race among the Western maritime powers led to a decline in Japan's relative naval strength from third to fifth among the maritime nations. More immediate was the emerging profile of the U.S. Navy as Japan's most likely future enemy, a situation caused less by any conflict of interest between the two nations than by the fact that they were now the Pacific's foremost naval powers. This fact became the strategic focus for Admiral Satō Tetsutarō, Japan's leading naval thinker, who formulated the concept of the "hypothetical enemy," which was based on a nation's *ability* to threaten the national security of another rather than on its *intentions* to do so. But the problem in Satō's identification of the U.S. Navy as Japan's top enemy was that it ran counter to the strategic priority of the Japanese army, which identified Russia as Japan's chief hypothetical enemy.

Japan's 1907 Imperial Defense Policy tried to eliminate this dichotomy and to coordinate the strategy of the two armed services. Ultimately, the 1907 policy only highlighted these fundamentally opposed approaches to grand strategy and designated two hypothetical enemies: Russia for the army, the United States for the navy.

Admiral Satō, having shaped the navy's strategy toward a naval conflict with the United States, next attempted to provide the navy with a formula by which Japan, as the lesser economic and industrial power, could deal with the quantitative superiority of its projected foe. His "solution" was to call for Japanese maintenance of a set ratio of naval strength vis-à-vis the U.S. Navy. Using historical precedent and mathematical calculation, Satō held that Japan's maintenance of naval power of 70 percent of American naval strength would be sufficient to defend Japan against the advance of a hostile American fleet. Although its assumptions were flawed, the 70 percent ratio became a bedrock policy of Japanese naval force structure for the next thirty years.

These twin policies—the U.S. Navy as the hypothetical enemy and the insistence on a 70 percent ratio vis-à-vis American naval strength—were paralleled by the navy's strategic and tactical preparations for the eventual naval conflict with the United States. The acquisition of newer capital ships was of prime importance, of course. Its manifestation was Yamamoto Gombei's "Six-Six Fleet"—six battleships and six battle cruisers to be built every six years, which was replaced in 1907 with the "Eight-Eight Fleet" concept that became the heart of Japanese naval planning from 1907 to 1922, in large part because Satō Tetsutarō was able to persuade his colleagues on the General Staff that a 70 percent ratio would be impossible without it. Yet clearly the Eight-Eight Fleet idea was ill conceived. In 1907 it was beyond the country's economic and material resources. Moreover, it undercut established Japanese foreign policy in that it provided no detailed explanation of the supposed American naval threat it was designed to counter. Indeed, the General Staff had almost arbitrarily selected the U.S. Navy as a likely opponent to justify the scale of naval strength the Japanese navy brass desired.

Meanwhile, the progress of Japanese industry and technology was providing the nation with the potential to build a fleet capable of challenging the United States for mastery of the Pacific. In 1910, with the design and construction of four major battle cruisers of the *Kongō* class, the Japanese shipbuilding industry took a quantum leap forward. The namesake of the class had been built in Britain to specifications that, in certain respects, were more demanding than those capital ships being built for the Royal Navy.

Kongō was the last Japanese warship built abroad. Her sisters were constructed in Japanese yards, and with their completion, Japanese naval construction came of age. Still the goal of an Eight-Eight Fleet lay just beyond the navy's reach in large part because of the resistance of an economy-minded Diet. Then, in 1916, with the sudden challenge of a new and massive American naval construction program, the Diet authorized an interim naval expansion plan that would have given the navy an Eight-Six Fleet and in 1918, the announcement of still another huge American building program shocked the Diet into actually approving funds (1920) for the Eight-Eight Fleet idea.

The navy's long-held ambition was not to be realized because, in 1921, the navy reluctantly joined the Washington naval conference, which was called to halt the emerging naval arms race between Britain, the United States, and Japan. The result of the conference, the Washington Naval Treaty, called for a moratorium on further construction of capital ships and, much worse for the Japanese navy, acceptance of a capital ship ratio of less than 70 percent of the Anglo-American navies. Although the navy's "antitreaty" faction seethed with rage, the naval high command accepted this major limitation in return for unfettered construction of cruisers, destroyers, and submarines, as well as certain restrictions on Anglo-American bases in the west Pacific which appeared to lessen the Western threat to Japanese national security.

Thus began the interwar "treaty era" (1922–1936) in international naval affairs. For the Japanese navy, its force structure and naval construction during this period were shaped by two determinants: the doctrinal concepts in place since the Russo-Japanese War and the navy's perceptions of the evolving strategy of the U.S. Navy, more than ever seen by the Japanese as their most likely future opponent. In turn, these determinants rested on six basic Japanese assumptions about the nature of a conflict with the United States: first, that a Japan-U.S. naval war would be determined by a single great battle-fleet encounter in the mid-Pacific; second, that victory in that encounter would be determined by superiority in big guns; third, that it was imperative that the war be short, since Japan, with its smaller industrial base, would eventually be overwhelmed in a protracted war under an avalanche of American ships and weapons; fourth, that to have any hope of defeating the United States in a naval war, it was imperative that Japan enter the conflict with at least 70 percent of the strength of the U.S. Navy; fifth, that as Japan would undoubtedly open the war by seizing the Philippines and the United States would undoubtedly react by sending a battle fleet and expeditionary force across the Pacific to reoccupy the islands, the site of the great big-gun duel would probably be somewhere in the western Pacific; and sixth, that because the American battle fleet would be numerically superior at the outset of the war, it would be vital for the Japanese navy to develop weapons and tactics that would reduce the American battle line to at least parity before the decisive encounter.

With more than seventy years' hindsight, we can see how badly the Japanese misunderstood the lessons of World War I. Although Japanese navy men (along with their opposite numbers in various Western navies) were transfixed by the big gun duel at Jutland in 1916, that battle was in fact a strategic and tactical dead end. The real import of the war at sea was the German U-boat campaign against Britain that nearly brought that nation to its knees. Of this campaign, the Japanese navy, even though it had had observers at the British Admiralty who sent back data on the German submarine peril, took little cognizance, obsessed as its leadership continued to be with big ships and big guns.

At the end of the war, the navy made a reassessment of the international situation and subsequently undertook the first revision of the Imperial Defense Policy of 1907, a revision that took note of the changes in the international balance in naval power: German naval power temporarily obliterated, Russian naval power dramatically shrunken, Anglo-French naval power in Asia and the Pacific sharply reduced, and American naval power massively increased. This last change reinforced the view of the U.S. Navy as Japan's prime hypothetical enemy and in this regard simply rekindled old disagreements with the army.

A matter of far greater import was the strategic recasting of the navy's force projection compelled by the Washington Naval Treaty of 1922. Obliged to abandon further capital ship construction, the Japanese navy turned to the next best substitute: the heavy cruiser. Devoting intensive research to the design and construction of these ships, the navy came to possess the most powerful warships of this type afloat.

But the navy did not stop at the cruiser. As torpedo units, destroyers and submarines were seen as potentially contributing to a powerfully enhanced capability to whittle away American numerical superiority in capital ships. This was a conviction stemming from Japanese operations in the Sino- and Russo-Japanese wars that relentless night torpedo attacks were the best way to reduce enemy heavy units. In the 1920s, this conviction was buttressed by the design of large, heavily armed destroyers and the most powerful torpedoes (24-inch) of any navy. By the 1930s, the Japanese destroyer, with its nine to twelve torpedo tubes, was a specialized all-out attack vessel, unlike its jack-of-all-trades counterparts in Western navies, and was seen as the most effective weapon to break through the enemy screen and throw the enemy's capital ships into disorder before the onset of the big gun duel. Throughout the 1920s and 1930s, in order to achieve this objective, the navy refined its torpedo techniques through relentless and often hazardous night exercises.

Submarines were expected to perform a roughly similar function, launching attacks on American fleet units from Japanese bases in Micronesia. During the interwar period, the Japanese navy built some of the world's largest submarines to extend Japanese reach to U.S. warships off the American West Coast. As a strategy, it might have worked for a while, but it was a high-priced gamble because the submarine as a devastating antifleet weapon had not been consistently tested in World War I. What had been tested and proven was the effectiveness of submersibles as raiders against merchant shipping. But despite the clear evidence of this fact, the Japanese navy saw commerce warfare as irrelevant to the Japanese warrior tradition. By setting aside what Japanese submarines could do to American shipping, the navy compounded its error by thus failing to understand what American submarines could do to Japanese merchant shipping, a failure that was one of the major reasons for Japanese defeat in the Pacific War.

But the Japanese drive to construct the world's most powerful cruisers sparked a new and heated building race between Japan and the United States, whose interests and positions in this category were deadlocked. Whereas the United States opposed any reduction in the tonnage of individual cruisers, destroyers, and submarines but supported reductions in the aggregate tonnage of these lesser ship types, the Japanese navy was adamantly opposed to reductions in aggregate tonnage, particularly in heavy cruisers, and was determined that it not be compelled to accept the sort of lesser ratio that had been forced on it at Washington for capital ships. In 1930 the British and American navies had called for a conference in London to do just that, in order to complete the system of naval limitations begun at Washington. The London conference did indeed result in a treaty that obliged Japan to accept a reduction in naval strength not only across the board but also an actual reduction in strength

PHOTO 5.1. The impressive lines of the heavy cruiser *Myōkō* in August 1934 before her last reconstruction. (NARA)

relative to the Anglo-Americans in cruisers, a category in which the Japanese navy had labored, with effort and skill, to obtain a lead. By 1934 the white-hot anger of Japan's "antitreaty" faction made clear its determination to take Japan out of the entire naval limitations system when it expired in 1936 and, in the meantime, to prepare for the furious new naval race that would erupt in a treatyless world. Until then, the navy had to deal with the realities created by the London Treaty. Its response, undertaken with skill and ingenuity, was to build to its allotted tonnage in each of the restricted warship categories and to strengthen those weapons and systems not covered by the treaty.

The first material results of this effort were a series of construction programs that came to be known unofficially as the "Circle Plans." There were four of them drawn up between 1931 and the outbreak of war in Europe in 1939. The first Circle Plan, in 1931, realized the ambition of the General Staff to give Japan a qualitative lead in cruisers by placing within a cruiser hull the maximum firepower allowed under the London Treaty. The result was the B-class cruiser of 8,000–10,000 tons. More heavily armed and armored than any Japanese "light" cruiser heretofore, these ships possessed greater firepower than any British or American cruiser of similar tonnage. Similar changes in design were undertaken across a range of lesser warship categories.

The addition of heavier batteries and deck armor resulted in excessive top weight and thus dangerous instability. The consequences of these defects were not long in coming. In March 1934 the torpedo boat *Tomozuru* capsized in a gale, and in September 1935 units of the Fourth Fleet, on maneuvers in the North Pacific, were caught in a huge typhoon and a considerable number sustained heavy damage or capsized in the mountainous seas. The *Tomozuru* and Fourth Fleet "incidents" sent shock waves through the navy, which redesigned ships under construction and retrofitted units already in service to give them greater stability. In this, however, these mishaps may have worked to the navy's advantage, since the modifications in design and construction were undertaken when the navy had the time and resources to make them.

But accidents at sea in the 1930s were not the only stimulus to retrofitting and reconstruction in the navy. Continuing modernization projects had been going on since World War I not just in the Japanese navy but also in all navies. During the 1922–1936 treaty era, all major units of the Japanese navy were rebuilt as part of a considered program of modernization. Beginning in the late 1920s through the end of the next decade, all Japanese capital ships went into the yard for improvements in main batteries, bridge structures, fire-control systems, deck armor, and antitorpedo protection. During these years, advances in steam engineering and fire control marked important technological improvements that contributed to the Japanese navy's tactical flexibility and strategic reach.

But similar advances in the British and American navies more than matched these improvements. Beginning in the early 1930s, the U.S. Navy in particular embarked on a major naval construction program. The United States' naval expansion programs shocked Japan. Its naval leadership, dominated by the vehement "antitreaty faction," had worked tirelessly to have their nation abrogate the naval arms limitations agreements and free itself from the Anglo-American imposition of a 60 percent ratio in major warship tonnage. A maritime world without agreed-upon naval arms limits, however, proved more threatening to Japan than its naval leadership had foreseen. The United States, also freed from treaty limits, could now put its industrial might into naval rearmament that surged far beyond those limits. The successive American expansion plans eventually extinguished Japanese hopes of attaining a 70 percent ratio (let alone parity) with the U.S. Navy.

Given this ominous reality, the Japanese navy's only recourse, as its leaders saw it, was acquiring exceptional weapons, further improving tactical skills, and making up for a deficit in quantity by means of quality. In the navy's post-treaty era, this conviction led to critical decisions, of which its "superbattle-ship strategy" is only the most famous.

That strategy emerged during consultations between the Navy General Staff and Navy Ministry in 1934 concerning the third "circle" plan by which the navy, freed of the former treaty restrictions, could build a fleet capable of overpowering the larger American maritime enemy. It comprised several elements: the continued modernization of existing fleet units, the construction of sixty-four new warships of various types, and the achievement and maintenance of parity in naval air power. But its chief component was the construction of two superbattleships—the *Yamato* and *Musashi*—designed to be superior in armament, armor, and speed over all other capital ships for years to come and thus capable of crushing any American capital ships in the long-projected great gun duel at sea.

It has become popular to view these two naval monsters as technological dinosaurs at the time of their design, doomed by air power, the weapons system that caused their destruction in the Pacific War. It cannot be denied that, as a type, the battleship had outlived its dominance and had been overtaken by air power by the opening of the Pacific War. But in the early years of the 1930s, when the two monsters were conceived and when aircraft were still relatively frail machines incapable of carrying ordnance of significant explosive power, the concept behind their design made a good deal of sense. The failure of the navy's superbattleship strategy lay rather in certain inherent defects in the design of these ships, in the rapid and inevitable advances in other technologies after they were conceived, particularly in the destructive power of aerial torpedoes, and most of all because the superbattleship strategy diverted the navy's attention and resources away from the most critical strategic problem confronting the navy and the nation: Japan's dependence on its overseas supply and communications routes and the vulnerability of shipping on those routes to submarine and aerial attacks.

B. MISSION
In 1936, when Japan abrogated the Washington treaty and set a course for renewed naval expansion, the navy's mission was now to contest the U.S. Navy for control of the entire Pacific. But even then this mission was reactive and regionally focused: a response against an American fleet moving westward to relieve or retake Guam and the Philippines threatened or seized by Japan at the outset of hostilities.

A real change in the navy's mission did not occur until Admiral Yamamoto Isoroku assumed command of the Combined Fleet in 1940. Soon after taking command, Yamamoto began his initial planning for a preemptive attack on the American Pacific Fleet in Hawaii, which would inevitably stretch the projection of Japanese naval power across the vast distances of the Pacific.

II. ORGANIZATION

A. COMMAND STRUCTURE

1. Administration

High Command. Any explanation of the organization and administration of the Imperial Japanese Navy has to begin with the Japanese sovereign. Theoretically, the emperor—whose person and authority, according to the Japanese constitution, was "sacred and inviolable"—reigned supreme over all government agencies and institutions, including both armed services, but in fact, his practical involvement and responsibility in the operation of government were limited by tradition and law.

Functioning beneath the emperor were the armed services, the civilian government headed by the prime minister, and certain prestigious but generally passive advisory bodies. The prime minister's cabinet included the ministers of the two armed services who were selected by and nominally responsible to the prime minister. In reality, the army and navy ministers looked to the chiefs of staff of their respective services for direction because they were usually officers on active service. They could, and sometimes did, bring down a civilian cabinet by refusing to serve in it. In any event, real power in both armed services resided not in the ministers, who were generally responsible for administration, but in their general staffs.

The Navy General Staff was composed of three divisions—operations, intelligence, and readiness—and was charged with the preparation of war plans, collection of intelligence, setting the requirements for the navy's force structure, drafting warship designs, and direction of operations at sea. The chief of the Navy General Staff, acting in the name of the emperor, held "the right of supreme command," which meant that he was responsible only to the emperor and not to the civilian government. In theory, all plans devised by the navy general staff required imperial sanction; in practice, the emperor approved them automatically. This meant that, with the exception of the submission of the navy's annual budget to the Diet, the navy was accountable to no one else.

This system had several baleful consequences. The first was the fact that, because the will of the emperor was "sacred and inviolable," all who acted in his name could not be obstructed in the conduct of their duties by anyone outside the navy—a recipe for chaos in the conduct of Japan's foreign policy. The second consequence was equally pernicious. Because of the untrammeled authority of the armed services, there was no effective civilian voice to raise an objection or to point out the folly or danger of a particular military initiative. This proved to be a crippling defect in the conduct of Japanese military operations in the Pacific War, beginning with the decision to go to war.

The Navy Ministry was the largest organization in the Japanese naval high command and was largely concerned with the administration of the navy, its finances, appropriations, personnel, training, and logistics. Within the ministry were a number of powerful and independent bureaus and departments, of which the Naval Affairs Bureau was the most important. The navy's appropriations process began with the Navy General Staff, which sent to the ministry its force requirements and its warship designs and specifications. The ministry, in consultation with both the staff and the Finance Ministry, translated these into monetary figures that were formed into an appropriations request that was submitted to the Diet. Although the Diet could theoretically reject the request or any part of it, by the 1930s it seldom did so because of the dominating position of the armed services and their strong public support. But in a period of increasing naval expenditures, such as World War II, the General Staff's relentless demands for expansion drove the civilian government to near bankruptcy. These arrangements help to explain how, over time, the Japanese navy, like its sister service, came to develop two insidious tendencies: first, its extreme reluctance to accept any compromise that appeared to infringe on its authority; and second, the evolution of its various divisions and departments into a web of bureaucratic satrapies, each jealous of its prerogatives and each less than devoted to the principle of interservice harmony and coordination. In the last two years before the Pacific War, the emergence of powerful ad hoc intraservice committees standing outside the navy's formal bureaucratic structure proved insidious creating additional fissures within the navy. Added to these internal tensions was the far more serious enmity between the two armed services that, like scorpions in a bottle, sought to inflict painful bureaucratic injuries on each other. It is because of this bureaucratic enmity that Japan never developed an effective coordinating body such as the Joint Chiefs of Staff in the United States. It was tried, of course, in the form of an Imperial General Headquarters (IGHQ), reestablished in 1937.[2] But the IGHQ never really functioned as an effective coordinating body. Its structure was too weak, it had no overall executive, and its two parts came together as bureaucratic rivals only to negotiate matters of strategy, as between independent states. This situation was symptomatic of one of the basic reasons for the Japanese defeat in the Pacific War: the inability of the army and navy to work out an effectively integrated strategy.

Fleet Commands. The Combined Fleet was in effect the overall command of Japan's oceangoing navy. In terms of fighting, it *was* the Japanese navy, comprising all combat elements except the China Area Fleet, the special naval landing forces, the land-based air groups, and the base units.

The Combined Fleet had been formed at the outset of the first Sino-Japanese War and disbanded at its conclusion. It was periodically reconstituted on a temporary basis for a specific purpose until 1924 when it was made a permanent command composed of the 1st and 2nd Fleets but without a headquarters staff of its own because the commander of the 1st Fleet served concurrently as commander of the Combined Fleet. In 1933, with tensions rising with China, a permanent headquarters staff was established and the Combined Fleet commander was made at least theoretically responsible to the Navy General Staff.

Subordinate to the Combined Fleet were the area fleets responsible for specific geographic areas. Area fleets usually comprised one or more fleets and air fleets. While area fleets possessed major warship types, most capital ships and carriers served with mobile fleets, and the 6th Fleet was composed entirely of submarines.

In addition to these semipermanent combat fleets, during the Pacific War the Japanese navy also formed temporary "mobile fleets" for specific operations. Operating under the overall command of a mobile fleet were one or more "strike forces," in concept not unlike the "task forces" of the U.S. Navy during those same years but with far less logistical "tail" and thus far less staying power at sea.

Japanese naval aircraft were formed into air groups (kōkūtai), either land-based or carrier-based. Carrier air groups were composed of three squadrons each of fighters, dive-bombers, and torpedo-bombers; several carrier air groups made up a carrier division (kōkū sentai) usually composed of two or more carriers. The land-base equivalent of a carrier division was an air flotilla (also kōkū sentai). Several air flotillas made up an air fleet (kōkū kantai) composed of either land-based aircraft, or, oddly, sometimes both land and carrier-based air groups.

2. Personnel

Both in peace and war, the navy met its manpower needs by relying on a small cadre of career officers and men who were highly qualified and rigorously trained rather than creating a professional core backed by a much larger reserve of men with some training who could be mobilized to swell the ranks in wartime. Over the decades, pursuing this personnel policy of quality over quantity, the Japanese navy built a small, elite force of some of the world's best trained, best disciplined, best motivated, and most experienced naval professionals. With such a cadre of officers and men, the navy had won two major naval wars in the first thirty years of its history.

Because of the rigors of the Japanese navy's training and because of its technical proficiency, during the treaty era, the Japanese navy's personnel were probably equal to and, in some cases, superior to those of the Anglo-

American navies. The difficulties began in the mid-1930s, when the navy launched its posttreaty expansion plans and found itself short of personnel to man a rapidly growing surface fleet, an expanding air service, sizeable naval landing forces, and all the elements of its shore establishment. As the navy began to pile one expansion program on top of another, the situation worsened. Between 1936 and 1941 the navy estimated it was roughly eight hundred to a thousand officers short. The real trouble came during the Pacific War, of course, when difficulty in manning new naval construction was compounded by mounting combat injuries and fatalities. By the middle of the war, when many of the midlevel officers had been killed, the problem reached crisis proportions. The creation of a strong, reasonably trained reserve in the prewar decades, such as the U.S. Navy had developed, would have considerably lessened this critical situation.

While the average Japanese naval officer was highly intelligent, heroically brave, and loyal unto death, Western naval historians have cataloged serious weaknesses in the navy's officer corps: the absence of independent and rational judgment in the average naval officer, his lack of assertiveness, the narrow tactical concerns that monopolized his higher naval education at the Naval Staff College, and the overweening pride of service that perpetuated the navy's continuing and destructive rivalry with the army.[3]

Training was rigorous for all sea service and combat personnel but particularly for air crews. Between the world wars, surface units trained ferociously under conditions that the navy attempted to make even more difficult, stressful, and dangerous than the combat conditions it anticipated. The consequent casualties caused by this extreme training deterred the navy high command not at all. In the naval air service, the demanding selection process weeded out all but the most perfect physical specimens; of those who washed out, many were in the horrendously demanding training with the Kasumigaura Air Group (basic flight training) or the Yokosuka Air Group (advanced and combat air training). Two parallel air training programs were the Pilot Trainee System, which recruited and trained noncommissioned officers, and the Flight Reserve Enlisted Trainee System, which drew its candidates directly from civilian life. In either case, such flight training involved relentless and rigorous drill through which only a small, elite group of pilots were able to pass.

By the eve of the Pacific War, therefore, the Japanese navy possessed some of the best fighter pilots in the world—many of them gained combat experience in the skies over China—but their numbers were shockingly small, and there was no large reserve of good but less brilliantly skilled pilots behind them. It was a personnel policy that was to work to the navy's great disadvantage in the latter half of the Pacific War.

The essential cause of the navy's crippling personnel policies was simply a lack of foresight. A policy that relied on entering combat with a small elite of highly trained professionals would have undoubtedly suited the kind of short conflict centered on the single battle that the navy planned to fight. It was a fatal defect in waging the extended war of attrition that the navy was actually obliged to fight.[4]

3. Intelligence

The navy's intelligence capabilities were central to Japanese victories in the spring of 1942, and its limitations were critical in the navy's greatest defeats thereafter. Both were the result of certain anomalies in the structure and status of the navy's intelligence organization. The first of these was the bifurcation of function at the highest level, the Navy General Staff, whose intelligence responsibilities were divided between its intelligence division, which performed most of the standard intelligence functions, and the communications division, charged with cryptanalysis and communications security. More important was the limited role and influence of the intelligence division in the formation of Japanese naval policy and strategy. The principal function of the division was to provide relevant and timely information to the operations division. Combining such information with communications intelligence and with tactical intelligence from various fleet units, the operations division could then prepare estimates of enemy capabilities and intentions. But, surprisingly, the intelligence division did not evaluate the information it collected and passed on. Moreover, within the operations division, information supplied by the intelligence division was often ignored as suspect or irrelevant. Worse, operations, fixated on its own agenda, sometimes initiated plans without even consulting intelligence. Because of this stunted development, intelligence, particularly after 1937, became an understaffed adjunct to operations and never developed into a coordinated body capable of collecting, possessing, and disseminating useful intelligence throughout all levels of the navy.

The limited influence of intelligence in the Japanese navy was a crippling drag on its specialized personnel and training. There were too few capable intelligence officers and little effort was made to improve their skills. Most naval officers regarded an intelligence billet as a career dead end and the navy made little effort to make intelligence work professionally rewarding. This situation affected all aspects of intelligence, including communications intelligence and photoreconnaissance, and was a failure for which the General Staff and Combined Fleet were both responsible. It was a defect that originated in the navy's fixation on combat to the neglect of critical but less heroic aspects of naval warfare.

Like most intelligence organizations, the intelligence division gathered its information from a variety of sources: translation of foreign books and journals, reports of naval attachés and clandestine operatives abroad, navy-run espionage centers in foreign countries, and reports from Japanese consulates concerning foreign ship movements. But the greatest source was interception of foreign radio traffic, the responsibility of the "special division" after 1940. Within that organization was a code-breaking research branch and a communications unit located southwest of Tokyo, which became the navy's chief radio intercept center—able, in the 1930s, to track the maneuvers of American fleet units in the Pacific. From the 1920s, the navy also began to experiment with fleet tankers as clandestine floating intercept stations, particularly off Hawaii. Still, with the exception of one or two mode breakthroughs, the Japanese navy was unable to make significant headway in reading American radio traffic before and during the Pacific War. Even the mid-level American code systems proved beyond the skills of Japanese cryptographers.

Unfortunately for Japan, the United States was superlatively successful in breaking certain Japanese systems before the war, particularly the Japanese diplomatic codes. The most important Japanese naval codes—the "Ko" and "Ro" systems—were more resistant to solution. The "Ko" or "flag officers code," used for its highest level communications, was never completely solved by the U.S. Navy before the war and was abandoned by the Japanese navy in favor of the "Ro" code (called JN-25 by the U.S. Navy), which became the Japanese navy's most widely used cryptographic system.[5]

One last comment may serve as a summary judgment on Japanese naval intelligence. It is undeniably true that, as of December 1941, the navy's tactical intelligence on the Allied military situation throughout the west Pacific and Southeast Asia was precise and comprehensive. What was critical and absent was any information or analysis of the broadest issues: the recuperative powers of the United States once it had absorbed the first Japanese blows, and the vast American industrial and military capacities that in the months to come would enable the United States to launch counterblows with a speed and force which the Japanese did not anticipate. For the Japanese navy and nation, this was the most critical intelligence failure of all.

B. DOCTRINE

1. Surface Warfare

There were, of course, certain tactical principles in the Japanese navy that predated the concept of "big ships, big guns" (*taikan kyohōshugi*). One dogma can be traced all the way back to Japan's traditional warrior culture—the concept of fearless, close-in attacks against the enemy—that can be summed up in one of the navy's tactical mantras: "press closely, strike home" (*nikuhaku hitchū*), a concept that first inspired the torpedo boats and destroyers of the modern navy in the Sino-Japanese war. This remained a cardinal tactical principle in the years before the Pacific War when the navy considered that the role of cruisers and even battleships was to blast a breach in the enemy heavy formations for the destroyers to exploit, rather than viewing the lighter craft as opening the way for capital ships, as in American tactical doctrine.

Nevertheless, the most influential voice in navy doctrine and force structure was that of the so-called gun club (*teppō-ya*), which insisted that the "big ships, big guns" policy was the quickest and surest means to win the great encounter at sea. The importance of the biggest guns was predicated on two assumptions: first, that such guns could fire the heaviest shells and fire them over the greatest distances, far outranging the enemy's ability to retaliate; and second, that improvements in technology would make it possible to concentrate that shellfire. By 1917 the concept had hardened into dogma, and over the next two decades, through simultaneous improvements in gunnery, "outranging" in the form of long-range concentrated shellfire became a basic doctrine of the Japanese navy.

The reader must not assume, however, that in the minds of Japanese tacticians the concept of outranging was limited to the heaviest ships. In the 1930s, to give medium and light surface units greater reach, the Japanese navy searched for means to give torpedoes greater range. After some years of intensive research, Japanese technicians devised a formidable new weapon: the famous Type 93 oxygen torpedo, which was wakeless and of greater size, speed, and payload than any available in any Western navies. Exploiting the potential of the new weapon, Japanese naval tacticians worked out a new torpedo tactic—long-distance concealed firing—and developed a new class of light cruiser to carry it out.

2. Aviation

Although the culture of the Japanese navy shaped its offensive mindset, until the mid-1930s the limited performance of aircraft around the globe—in speed, range, ceiling, and payload—meant that aviation was not seen as an offensive asset. In the early 1930s, Japanese naval orthodoxy held that "command of the air" was meaningful only in relation to support for the surface fleet as it prepared for the great gun duel at sea, in other words, for reconnaissance and spotting for naval gunnery.

Not surprisingly, during these years, Japanese naval aviation was subject to some of the same tensions and controversies that troubled naval air services in the West. Chief among these was the difference of opinion about the relative performances of fighters and bombers. Fighter aircraft had dominated the skies over western Europe in World War I, but by the early 1930s bombers were seen as superior in performance for offensive operations, and fighter aircraft were relegated to fleet air defense.

Out of numerous practices and exercises in the 1930s, the navy reached four conclusions about carrier warfare: first, that the winning side would be the one that got in the initial blow; second, that such a blow must "outrange" the enemy; third, that such a blow must be delivered by carrier attack aircraft—dive and torpedo-bombers; and fourth, that it was less important to try to sink an enemy carrier than it was to destroy its flight deck because a carrier without aircraft was as harmless as a tennis court.

By the end of the decade, given the navy's traditional preference for offensive operations, some observers foresaw the eventual extinction of the fighter from the navy's inventory. But this situation was reversed in 1940 with the appearance of the Mitsubishi Type 0 A6M (Zero) carrier fighter. In the wild combat in the skies over China, the navy's pilots brilliantly displayed the amazing capabilities of this aircraft as well as their own superlative flying skills and exquisitely honed teamwork. Yet, if the Zero was emblematic of the cutting edge of Japanese naval aviation on the eve of the Pacific War, it was also symptomatic of the weaknesses of that service. An inadequate power plant and lack of protection for pilot and fuel tanks were ultimately to prove fatal in combat with American fighter aircraft, and these defects made no sense in relation to the precious handful of pilots the navy possessed.

3. Antisubmarine

Protection of merchant shipping and overseas trade routes should have been a natural and logical priority for Japan. Despite building a significant number of oceangoing submarines that could blockade ports on the American West Coast, Japanese naval strategists never seem to have considered the possibility that Western navies could do the same to Japan. Little thought was given to constructing quantities of cheap antisubmarine warfare (ASW) vessels or to upgrading existing ASW tactics, techniques, or weapons.

4. Submarine

The story of the Japanese submarine force is the story of missed opportunities. Although Japan acquired a formidable collection of submarines whose numbers included some of the largest of their type as well as midget submarines that could be carried aboard surface ships or larger submarines, Japanese submersibles did little to affect the course of World War II.

The problem began with the fact that the navy gave its submarine force a flawed mission: the long-distance interception of American fleet movements in the Pacific. Although Japanese submarines did score some dramatic sinking of American warships (the carrier *Yorktown* at Midway and the heavy cruiser *Indianapolis* at the end of the war, for example), too often American surface warships were too fast and too evasive for the Japanese navy's standard pursuit, contact-keeping, and attack formulas.

These difficulties related to an essential problem in submarine tactics for all navies prior to and during the war: the opposing requirements of stealth and surprise through subsurface concealment on the one hand and, on the other, aggressive action that obliged a submarine to come at least to periscope depth where its periscope and torpedo wakes might give away its position. Forced to choose between these two, Japanese submarine commanders often chose stealth over boldness, which meant that they usually failed in their missions as enemy fleet units raced by unscathed.

The most glittering opportunity presented to the submarine force came early in the Pacific War: the chance for a major blow to the American conduct of the war by attacks on shipping to and from the American West Coast. Had the Japanese navy concentrated its submarines in such operations in the spring of 1942 at the same time that the German navy was massacring shipping along the East Coast, such a coordinated assault might have set back American strategy in both the Pacific and Atlantic by many months. But, caught up in its early victories in Southeast Asia and in its fixation with the great surface battle in the mid-Pacific, the navy let that opportunity slip by.

5. Amphibious Operations

Whereas aviation, submarine, and antisubmarine warfare all had significant successes in World War I, the Allied landings at Gallipoli, the war's most ambitious amphibious operation, had been a disastrous failure. After the war, most military and naval establishments—the U.S. Marine Corps excepted—viewed Gallipoli as a confirmation of the extreme difficulty, if not impossibility, of conducting a landing from the sea in the face of an armed, entrenched, and determined enemy.

Yet early in the interwar period, the Washington Treaty had given both the United States and Japan an incentive to maintain an amphibious capability in the Pacific. As the treaty prohibited both the construction of new bases in the western Pacific and the strengthening of existing bases there, any conflict between the two powers would require the occupation of enemy bases or the recapture of bases lost to the enemy. It was not that the Japanese knew nothing about amphibious operations. Nearly all of Japan's modern wars had involved army landings on an enemy coast and had required navy transport and fire support. Indeed, Japan was one of the first nations to understand the importance of modern amphibious capabilities without which it could not have established a military presence on the Asian continent. But the army's mission in these conflicts was principally devoted to the great land battles inland. The navy maintained a modest ability to project power ashore.

Beginning in China, the navy assigned landing operations to ad hoc landing parties (*rikusentai*). These units were usually composed of personnel from Japanese gunboats plying Chinese rivers. The sailors selected were given a modicum of infantry and small arms training and were put ashore when the need arose. Later, in the 1930s, standing landing parties were stationed permanently ashore in barracks and armed with heavy weapons, including 3-inch howitzers.

The army gave hardly any thought to amphibious doctrine until after World War I. In the late 1920s, it collaborated with the navy in a series of joint exercises in the western Pacific where some of the problems of combined amphibious operations were worked out. By 1932 the two services had developed a series of guidelines for such operations, and that same year the navy created a permanent, specialized naval landing force for small-scale amphibious operations. By the outbreak of the Pacific War, the two services had developed a set of three simple doctrinal principles for their amphibious operations: land on essentially undefended shores; land at night, or at the latest, at dawn; and land at several places simultaneously. These were the tactics used by the Japanese in their flood tide of advance through Southeast Asia in early 1942. Their landings, often at night, were carried out with speed, surprise, and economy of force by units that landed separately but concentrated at the point of attack. Their effectiveness was clearly measured by the consequent confusion and demoralization sown among the Dutch, British, and American defenders of those tropical shores.

But as effective as such operations were, it is clear that they were essentially unopposed landings, not amphibious assaults—heavily armed frontal attacks out of the sea in daylight in the teeth of determined resistance by an alerted, entrenched, and well-fortified enemy. The Japanese never mastered that mission before the war because it must have seemed to them that it would not be necessary. Yet, in the long run, they paid dearly for their ignorance of this more violent face of amphibious warfare. Certainly, that ignorance is one of the principal reasons why, during the entire war, the Japanese were never able to retake an island base once lost to the American enemy.

6. Trade Protection

Given the vulnerability of the Japanese home islands to naval blockade and the potential danger to its overseas commerce from naval attack, the Japanese navy's indifference to these perils is incredible. On a theoretical level, of course, the navy acknowledged the problem of protecting the nation's maritime trade, but it undertook few concrete measures that would make such protection effective. There were multiple reasons for this: restricted budgets, the priority given to major surface combat, and preparations for the anticipated great gun duel at sea.

The navy entered the Pacific War with a feeble understanding of the basics of trade protection. Essentially, the navy had regarded it as an extension of the problems of coastal defense, a view that might have had some marginal relevance when the nation's interests were confined to the shorelines of the home islands but that made absolutely no sense when those interests had thrust onto the Asian mainland or, later, into Southeast Asia. Thus, on the eve of Japan's conflict with the United States, the Navy General Staff, in its Olympian complacency concerning the safety of Japanese shipping in the event of war, had given little thought to the general problem of trade protection, or to its subsidiary elements—the requirements of ASW, the tasks of convoy and convoy escort, and the need for relevant and accurate intelligence concerning American submarine doctrine and capabilities. It had little in the way of organization, weapons, tactics, training, personnel, or doctrine that could effectively defend the nation's maritime transport. In consequence, disaster awaited.

7. Communications

The advent of ship-borne radio or, more exactly, radio telegraph provided Japanese commanders at sea a rapid and effective means of communicating with their forces, thus exercising more effective tactical control over them. Radio was a great asset to Admiral Tōgō in his victory over the Russian Baltic Fleet in 1905.

The great weakness of radio, of course, was the vulnerability of communications to interception. The attempt to protect radio communications through encoding and encryption inevitably provoked counterefforts by other naval establishments for the decoding and decryption of such messages. In this context, the Japanese navy, lacking the appreciation of the importance of this "intelligence revolution" wrought by radio communications and failing to mobilize knowledgeable civilian talent for such encryption and decryption, increasingly fell behind the western maritime powers.

In the late 1920s, the navy began the first serious attempts to develop radio communications for its aircraft. In 1929 the first Japanese-designed radio equipment was produced and a communications unit was added to each air group. But the navy's airborne communications were spotty, as they were for the air services of all nations between the world wars. Crystal-controlled equipment maintained selected frequencies accurately but operated on only a few such frequencies. Analog equipment covered relatively broad frequencies but drifted frequently because of vibration and the idiosyncrasies of electronics.

Photo 5.2. A prewar shot of Japanese "Sea Scouts" practicing semaphore on the deck of *Mikasa*. (U.S. Naval Institute Photo Archives)

III. MATERIEL

A. SHIPS

At the opening of the Pacific War the Japanese navy possessed warships that were among the world's best in nearly every category. Of course, to assess what is the "best" warship is a problematical task given that ship design, like aircraft design, requires a series of trade-offs among performance capabilities. Any particular design will perform better in certain combat tasks and environments than in others. That said, it is clear that Japan's monster battleships *Yamato* and *Musashi* were the most heavily armored and the most powerful gun platforms ever launched. While they had serious defects, the ultimate futility of their creation lay not in their design but in the foolish uses for which they were employed in their relatively short lifetimes. Both succumbed to aerial assault and were never employed in a Japanese battle line confronting American capital ships—the scenario for which they were originally conceived.

Whereas these two superbattleships represented the apogee of capital ship construction, the navy's other battleships and battle cruisers contributed substantially to the Japanese navy's awesome reputation as a fighting force. Its four *Kongō*-class battleships were among the world's most formidable (eight 14-inch guns and twenty-seven- to thirty-knot speed) when they were launched just before and during World War I, and all underwent extensive modernization

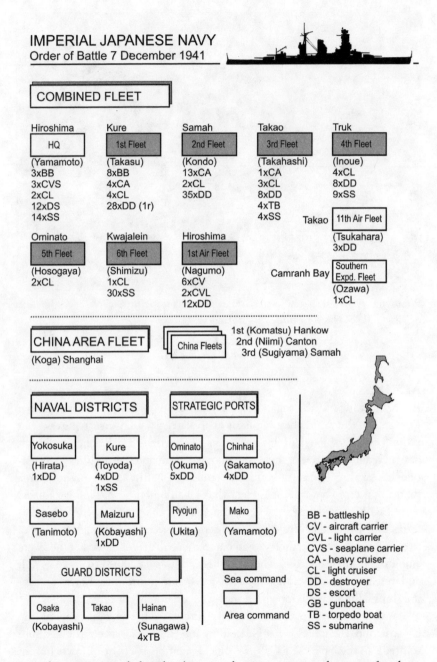

IMPERIAL JAPANESE NAVY
Order of Battle 7 December 1941

COMBINED FLEET

Hiroshima
HQ
(Yamamoto)
3xBB
3xCVS
2xCL
12xDS
14xSS

Kure
1st Fleet
(Takasu)
8xBB
4xCA
4xCL
28xDD (1r)

Samah
2nd Fleet
(Kondo)
13xCA
2xCL
35xDD

Takao
3rd Fleet
(Takahashi)
1xCA
3xCL
8xDD
4xTB
4xSS

Truk
4th Fleet
(Inoue)
4xCL
8xDD
9xSS

Takao — 11th Air Fleet
(Tsukahara)
3xDD

Ominato
5th Fleet
(Hosogaya)
2xCL

Kwajalein
6th Fleet
(Shimizu)
1xCL
30xSS

Hiroshima
1st Air Fleet
(Nagumo)
6xCV
2xCVL
12xDD

Camranh Bay — Southern Expd. Fleet
(Ozawa)
1xCL

CHINA AREA FLEET
(Koga) Shanghai

China Fleets
1st (Komatsu) Hankow
2nd (Niimi) Canton
3rd (Sugiyama) Samah

NAVAL DISTRICTS

Yokosuka
(Hirata)
1xDD

Kure
(Toyoda)
4xDD
1xSS

Sasebo
(Tanimoto)

Maizuru
(Kobayashi)
1xDD

STRATEGIC PORTS

Ominato
(Okuma)
5xDD

Chinhai
(Sakamoto)
4xDD

Ryojun
(Ukita)

Mako
(Yamamoto)

GUARD DISTRICTS

Osaka
(Kobayashi)

Takao

Hainan
(Sunagawa)
4xTB

Sea command

Area command

BB - battleship
CV - aircraft carrier
CVL - light carrier
CVS - seaplane carrier
CA - heavy cruiser
CL - light cruiser
DD - destroyer
DS - escort
GB - gunboat
TB - torpedo boat
SS - submarine

over the next several decades (increased armor, greater elevation for their main batteries, and added fire control platforms).

The two *Nagato*-class ships, which had been laid down during World War I, were also modernized in the 1930s. The two *Ise*-class and the two *Fusō-*

Photo 5.3. The light cruiser *Tenryu* dressed for a prewar occasion. (The Boris Lemachko Collection)

class battleships (twelve 14-inch guns) were famed for their towering super-structures. The *Fusōs* slugged it out with American forces in the battles in Leyte Gulf in October 1944, with the loss of *Fusō* and *Yamashiro*.

Given the moratorium on new capital ship construction dictated by the Washington Treaty, the Japanese can be credited with maintaining a capable capital ship fleet during the interwar period. That these ships were eventually overwhelmed by their American enemy had less to do with their design and construction than with the overpowering quantitative superiority of American industry and the fact that they lacked certain technological advantages, such as the latest and most effective surface radar of the kind installed on their American counterparts.

Japan's participation in the Washington Treaty obliged the navy to consider what other warship types might be designed as substitutes for the battleship and battle cruiser. The navy's solution was the development of the "A" class, or heavy cruiser, which was permitted under the terms of the treaty to be of up to 10,000 tons displacement and armed with main batteries of not more than eight inches.

Immediately following World War I, the Japanese navy had already experimented with the light cruiser, a warship type capable of acting either as a fleet scout or as a destroyer flotilla leader. Some seventeen ships of this type, designed for this dual purpose, were constructed in the *Tatsuta*, *Kuma*, *Nagara*, *Sendai*, and *Yubari* classes in the 1920s. But the navy's search for an all-purpose substitute for the capital ship continued and eventually led to a series of heavy cruiser classes constructed during the interwar "treaty era." The Japanese successes in designing a cruiser that would combine high speed and heavy armament within a hull of modest proportions was due to the imagination and exacting calculations of the navy's technical department, specifically to the chief of its basic design section, Hiraga Yuzuru. Hiraga's original design, if unexceptional in its armament, was ingenious in its hull structure and armor arrangements. These incorporated the armored elements (composed of high tensile and hardened chromium steel) in the hull's internal structure rather than bolting them onto existing plates and beams. This not only reduced the weight of the hull but also added to its strength.

The first "A"-class cruisers were *Furutaka* and *Kako*, whose greatest offensive punch was provided by their twelve 24-inch torpedo tubes. Improved Class "A" cruiser classes were added one after the other. The two 7,000-ton cruisers of the *Aoba* class were given six 8-inch guns in three turrets. But even before the *Aoba* and her sister *Kinugasa* were laid down, the navy set out to design a cruiser that would not only reach treaty specification limits but would also be superior to every other cruiser afloat. The result was the *Myōkō* class of four heavy cruisers, ships of great speed (thirty-five knots), heavy armor, ten 8-inch guns, and twelve fixed 24-inch torpedo tubes. In the design of the *Myōkō* class, however, the General Staff's insistence on heavy armor and on mounting the torpedo tubes within the hull not only made the ships heavier than treaty limits allowed but also made them so dangerously top-heavy and unseaworthy that these defects had to be corrected by substantial reconstruction in the 1930s.

By the end of the 1920s, heavy cruisers had come to occupy a central place in the navy's operational planning. A first division of heavy cruisers—the four ships of the *Myōkō* class—was formed early in the 1930s. Then, in 1935, the General Staff established a second and even more powerful cruiser division, one composed of the four ships of the *Takao* class. These were 10,000-ton vessels, armed with main batteries of ten 8-inch guns, capable of more than thirty-three knots, and a range of eight thousand miles at fourteen knots.

The ships of this class were to serve as an advance guard for the fleet, as an attack force to break into the elements supporting the enemy's battle line, or individually, in a reconnaissance role. Most importantly, they were expected to function as flagships for the fleet during both day and night combat involving torpedoes and long-range gunnery. The increasingly complex installations required to direct these various operations were grouped together in an enormous bridge complex, a centralization of command applications achieved at the cost of great topside weight and a higher profile for enemy gunnery.

Aviation was one of the few components of sea power in which the Japanese navy did not have to scramble to catch up with the Anglo-American maritime powers because Japan's first efforts in this element were roughly contemporaneous with Western initiatives in the decade after World War I. To be sure, it posed a set of difficult tasks and uncertain assumptions for both naval architects and tacticians in all the major navies. In addition to the usual problems of propulsion, hull structure, seakeeping, and crew accommodations, aircraft carrier designers in both the U.S. and Japanese navies had to deal with a host of difficulties posed by flight operations. As aircraft developed greater engine power and speed, they needed increasing flight deck length for take-off. Moreover, the still uncertain function of carriers and their place relative to the battle line left open the question as to whether they needed deck guns for self-defense.

These problems were manifest in the construction of the Hōshō, Japan's first and essentially experimental aircraft carrier. From the perspective of later years, the Hōshō, at less than 8,000 tons and with a flight deck of only 552 feet, was a very small carrier. The configuration of her hanger deck was such that it permitted the embarkation of only twenty or so aircraft. As larger and faster attack aircraft were developed, her modest size meant that she could embark only fighters and that her function had to be limited to training or, at best, to contribute to the fleet's air cover. But as the navy's laboratory for carrier design, construction, and flight operations, she justified the cost of her construction.

With the acquisition of the carriers Kaga and Akagi, originally laid down as capital ships and then converted to aircraft carriers, Japan acquired its first fleet carriers. Still experimenting with carrier design, the navy added certain features, such as deck guns and triple flight decks, that eventually proved impractical and were eliminated or altered in subsequent reconstruction of both ships in the 1930s. During their lifetimes, however, the Kaga and Akagi demonstrated the great potential of carrier aviation in the war with China, in the Hawaii operation, and in the grand sweep in the northern Indian Ocean in the spring of 1942.

Because construction of these ships had already accounted for 54,000 tons of the 81,000 aggregate tonnage allowed Japan for carrier construction under the terms of the Washington Treaty, the navy decided to use the remaining permitted tonnage in the building of a carrier of under 10,000 tons displacement. The result was *Ryūjō*, Japan's smallest carrier since *Hōshō*, a vessel with almost no armor protection and only one hanger. Later improvements, including the addition of a second hanger, made the ship less stable. That in turn put her twice into dry dock in the mid-1930s to improve her stability, but given her small air group, she was never an efficient fleet unit.

The lessons learned in the construction and reconstruction of the *Ryūjō* were applied to the two carriers of the 16,000-ton *Sōryū* class. They were designed with cruiser hull configurations and thus were fast ships, capable of thirty-five knots. *Sōryū* was built with a small island on her starboard side; her sister, *Hiryū* had it located on the port side. *Sōryū* could embark sixty-eight aircraft of various types, and *Hiryū*, seventy-three.

With the expiration the Washington Treaty in December 1936, Japan was now free to build as many ships of all classes as it could afford, including carriers of unprecedented size and performance. During the five years before the Pacific War, the navy added *Shōkaku* and *Zuikaku*, the finest carriers that Japan ever built. They were conceived as forming a carrier group able to operate with *Yamato* and *Musashi*, a mission that called for large, fast carriers capable of mounting a powerful aerial strike force and able to defend themselves with their own air cover. Their specifications called for the same aircraft complement (ninety-six) as the remodeled *Kaga* and *Akagi*, a top speed of thirty-five knots, and a range of ten thousand miles at eighteen knots. Because of their main deck armor, they were ten thousand tons heavier than the *Sōryū* class but still had excellent stability. Their engines delivered ten thousand more horsepower than even the superbattleships. Until the wartime entry of the American *Essex*-class carriers, *Shōkaku* and her sister outclassed every other carrier. Indeed, so valuable did the Japanese consider them that the decision to mount the attack on Pearl Harbor was based in part on their availability for that operation.

Ships that entered service after the war started include *Taiho* and *Shinano*. The 29,300-ton *Taiho*, designed as the Japanese answer to the British *Illustrious* and American *Essex* classes, was Japan's first carrier with an armored flight deck. With a thirty-three-knot speed and a capacity for sixty aircraft, she could have been an effective asset but was torpedoed by an American submarine in June 1944, only three months after she was commissioned. *Shinano*, the largest carrier Japan ever built, was designed and laid down as the third of the *Yamato* class of superbattleships but was converted during the war to a carrier. At 62,000 tons, she was a potentially awesome platform for air operations, but with her great fuel and ordnance stowage capacity, she was to have been fitted out as a replenishment and support ship for carrier task forces. But she did not live long enough to fulfill this function; an American submarine torpedoed her in November 1944, ten days after completing trials.

There were also a number of lesser carriers drawn from the navy's "shadow fleet" of auxiliary and merchant vessels designed to be quickly converted into aircraft carriers as needed. As a group, these conversions were not a success because their minimum protection, modest aircraft capacity, slow speed, and inadequate power from their diesel engines made them ineffective as fleet carriers.

By a number of standards, the Japanese had been innovators in carrier design; in 1941 the two Shōkaku-class ships—the culmination of prewar Japanese carrier design—were superior to any carrier in the world then in commission. They had certain defects, certainly, some of which they shared with American counterparts, some of which were unique to their own service. Like American carriers, they sacrificed armored decks in order to embark more aircraft and thus more offensive power. Their flight decks consisted merely of wooden planking lengthwise over thin steel decks. Again like American carriers, their flight decks were for the most part simply superimposed upon the hull rather than being constructed as strength decks supporting the hull as in contemporary carriers in the Royal Navy.

But there were differences, too, between Japanese and American carrier design and construction. The first had to do with maximum aircraft capacity. As in the Royal Navy, Japanese carrier aircraft capacity was determined by the size of the hangar rather than the flight deck because Japanese carriers stored their aircraft in hangars rather than on the flight deck, as did the Americans. Second, the hangars in Japanese carriers were enclosed by storerooms so that aircraft and ready crews were shielded from wind and weather, but when enemy bombs penetrated the hangars, the resultant blast pressures could be disastrous to the integrity of the ships' structures. Moreover, the enclosed spaces prevented the disposition of fuel and ordnance over the side in case of fire and complicated the easy insertion of fire hoses from screening ships in order to fight fires. The final difference lay in flight operations. American carriers used crash barriers to separate parked and landing aircraft whereas the Japanese needed to clear flight decks during flight operations. Thus, during continuous flight operations, elevator cycles governed launch and recovery speeds.

In the long run, however, it was not carrier design that determined the outcome of the naval air war in the Pacific but simply the overwhelming quantitative superiority of the United States to turn out carriers, aircraft, and air crews. Comparative data demonstrate this awesome disparity. From 1942 to the end of the war in the summer of 1945, the Japanese navy constructed and acquired by conversion 15 aircraft carriers. During that same period, the U.S. Navy added 141 carriers.

As earlier noted, the Japanese navy placed a greater premium on night combat, particularly night torpedo operations, than any other navy in the interwar period. By World War I, the principal warship for such operations was the destroyer, a type on which the navy relied for the delivery of relentless torpedo attacks even at the cost of heavy losses.

Despite having several destroyer classes of excellent design, the onset of World War I found the navy with too few of these ships for patrol and escort duty. Beginning in 1914, therefore, the navy undertook an emergency program of destroyer construction, the best of which was the fifteen-ship *Minekaze* class, a new type of destroyer constructed between 1917 and 1922. They were fast vessels (thirty-nine knots) capable of weathering the frequent heavy seas of the north Pacific because of their long hulls and the retention of the turtle deck construction of Japan's older destroyers, carrying their torpedo tubes directly behind the forecastle and having their unshielded guns as high as possible to maximize their use in heavy weather. The *Minekaze* class and the twenty-one units of the *Kamikaze* and *Mutsuki* classes formed the backbone of Japanese destroyer flotillas during the 1920s until replaced by the famous *Fubuki* class at mid-decade.

The *Fubuki* class owed its creation to the Japanese search for a radically enhanced surface capability—largely that of torpedo units—to spearhead the navy's strategy for the distant attrition of any westward-moving American fleet at the outset of the war. The twenty-four ships of this class built between 1922 and 1931 with their 1,600-ton displacement and their nearly 400-foot length were the most advanced and powerful destroyers of their day and the archetype of most Japanese destroyers that saw action during the Pacific War. Because of their enclosed bridge, fire-control spaces, and gun mounts, their fighting qualities were outstanding even in heavy seas and bad weather. Their six 5-inch guns, mounted in pairs in three turrets, were not only weatherproof but also splinterproof. Ammunition for this ordnance was brought up on hoists directly from the magazine under each turret, thus providing a high rate of fire. Indeed, these arrangements for their main batteries (years before such arrangements were adopted for destroyers in other navies) gave the *Fubuki* class fire power equal to that of many light cruisers.

But it was the greatly increased torpedo armament that made the *Fubuki* class the most powerful destroyers afloat. Each ship carried eighteen 24-inch torpedoes, two each for the nine torpedo tubes housed in three triple mountings, an arrangement that provided a larger torpedo salvo than available on destroyers of any other navy.

By the 1930s, therefore, the Japanese destroyer, with its nine to twelve torpedo tubes, was an all-out attack vessel. Its dominant role was its original torpedo boat function, a purpose considerably more specialized than the typical destroyer in the U.S. and British navies, which had become a jack-of-all-trades warship. Throughout the interwar period, the Japanese navy took advantage of its outstanding destroyer classes and refined its night torpedo tactics through continued, relentless, and often hazardous exercises and, by the outbreak of the Pacific War, had forged a formidable offensive asset. But the navy would come to regret that, in burnishing so bright a specialized weapon, it had neglected the less glamorous duties of a destroyer: scouting, convoy escort, patrol duty, and antisubmarine warfare.

B. AVIATION

Immediately after World War I, such was the promise of aircraft to project naval power beyond the range of ship-borne weapons that the world's three major navies, which now included Japan, felt impelled to create a naval air arm in one form or another. By the 1920s each had constructed at least one prototype aircraft carrier as well as designed carrier-based, water-based, and land-based aircraft.

Initially the modest abilities of these first naval aircraft hardly seemed a serious threat to naval surface units. Until the 1930s, they were so limited in their capabilities in terms of speed, range, ceiling, and payload that, in the Japanese and Anglo-American navies, "command of the air" was viewed by the battleship-oriented brass only in relation to the decisive surface engagement.

While none of the trials of naval aviation in World War I had proved decisive and much of aviation's potential remained speculation, the Japanese navy was not slow to grasp the significance of new aviation technology and, even before the end of the war, had begun to develop some of its own aircraft. Yet the gap in aviation technology between the West and Japan had widened considerably since Western belligerents had gained practical understanding of the design requirements for combat and valuable experience in the mass production of aircraft. The postwar decade in Japanese aviation technology was therefore marked by two intensive and interrelated initiatives: the infusion of Western technological assistance and vigorous domestic efforts to establish a Japanese aircraft industry. The first was realized by the invitation to Japan of a British civil aviation delegation—the Sempill Mission—that provided the navy with the latest Western aviation technology as well as the latest air combat tactics and techniques. Japanese efforts to establish its own fledgling air industry were facilitated by a number of institutional innovations: the granting to the Navy Technical Department, in 1921, the authority to issue competitions for the design of aircraft according to specifications laid down by the

Navy General Staff; in 1927 the creation of the Naval Aviation Department made responsible for the development (but not the production) of air frames, engines, ordnance, and equipment; in 1932 the establishment of the Naval Air Arsenal to coordinate aircraft design and flight testing; and the institution of the navy's "Prototypes System," a managed competition in the design and development of naval aircraft by the Japanese aircraft industry.[6] These organizational details are important because they are basic to an understanding of the navy's ability to develop some of the finest combat aircraft in the world in the 1930s, which moved aviation from the margins to the center of naval power by the opening of the Pacific War.

1. Ship-based

Carrier Aircraft. In 1934 the navy began a search for a new single-seat carrier aircraft to replace its current biplane fighter. Because of the stringent requirements imposed by carrier flight operations, a successful design demanded a careful selection of performance priorities within the specifications set forth by the Navy General Staff. The Mitsubishi A5M Type 96 carrier fighter brilliantly satisfied the greater number of these priorities. It was an all-metal, open-cockpit, low-wing monoplane powered by a 500-hp radial engine and armed with two machine guns mounted in the engine cowling. Its aluminum construction, flush rivets, and smooth contouring sufficiently reduced air drag so the designers were able to retain its fixed landing gear. The A5M's superb maneuverability underscored the navy's emphasis on dogfighting although its speed (280 mph) and rate of climb (16,000 feet in six and a half minutes) were also unprecedented in Japanese aviation. The appearance of the A5M, along with the G3M medium bomber (see below) marked the emergence of an ambitious program of aircraft reequipment for the navy and signaled the entry of Japanese aviation into an era of self-sufficiency.

Even as the A5M was scoring triumphs in the skies over China in the summer and fall of 1937, the navy was moving ahead with the design of an aircraft that would surpass it in performance. In the opinion of the front-line pilots in the China War, the need was for a fighter with the speed and firepower to destroy enemy bombers, the range and endurance to escort the navy's own medium bombers, and the maneuverability to deal with any enemy fighters along the way. They also wanted a fighter that would meet the challenging demands of carrier flight operations. To satisfy these requirements, the Naval Aviation Department proposed a carrier fighter whose design specifications were of unprecedented difficulty because they were so contradictory. The Mitsubishi team that had created the A5M won the design contract and now created the A6M, eventually known throughout the world as the "Zero" fighter, solving most of the competing staff specifications through a series of ingenious adjustments in structural components, revolutionary advances in construction methods, and the use of innovations such as retractable landing gear and fuselage streamlining. In 1940 the Zero was one of the most ingeniously designed aircraft in the world. In speed, radius, firepower, rate of climb, and turning radius, it was one of the premier combat aircraft in the world. Initially thrust into the fighting in the skies over China during 1940–1941, it decimated Chinese air units, successes that were to be repeated in the Japanese sweep through Southeast Asia in early 1942. Its dangerous weaknesses—structural fragility, the vulnerability of it fuel tanks to enemy fire, and the modest output of its engine—were not revealed until it met the more rugged and more powerfully engined American aircraft during the latter half of the Pacific War.

During the late 1930s, the navy developed two categories of attack aircraft to arm the flight decks of its carriers: torpedo- and dive-bombers. By 1937, in the Nakajima B5N Type 97 torpedo-bomber, it had an aircraft that could undertake multiple roles: torpedo attacks, reconnaissance, and high-level bombing. After its adoption by the navy, the B5N almost immediately went into carrier service; as a participant in the assault on Pearl Harbor, a B5N is credited with dropping the killer bomb that sank the battleship *Arizona*. The plane also saw service in China where it performed well in supporting Japanese ground operations.

The Aichi D3A Type 99 carrier dive-bomber was remarkably rugged for a Japanese combat aircraft. In range and structural integrity, it compared favorably with the American Douglas Dauntless (although it was slower) and with the German Stuka. In the first year of the Pacific War, it sank more Allied warships than any other Axis aircraft.

Long-range Flying Boats. During the interwar years, the Japanese navy recognized the need for long-range over-water reconnaissance. For this purpose, it developed the large flying boat. The experience of the Kawanishi Aircraft Company in developing this type of airplane led to the creation of the H6K Type 97 flying boat, which the navy adopted in 1938. A parasol-winged aircraft powered by four radial engines, its range of 2,200 miles gave it a dramatic reach over vast oceanic distances early in the Pacific War. But its vulnerability to enemy fighter attack eventually led to its replacement by its hardier successor, the Kawanishi H8K Type 2 flying boat, a high-winged aircraft also powered by four radial engines but with a range of almost 4,000 miles. It was for a time the world's best flying boat.

2. Shore-based

In 1930, when Yamamoto Isoroku assumed direction of the technical bureau of the Naval Aviation Department, one of his first priorities was the development of an effective land-based long-range bomber. After a year (1935–1936) of Mitsubishi's testing an ever-improving series of bomber prototypes, the navy accepted an advance model of the Mitsubishi G3M Type 96 medium bomber in June 1936. A sleek, all-metal, twin-engined monoplane bomber with a payload of either 800 kilograms of bombs or a single torpedo slung under its fuselage, its range of 2,300 miles and its ceiling of 30,000 feet were unprecedented except for the contemporary American B-17 Flying Fortress. But like other Japanese aircraft, its weaknesses—the absence of protective armor, and inadequate defensive armament—were revealed in its combat operations over China, 1938–1939.

In any event, even as the G3M entered combat, the navy began working on a successor that would have better power plants, greater speed, increased payload, increased range, and better defensive armament. In early 1940 the navy accepted the G4M Type 1 medium bomber. During the first six months of the Pacific War, the G4M spearheaded Japanese offensives in the west Pacific and Southeast Asia. It was, early in the war, a formidable weapon and achieved some remarkable successes: raids deep into central China in 1941, the sinking of the British capital ships *Repulse* and *Prince of Wales* at the opening of the war, and the bombing of Port Darwin in Australia in 1942. Nevertheless, the old nemeses of Japanese aircraft design—structural fragility and vulnerability to enemy fire—often proved fatal to the aircraft in combat situations. Indeed, the G4M caught fire so easily that its aircrews gave it an ominous sobriquet, "The Flying Lighter," and American fighter pilots gave it the dismissive name of "Zippo."

At the time of their appearance, the small group of Japanese naval aircraft displayed some of the most advanced aviation technology in the world. Flown by highly skilled aircrews, the navy's planes collectively constituted an immensely dangerous offensive force. Yet they also collectively demonstrated the fatal weaknesses of Japanese naval air technology. Of these, the most serious was the failure of Japanese industry to keep up with the West in the development of powerful, lightweight aircraft engines. This in turn was the consequence of Japan's inability to have access to strategic alloys essential to the development of such engines. The superior power plants of American aircraft were a major reason for the increasing losses of Japanese aircraft in combat in the latter half of the Pacific War. But there were also serious problems in the design of Japanese aircraft. Considerations of speed, range, and maneuverability so monopolized the concerns of Japanese engineers and aircrews that the Japanese aircraft discussed herein were bereft of all but the most minimal protection and defensive armament. These deficiencies would have been serious even if Japan had had a limitless pool of highly trained aircrews. With the small number of such personnel available, they would prove fatal to Japanese prospects in their combat with their sturdier American opponents in the skies over the Pacific.

C. WEAPON SYSTEMS

1. Gunnery

That the Japanese navy devoted much time and attention to gunnery in its early decades was evident in the effectiveness of its gunfire in the naval battles of the Sino- and Russo-Japanese wars. Of course, in an era when fire control was still in its primitive stages in all navies, in these encounters the Japanese achieved a fraction of hits by their main batteries out of the total number of shots fired. That said, that fire, particularly at the Battle of Tsushima in 1905, was awesomely destructive due to the force and explosive power of Japanese shells. Admiral Tōgō's annihilating victory at Tsushima proved to be a milestone in naval warfare because it proved the primacy of long-range firing (6,000–10,000 m) and thus heralded the dominance of the biggest guns.

In the near-decade between the Russo-Japanese War and the outbreak of World War I, the problems of surface fire control in naval gunnery were beginning to be understood in the major navies but insufficiently solved to exploit the potential ranges of rifled ordnance. While, by 1905, primitive fire-control systems had advanced partial solutions to the problems of target tracking, predicting range and bearing, and correcting aim based on observation, such systems were slow and imperfectly integrated. For the Japanese navy, the period 1905–1914 was not one of great technological innovation in fire control, and the Japanese relied largely on advances by the British navy in this regard.

During World War I, however, the Japanese did attempt to develop fire-control instruments, and this program laid the foundations of the navy's fire-control systems between the world wars. In the 1920s, the navy's increasing obsession with "outranging"—striking the enemy at the outset of a battle from a distance at which he could not retaliate—led to several technological improvements that made it possible to coordinate the long-range fire of main battery ordnance. By mid-decade the navy had sufficient confidence in its guns and gunnery that it believed its main force units could outrange those of the U.S. fleet by four to five thousand meters. However, the course of this technological development in these years was at a slower pace than in the American and British navies. During the first year of the Pacific War, the superior quality of Japanese optics and the training and skill of Japanese gun crews enabled Japanese gunnery to more than match the American enemy, but thereafter, as the U.S. Navy fully exploited its advances in fire-control radar and high-powered servomechanisms, Japanese gunnery could no longer hold its own.

Electronics, particularly radar, was the most vital field of technology in the naval side of the Pacific War. Disastrously for the Japanese navy, the development of electronics was a case of too little, too late. This is ironic because Japanese research in the field had begun in the early 1930s, at almost the same time as in Britain and the United States. Yet official indifference, haphazard mobilization of civilian scientific expertise and talent, and (as always) the absence of interservice cooperation fatally delayed the practical application of Japanese radar research.

With the outbreak of the war in Europe and the recognition by the navy of some of the advances in radar made in the West, the navy's interest in this new technology accelerated to the point when, in August 1941, the Navy Ministry finally ordered a crash program in radar development. The first meter-length air-search radar set was ready in late November 1941, but it was an electrically and mechanically crude device by Western standards. By the opening of the Pacific War, the navy still had no shipborne surface search or fire-control radar. Confident at the outset of hostilities in its night combat doctrine and equipment (powerful optics and searchlights), the Japanese navy found itself a year into the Pacific War fighting like a man blindfolded.

Despite the urgent demands of the Navy General Staff for accelerated development of radar, the inability of Japanese naval researchers to produce centimeter wavelength magnetrons and the severe staff specifications for radar sets made it impossible for the navy's research staffs to develop effective radar models in the time they were given. Without doubt, prewar American advances in radar and the Japanese failure to match them were among the reasons for American naval victory and Japanese naval defeat in the Pacific War.

2. Torpedoes

Torpedoes were a favored weapon in the Japanese navy from its early years, and most of its warships were equipped with torpedo tubes by 1893. The torpedoes used by the navy in the Sino-Japanese conflict were of German manufacture based on the original Whitehead design, but in 1897 the navy began producing its own Whitehead-type torpedoes at the Tokyo Naval Arsenal.

The torpedo remained a weapon of choice for the navy well into the twentieth century and was a central element in the navy's night operations exercises. But these exercises revealed a serious problem: the potentially prohibitive losses among the destroyer units assigned to undertake them.

The solution was for destroyers to fire their torpedoes at long range, for which the navy needed a powerful, wakeless torpedo. The navy undertook intensive research on and testing of such a weapon in the 1920s and early

1930s and by the latter half of the 1930s had developed the formidable Type 93 oxygen torpedo. This appeared to be the navy's ideal weapon for outranging the enemy and was installed on many Japanese cruisers and destroyers by 1940. In addition to the Type 93 for surface vessels, the navy later developed an aerial version, the Type 94, and a submarine version, the Type 95.

3. Antisubmarine Warfare

Given the prewar Japanese complacency toward trade protection and ASW, it is not surprising that its ships, weapons, and the equipment to deal with these matters were too few in number and poor in quality. The marginal attention given to protection of sea transport was reflected in the paucity of naval construction devoted to it. Just before the London Naval Treaty, the navy briefly considered building a sizeable force of specialized vessels for trade protection, but budgetary limitations (at a time when the navy was considering its super-battleship strategy) aborted the plan and the navy built only four small multi-purpose coast defense vessels whose size (860 tons), speed, and armament were inadequate for an ASW mission. Fourteen vessels of an improved type were planned, but none had been completed when the Pacific War began.

Not only was the number of vessels assigned ASW duties inadequate for their mission, their weapons and equipment were largely ineffective for any such task. They had no forward-thrown ASW weapons, and their main armament was inferior to the larger deck guns of American submarines. Their underwater detection gear was obsolete, their sonar was rudimentary, and the settings for their depth charges were faulty (too shallow because Japanese intelligence had underestimated the maximum diving depth of most American submarines).

4. Mines

Mines had been in the navy's arsenal from its early days but were used with modest success only in the Russo-Japanese War when they sank a Russian battleship. By the 1930s, due to the navy's increasing emphasis on aircraft and to its protective improvements for surface warships, mines had become obsolete weapons.

D. INFRASTRUCTURE

1. Logistics

Until it initiated the Pacific War, the Japanese navy had been only marginally concerned with logistics.[7] In its first two combat tests—the Sino- and Russo-Japanese wars—the navy's logistical requirements were simple and adequately met. But these were conflicts of short duration against close-at-hand enemies. A naval war with the United States fought over vast oceanic distances against an enemy formidably supplied by an enormous industrial base confronted the

Japanese navy with huge logistical problems. Beyond the critical question of oil stocks, there was a serious shortage of ammunition, particularly in aviation ordnance. Although the navy maintained the flow of ordnance at the start of the war, it was haunted by ammunition shortages throughout the remainder of the conflict.

Turning to logistical procedures, the navy high command had clearly not anticipated the need for materiel and expertise required for the construction of forward bases in the Pacific. Specifically, the navy lacked the specialized organization, training, and equipment to make such construction possible. In particular, it lacked the requisite equipment—bulldozers, earthmovers, and steam shovels—of modern civil engineering; therefore, nearly all of its construction was by hand. As the tide of the Japanese advance swept through the southwest and central Pacific, the navy came to recognize the need for specialized units to build airfields and other advance base facilities. The first such construction units (setsueitai) were organized in November 1941, but they were only semimilitary in character and had scant combat value with little of the expertise, training, equipment, or weapons possessed by the U.S. Navy's Seabees. As the tide of the Japanese offense slowed and then stopped, the mission of the setsueitai was redirected to the construction of defensive works on the islands they had captured. But overwhelmed in a series of futile defenses as the American counteroffensive began to roll westward through the central Pacific, they were immolated in the bunkers they had helped to construct.

The fundamental cause of the Japanese navy's prewar failure to recognize in advance the logistical problems in a war with the United States was again the navy's fixation on the long anticipated great gun duel at sea. Only less capable or more physically limited officers were assigned to grapple with the difficulties of transport, supply, and construction, and their views were rarely sought by those officers planning and directing combat operations. Hence, the latter tended to frame their plans without relation to logistical resources and their plans often failed disastrously.

2. Bases

From its earliest years, the Japanese navy maintained several types of base commands, each headed by an officer formally subordinate to the direct authority of the emperor. By the 1890s, the coastal defense of the islands was entrusted to three separate naval districts, each centered on a naval base that served as both a "primary port" and the naval headquarters of the district. The port included building yards, fuel and supply depots, naval barracks, and the anchorage for guard and coast defense vessels. In peacetime each district was under the authority of the Navy Ministry; in wartime it came under the direct command of the area fleet attached to the district. Within each district were

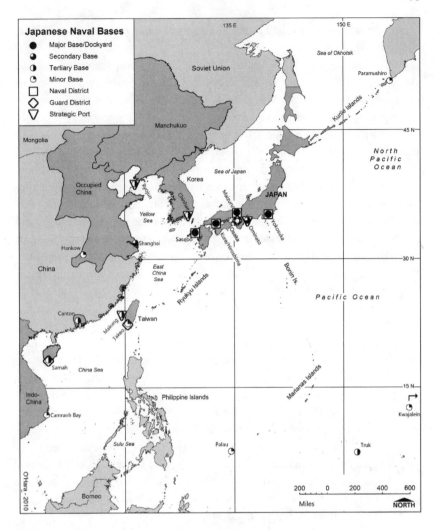

also "naval ports," a secondary type of base that included repair shops, naval hospitals, and an anchorage for more coast defense vessels.

As Japan acquired overseas possessions, it also established "strategic ports," which were the overseas equivalent of a domestic naval base. After the League of Nations awarded Japan a mandate in Micronesia following World War I, the navy began eyeing the possibility of establishing bases in the Mariana and Caroline islands as well. With its entry into the air age, the navy also began establishing air bases that would provide not only airfields but also headquarters for its various land-based air groups. There were twelve of these in the home islands and one in Korea by 1937. These air bases were established at the moderate pace compelled by the traditional pick-and-shovel construction that the navy practiced.

After the outbreak of the Pacific War and Japan's sweep through Southeast Asia, the navy took over existing air and naval bases established by Western colonial powers. The real difficulties for the navy began when the course of the war entered the central and southwestern Pacific and the navy was confronted with the need to construct bases on undeveloped coral atolls and in remote tropical bays. To level the ground, build docks, lay down airstrips, and erect buildings and revetments the navy had little earth-moving machinery and slight expertise of the sort enjoyed by the American Seabee construction battalions. This deficiency was not a critical problem initially as the navy swept eastward in the Pacific, but it became so after the tide of war turned and the first American amphibious counteroffensives surged westward. Without avail, the Japanese navy attempted to throw up effective land defenses in the Pacific, but these were overwhelmed by storms of American naval gunfire, air bombardment, and waves of landing infantry.

3. Industry

Japan's defeat in World War II is often explained entirely by the avalanche of American resources, materiel, and weapons that simply buried Japanese forces. Certainly, the enormous output of American industry after 1942 makes this a plausible explanation. But the serious incapacities of Japanese industry during the period 1942–1945 are just as important in assessing the awesome material disparity between the two combatants.

The workings of Japan's war industry are too complex to be analyzed comprehensively here, particularly since we have Jerome Cohen's *Japan's Economy in War and Reconstruction*, which remains the classic English-language study on the subject.[8] Much of what is said here is drawn from the most salient points in his chapter on Japanese industry.

Initially, Cohen asserts, the Japanese high command, specifically including the navy, made the decision to go to war with great confidence that Japan had an adequate supply of weapons and equipment of all types that it would need for the conflict. From their Olympian perspective, they noted that munitions output currently exceeded expectations and that naval construction had surged during the previous decade. But this confidence was based on the nation's experience in its war in China, which had largely involved conventional land weapons and which had been fought against a materially inferior enemy. A conflict with the United States would be principally a maritime conflict, one requiring not only warships of every size and type but also a vast array of aircraft, electronic devices, and antiaircraft weapons; mountains of ammunition of all calibers; hundreds of cargo ships and tankers; and oceans of naval fuel and aviation gasoline. Moreover, the changing tides of war would require unanticipated shifts in the kind of ships, aircraft, weapons, and equipment needed, which would in turn necessitate alternative production plans during the course of the war and would thus slow industrial output across the board.

Japan encountered this last difficulty by the end of 1942, when it appeared that Japan's greatest need was for cargo vessels to bring to Japan the great treasure house of strategic raw materials that it had captured in Southeast Asia and that were now desperately needed by the industrial machine in the home islands. In this regard, wartime Japan depended on its merchant shipping even more than beleaguered Britain (which, after all, was largely kept in the war by American supply convoys). At the beginning of the China war, Japan had one of the world's largest merchant fleets and thus turned its shipbuilding industry to strengthening its naval forces through modernization of older vessels and construction of new ones. But because Japan's available stocks of steel were limited, new or reconstructed warships came at the sacrifice of further merchant ship construction. This would have posed a difficult dilemma for the navy in any event, but the mounting losses of both warships and merchant shipping to American submarine and air attacks soon made the situation critical. By 1944 an overriding need was for more tankers to import Southeast Asian petroleum for a thirsty navy. Even before the war, Japan had had too few large tankers, and as American submarines began to sink tankers as a target priority, the need for such vessels rose dramatically. In addition to the problem of limited stocks of steel and other metals used in ship construction, there were insufficient shipbuilding facilities. Good sites for ship construction—expanses of flat land near both rail links and deep water—were rare; where they did exist, they were usually located on city waterfronts where any expansion of dockyards was difficult and expensive. In consequence, expansion of existing facilities usually caused congestion, confusion, and disruption of a smooth and systematic flow of construction output. Newer yards, often specialized in their construction functions, avoided some of these difficulties, but they usually had a smaller and less experienced workforce, a condition that created its own problems.

As the war progressed, the growing number of ship losses in both naval and merchant vessels put a terrific strain on Japanese industry to make up for them. But after the first year of the conflict, there were never enough materials, facilities, or skilled workmen to meet the nation's needs. Equal to problems of low stocks of material was the question of manpower and its effect on the production of everything from radios to battleship turrets. Here the demands of the military were both dominant and shortsighted. All too often the military drafted skilled workmen and technicians to serve as ordinary seamen or common soldiers, a policy that contributed to the chaotic course of industrial production.

Japan's aircraft industry was shockingly vulnerable to aerial destruction as well as to disruption from lack of planning. To begin with, the industry's factories were extremely concentrated. For example, 72 percent of aircraft output was located within a thirty-five-mile radius of three large cities—Tokyo, Nagoya, and Osaka—and only four aircraft companies produced more than two-thirds of all aircraft during the war. Two of the largest aircraft plants located in Osaka produced 92 percent of Japan's aircraft between 1941 and 1945.

Even more than shipbuilding, the Japanese aircraft industry suffered from interservice friction and duplication as well as an ever-shifting emphasis in combat unit demands. Added to shortages of strategic metals and skilled labor, such chaotic conditions lowered production efficiency, not to mention the failure to keep abreast of Western advances in aircraft design and technology.

Part of the problem, of course, was that the Japanese lacked the vast research capacity available in the United States. While the United States enjoyed the findings of numerous commercial research laboratories such as Bell, RCA, Argonne, and Westinghouse as well as a number of government research institutions, Japan had very few of these. This meant that the number of specialists available to think through problems in technology, communications, logistics, and intelligence was far smaller in Japan than in the United States; thus the nation lagged behind its enemy in these important fields, with adverse consequences both in staff planning and on the fighting fronts.

Such knowledgeable advice might have avoided some of the grave mistakes by the military at the start of the war, particularly the failure to connect plans for airframe and engine production with the realities of materiel requirements. Before 1942, according to Cohen, there was no real effort to determine the exact raw-material requirements for the aircraft industry as a whole. Nor had the navy made any effort to stockpile rare alloys used in the making of high-tensile-strength special alloy steels. Shortages of nickel, copper, chromium, tungsten, cobalt, and other strategic materials eventually led to a decline of alloy steels for aircraft engines, fuel systems, motor mounts, and landing gear. Such material shortages, in combination with the deteriorating quality of workmanship eventually caused a significant drop in the operational availability of Japanese naval aircraft. At the outset of the war, the navy was able to count on the availability of 80 percent of its aircraft. That percentage dropped to 50 percent midway through the war and for some air groups to only 20 percent.

Shortages in fuel stocks also contributed to the decline in the quality as well as quantity of Japanese naval aircraft. Low stocks of aviation gasoline meant that the navy tested engines less frequently. Early in the war, the navy tested its newly built engines for nine hours; by the end of the war that figure was down to two hours, and only one out of ten engines was being tested.

IV. RECAPITULATION

A. WARTIME EVOLUTION

For more than three decades, between the Russo-Japanese War and the Pacific War, the Japanese navy planned, trained, and armed itself for combat with a single opponent, the U.S. Navy. In assessing these preparations, one should survey, if only briefly, the course of the naval war in the Pacific.

For the first two years of the war, the Japanese navy fought, often with great success, using the tactics and technologies it had perfected during the interwar period. From early 1944, however, it suffered calamity in the face of the enormous buildup of American forces and the U.S. Navy's extraordinary technological advances in naval warfare. From that time forward, the Japanese navy waged a war of desperation, largely abandoning its prewar tactical and strategic thinking.

The outset of hostilities was initiated by the navy's thunderous attack on the U.S. Fleet at Pearl Harbor, which remains to this day a marker for tactical triumph and strategic error. Had the Japanese concentrated their effort on the conquest of Southeast Asia—which was, after all, their primary strategic objective, not the Pacific Fleet at Hawaii—the American fleet would have come lumbering westward across the Pacific, very likely to have been sunk in deep water by Japanese bombers based in Micronesia.

In the first months of the war, the Japanese navy essentially limited itself to the strategic goals set forth in its immediate prewar planning. In this, the conquest of Southeast Asia was accomplished with a speed that surprised even the Japanese themselves. After its strategic successes in the first half of 1942, the navy turned to the second phase of its plans: the elimination or neutralization of those strategic points from which the Allies could launch counteroffensives against the periphery of Japanese conquests. There the Japanese met for the first time with serious strategic reverses, first at the Coral Sea, when they were forced to abandon their effort to isolate Australia; then at Midway, when their attempt to establish a steppingstone for an assault on Hawaii resulted in the loss of four carriers; and finally, in the seven-month-long fight to control the Solomon Islands, in which the navy ultimately lost a campaign of attrition. In each of these campaigns, Japanese naval operations followed a pattern that significantly undercut the prospects for success: a failure to concentrate its forces at a time when it still held superiority in the Pacific. This was particularly critical in the Japanese defeat at Midway.

After Midway, the navy once more turned its attention to the southwest Pacific. There, in a campaign centered on the struggle for Guadalcanal, both Japanese armed services lost ground, ships, aircraft, men, and materiel through piecemeal commitment of their forces. The consequent loss of strategic initiative made the Solomons campaign the decisive period of the war. But more serious to Japanese prospects than the destruction of the navy's men, ships, and aircraft in that campaign was the gift of time and space it gave to the United States. During 1943, with the battle lines in the Pacific at a standstill, America was able to gather and reorganize its forces. Most critically, thereafter, the United States' vast industrial plant and array of scientific skills began to affect the outcome of combat.

Once halted in their drive to expand Japan's strategic periphery beyond the limits of prewar planning, in 1943 Japan's armed services turned their energies to the defense of the perimeter of their earlier conquests. But Japanese preparations to rush to completion a barrier against the American amphibious counteroffensive were puny compared to the enormous scale of the force gathering against them. The United States launched against the overextended Japanese a type of sea power so revolutionary and so massively armed and equipped that the Japanese navy was unprepared to respond at any level—strategic, operational, or tactical. At the end of 1943, this offensive power was turned against Japan's defensive zone in the Pacific and, over the next six months, overcame or bypassed its island bases one after another.

By the summer of 1944, the Japanese defensive line had failed to hold, and the Combined Fleet, so carefully husbanded for the opportunity to fight the long-sought decisive battle, could no longer muster sufficient strength for a counterattack. By that autumn the Japanese navy was faced with a stark choice: to conserve what remained of the Combined Fleet without confronting the cresting wave of American naval power and thus witness the United States take one Japanese bastion after another, or to throw the fleet in front of the American advance and risk its annihilation. The disasters at the Philippine Sea and Leyte Gulf in 1944 were the consequences of Toyko's attempts at the second alternative. By May 1945, most ships of the once mighty Combined Fleet had been sunk and its assorted remnants were cowering in the bays and anchorages of the home islands under a rain of American bombs. By the time that the USS Missouri dropped anchor in Tokyo Bay, the cost in Japanese ships and men had been tremendous: 334 warships and well over 300,000 officers and enlisted men.

B. SUMMARY AND ASSESSMENT

The Japanese navy's conduct of the Pacific War hinged on its strategy, and the most fundamental aspect of that strategy was the disconnection between the war that the navy planned for and the war that the navy initiated. As a continent-oriented force for most of its existence, it was used to thinking in regional and limited terms. Its successes in the Sino- and Russo-Japanese wars had been waged against regional foes and in carefully limited theaters of operation. In plotting the opening moves of the Pacific War, the Navy General Staff may have believed it was planning for a limited conflict, but by its surprise attack on Pearl Harbor it created a political, psychological, and strategic climate in the United States that made total war inevitable.

Cocooned in self-confidence, the Japanese naval high command also mistakenly assumed that it would be able to determine the pace as well as the direction of the war. But after 1942, the navy became increasingly frustrated by the growing ability of the American enemy to move farther, faster, and with greater force, as well as by the navy's own inability to prevent the enemy's strategic moves.

Moreover, the Japanese navy failed to think through what was entailed in the second phase of its strategy because it failed to appreciate the vast size of the arena it had chosen to defend. The navy's strategy of trying to defend a chain of widely separated island bastions with locally deployed air units was basically unsound. The navy simply lacked the means to hold such front-line positions in depth or the strength to support those forces committed to that defense.

As late as mid-1944, the Japanese navy still counted on a single great naval victory to turn the war around. Other elements of sea power—including convoy protection and antisubmarine warfare capabilities—were often sacrificed to this concept. The navy's dogged pursuit of this chimera not only warped its force structure, it also limited its chances for success in several major engagements it did fight. Indeed, the abject demise of both the *Musashi* and the *Yamato* under aerial bombardment without having fired a shell at a worthy target demonstrates the futility of the decisive battle idea. It also exemplifies the navy's failure to think of alternatives.

If the Japanese navy vainly chased the chimera of decisive battle across the Pacific until late in the Pacific War, early on it was forced to confront the reality of attrition. During the conflict, attrition—that is, attacks from submarines and aircraft other than those in a major named engagement—was the cause of the destruction of the Japanese merchant marine. Here the Japanese navy was slow to adjust to the mounting danger. In the first year of the war, while America's submarine operations were still limited by technological, tactical, and command problems, the Japanese navy did little to strengthen its ASW capabilities. The 900,000 tons of Japanese shipping sunk in 1942 should have been a warning. By the beginning of 1944, when American submarines were scouring the west Pacific in great numbers, the situation was too late to reverse. At war's end, Japan had only 1.5 million tons of merchant shipping left out of a prewar total of 6.4 million tons. But attrition also accounted for nearly half the navy's losses in surface warships.

PHOTO 5.4. The face of defeat. The Japanese battleship *Haruna* wrecked in Kure Harbor immediately postwar, festooned with ineffective camouflage. (U.S. Naval Institute Photo Archives)

If American submarines were initially hampered by a range of technological problems, their Japanese counterparts were tethered by an ineffectual doctrine. Focused on fleet operations, their commanders' failure to attack American troop and supply ships was a major oversight because such operations, pressed home aggressively, would have enormously complicated Allied counteroffensives during the middle and later stages of the war.

No aspect of the Japanese navy's prosecution of the war was more wasteful of its energies and resources than the interservice feud endemic to both services since the early years of the twentieth century. The services' latent distrust of each other turned to active hostility as the war situation worsened. It inhibited overall strategic planning, it often hindered operations, and it resulted in tremendous duplication of effort in the development and production of technology.

If the weak point of the Japanese navy in World War II was strategy, its strength was tactics. During the first two years of the war, the navy frequently showed itself the tactical superior of its American enemy. After that, no matter how well or poorly the navy conducted its battles, the overwhelming might of American sea power made tactics irrelevant in determining the outcome. In the campaigns for the Solomon Islands, one can best evaluate the navy's tactical performance in a period when Japanese and American naval forces were roughly in balance. In the seven engagements of the campaign (eight, if one divides the night actions off Guadalcanal between the battleship and cruiser engagements), the Japanese were usually able to exchange blow for blow. Four actions (Savo Island, Cape Esperance, the battles off Guadalcanal, and Tassafaronga) were night surface engagements that demonstrated that the Japanese were better prepared for night combat than the Americans were. The Japanese navy's tactical successes in these engagements were clearly the result not only of the superior professionalism of the Japanese commanders on the spot but also of the navy's officers and men who, across the board, were intelligent, superbly trained, physically tough, highly motivated, and obedient unto death. No doubt, the navy's emphasis on *seishin* (spirit) was a significant element in the capabilities of all branches of the navy.

Although *seishin* eventually led to dangerous overconfidence and thus contributed to eventual defeat, toward the end of the war, when the navy was shattered, *seishin* held its remnants together far longer than would have been possible in any other navy faced with similar ruin. In the long run, however, quality in training and morale could not compensate for inadequate quantity worsened by mounting casualties and combat fatigue. This was particularly true in the navy's air arm, in which, as the ranks of seasoned aircrews thinned rapidly in the last years of the war, large numbers of inadequately trained pilots were rushed into combat with predictably disastrous results.

The tactical schemes of the interwar decades yielded a wide range of results. The navy's single most impressive tactical innovation in the prewar years was the concentration of carrier air power manifested in the formation of the First Air Fleet, which, when it was formed in April 1941, was the single most powerful agglomeration of naval air power anywhere in the world. But it represented a hit-and-run strike force concept that was soon superseded by the American task force—a multicomponent fleet supplied by a mobile fleet train and able to provide round-the-clock offensive operations against a target. Some tactical innovations studied and practiced by the navy in the prewar years were employed, at least for a while, with reasonable success. In particular, night combat tactics and technologies (particularly Japanese optics) were quite effective in the early battles in the southwest Pacific. Others were far less successful. The midget submarine idea proved to be a bust, as did plans to use submarine-launched aircraft for reconnaissance and long-distance concealed firing by the navy's surface torpedo units. The merits of "outranging" are hard to judge. Although the Japanese navy's long-sought apotheosis, the great gun duel between *Yamato*-class battleships and the American battle line, never took place, the idea—embedded in the design of a variety of Japanese weapons, ships, and aircraft—was sound enough. But often the Japanese ability to outrange the enemy was simply vitiated by ineffective Japanese strategy, as in the case of Japanese submarine doctrine.

Given the ultimate scale of the American superiority in industrial power and the utter annihilation of the Combined Fleet by war's end, it is clear that Japan was doomed to defeat and that, after 1943, there was little the nation and the navy could have done to avoid that defeat. Yet various strategic and doctrinal decisions not taken could have improved the odds for the navy and could have prolonged the struggle. Several examples come to mind. As discussed earlier, the surprise attack at Pearl Harbor was of questionable strategic value. If the navy had paid greater attention to the vulnerability of the home islands and of Japan's commerce and communications routes to submarine blockade, it would have not been so quickly cut off from its overseas strategic resources. If it had directed its own submarine strategy toward the interdiction of supply and communications routes between the American West Coast and American advance bases in the Pacific, the U.S. amphibious counteroffensive in that ocean might have been seriously delayed.

Yet a balanced view of the Japanese navy's performance in the Pacific War requires a careful consideration of the first two years of the conflict. During that period, the navy waged the sort of war for which it had planned and trained. If one concentrates on tactical outcomes, the navy's record is rather good. Excluding both the Pearl Harbor operation and the massacre of a Japanese convoy by U.S. Army Air Corps bombers in the Bismarck Sea, there were seventeen engagements between American and Japanese naval forces during the first two years of the Pacific War. Four were carrier battles, of which the Japanese lost one (Midway) decisively and fought the others to a draw. Of the remaining thirteen ship-to-ship encounters, the Japanese won six; the U.S. Navy, four; and three were draws. That record is proof that when pitted against naval forces also employing tactics and technologies developed between the world wars, the Japanese navy was a formidable fighting force. It was not until the introduction of revolutionary tactics and technologies by the U.S. Navy and the exertion of preponderant American naval power early in 1944 that the tide turned decisively against the Japanese navy.

C. REFLECTIONS ON THE JAPANESE NAVY

When the Japanese navy initiated the Pacific War, it was indeed a formidable fighting force. It comprised 10 battleships, including the first of the 2 greatest battleships ever built; 10 aircraft carriers; 38 cruisers, heavy and light; 112 destroyers; 65 submarines; and numerous auxiliary warships of various sizes. Japanese naval aviation was world-class; its air crews were the best trained and the most experienced. The personnel of the navy, both officers and enlisted men, comprised a professional elite unsurpassed in training, bravery, and dedication. Yet certain strategic, organizational, and technological decisions made by the navy in the interwar period proved fatal. To those decisions should be added certain inherent national impediments, many of which were beyond the navy's control but which in the end were ruinous to the navy's prospects in fighting a modern naval war.

It is a stark fact that Japan's resource base was inadequate not only in terms of the obvious resources of oil and rubber but also in specialized materials such as high-performance metals, which hampered Japanese naval and aviation technology, for example, the production of light-weight but powerful aircraft engines or ship power plants that could handle the highest steam pressures. Japan's shortage of these resources was worsened by the fact that it had to import most of them from overseas and by the vulnerability of the shipping that brought them to Japanese industry in the home islands.

Japan also entered hostilities with woefully inefficient transportation and distribution systems. The consequence was exemplified by the fact that the first production model of its finest fighter aircraft, the Mitsubishi Zero fighter, was taken by oxcart from the Mitsubishi aircraft factory to the nearest airfield for flight testing. In the latter stages of the Pacific War, the production of small parts for various equipment and weapons was undertaken in hundreds of small workshops scattered throughout the home islands, resulting in colossal inefficiencies in the distribution of raw materials to these mini-factories and in the distribution of the finished products to the naval and air units that needed them.

A crippling disadvantage to the navy in amassing ships, aircraft, and weapons was the fact that Japan operated from a much smaller and temporally shorter base of technological expertise. Whereas the U.S. Navy could call upon a host of private research laboratories as well as its own research facilities, the Japanese navy essentially had to rely on its own technological research centers, which were few in number. This situation was worsened by the fact that the navy had given too little thought to the mobilization of the scientific and industrial assets it did possess and by the duplication of effort and inefficiencies caused by its hostile relations with the army. Japanese failure to keep up with the Western allies in radar is more than partially explained by these deficiencies. A related problem was the inadequate number of naval dockyards in Japan compared to the United States. Japan had far fewer dockyards, both commercial and navy, in its ports.

The consequent disparity in production figures is exemplified by the construction of destroyers in Japan and the United States during World War II: 61 destroyers were built in Japan during 1942–1945, and 354 destroyers were built in the United States during the same period. Part of the problem for the Japanese navy was that there were too few ships of any particular design and too few ships per dockyard. The result was that the Japanese did not develop efficiencies of production as rapidly as their American counterparts did.

Yet it is undeniable that through its understanding and eventual mastery of the basic principles of Western technology, the Japanese navy designed and produced outstanding warships, combat aircraft, and weapons. Among these are the two superbattleships *Yamato* and *Musashi*, the *Fubuki*-class destroyers, the Mitsubishi Zero fighter, the G3M medium bomber, and the Type 93 oxygen torpedo. When introduced, they were worldclass technologies. But they were older, "first generation" technologies that Japan had brought to perfection, and, like all technologies, they were bound to be overtaken by other technologies. Therein lay a serious problem for the Japanese navy. Because of scarce resources and limited facilities for technological innovation, made worse in wartime when Japanese manufacture found it hard just to replace combat losses, it was difficult to develop, test, and produce new weapons and equipment. Even more importantly, the limitations on Japanese science and technology prevented Japan from developing complex and critical "second stage" technologies that were introduced by the United States including radar, the VT (proximity) fuze, and forward-thrown antisubmarine weapons.

Exacerbating these scientific and industrial limitations was a basic defect in the thinking and preparations of both Japanese armed services but particularly in the navy: a fundamental miscalculation of the relationship between strategy, force structure, and the nation's industrial base. Counting on surprise, speed, and overwhelming fire power, the navy planned for a lightning offensive of war of short duration that would culminate in a single, swift, and annihilating victory.

This assumption led to the design of a small number of superior ships and aircraft whose quality was counted on to defeat a larger number of enemy ships and aircraft of inferior quality. Once the impetus of the navy's strategic offensive was halted and the conflict turned into a serious war of attrition of men and material, not only did the navy have too little of everything but it also found that its human and technological assets were unsuited for attritional warfare.

There was also another fundamental error in Japanese naval thought: the belief that quality could always overcome quantity. Indeed, one can argue that this belief was one of the most essential principles of Japanese naval doctrine and as such shaped much, if not most, of Japanese naval technology. The design and development of a range of weapons, ships, and aircraft were predicated on the notion that they would be decisively superior to their enemy counterparts. This imbalance between doctrine and technology had evil consequences even before the outbreak of the Pacific War. It could be seen in the extreme demands by the Navy General Staff for certain design specifications relating to armor and fire power that made a number of Japanese warships seriously unstable.

"Quality," in any event, is a complex proposition. It can be judged in relation to how well a particular system performs one particular function—which was the Japanese approach—or how effectively a system is able to confront a range of problems it might meet—the American approach. Moreover, the Japanese confidence that quality was always preferable to quantity was a dubious assumption from the beginning. In the history of modern war, no conflict was ever won exclusively by technologically superior weapons. Rather, most modern wars have been won by superior planning, organization, logistics, staff work, industrial output, and political leadership. Stalin probably had it right when he pronounced that "quantity has a quality all its own."

For much of its seventy-five year history, the Japanese navy demonstrated the solid application of scientific methodology to the development of its tactics. In the late nineteenth century, the navy had been at the forefront of tactical innovation. But gradually Japanese doctrinal thought began to atrophy and, by the 1920s, rigidity overtook the navy's tactical doctrine. By the 1930s that trend had hardened into extreme dogmatism, allowing no criticism of the navy's orthodox tactical assumptions or consideration of new approaches to naval warfare.

With such a mindset it is not surprising that the navy's study of naval warfare during World War I focused only on the Battle of Jutland, with little attention given to broader strategic, economic, political, and industrial matters that had in fact marked the margins of victory and defeat. It is obvious that strategy was the Japanese navy's weakest understanding. In the beginning, at the navy's genesis, its strategic priority was clear enough: control of the surrounding seas. Its strategic posture was therefore defensive, regional, and limited in scope. Japan's imperial expansion on the Asian continent complicated this approach, although in its wars with China and Russia, Japan carefully calculated the odds and fought for limited, near-at-hand objectives. But the navy's support for a permanent Japanese presence on the Asian continent led to a new strategic rationale: projection of national power on the high seas. In turn, this new raison d'être for the navy led to a serious contradiction between regional power, which was attainable, and global reach, which was not.

In the long run, the most critical failing of the Japanese navy was to mistake tactics for strategy, and strategy for the general conduct of modern war. The navy's over-arching concern was for decisive battle—the one great surface battle on which would ride the fate of the nation. Indeed, it can be argued that in December 1941, the navy was not prepared for war; it prepared for battle. But the idea of decisive battle no longer had much validity in the twentieth century. By then, national destinies were determined not by single encounters but by the strength or weakness of national power beyond pure military might: diplomacy, industrial structure, scientific and technological competence, political leadership, civilian morale, and other elements that had come to comprise total war. The navy gave them little attention—far less, even, than did its sister service. This was due in large part to the dead weight of the Japanese martial tradition with its particular emphasis on "spirit" as equivalent or superior to material assets. Whereas "spirit" accounted for unrivalled bravery by the men who served in the navy, it also led to an arrogance that ignored or discounted enemy capabilities and a blindness to material realities that bordered on the irrational. This, then, was the Imperial Japanese Navy's ultimate failure to the Japanese nation it served so bravely: the failure to understand and prepare for modern war.

chapter six

USA: The United States Navy

I. BACKSTORY

A. HISTORY

Founded in 1775, the U.S. Navy began as a small force. In its early wars, it fought minor actions with little bearing on strategy and tactics, but in these fights the energetic young republic showed that it could field officers and sailors who, like those of frigate *Constitution*, were the equal of their European counterparts.

Through the nineteenth century, the U.S. Navy remained focused on coastal defense and minor operations. The American Civil War provided the first real opportunity for the Navy to exert strategic influence. The important role naval operations played in the Civil War is frequently overshadowed by the history of the land campaigns, but the supremacy the Federal forces enjoyed on the sea and inland waterways was an important key to victory. Success in numerous operations that would today be described as "joint," like the Peninsular Campaign of 1862 and the seizure of Mobile Bay in 1864, provided valuable experience and ultimately led to the philosophic underpinnings for the strategic concepts that brought victory in World War II. The most important naval strategist of modern times, Alfred Thayer Mahan, graduated from the Naval Academy in 1859 and developed theories that stressed the fact that dominance of the seas was a means to an end, a prerequisite for strategic power that could decisively influence wars on land. The examples he chose in his most important work, *The Influence of Sea Power upon History, 1660–1783*, illustrate this concept.

In the late nineteenth and early twentieth centuries, in parallel with the increasing influence of Mahan's theories, the Navy began to expand and modernize. Victory in the war with Spain made the United States a Pacific power, increasing the likelihood of a future conflict with Japan. The voyage of the Great White Fleet proved that the Navy's modern steamships could operate

globally, like their wind-powered predecessors. By 1917, when America entered
World War I, the Navy had become one of the most powerful and modern
forces in the world.

World War I provided valuable experience with new technologies, submarines, aircraft, and modern fire-control systems. Through close cooperation
with Britain's Royal Navy and real operational experience, the Navy validated
the correctness of many procedures and modified or rejected those that were
inadequate.

After the war, with the political climate ripe for a reduction of military
spending, the great powers met in Washington, D.C., in 1922 to discuss the
possibility of limiting naval armaments. The Washington Treaty and others
that followed were an essential part of the strategic backdrop of World War
II. By canceling postwar building programs, terminating the alliance between
Japan and Great Britain, fixing the capital ship ratios of the major powers,
and preventing the fortification of most islands in the Pacific, the Washington
Treaty dramatically altered the status quo and provided a new framework for
the development of Pacific strategy.

Mahan's theories provided the context for this development; throughout
the interwar period, the Navy conducted its planning within a strategic framework that emphasized naval power as a means to an end—the ultimate defeat
of Japan through isolation and blockade. The problem that planners had to
solve was how to move a large and powerful fleet across the Pacific in the face
of Japanese opposition, seize the necessary bases along the way, and defeat the
Japanese at a time and place of their choosing.

B. MISSION

The Navy's mission varied according to the potential enemy. In the American
system of strategic planning, each potential enemy was color-coded. Orange
was the color for Japan, and in the interwar period, the Navy was focused on
War Plan Orange, a war in the Pacific with Japan. The basic concept was
developed before World War I, but planning began in earnest between the
world wars. Of the numerous influences on the Navy's approach, none was
more important than the restrictive environment imposed by the adoption of
the treaty system in Washington in 1922.

The Washington Treaty and those that followed—the London Treaties
of 1930 and 1936—limited the size, number, and offensive power of combatant ships. The most famous of these limitations were the ratios imposed on
battleships and, ultimately, other classes of combatants. For every five battleships the Americans were allowed, the Japanese were permitted only three.
This 60 percent ratio was necessary to give the Navy a realistic chance of victory in a naval war with Japan. Prevailing theories held that a fleet would lose

10 percent of its strength for every thousand miles it traveled from its bases in wartime. Allowing for distance, the American fleet would need a 40 percent margin of superiority to fight a battle in the western Pacific on equal terms, resulting in a 60 percent ratio for Japan. Using similar logic, the Japanese Imperial Navy argued for a 70 percent ratio.

Bases further complicated the issue. In 1922, the Navy had western Pacific bases at Cavite in the Philippines and Guam in the Marianas. Plans were in place to improve their defenses. Article XIX of the Washington Treaty—known as the "fortification clause"—made it illegal to do so, and in light of the strategic situation after World War I, the inability to add fortifications made it virtually inevitable that in the event of war, Japan would isolate and overwhelm them.

This was because the Japanese, having joined the Allies in World War I, seized the German possessions in the Central Pacific, the Marshall and Caroline island groups. Japan was granted a mandate over these islands by the terms of the armistice agreements. Collectively, they became known as the "Mandates." They straddled the most direct route across the Pacific from the United States' West Coast bases to her Pacific possessions. Although Article XIX restricted fortification of these islands, the islands offered numerous anchorages and potential air bases from which an active defense could be mounted.

The Americans devoted extensive planning to these problems, and two basic approaches ultimately emerged. "Thrusters" argued for a rapid advance to the western Pacific to relieve the Philippines and bring the war to a rapid conclusion. They were opposed by "Cautionaries" who held that a more methodical, step-by-step approach was the proper strategy. The more cautious approach was ultimately adopted. However, the call of the Thrusters did not go unheeded, and advancements in tactics and technology allowed the Pacific Fleet to meld the two approaches.[1]

II. ORGANIZATION

A. COMMAND STRUCTURE
1. Administration
Civilian control always has been a fundamental principle of the United States armed services. Ultimate authority rests with the president, and in Franklin D. Roosevelt, the Navy had an enthusiastic supporter. Sworn into office in March 1933, he displayed an affinity for the Navy, tempered by his long service as assistant secretary of the Navy in Woodrow Wilson's administration.

Roosevelt was aided by adept bureaucrats. Administration of the Navy Department was the responsibility of the secretary of the Navy, who, prior to 1947, reported directly to the president. Roosevelt was aided by three secretaries who prepared the Navy for war and saw it through the conflict. Charles Edison served from November 1937 to January 1940; Frank Knox replaced Edison in July 1940 and served until his death in April 1944; and James Forrestal, from April 1944 until 1947, when he went on to serve as the first secretary of defense.

Assisting the secretary was a complex arrangement of civilian administrators and military officers. The assistant secretary was responsible for "shore establishment matters, civilian personnel in general, and the housekeeping of the Navy Department." Charles Edison created the office of undersecretary of the Navy. He saw the need for improved coordination in procurement, particularly in light of the extensive building programs initiated in the years before the war. Forrestal was appointed the first undersecretary of the Navy in August, 1940; he "excelled in the ability to analyze administrative problems and to think constructively about the business aspects of naval administration."[2]

The details of procurement were the responsibility of the Navy bureaus. At the dawn of the Roosevelt administration, there were nine bureaus—yards and docks, navigation, ordnance, construction and repair, engineering, supplies and accounts, medicine and surgery, and aeronautics. They provided technical advice to the civilian administrators and had responsibility for specific procurement functions in their area. The Bureau of Ordnance, for example, "was responsible for the armament of ships, for ammunition, and, in general, for the armor protection of ships."[3] Similarly, the Bureau of Aeronautics was responsible for matters related to aviation, including the procurement of aircraft.

In addition to convincing Congress to create the office of the undersecretary, Edison further increased efficiency by combining the Bureau of Engineering with the Bureau of Construction and Repair, resulting in the Bureau of Ships. This greatly simplified the procurement problem because now there was a single bureau responsible for the design and construction of ships.

Additional advice, on technical concerns and other matters, was provided by the General Board. Staffed with "senior and mid-grade officers of proven experience and promise," the board proved to be collaborative, open to experimentation, and flexible.[4] It helped shepherd the Navy through the restrictions of the interwar period and assisted innovation by influencing the number, type, and characteristics of the Navy's ships.

As talented as Knox and Forrestal were in their roles as secretary and undersecretary, they were greatly aided by an effective and efficient military command structure created after the outbreak of war. At the time of the attack on Pearl Harbor, three commanders in chief held command of the Navy's operating forces, the Atlantic, Pacific, and Asiatic. One of these officers was given overall command and designated Commander in Chief, U.S. Fleet (then

Photo 6.1. Admiral Ernest J. King, then commander of the Atlantic Fleet, and Secretary of the Navy Frank Knox aboard the cruiser *Augusta*, September 1941. (NH56978)

abbreviated CINCUS). Admiral Husband E. Kimmel, Commander in Chief of the Pacific Fleet, was also CINCUS.

Kimmel was relieved of command soon after the disastrous attack on Pearl Harbor. Knox chose not to appoint a direct successor; he recognized that a global conflict and the Navy's rapidly increasing size would necessitate a higher level of command to ensure proper coordination of naval forces across several oceans. This authority needed to be located in Washington, where the commander and his staff could work seamlessly with the civilian leadership and their counterparts in the Army. The result was Executive Order 8984 of 18 December 1941. Two days after issuing the order, Roosevelt chose Admiral Ernest J. King for the role, now abbreviated COMINCH. In March 1942 King's authority was increased; Executive Order 9096 combined the roles of commander in chief and chief of naval operations. King was the first to hold both positions simultaneously.

While Knox and Forrestal concentrated on vital administrative efforts, King ran the Navy's war. Forceful, driving, and frequently abrasive, King was unique. Described as a man of "superlative competence," King thoroughly embraced the aggressive nature of the Navy's tactical and operational doctrines.[5] He understood the importance of the initiative and drove his

subordinates to seize it and come to grips with the enemy. King did not toler-
ate ineffective admirals and relieved those whom he believed had failed.

However, King developed effective subordinates, delegating authority to
them and encouraging their initiative. These were important tenets of King's
command style and are evident in orders he issued while commanding the
Atlantic Fleet in 1941.

> I have been concerned for many years over the increasing tendency
> . . . of flag officers and other group commanders to issue orders and
> instructions in which their subordinates are told "how" as well as
> "what" to do. . . . If subordinates are deprived . . . of that training
> and experience which will enable them to act "on their own"—if
> they do not know, by constant practice, how to exercise "initiative of
> the subordinates"—if they are reluctant (afraid) to act because they
> are accustomed to detailed orders and instructions—if they are not
> habituated to think, to judge, to decide and to act for themselves in
> their several echelons of command—we shall be in a sorry case when
> the time of "active operations" [war] arrives.[6]

King's approach to command was not unique; it reflected cultural norms the
Navy had embraced for years, and the practice of delegating authority and
encouraging individual initiative was a fundamental component of the Navy's
tactical doctrines.

To salvage the morale of the Pacific Fleet after Pearl Harbor and ultimately take the war to Japan, Knox and Roosevelt chose Admiral Chester W.
Nimitz. Although not first in line for the position, Nimitz was an excellent
choice. A graduate of the Naval Academy class of 1905, Nimitz lacked King's
brusque nature but understood the importance of aggressive offensive action
and operational tempo. Nimitz was able to temper King's strategic vision with
methodical planning and execution.

Nimitz was also gifted when it came to personnel matters. As head of the
Bureau of Navigation, Nimitz had been responsible for personnel administration before the war. He was therefore familiar with the Navy's talent base, particularly its officer corps, and would ably select subordinates for the Pacific Fleet.
Like his superior, Nimitz was ruthless with ineffective subordinates but exhib-
ited a greater humanity in his approach and proved an inspirational leader.

To command the Atlantic Fleet, King chose Rear Admiral Royal E.
Ingersoll. Ingersoll placed fourth in the class of 1905, three ahead of his
classmate Nimitz. Ingersoll was responsible for the campaign against the
German U-boats until the formation of the dedicated Tenth Fleet in May
1943. "The public knew nothing of him; even to most of the Atlantic Fleet,

he remained a shadowy, almost a legendary figure. But to Admiral Ingersoll's sagacity . . . the Allied nations owed in large measure their progress against the submarine in 1942–1943."[7]

Command of the Asiatic Fleet remained in the hands of Admiral Thomas C. Hart, promoted to the position in July 1939. In prewar plans, the Asiatic Fleet had two objectives: to further the advance of the Pacific Fleet toward the western Pacific and, in conjunction with the Army, to defend the Philippines. Both of these would prove beyond its capabilities. Hart and his forces fell back and became part of the ill-fated American-British-Dutch-Australian (ABDA) Command. As the situation deteriorated in February 1942, Hart was recalled. Soon thereafter, his surviving ships were absorbed into other commands, and the Asiatic Fleet ceased to exist.

2. Personnel

The Navy's traditional approach to filling its ranks was to recruit volunteers. During the Great Depression of the 1930s, the Navy had a surplus of young men seeking to join the service and was able to accept only those candidates who had a high school diploma or equivalent. This led to a highly trained cadre of recruits, "giving the service some of the most capable enlisted men in its history."[8] The available surplus facilitated the Navy's rapid increase in size during the last years of peace. In 1939 the authorized strength was increased to 145,000; by the time of Pearl Harbor the number in service had grown to 290,000.

The situation with officers was far different. The primary source of new officers was the Naval Academy, and although graduating classes were larger than the number of officers retiring, there were too few officers available to meet peacetime demands, let alone those of war. This problem was particularly acute at higher grades. The number of officers that could be promoted to higher ranks was based on a percentage of officers available, not the number of open positions.

The issue was compounded by the fact that junior officers were promoted based on seniority rather than merit. Merit was a key component of promotion for the senior ranks; selection boards chose officers for these positions, ensuring the best advanced. No such system existed for junior officers. The problem became particularly acute in the 1930s as the large number of officers commissioned during World War I began to clog the system, holding back younger and more talented individuals.

In 1934 Representative Carl Vinson of Georgia introduced legislation that granted the secretary of the Navy more discretion. Roosevelt signed it into law. The percentage approach was discarded and selection boards were introduced for the lower grades. By removing the dependency on seniority, the best candidates would advance.

These changes alone did not resolve the issues. In 1935 the authorized strength of the officer corps was 6,531, but only 6,320 were in service. Nearly 8,000 would be needed to meet the requirements of new construction. Compromises were being made. "The acute demands for officers had meant reducing officers at the postgraduate school, the Naval War College, and other educational activities—thus meeting short-term requirements damaged long-term development."[9]

The number of authorized officers was increased again in 1938, but as the size of the fleet continued to grow, the number of officers lagged behind. The dramatic increase in the size of the Navy authorized in 1940 invalidated all prior approaches to resolving the issue, which forced the temporary augmentation of the regular officer corps with reserve, retired, and fitted officers. This measure, however, was still insufficient to meet the needs of wartime expansion.

Reserve officers were provided through the Naval Reserve Officers Training Corps (NROTC). Established in 1925, the program grew from humble beginnings to a large program during the war. There were nine civilian universities participating in 1940, which produced about two hundred reserve ensigns a year. By 1945, fifty-two universities participated and the number of graduating officers had increased tenfold.

As large as this output was, the Navy needed other sources. The V-12 program, a collaborative effort between the armed services and the American educational system to make "maximum utilization of the educational facilities of the United States in furthering the war effort," was the solution.[10] An evolution of earlier similar efforts, the program went into operation on 1 July 1943 and, in the last two years of the war, produced around 50,000 reserve officers.

To indoctrinate new recruits and prepare for war, the Navy took its ships and men through an annual series of exercises, which gradually increased in scale and complexity until culminating in the "Fleet Problem" held in the late winter or early spring. These annual exercises rated the ability of each ship relative to her peers; they covered areas such as gunnery, signaling, engineering, and torpedoes. There were prizes for the winners of these competitions, which augmented one's prestige and pocketbook. The goal was to improve efficiency by introducing healthy competition, but the system encouraged preparing for the annual competition, not the challenge of war.

In many respects, the Navy's training regimens were heavily dependent on the knowledge and talents of individuals; specific approaches varied from ship to ship until the demands of war forced greater standardization and uniformity. Nowhere was this more apparent than the process for making a ship ready for service during the shakedown cruise. Before the war, this process was

PHOTO 6.2. Battleship *Oklahoma* leading the U.S. battle line during a prewar exercise. (NARA)

managed by the captain and his senior officers. For important new vessels, the most talented officers were selected, and they, based on their knowledge and experience, brought the ship up to the desired level of efficiency. Different ships experimented with different techniques.

The Bureau of Personnel established Instructor Training Schools in 1943, which began to formalize the process of making a ship and its crew ready for action. The problem of how to conduct effective training had been a thorny one; there was a need to impart lessons from the fighting forces, but there was no established procedure to do so, and there were too few men available with wartime experience. By 1943, men from the fleet were rotating to shore billets. Many were assigned to the new schools where they learned to be instructors and share their knowledge and experience.

3. Intelligence

The Navy recognized the importance of intelligence and took steps to acquire and disseminate it at multiple levels and in numerous forms. The Office of Naval Intelligence (ONI), a subordinate to the Chief of Naval Operations, was mainly a "post office" in World War II, "charged with forwarding Intelligence reports and other data to the activity in the Navy Department most likely to need and make use of the information."[11] The communications division would do the famous work of breaking enemy codes and decrypting their messages.

Work began prewar. Practice was obtained in early Fleet Problems; each side developed ciphers and attempted to break those of their opponents. In the 1930s this practice was curtailed because it was feared this would reveal too much about the Navy's capabilities and intentions to any foreign groups that might be listening in. Code breaking moved onshore, and by September 1940 the Navy was able to read Japanese diplomatic messages in their latest cipher.

The Imperial Japanese Navy's codes proved more resistant but ultimately succumbed, leading to a series of intelligence coups. Aided by a delayed transition to a new cipher in 1942, the cryptologists under Commander Joseph Rochefort broke the Japanese fleet code they called JN-25 and gained insight into Japanese plans before the Battle of Midway, which allowed Nimitz to spring a trap with his remaining carriers. Another decoded message led to the ambushing of Admiral Yamamoto Isoroku, commander of the Combined Fleet, in April 1943.

Code breaking also played an important role in the Battle of the Atlantic. German ciphers proved more difficult to crack than those of the Japanese, but the Americans and their British allies were aided by the great volume of traffic necessitated by Germany's centralized control of her U-boat fleet. Eventually the German codes were broken, which allowed the Allies to route convoys around concentrations of U-boats and send hunter-killer groups to destroy them.

Before the German codes were compromised, signals intelligence methods were used to locate their submarines. The Navy had worked extensively on direction-finding techniques during the interwar period, experimenting with specific approaches in the Fleet Problems. The introduction of high-frequency (three MHz and above) radio communications made this more difficult, but the Navy responded by developing high-frequency direction finders that worked on these frequencies. Cutting-edge technology at the time, they were being installed on ships in the years immediately before the war.

Direction-finding stations were also established on shore. When the United States entered the war, a network of these stations existed on the Atlantic coast and they were quickly put to good use. Direction finding was also used against the Japanese; in June 1944, during the preliminary stages of the Battle of the Philippine Sea, direction finders estimated the position of the Japanese main body.

Signals intelligence work was complemented by efforts to capture, translate, and exploit enemy material. There are several noteworthy examples. In November 1944, the Japanese heavy cruiser *Nachi*, flagship of Vice Admiral Shima Kiyohide's Second Striking Force at the Battle of Leyte Gulf, was sunk in Manila Bay. The wreck was located and examined by a field team from ONI in April 1945, who found a treasure trove of orders and plans. In the Atlantic, the famous capture of *U-505* in May 1944 was a similar intelligence coup, providing the Navy with not only the latest German ciphers but also an operational U-boat.

Intelligence was disseminated to the combatant forces through numerous means. Real-time information provided by code breaking was distributed through the code name "Magic"; to limit the chances of the enemy discovering the vulnerability, only select individuals had access. Direction-finding information was also provided in real time but was not guarded with the same precautions. Less time-sensitive material was issued in a variety of ways, including regular publications issued on a weekly basis such as *ONI Weekly* and the Joint Intelligence Command Pacific Operating Areas bulletin *Weekly Intelligence*.

Once battles were over, the Navy did its best to accumulate and evaluate all available information and reconcile action reports with other sources of intelligence. Early failures taught the Navy to be skeptical of contact and battle reports. This led to more intense training in recognition and more realistic assessments of enemy losses. After the Battle of Kula Gulf in July 1943, for example, Rear Admiral Walden L. Ainsworth believed that his force had sunk six enemy destroyers and forced another to beach. Actual Japanese losses were two destroyers. The Navy's assessment was not far off this mark, estimating that three destroyers had been lost. Critical evaluation of battle reports prevented unrealistic assessments of enemy losses and aided a more effective evaluation of the Navy's own capabilities.

B. DOCTRINE

Over the course of the interwar period, the Navy developed a sophisticated tactical doctrine based on experimentation in live exercises and tabletop maneuvers at the Naval War College. One of the reasons these maneuvers and exercises proved effective tools was the flexibility provided by the Navy's approach to doctrinal development. Low-level commanders were encouraged and expected to come up with specific doctrines for their own forces that reflected their strengths and weaknesses as well as those of the enemy. This led to experimentation and innovation in tactical exercises as commanders attempted to develop more effective doctrines.

1. Surface Warfare

The focus of surface warfare doctrine before the war was fleet action, or, as it was termed, "major tactics." An important milestone in the development of major tactics was the publication in 1930 of *Tentative Fleet Dispositions and Battle Plans*, which introduced the basic framework for all the major action plans the Navy would employ throughout the war.

The most significant innovation that the new plans introduced was the way in which they could be communicated to the fleet. Each plan had a short designation so it could be quickly transmitted to all the vessels and immediately put into action. Different plans could be used depending on the specific circumstances or stage of the battle. The Navy expected to be able to react quickly to developing situations and take advantage of fleeting opportunities with this flexibility.

These plans were tested under realistic conditions during the Fleet Problems of 1930 (X and XI) and found to be quite effective. The positive experience led to their formal adoption. In 1934, they appeared in an official manual, *F.T.P. 142 General Tactical Instructions*. The plans were repeated in the 1940 update to the same manual, *F.T.P. 188 General Tactical Instructions*. Details of the 1940 plans are summarized in table 6.1.

The division of the battle plans into four specific range bands reflected assumptions about Japanese tactics and the perceived strengths and weaknesses of battleships on both sides. The Navy believed that it had a significant advantage at extreme range; its five most modern battleships—the "Big Five" of the *Colorado* and *Tennessee* classes—could engage at those ranges. The Japanese had only two ships that could fight at extreme range. Long range was disadvantageous; all Japanese battleships could engage at long ranges, but the Navy's battle line, with gun elevations on the older ships restricted to fifteen degrees, would have to rely on the Big Five. Prior to modification of the older Japanese battleships, this assumption was correct. Only *Nagato* and her sister *Mutsu* had extreme range capability. However, as Japan modified its older ships, they were all given the increased gun elevation necessary to reach extreme ranges.

Starting in the late 1920s, the older U.S. battleships were also modernized and given increased gun elevation, which allowed them to reach extreme ranges. Extreme range-fire at the outset of an action to disrupt an enemy deployment or secure an initial advantage received significant emphasis.

TABLE 6.1 Standard Battle Plans

Plan	Engagement Range in thousands of yards	Deployment Course	Objective	Light Force Instructions
1E	Extreme, 27 and beyond	Parallel to enemy	Attainment of initial advantage before enemy can close to unfavorable ranges	Defend battle line
2E	Extreme, 27 and beyond	Opposite to enemy	Attainment of initial advantage before enemy can close to unfavorable ranges	Defend battle line
1L	Long, 21–27	Parallel to enemy	Shortening the time during which battle line may be compelled to engage at unfavorable ranges	Attack enemy battle line
2L	Long, 21–27	Opposite to enemy	Shortening the time during which battle line may be compelled to engage at unfavorable ranges	Attack enemy battle line
1M	Medium, 17–21	Parallel to enemy	Continue engagement at favorable ranges	Defend battle line
2M	Medium, 17–21	Opposite to enemy	Continue engagement at favorable ranges	Defend battle line
1C	Close, under 17	Parallel to enemy	Concentration on enemy battle line	Attack enemy battle line
2C	Close, under 17	Opposite to enemy	Concentration on enemy battle line	Attack enemy battle line

"Fire should be opened, normally, at the maximum range at which an effective fire can be delivered under the conditions which exist at the time. The advantage of an initial superiority is so great that every effort should be made to establish early hitting."[12] Fire at these ranges required aerial spotting, and although hits would be fewer, the damage those hits could inflict would be great. Steeply plunging shells would penetrate deck armor and detonate in the vitals of the target.

Figure 6.1 graphically illustrates the advantages of long-range plunging fire. The large area of Zone 2, in which an opponent's deck armor would be penetrated, dwarfs Zone 5, which represents the area of belt armor penetration with an intact projectile, one that could explode inside the target. Zone 5 is small because of the close ranges necessary to penetrate thick belt armor, and it is narrow because the Navy's projectiles were originally not designed to penetrate such armor at angles greater than fifteen degrees. In Zone 4, penetration of the belt would occur, but the projectile would break up; little damage would result. Zone 3 represents the "immune zone," ranges and angles at which penetration would not occur.

Even after all the front-line battleships had been modernized, the Navy considered the long-range band disadvantageous. The Japanese were expected to fight at these ranges, and the Navy planned to disrupt their preparations. If forced to fight at long range, aerial and light force attacks would limit the effectiveness of Japanese fire and allow the Navy's battleships to close to more decisive ranges.

Once medium ranges were achieved, the air force and light forces would hold back and allow the guns of the battle line to engage the enemy. At these ranges, battleship gunnery would be decisive and the Navy's superior numbers would bring victory.

Engagement at close ranges would be more risky; while the Navy's battle line enjoyed a clear superiority, attacks of light forces would be very effective and difficult to stop. A chaotic engagement would ensue, which would be to the advantage of the inferior force. To make the most of any potential opportunities, planes and light forces would attack immediately.

No matter what the range, the Navy's battle formation would be generally similar to that presented in figure 6.2, a linear formation with the battleships at the center and light forces on either flank. Dedicated attack and defense groups would be provided if the necessary forces were available. If not, these roles would be combined.

In the months before the war, a sophisticated plan based on these principles was outlined by Admiral Kimmel. Should war erupt in the Pacific, he intended to strike into the Marshalls and initiate a fleet action. He planned to counteract the powerful battle cruisers and heavy cruisers the Japanese were

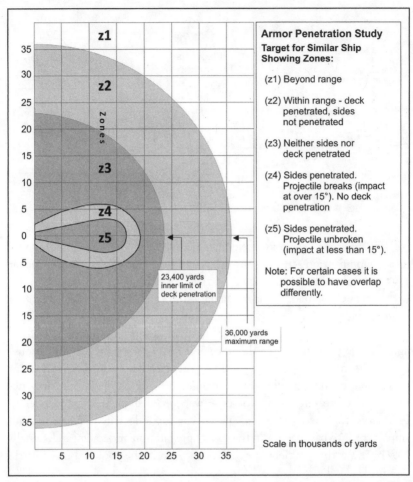

Armor Penetration Study

Target for Similar Ship Showing Zones:

(z1) Beyond range

(z2) Within range - deck penetrated, sides not penetrated

(z3) Neither sides nor deck penetrated

(z4) Sides penetrated. Projectile breaks (impact at over 15°). No deck penetration

(z5) Sides penetrated. Projectile unbroken (impact at less than 15°).

Note: For certain cases it is possible to have overlap differently.

23,400 yards inner limit of deck penetration

36,000 yards maximum range

Scale in thousands of yards

Source: Commander G. L. Schuyler, "Recent Developments in Ordnance," Naval War College, Newport, RI, 12 March 1924, Illustrative Diagram, 16. Box 11, Strategic Plans Division Records, Record Group 38, National Archives.

sure to place in their van by reversing direction at a critical moment and initiating a reverse action. Kimmel would conceal the maneuver with light force attacks on the Japanese van and center.

Like the *Gefechtskehrtwendung*, the battle turn-away performed by the Germans at Jutland, Kimmel's reversal of course would begin at the rear of his line. And just as the Germans' turn had left the British wondering what had happened, Kimmel expected the maneuver to take the Japanese by surprise. He planned to use the momentary confusion to fall on the rear of the Japanese line and crush it decisively. With the rear of the Japanese line in disarray, victory was expected to follow.

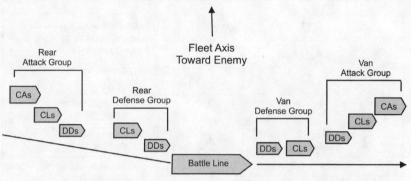

Source: U.S.F. 10, Current Tactical Orders and Doctrine, United States Fleet, 1941, Diagram Number One, 33, NHC, WW2 CF, Box 270.

The basic structure of these prewar plans continued to be employed with minor modifications throughout the war. They were a core feature of wartime tactical publications. However, the lack of a major surface action during the war prevented a proper evaluation of the Navy's prewar investment in major tactics.

"Minor tactics" were the subject of much less attention before the war, and the Navy's approach to the development of minor tactics was seriously tested within its first year. The flexible approach that stressed individual initiative and relied on small task force commanders for battle doctrine was ineffective. The pressures of a two-ocean war forced ships and commanders to be thrown together without adequate time for indoctrination. As a result, ships went into battle without the proper preparation and fought individually. Nowhere was this problem more apparent than in the confused night battles off Guadalcanal.

Poor planning and inadequate indoctrination resulted in high losses. A new approach was needed; planning and indoctrination for minor tactics could no longer be left to commanders in the field. The solution was centralized development—the fleet would create plans that could be learned by all ships.

Nimitz's Pacific Fleet was the first to realize this need and the result was the publication of *P.A.C. 10* in June 1943. The office of CINCPAC was now driving doctrinal development for the Navy. The challenge presented by the Japanese had forced innovation, and rather than waiting for changes to be assimilated by the traditional agencies that developed doctrine—the Naval War College and COMINCH—Nimitz led the way. King followed his lead. *U.S.F. 10A*, a revised version of *P.A.C. 10* issued to the entire Navy, was issued in February 1944. It was followed by *U.S.F. 10B* in May 1945, which included additional wartime lessons from the Pacific Fleet.

These manuals expanded on the foundation provided by prewar material. They adapted the existing battle plans to smaller task forces and provided the ability to throw disparate ships and task groups together for battle at a moment's notice. This was essential to the success of the Central Pacific offensive initiated by the invasion of the Gilbert Islands in November 1943.

During the offensive, ships were organized into carrier task groups. These were very effective for making the most of the carrier's air power, but not for combating surface threats. In order to fight a surface action, ships would have to be taken from their carrier groups and brought together with no chance for indoctrination. *P.A.C. 10* and its successors obviated the need for such indoctrination.

The ultimate test of the new approach to minor tactics came at the Battle of Leyte Gulf in October 1944. On 24 October, the Japanese "southern force" was approaching the gulf and expected to enter through Surigao Strait that night. Vice Admiral Thomas C. Kinkaid, commander of the Seventh Fleet and the Leyte invasion forces, ordered Rear Admiral Jesse B. Oldendorf, commander of his surface action force, to block the strait. Oldendorf employed ships from four different task groups; he coordinated their actions through a succinct battle plan and a typical formation from *U.S.F. 10A*. The Japanese southern force was all but annihilated in the Battle of Surigao Strait.

2. Aviation

The development of the Navy's aviation doctrine was channeled by the agreement struck between Chief of Naval Operations Admiral William V. Pratt and Army Chief of Staff General Douglas MacArthur in 1931. Under the terms of the agreement, the Army assumed responsibility for coast defense, and the Navy agreed not to develop large land-based planes. Instead, the Navy focused on fleet aviation, planes that move with the fleet across the oceans. This led to the development of carrier planes and tender-serviced seaplanes.

The rapid pace of technological advancement, in particular the increasing size, power, and range of aircraft, made the development of doctrine a complex problem. Tactics had to remain fluid; the next generation of aircraft could render specific approaches obsolete. However, a fundamental guiding principle of the Navy's aerial doctrine remained a constant—the need to "attack effectively first."[13]

Early experimentation with aircraft carriers illustrated that the best way to win a carrier duel was to locate and attack the enemy carrier, disabling its flight deck. Once a strike was in the air, it was difficult to intercept and even more difficult to stop. Antiaircraft techniques were unsophisticated. Radar did not exist, and the concept of fighter direction had yet to be invented.

The bombers were expected to get through, and in the tactical exercises of the day, they often did.

When airframes were light and bomb loads small, planes focused on achieving aerial superiority by disabling enemy carriers and then augmenting the accuracy of battleships in the main action. Aerial superiority could be decisive. Without aerial spotting, the maximum range of battleship guns was about 22,000 yards; with it, battleships could fire to the limits of their range. In mock battles, the side that achieved aerial superiority was almost always victorious.

As larger and more powerful airframes increased the potential of carrier aircraft and made them powerful weapons, they became a core element of the Navy's offensive doctrine. In fleet exercises, carrier aircraft began to contribute to the destruction of capital ships, damaging them before and during gunnery actions. Carriers themselves began to operate independently from the main fleet, using their higher speeds to avoid detection and seek out their opposite numbers.

For much of the interwar period, the Navy had only two large carriers capable of leading an independent task force. These were *Lexington* and *Saratoga*, the sisters built on battle cruiser hulls. In most tactical exercises, they were on opposite sides. This made for effective adversarial investigations of carrier tactics but prevented the Navy from developing more sophisticated doctrines for the coordination of multiple carriers.

The positive and negative aspects of this approach were displayed at Midway. Although *Yorktown*, *Enterprise*, and *Hornet* were close enough to coordinate their activities, each carrier launched its strike independently. Those squadrons that arrived at the target—and not all of them did—attacked piecemeal. The contrast with Japanese tactics is significant. The Americans did not demonstrate the ability to coordinate the activities of multiple carriers in a single task force until late 1943.

By that time, fighter direction techniques enabled by modern radars and combat information centers had dramatically increased the defensive capabilities of American carrier task forces. These new techniques were the outgrowth of wartime experience—hard lessons learned in the battles of 1942—and cooperation with the British. They were incorporated in the new Pacific Fleet tactical manual, P.A.C. 10, and its successors. These new techniques changed the paradigm of carrier battles and allowed the decisive defeat of Japanese attacks in the Battle of the Philippine Sea in June 1944.

Carrier bombers were not the only aerial striking force the Navy possessed. Before the war, there were high expectations for the seaplane patrol bomber. Defensive machine guns would fend off enemy fighters while the sophisticated

Norden bombsight and salvo fire—an entire flight of planes dropping their bombs at once—were expected to solve the problem of accuracy.

Neither assumption was correct, although the PBY Catalinas of the Asiatic Fleet's Patrol Wing Ten tried to prove the theory early in the war. Japanese fighters shot them down and broke up their formations. Bombs delivered from high altitude against ships invariably missed. In their final attacks, the planes of Patrol Wing Ten resorted to individual heroics and glide bombing.

But the concept of the patrol bomber survived and proved more effective in modified circumstances. Radar and the cover of darkness gave the PBY new life and the "Black Cats" dogged Japanese ships in the Solomons, tailing them, reporting their movements, and occasionally attacking.

This mix of reconnaissance and attack was a hallmark of the Navy's patrol bombers. The longer-ranged PB4Y, the naval version of the B-24 Liberator, demonstrated it against Japanese reconnaissance aircraft, shooting them down when encountered. Even in these isolated aerial combats, the recurring theme of the Navy's doctrine—aggressive offensive action against the enemy to seize the initiative and keep him off balance—is evident.

3. Antisubmarine

The Navy's antisubmarine warfare doctrine was, like its battle doctrine, focused on the main fleet and its movement through the Pacific. The primary tools for detecting and thwarting submarine attacks were destroyers equipped with the latest sonar and airplane patrols over the fleet.

These tools proved very effective in fleet exercises. Submarine commanders found it difficult to approach close enough for an attack without being detected and declared sunk. The solution was to attack at night—when the planes would be grounded—and on the surface. This was tried in Fleet Problem XV of 1934 and it worked, but it was not adopted as a model for future attacks because of the dangers involved and a mistaken belief that it would be less effective in wartime.

The Germans illustrated the folly of this assumption, and the success of their submarines in the first months of war came as a shock. The Navy reacted according to doctrine and focused its efforts on offensive patrols, but these proved ineffective. A convoy system had to be introduced, and offensive patrols were abandoned.

The offensive doctrine remained dormant for two years, but in 1943, as more escorts, escort carriers, and planes became available, a renewed emphasis was placed on hunting the Axis sea-wolves. Escort carrier groups began to be freed from their convoys so they could pursue U-boats, leading to numerous successes. Similar groups were employed in the Pacific to destroy Japanese submarine pickets. In concert with these surface task forces, patrol planes aggressively pressured Axis submarines. Specific emphasis was placed on the Bay of Biscay, and in one six-day period between 28 July and 2 August 1943, Navy planes sank nine German boats in those waters.

4. Submarine

Officially, the Navy's submarine doctrine emphasized the coordinated use of submarines with the fleet, for scouting operations ahead of the fleet's advance and for attacks on enemy surface combatants. Commerce destruction was deemphasized. International law held that submarines must surface and declare their presence before attacking merchant ships, thereby ceding their best advantage—stealth. In exercises, submarines did not prove particularly effective in their assigned roles. The available vessels were too slow to operate as effective scouts, and coordination with the main body of the fleet was very difficult. Attacks on protected warships were relatively ineffective; the slow speed of the submarines made it difficult to get into an attack position. If they achieved it, inner air patrols forced them below the surface outside of range or sank them as they approached. These problems had not been resolved by the time war was declared.

Ultimately, the solution would be to free submarines from these roles and allow them to attack Japanese commerce. After Pearl Harbor, national outrage made it easy to discard prewar objections to unrestricted submarine warfare, and the obvious vulnerability of Japan to such a campaign—which had been noted by Navy planners immediately after World War I—led to its immediate adoption. The campaign was undertaken by the new "fleet submarines," the ships of the *Gato*, *Balao*, and *Tench* classes, which started joining the fleet in 1941. Their precursors of the 1930s, starting with the *Porpoise* class of 1934, had evolved along with the new Torpedo Data Computer, a fire-control system for submarine torpedoes. Designed to overcome the deficiencies apparent in interwar exercises, the new boats were larger, faster, and well suited for the Pacific. The new computers helped make them even more deadly.

Revised doctrines and new technologies allowed submarines to operate effectively in the traditional roles of scouting for and attacking enemy warships. Instead of operating with the fleet as they had in prewar exercises, submarine scouts were positioned by commanders ashore. They monitored choke points and concentrated in areas where the enemy was likely to be found. Radar gave them better "eyes." Submarines made valuable contributions in the battles of Philippine Sea and Leyte Gulf, sinking two Japanese carriers and sending numerous contact reports.

5. Amphibious Operations

The Navy recognized that the Philippines and Guam were likely to be lost soon after the outbreak of war, and a campaign against Japan would have to be supported by the capture of strategic positions as the Navy moved west. An advance through the Japanese Mandates, where small atolls could be turned into mazes of pillboxes and machine gun nests, would require the ability to land forces directly into the teeth of opposed defenses. The concept of an "assault landing" became an element of Navy and Marine Corps doctrine. "In 1933 the Fleet Marine Force was established and a series of annual fleet landing exercises was begun. They dealt with problems of transportation of troops in naval vessels, of ship-to-shore movement, of assault landings, of naval gunfire support, of aviation support, and of development of suitable landing craft."[14]

The creation of the Fleet Marine Force (FMF) was an important milestone in the development of amphibious warfare doctrine. It was an integral part of the fleet, which meant that it could be dedicated to training, preparing, and equipping for amphibious assaults. This helped focus the Marine Corps on its role in a Pacific campaign. The FMF grew from a complement of two regiments and 3,186 men in 1933, to two divisions and 22,786 men by February 1941.

The concept of amphibious operations was further augmented in 1934; in that year, the Marine Corps's school published *Tentative Manual for Landing Operations*. The new manual considered the fleet a supporting element for the landing forces, a revolutionary concept. In 1938 the Navy officially adopted it by publishing a revised version of the manual, *F.T.P. 167 Landing Operations Doctrine*. Unfortunately, when war came, the Navy was unprepared to implement it.

The invasion of Guadalcanal in August 1942 illustrated the problem. The Navy lacked the strength to provide fleet support for the landings long enough to ensure that the captured airfield was operational, particularly after the decimation of the covering force at the Battle of Savo Island. As a result, the Marines were left to fend for themselves in the face of Japanese countermoves.

The first true test of the new "assault landing" concept would come at Tarawa Atoll in the Gilberts in November 1943. The assault on Tarawa illustrated how far the Navy had come since Guadalcanal. At Tarawa, ships and planes were dedicated to the capture of the objective and remained until it was secure. Prewar planning and doctrine helped lead to this success, but significant improvements were still necessary. Tarawa was a costly first step; future assaults would benefit from its lessons.

Future attacks would also benefit from the growing number of specialized amphibious assault ships. Prewar exercises had shown the need for these types, and by the start of the war, the first attack transports and specialized landing craft were coming into service. Tarawa saw the introduction of the tracked landing vehicle, the LVT. Additional types would join the fleet in vast numbers as the war went on. Most carried men and material, some were dedicated fire support ships, and still others housed the communication facilities necessary to coordinate massive amphibious operations.

The U.S. Army was an active participant in the development of amphibious doctrine and operations. With the fall of France in 1940, it became apparent that the war, when it came, would require amphibious operations against continents as well as Pacific islands. There was competition for resources in the immediate prewar period, but a coherent plan was quickly established. Responsibility for operations was logically divided, with the Army taking the lead for continental assaults—such as those against North Africa, Sicily, Italy, and France—while the Navy and Marines led the island campaigns in the Central Pacific. Southern Pacific operations, culminating in the landings in the Philippines, were led by General MacArthur's joint command.

6. Trade Protection

The Navy's approach to commerce protection was limited by the emphasis given to fleet action. While the importance of trade and commerce to strategic power was recognized, the best protection was considered a powerful fleet that could ensure dominance of the seas. Direct protection of commerce was neglected by the Navy in the interwar period.

Nowhere is this oversight more apparent than in the success enjoyed by Operation Drumbeat, the German submarine offensive against the American East Coast. The Atlantic Fleet, still effectively under the direction of Admiral King, relied on "offensive patrols by surface and air forces, protected lanes, and independently routed coastal shipping to defeat the U-boat menace."[15] The result was a disaster for merchant shipping and a second "happy time" for the U-boats.

The wartime Navy had to quickly relearn existing lessons from World War I and new lessons from its British ally to counter the U-boats. Convoys were hastily introduced, but the lack of attention given tactics, techniques, and weapons in the interwar period meant that more than a year would elapse before adequate means were in place to fight the U-boats on equal terms.

However, the Navy did prove capable of protecting strategically important convoys for vital operations. Nothing illustrates this better than the success of Operation Torch, the invasion of North Africa in November 1942. Both the training for the operation and the invasion itself were performed without major interference from enemy submarines.

By mid-1943 the Navy and its British ally were beginning to master the situation in the Atlantic. Adequate numbers of escort vessels—the new destroyer-escorts—were becoming available; escort carriers, purpose-built to provide air cover for convoys, were joining the fleet; and longer-ranged land-based planes were being deployed. This new equipment was augmented by better training, new weapons, microwave radar, and more effective intelligence. Losses of merchant vessels declined, and U-boat losses increased dramatically.

7. Communications

In the interwar period, the Navy struggled with the best way to conduct tactical communications. Fleet Problem I of 1923 illustrated the limitations of traditional methods—signal flags, semaphores, and blinker tubes. They could not be seen far enough away for effective control of a large fleet. Searchlights offered a temporary solution, but the Navy needed a short-range, super-high-frequency radio system.

Test super-frequency radio sets were installed on two battleships in 1929, but it took six more years of experimentation before the Navy was ready to issue contracts for such equipment. The CXL set was available the next year. It worked well in fleet tests but lacked the required security; its signals could be intercepted "well beyond the horizon."[16]

Talk Between Ships (TBS) was the solution. Introduced in 1939, it was created by the Naval Research Laboratory and produced by RCA. It operated on a frequency range of sixty to eighty megahertz, which gave it a shorter range and ensured that its transmissions would be more difficult to intercept than those of the CXL. By 1941 TBS was installed on all of the Navy's major combatants; it was the primary ship-to-ship communication mechanism for all of World War II.

III. MATERIEL

A. SHIPS

The treaty system restricted the Navy's ability to build a balanced fleet. As a result, the ships of the fleet on the eve of war can be grouped into three broad categories. "The first, built before, during, and right after World War I, was composed mostly of battleships, destroyers, and submarines. The second, whose shape was molded by the [Washington] Treaty . . . of 1922, was composed almost entirely of heavy cruisers, two battle cruisers converted to carriers, and one aircraft carrier designed and built as such. The third, influenced by both the London Naval Treaty of 1930 and the Great Depression of the 1930s, consisted mostly of light cruisers, destroyers, two battleships, three aircraft carriers, and submarines."[17]

The centerpiece of the Navy's strength immediately before the war was the battle line. Composed of the twelve most modern battleships—the *Nevada*, *Pennsylvania*, *New Mexico*, *Tennessee*, and *Colorado* classes—they could all fire to extreme ranges. The five newest remained much as they had on commissioning. The others had all been rebuilt with increased gun elevation, augmented deck armor, enhanced fire control systems, and new machinery. Most of these ships were sunk or crippled at Pearl Harbor.

Three older battleships remained in commission, *New York*, *Texas*, and *Arkansas*. They were relegated to duties in the Atlantic at the outbreak of war. These old ships gave sterling service as shore bombardment and convoy escort vessels but would have been of limited use in a surface action.

All of these battleships were too slow to keep pace with carrier task forces; fast battleships were necessary for the modern form of mobile warfare the Navy would pioneer in the Pacific. Ten fast battleships were built, divided among three classes—two of the *North Carolina* class, four *South Dakota*, and four *Iowa*. The combination of advanced fire-control systems, radars, and "super-heavy" shells made these ships among the most powerful in the world.

The Navy's carriers on the eve of war were a mixed group. The two large carriers—*Lexington* and *Saratoga*—were conversions on battle cruiser hulls. They were useful platforms for experimentation but an inefficient use of tonnage; they carried no more planes than later carriers half their size—in peacetime, *Lexington* carried seventy-nine planes on a full load displacement of 43,000 tons. *Wasp*, with a full load displacement of only 19,100 tons, carried seventy-four. The Navy's first purpose-built carrier, *Ranger*, proved to be too small. She was relegated to the Atlantic and dedicated to training purposes after 1943. *Wasp* was similar but larger and capable enough for Pacific operations. *Yorktown*, *Enterprise*, and *Hornet* were larger still. Although limited by treaty, they were very efficient designs.

In 1943 the new fleet carriers of the *Essex* class began to appear. Larger and improved versions of the *Yorktown* group, they were the first carriers freed of treaty restrictions. *Essex* and her sisters were the core of the fast carrier task forces that ultimately took the war to Japan.

The fleet carriers were augmented by an emergency program to build light carriers on cruiser hulls. These ships, the *Independence* class, filled out the task groups and freed the larger carriers for strike operations by assisting with combat air patrol and scouting duties.

Air cover for convoys, auxiliaries, and antisubmarine warfare (ASW) hunter-killer teams was provided by escort carriers. The Navy built seventy-seven of these ships in six classes during the war; many more were built for the Royal Navy. They performed vital service in both the Atlantic and Pacific.

UNITED STATES NAVY
Order of Battle 7 December 1941

FLEET COMMANDS

Pearl Harbor

| Pacific Fleet | (Kimmel) |

Norfolk	Cavite
Atlantic Fleet	Asiatic Fleet
(King)	(Hart)
8xBB (1r)	1xCA
4xCV	2xCL*
1xCVE	13xDD (2r)
5xCA	29xSS (2r)
8xCL (1r)	*from
99xDD (1r)	Pacific
58xSS (r)	Fleet

	Battle Force		Scouting Force
	(Anderson)		(Newton)
	9xBB (2r)		12xCA (2r)
	3xCV		1xDD
	9xCL (3r)		24xSS (4r)
	49xDD (8r)		
	8xDM (4r)		
	13xDMS (1r)		

NAVAL DISTRICTS

Boston	New York	Philadelphia	Norfolk	Charleston	Jacksonville
1st	3rd	4th	5th	6th	7th
(Tarrant)	(Andrews)	(Watson)	(Simons)	(Allen)	(Allen)
5xDMS			2xPG		
2xPG					

New Orleans	Chicago	S. Juan, PR	San Diego	S. Francisco	Seattle
8th	9th	10th	11th	12th	13th
(Allen)	(Downes)	(Hoover)	(Blakely)	(Greenslade)	(Freeman)
			4xDD		5xDD

Honolulu	Balboa, CZ	Cavite, PI
14th	15th	16th
(Bloch)	(Sadler)	(Rockwell)
2xPG	10xDD	2xPG
	1xPG	

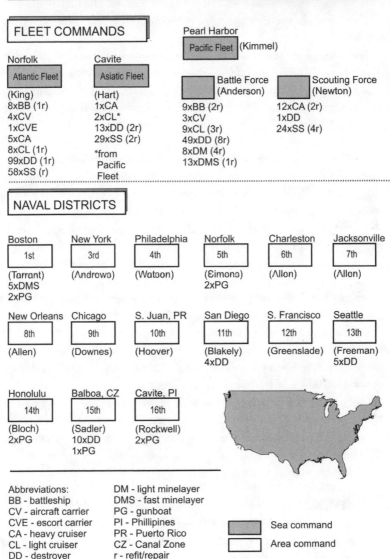

Abbreviations:
BB - battleship
CV - aircraft carrier
CVE - escort carrier
CA - heavy cruiser
CL - light cruiser
DD - destroyer

DM - light minelayer
DMS - fast minelayer
PG - gunboat
PI - Phillipines
PR - Puerto Rico
CZ - Canal Zone
r - refit/repair

Sea command

Area command

The Navy's treaty cruisers—heavy and light cruisers built to the 10,000-ton limit of the interwar treaties—were the core of the mixed task forces that blunted Japanese bombardment and resupply operations at Guadalcanal. The Treaty Cruisers can be grouped into three broad categories. The first attempts to meet the limitations, the eight ships of the *Pensacola* and *Northampton* classes, were underweight and emphasized firepower over protection. The next batch had increased armor with no loss of offensive capabilities; these were the nine ships in the *Portland* and *New Orleans* classes. The final evolution of prewar designs was the *Brooklyn* class of light cruisers and their heavy near-sister, *Wichita*.

Before the treaty restrictions were lifted, another type was introduced, the small cruisers of the *Atlanta* class. These were light ships with large batteries of dual-purpose weapons; unlike most American cruisers, they mounted torpedoes. *Atlanta* and her sisters were useful as antiaircraft vessels but less effective in surface engagements.

With treaty regulations lifted, construction emphasized more balanced designs. The *Cleveland* class of light cruisers and *Baltimore* class of heavy cruisers reflected the best of prewar experience. Wartime lessons led to minor changes in the designs, resulting in slight variations between the first ships produced and the final ones completed after the war.

During most of the interwar period, the Navy relied on the flush-decked destroyers of World War I vintage; some of these were still in service at the outbreak of war. Starting in 1934, a new series of vessels began to replace them. The *Farragut* class and those that followed were built in small groups; they experimented with different torpedo and gun arrangements in an attempt to improve on the original design. The *Sims* class began to join the fleet in 1938. This was the first with the highly successful dual-purpose Mk 37 director. The *Benson*, *Livermore*, and *Fletcher* classes built on this model and formed the core of the wartime destroyer force. The late-war *Sumner* and *Gearing* classes were larger and introduced twin dual-purpose mountings.

Submarines, like destroyers, were built in small classes as war approached. Existing submarines were too small for the demands of war in the Pacific. Large submarines built in the 1920s and 1930s proved too unwieldy. Ultimately, the Navy focused on the "fleet submarine" introduced in the *Gato* class and built them in large numbers.

B. AVIATION

The Navy established an effective partnership with industry during the interwar period that allowed it to keep abreast of the rapid developments in aircraft technology and harness them for military use. A key component of this was the purchase of different, and often competing, aircraft to fulfill the same roles. The Navy purchased small numbers of the most modern designs and refrained from mass production of standardized types until the international situation deteriorated. The results were impressive. By 1943 the Navy was able to field very large numbers of superior aircraft designed in the final years of peace.

1. Ship-based

The Navy used four basic types of ship-based aircraft. Aircraft carriers accounted for three of these—fighters, dive-bombers, and torpedo-bombers. The fourth was the observation seaplane carried on battleships and cruisers. These planes were modern and rugged, with self-sealing fuel tanks and armor for the crew. Conscious of the value of skilled pilots and crewmen, the Navy traded performance and range for survivability. It was an appropriate decision. Later models with more powerful engines would make up the performance differences with their adversaries and would place their Japanese opponents at a distinct disadvantage.

In 1941 there were two first-line carrier fighters in the Navy's inventory, Brewster's F2A Buffalo and Grumman's F4F Wildcat. The F4F was the superior of the two, and the F2A was quickly moved out of front-line service. Although inferior to the Mitsubishi A6M, the F4F proved surprisingly effective against its Japanese adversary in the first year of the war. The explanation lies in the high quality of the Navy's fighter pilots and superior team tactics.

While the F4F could fight the A6M on roughly equal terms, the next generation of Navy aircraft surpassed it. Grumman followed the F4F with the F6F Hellcat; Chance-Vought provided a comparable design in the F4U Corsair. Both were significantly larger, more powerful, and better armed than the F4F. As the quality of Japanese pilots decreased during the war, these newer fighters achieved aerial supremacy over the skies of the Pacific.

Interwar fleet exercises and tactical problems revealed the vulnerability of the aircraft carrier; the side that could find the enemy and strike first would have a distinct advantage. This led to the concept of the "scout-bomber," a plane that could scout with a bomb load, attacking immediately after sighting the enemy and sending a contact report. This vision combined with the Navy's pioneering work in dive-bombing techniques to culminate in the Douglass SBD Dauntless, the Navy's premier scout- and dive-bomber in 1941. While the scout-bomber concept did not prove decisive, the SBD proved its worth at the Battle of Midway.

Like the second generation of fighters, the SBD's replacement was larger and more powerful. Starting with the Central Pacific Offensive in November 1943, the Curtiss SB2C Helldiver became the Navy's primary dive-bomber. Nicknamed "the Beast" by its crews, the Helldiver had poor handling characteristics and was ultimately a disappointment.

The Navy's principal torpedo-bomber on the eve of war was approaching obsolescence. The Douglas TBD Devastator was the Navy's first all-metal low-wing monoplane. It was state-of-the-art when it entered service in 1937 but was slow and vulnerable by 1941. Limited fighter cover and poor Japanese antiaircraft doctrine permitted the TBD a moment of glory at the Battle of the

PHOTO 6.3. SBD-3s of Bombing Squadron Five warm up on the deck of aircraft carrier *Yorktown* as she steams in the Coral Sea, April 1942. (NH95571)

Coral Sea, but at Midway, the aircraft's limitations would be fully exposed. Of forty-one planes that reached the Japanese fleet, only six returned.

Midway also saw the introduction of the Devastator's replacement; the Grumman TBF Avenger flew from Midway Island with Torpedo Squadron Eight. Larger, faster, and with more defensive gun positions, the TBF took advantage of improvements in the Navy's aerial torpedoes, which allowed drops at higher altitudes and faster speeds, to wreak havoc on Japanese shipping.

Complementing these fighters and bombers were observation and reconnaissance aircraft launched from battleships and cruisers, such as the Vought OS2U Kingfisher, the Curtiss SOC Seagull, and Curtiss SC-1 Seahawk. These planes were used for gunnery spotting, the rescue of downed pilots, ASW patrols, and many other duties.

2. Shore-based

Although the Navy's carrier-based aviation has received far more attention, the land-based component was also essential to victory. The pace and drive of the Central Pacific Offensive was sustained by land-based planes when the fast carriers were regrouping and refitting, and it was on land-based patrol aircraft that the fight against Axis submarines largely hinged.

The Navy began the war with one of the most effective medium-range amphibious patrol bombers, the Consolidated PBY. Designed to replace patrol bombers of the early 1930s, the PBY first flew in 1935. Production lasted through the war and eventually totaled more than three thousand aircraft. The PBY was used for reconnaissance, attacks against surface ships and submarines, and rescue operations.

The PBY was supplemented by nonamphibious models. Because the Navy had been restricted from developing its own land-based planes, extensive use was made of the Army's Consolidated B-24. In Navy service, it was designated PB4Y. These long-ranged planes were used for patrol, photoreconnaissance, and bombing missions. They provided vital intelligence for amphibious operations. On these missions, Navy planes typically took photographs while Army B-24s provided escort, shooting down Japanese planes that threatened the flight.

The PB4Y was also used in the Atlantic, where it was aided in the fight against the U-boats by the Lockheed PV-1, a patrol bomber developed from a commercial aircraft. The British were the first to see its value, and the Americans adopted it soon afterward. Smaller and more agile than the PB4Y, the PV-1 sank numerous U-boats. Combined across all types, the Navy's land-based planes sank or assisted in sinking forty-eight Axis submarines in the Atlantic and European theatres.

C. WEAPON SYSTEMS

1. Gunnery

Just as the battleship was considered the preeminent ship type, guns were accorded the most emphasis in doctrine and training. But the emphasis was not limited to surface gunnery. Antiaircraft gunnery received significant attention, particularly in the years immediately before 1941, when exercises revealed unexpected flaws in its effectiveness.

Surface. The Navy's surface gunnery capabilities were outstanding. Guns were the most visible element of the system, but behind them were sophisticated analog computers, advanced directors and radars, and new heavyweight shell designed to enhance their destructive power. These components, when coupled with the human elements of the system—spotters, fire-control men, turret crews, and gunnery officers—combined to make the Navy's surface gunnery among the most potent in the world.

The heart of the Navy's fire control systems was an analog computer, a rangekeeper. The earliest versions were developed before American entry into World War I. In those years, increasing battle ranges necessitated the introduction of computing mechanisms to predict the motion of the target.

The computer was coupled to a director, which tracked the target and provided its bearing. Experience in World War I convinced the Navy that its
basic approach was sound. During the interwar period, the Bureau of Ordnance
concentrated on refining it.

These refinements led toward a system that was increasingly automatic
and decreasingly subject to human error. The first major improvement was the
introduction of a self-synchronous system for transmitting data between the
director, rangekeeper, and turrets. This was introduced with the battleships of
the *Colorado* class. It prevented the need for resyncing the various elements
of the system and allowed the seamless transition from one rangekeeper or
director to another in the event of casualty, a major advantage.

A second innovation introduced in the *Colorado* class was the stable vertical, an artificial horizon, which allowed stabilization without the need to
observe external references, such as the horizon or the target. This was a significant step forward because it allowed more accurate fire at extreme distances where the target would be more obscure or potentially hidden, and
spotting information would be reported by aircraft.

During the treaty period, the new cruisers received the most modern systems. The Mk 5 Rangekeeper installed in the *Pensacola*-class cruisers received
and transmitted more data automatically. The Mk 6 Rangekeeper introduced
gyros to allow steady references in the horizontal and vertical dimensions,
allowing indirect fire even when turning. The Mk 8, the last major revision,
was built upon this concept. Introduced with the *Portland* class, it could fire
on the cross-level, meaning that as long as the guns were in the correct position, the angle of the ship would not matter.

Coupled with the next generation of modern directors, the Mk 8 was the
centerpiece of the Navy's wartime fire control systems. Cruisers and rebuilt
battleships employed it in concert with the Mk 34 director. Introduced in the
light cruisers of the *Brooklyn* class, the Mk 34 evolved from earlier directors
that rotated separately from the housing surrounding them. As the Mk 34 was
modified, first with a large stereoscopic rangefinder and later with radar antennae, it was essential to keep these additions pointed in the same direction as
the director itself. These additions turned what was originally designed as a
light outer shell into a heavy shield; the resulting system was overloaded but
ultimately very capable, as the performance of the Navy's cruisers and modernized old battleships showed.

The modern battleships mated the Mk 8 rangekeeper to the Mk 38
director. Designed from the beginning to incorporate a large stereoscopic
rangefinder and stabilization, the Mk 38 did not face the same issues as the
Mk 34. Together, the Mk 8 and Mk 38 were the pinnacle of prewar fire-control

systems, their accuracy enhanced by automatic control of the director, both in train and elevation, by outputs from the rangekeeper.

Automatic control was not confined to directors. During the interwar period, automatic control of guns was introduced. Previous systems transmitted elevation and bearing data to the gun mounts. By the mid-1930s, the guns themselves were being automatically controlled. These systems were introduced in the Navy's most modern ships, the fast battleships, modern cruisers, and destroyers. Increased automation eliminated the potential errors of earlier follow-the-pointer systems, which relied on gun layers and trainers to match their dials with those of the computer. With humans out of the loop, guns could be moved faster and more accurately, particularly in situations when crews were subject to fatigue—at night and during extended operations.

Like the systems controlling them, the Navy's guns became more sophisticated in the years before World War II. Guns of all sizes became lighter as construction techniques improved and designers sought to cram the most efficiency into treaty-limited ships. Super-heavy shells designed to increase striking power, particularly at long ranges, were introduced for large-caliber weapons. Semifixed ammunition was introduced for medium-caliber weapons, increasing their rates of fire.

The 6-inch/47 gun introduced in the *Brooklyn* class was one of these medium-caliber weapons. A semiautomatic sliding breechblock and semifixed ammunition allowed very high rates of fire with firing cycles as low as six seconds. The *Brooklyn* class was designed to defend the battle line against enemy destroyer attack, and it was thought that a single *Brooklyn* could break up the attack of a four-ship destroyer squadron before it could enter torpedo range.

The modern 16-inch/45 that equipped the battleships of the *Washington* and *South Dakota* classes provides the best example of the super-heavy shell. Typical 16-inch shells weighed about 2,100 pounds; the shells for these new weapons were nearly 30 percent larger, at 2,700 pounds. Maximum range was decreased, but the sacrifice was considered worthwhile given the increased striking and penetration power. Shell weights for the older weapons were also increased. See appendix 1 for the characteristics of the Navy's main surface guns.

Immediately before the war, the Navy's Bureau of Ordnance was experimenting with radar, incorporating it into fire-control systems and installing prototype sets in the fleet. These early prototypes quickly led to the Mk 3 (FC) radar, which proved its effectiveness in the night battles off Guadalcanal. But the Mk 3 was limited. Although it generated accurate ranges, its beam was too wide to generate sufficient accuracy for true blind fire. Fire-control teams still needed visual bearings.

The introduction of centimetric radars removed that limitation. The first of these, the S-band Mk 8 (FH), was introduced in 1943 and played a part in the victory at Empress Augusta Bay in November of that year. It enabled complete blind fire with accurate ranges, bearings, and spotting of shell splashes from the radar alone. It also introduced a new visual display that gave operators a virtual bird's-eye view of the area around the target. Targets appeared as glowing ovals on the screen. Shell splashes showed up as temporary "pips" around the target. The top-down view made it very easy for radar operators to quickly determine if shells were long, short, or off in train.

Increased power and a new antenna improved accuracy still further. The Mk 8 Mod 3 and its successor, the Mk 13, operated in the X-band. Their beams were much narrower, which allowed "better bearing accuracy, bearing discrimination, and deflection spotting accuracy."[18] Internal arrangements were also improved, which reduced the weight of equipment in the director.

Radar integrated relatively easily into the Navy's fire-control systems because of the prior investment in automatic mechanisms. Radar replaced the earlier approach of visually spotting the fall of shot and observing the target but did not fundamentally alter Navy's approach to fire control. What it did do was permit the Navy to reap the full promise of the sophisticated systems it had developed and harness the deadly accuracy of its surface gunnery under nearly all conditions.

Antiaircraft. The Navy was unequalled in the effectiveness of its antiaircraft armaments. While some of this is due to the sheer number of antiaircraft guns carried by the Navy's ships by the end of the war—ships literally bristled with them—the quality of the ordnance and the accuracy of the systems behind them were largely responsible.

The Navy's antiaircraft fire-control systems were an outgrowth of the surface systems, with similar dependence on a director and computer (range-keeper). The Mk 19 director was the first of these; work started in 1926 and was completed three years later. It guided the 5-inch/25 antiaircraft guns of the old battleships and treaty cruisers. The Mk 28 and Mk 33 were incremental improvements on the basic principle; both of them were self-contained, with director and computer in a single unit.

A dramatic improvement came with the Mk 37, introduced in 1938. The increasing emphasis on automation in surface fire control influenced the development of the Mk 37. The computer was moved belowdecks and information was transmitted between it and the director automatically. Since the director was lighter, it could move faster, acquiring and tracking targets more effectively.

The Mk 37 was coupled to a new dual-purpose gun, the 5-inch/38. Firing semifixed ammunition with a high rate of fire, the 5-inch/38 became the

Navy's most ubiquitous gun mounting. It equipped all manner of ships, from destroyer escorts and auxiliaries to battleships and cruisers. It was the most successful dual-purpose gun of the war. The combination of the 5-inch/38 and Mk 37 was superior to all other comparable systems. However, by the end of the war, Japanese kamikazes had exposed the system's limitations.

The Mk 37 director was designed specifically to accommodate radars; the Mk 4 radar, a parallel development to the Mk 3, was integrated in early installations. Later, the Mk 12 coupled with the Mk 22 height finder became standard. As with surface fire-control systems, radar increased accuracy and performance by providing better inputs to the men and machines at the heart of the system.

At least as important as the addition of radar was the incorporation of a variable time (VT) proximity fuze into the shells of the 5-inch/38. Prior fuzes had to be set for time delay based on the estimated height and range of the aircraft. This step introduced a delay and increased the possibility for error. It also made it far more difficult to shoot down a maneuvering target. The proximity fuze, triggered by a small radar in the nose of the projectile that detonated when it approached a target aircraft, eliminated these concerns and dramatically increased the system's potency, increasing the effectiveness of individual guns three or four times.

Antiaircraft batteries were augmented by smaller, automatic weapons. The Navy first introduced these in the early 1930s, when .50-caliber machine guns were installed to combat strafing planes. During the war, these were replaced by 20-mm cannons of an Oerlikon design. The accuracy of these was enhanced by the Mk 14 gun sight, a simple fire-control computer that measured the rate of movement and predicted the necessary lead angle to hit the target.

An intermediate automatic weapon was also needed, and orders were placed for a 1.1-inch gun in 1934. It was a four-barreled, water-cooled weapon. Development took a long time; the system was complex, and although it was mounted on many ships in 1941, the 1.1-inch was unsuccessful.

The 40-mm Bofors was ultimately selected to be the Navy's principal medium antiaircraft gun. Interest in the gun began in 1939, and after samples were received the next year, it was apparent that the Swedish gun was superior to "all similar guns."[19] It was produced in quadruple, twin, and single mountings. Unfortunately, its shells were too small to take the VT fuze and insufficient to guarantee destruction of a kamikaze. But it was reliable and mounted everywhere. By sheer volume of fire, the Bofors destroyed more kamikazes than any other antiaircraft gun. It was linked to the Mk 51 director, which incorporated the same Mk 14 sight that aimed the Oerlikon.

2. Torpedoes

The Navy began the war with the most ineffective torpedoes of any major combatant. Secrecy surrounding the magnetic exploder and limited testing, particularly with live warheads, prevented the problems from being discovered before the war. Resistance of the Bureau of Ordnance to evidence of those problems further delayed the introduction of satisfactory weapons.

At the outbreak of war, the Navy had three standard torpedoes, the Mk 13 for aircraft and patrol torpedo boats, the Mk 14 for submarines, and the Mk 15 for surface ships. Both the Mk 14 and Mk 15 were served by the sophisticated Mk 6 exploder, which had two modes of operation. The primary exploder was magnetic. The torpedo was intended to run about five to ten feet below the target. When the torpedo crossed underneath, the magnetic influence of the target's hull would set off the exploder. The resulting detonation, below the hull, would be far more damaging than a traditional impact against the side. The theory was excellent, but in practice, it did not work. The detonator was too sensitive, causing numerous premature explosions. In July 1943, the Pacific Fleet ordered the magnetic exploders deactivated.

Many crews had already chosen to exclusively rely on the secondary exploder, a traditional system that initiated on impact with the target, but it had its own problems. Frequently, the torpedoes ran ten feet below their depth setting and passed under the target, defeating the contact exploder entirely. When the torpedoes did hit the target, the exploder had a tendency to fail at impact angles close to 90 degrees. The Bureau of Ordnance solved the depth problems, but the Pacific Fleet led the way in addressing the failures of the exploder. By September 1943, the problems had been resolved.

The Mk 13 proved more reliable, but in its original form, it placed serious limitations on the planes carrying it. They had to slow to 110 knots and drop from a height of fifty feet. This forced a long, slow run on the pilots of the TBD and contributed to their high losses at Midway. Improvements were introduced, and by February 1944, high-speed drops from one thousand feet could be made by the TBF. Progress continued, and by the end of the war, drops from as high as five thousand feet and from speeds of 410 knots were possible.

More advanced torpedoes were introduced as the war went on. The first innovation was an electric torpedo for submarines, the Mk 18. Slower than the Mk 14, it was slightly less effective against merchant ships, but the lack of a wake—there were no tracks to point back to the firing submarine—made it far more popular. In the last six months of the war, it represented 65 percent of all submarine torpedoes fired.

The second innovation was a homing torpedo for submarines to use against attacking escorts. This was the Mk 27. It was slow and had a small warhead, but the passive acoustic guidance made it deadly. Of 106 fired, 33 hit and 24 of those hits were fatal. A similar torpedo was developed for ASW aircraft and will be discussed in the next section. See appendix 1 for specific details of the Navy's torpedoes.

3. Antisubmarine Warfare

At the beginning of the war, the standard Navy ASW weapon was still the depth charge. There were a number of varieties, all basic and ultimately inadequate. In 1941, Mk 6 and Mk 7 were standard, with bursting charges of three hundred and six hundred pounds, respectively. Both of these weapons were shaped like barrels, sank relatively slowly, and had maximum depths of three hundred feet. Submarines could avoid them by rapid maneuvers or deep dives. Later versions increased sinking speeds and maximum depth, but the overall poor quality of these weapons had an adverse effect on ASW tactics.

In early 1941, development began on the Mk 9; by the latter part of the war, it had become standard. With a hydrodynamic teardrop shape, it sank much faster, and fins at the rear made it spin, which stabilized its descent. Initial versions could reach depths of six hundred feet; this was later increased to one thousand feet. The bursting charge was two hundred pounds of Torpex. When it entered service in the spring of 1943, it increased the lethality of Allied escorts. The Mk 9 outnumbered a companion model with a proximity fuze, the Mk 8, which proved unreliable and difficult to maintain.

Unlike depth charges, the Hedgehog, a 24-spigot mortar of British origin, fired ahead of the launching destroyer. This made sonar attacks simpler and more accurate. The Navy had placed it into production by late 1942. There were two versions. Mk 10 fired an elliptical pattern and Mk 11 a circular one. Range of both was about 250 yards. On impact with the water, the projectiles sank rapidly. They were contact fuzed and had a bursting charge of thirty pounds of TNT or thirty-five pounds of Torpex. Hedgehogs proved twice as effective as depth charges. Mousetrap, a lighter, rocket-based alternative, was developed for smaller vessels.

Aircraft were a potent weapon in the struggle against Axis submarines. Initially they employed a specially adapted version of the Mk 6 depth charge, but soon specific aerial weapons were under development. The earliest of these was the Mk 17, which had a contact fuze in the nose and a depth charge hydrostatic fuze farther toward the rear. It had a charge of 227 pounds of TNT. Gradual improvements in later marks increased this. The Mk 53 was the last of this line to see wartime service, with an improved shape, fuze location, and 250-pound Torpex charge.

The most important development in aerial ASW weapons was the Mk 24 mine, also known as "Fido." It was not a mine at all but a passive acoustic homing torpedo. Work on the weapon began in the fall of 1941, and less than two years later it was ready. It proved very effective. For 346 weapons dropped, sisty-eight submarines were sunk and another thirty-three damaged. Use would have been more extensive if not for the security concerns surrounding the weapon; it was essential that it not be captured, lest the Axis develop a countermeasure. The range was 4,000 yards at 12 knots. It carried a 92-pound Torpex warhead.

4. Mines

Mines were primarily an offensive weapon for the Navy. The Mk 12 was a magnetic ground mine that could be planted by submarines, surface vessels, or aircraft. Some of these were available to the Asiatic Fleet in 1941, but they were dumped in deep water without being used to prevent the Japanese from exploiting them. They were an important part of the submarine offensive by late 1942. The warhead was either 1,060 pounds of TNT or 1,200 pounds of the more powerful Torpex.

TBF torpedo bombers began laying Mk 12 mines in March 1943, but far more were delivered by land-based planes, such as the PB4Y and B-29. The Mk 13 and Mk 25 were developed specifically for use by aircraft. The Mk 13 was intended for use without a parachute and doubled as a bomb. It had a warhead of 640 pounds of TNT or 710 pounds of Torpex. The Mk 25 was larger, with a 1,274-pound Torpex charge.

In all, over 25,000 aerial mines were dropped in Japanese controlled waters. Operation Starvation was responsible for nearly half of these. Starvation was a five-stage campaign to eradicate naval traffic in and around the home islands. It was aptly named. Beginning in March 1945, the operation "virtually severed Japan's lifeline to the continent," paralyzed industry, and, had the war continued another year, an estimated 10 percent of Japan's population would have starved.[20]

D. INFRASTRUCTURE

1. Logistics

The Navy recognized that logistics would play a critical role, particularly in a Pacific War. The voyage of the Great White Fleet provided valuable experience and helped initiate a trend toward self-sufficiency within the fleet that was reinforced by the experience of World War I. Soon thereafter, the Base Force, later named the Service Force, was established with the specific role of providing mobile logistic support to the fleet.

Interest in the Base Force in the early interwar years was an outgrowth of the fortification clause of the Washington Treaty. Prevented from developing secure bases in the Philippines and Guam, the Navy recognized that any return to the Western Pacific would depend on the ability to seize and develop advance bases in the Mandates.

The early years of the war proved the theory and the value of investment in the Base Force. Bases in the South Pacific were rapidly built up and put into service. After the invasion of Guadalcanal, the Navy quickly moved to exploit the harbor at Tulagi; it was turned into a forward base and used to repair damaged ships even as the surrounding waters were still being contested. The advance base concept had worked, but the rapid advances planned for the Central Pacific required a new model.

For the Central Pacific Campaign, the Navy needed truly mobile bases that could keep up with the fleet's carrier and amphibious forces. The Service Force of the Pacific Fleet set their minds to providing the solution. Their prototype became Service Squadron 4.

Commissioned on 1 November 1943 specifically to support the invasion of the Gilberts, Service Squadron 4 was the "first floating base in any navy." With a combination of standard auxiliary types and specialized barges, the squadron kept the fleet off Tarawa and Makin well supplied with food and ammunition. "A mobile supply base was the logistic counterpart to the airplane carrier. While flattops projected naval air power within striking distance of the enemy, Servrons 4 and 10 acted as a logistic annex to Pearl Harbor for servicing the Fleet at sea. Advanced naval bases were still needed; but it was the mobile base, in conjunction with the fast carriers, that permitted leapfrogging with seven-hundred-league boots."[21]

Carriers and their escorts also needed fuel. Fuel had been a factor in the early departure of the carriers from Guadalcanal the previous year, and steps were taken to prevent it from happening again. Service Squadron 8 provided thirteen oilers for the attack on the Gilberts, which "became the first operation in history in which an entire fleet was refueled at sea, eliminating the need for warships to leave the combat area for fuel."[22] The model would be repeated and improved for later offensives.

The wartime service squadrons were the culmination of prewar strategic insight. The prewar planners recognized that the lack of a defensible base in the Western Pacific and the sparse atolls of the Mandates would necessitate logistical mobility that could only be provided by an element of the Fleet. This led to the Base Force. The need to integrate these concepts with the rapid pace of operations desired by the Pacific Fleet prompted the creation of the Service Force, which became an essential component of the Central Pacific campaign.

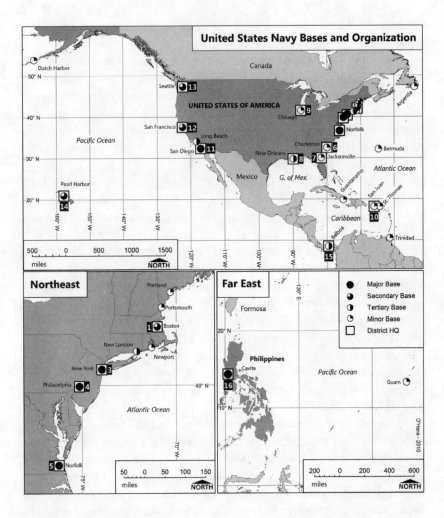

2. Bases

A fundamental difficulty presented by the strategic situation in the Pacific was the limited number of bases. Extensive facilities were available on the West Coast of the United States, at Puget Sound, Mare Island, San Pedro, and San Diego. The base at Pearl Harbor was improved over the interwar period, but no amount of improvements could bring it closer to the combat zones in the Mandates and Western Pacific. Cavite and Guam, 4,767 and 3,318 miles from Pearl Harbor, respectively, were closest to Japan but would inevitably be lost soon after the outbreak of war.

The problem would be solved by the mobile logistical capabilities introduced by the Service Force, but before Service Squadron 4 was created, the Pacific Fleet was very dependent on bases. The campaign for Guadalcanal and

Photo 6.4. Wartime recreation. U.S. Coast Guardmen, members of the crew of a combat transport, swim under the bow of *Kinugawa Maru*, a Japanese transport beached and sunk in the November 1942 battles for Guadalcanal. (U.S. Naval Institute Photo Archives)

operations in the South Pacific were sustained by a string of advanced positions—Bora Bora in the Society Islands, Nandi and Suva in the Fijis, Nouméa on New Caledonia, Havannah and Fila in Efate, Segond Channel in Espiritu Santo, and Wellington in New Zealand. These were staging grounds for logistic needs of all sorts, and preliminary repair facilities for damaged ships.

Even with a mobile base to support the carrier forces, Pearl Harbor remained an essential key to the campaign. Enhancements to the facilities accelerated after the outbreak of war; it became a staging point for the major offensives in the Central Pacific, providing storage for food, fuel, and men. Distant as it was from the combat zone, it was still the closest large base available for attacks on the Marshalls and Marianas.

The War in the Atlantic did not face the same challenges. The distances were less, the British Isles provided effective bases on its far side, and numerous established bases and shipyards lined the Atlantic coast. It was from these yards that the Navy's modern major combatants emerged. The yards at Philadelphia, New York, Newport News, and Quincy built the modern carriers and battleships that formed the backbone of the fleet. Smaller combatants emerged by the score, and many allied vessels were refitted in these yards.

3. Industry

The Navy's war effort benefitted greatly from its relationship with industry. Victory in both oceans was enabled by massive shipbuilding programs initiated before and during the war. The output of these programs, which exceeded the wartime production of all other navies combined, is frequently attributed to the size of the American industrial base, but its full potential would not have been realized without the efficient management of the Navy Department. As one expert wrote, "The Navy . . . gained a great deal of knowledge about logistics and procurement of material. It learned that in order to fight a modern naval war much more extensive industrial planning on the Navy's part was necessary than had been anticipated. Not only was close and continuous cooperation with the government agencies entrusted with the industrial mobilization necessary but far more aid to the individual manufacturer in terms of engineering advice, financial assistance, and scheduling was needed in World War II than ever before."[23]

Forrestal, in his position as undersecretary, was primarily responsible for the successful use of the industrial base. He and his office worked to identify and remove those bottlenecks that would have prevented the Navy from harnessing its full potential.

The results were truly impressive. American shipyards produced more than 130 aircraft carriers of all types, more than 300 destroyers and 400 escorts, and more than 56 million tons of merchant shipping. The latter was the work of the U.S. Maritime Commission, which, in late 1938, under the leadership of retired Admiral Emory S. Land, began an extensive program of merchant ship construction. The Maritime Commission ships enabled the campaign in two oceans, supplying simultaneous offensive campaigns on the continent of Europe and in the Pacific.

V. RECAPITULATION

A. WARTIME EVOLUTION

The prewar Navy had disappeared by 1944. It was not a casualty of the fighting but was lost in the rapid influx of new officers, sailors, ships, and planes
during the war. This rapid expansion forced the Navy to revise its approach to
personnel and training and abandon traditional procedures and doctrines that
relied on individual initiative for their effectiveness. Reliable and repeatable
processes that obliterated prewar approaches were introduced.

The expansion of naval personnel dwarfed prewar estimates. In July
1940 there were 13,162 officers; by August 1945, this number had ballooned
to 325,074. The growth among enlisted ranks was similar, expanding from
144,824 to 3,009,380 over the same time. The large shipbuilding programs
have already been mentioned; planes were produced on similar scales.

The impact on doctrinal development was substantial. The flaws inherent in the prewar approach, exposed by the fighting off Guadalcanal, have
already been discussed. The result was greater centralization and standardization of procedures. Sound fundamentals of the prewar approach—reliance
on individual initiative, aggressive offensive action, and coordinated action
against the enemy—were retained, but the method of applying these principles was standardized.

Training programs were also revised with a similar emphasis on uniformity
and standardization. While the new procedures ensured a standard approach
and a common level of efficiency, they hindered the effectiveness of more talented officers and encouraged a tendency to focus on procedures more than
significant matters.

Increasing standardization appeared in other areas, and nowhere is the
difference between prewar and wartime procedures more striking than in
the Navy's manuals. Before the war, manuals relied heavily on theory, present-
ing the underlying principles of the topic at hand. They had more equations
than pictures and were often exhaustive in their approach. They provided
concepts, the theory behind a problem. Wartime manuals placed far more
emphasis on practical problem solving. Pictures became much more common,
the size of manuals was reduced, unnecessary complexities were eliminated,
and the underlying theory appeared in the context of real-life examples.

By 1944 the Navy had become a modern institution. War had stripped
away old traditional procedures for doctrinal development, training, administration, and the introduction of new technology. The Navy that emerged from
the war was modern, efficient, and ultimately, victorious.

B. SUMMARY AND ASSESSMENT

By the time of the attack on Pearl Harbor in December 1941, the U.S. Navy had become the most powerful in the world. The backbone of that Navy—the Pacific Fleet's battle line—was shattered in Japan's attack on the fleet's Hawaiian base, but sufficient investments had been made in "balancing" the fleet and the Navy was able to wrest the initiative from the Japanese before the end of 1942 in a series of hard-fought battles. Victory in these early actions was won almost exclusively by the ships and men of the prewar Navy.

The sacrifice necessary to gain the initiative and blunt the initial Japanese offensives has been used to suggest that the Navy was unprepared, that it wasted the years of peace and had to learn hard lessons as it went in the first year of war. A realistic assessment is more balanced.

Prewar preparation was effective and recognized the decisive influence of new technologies, such as aircraft, radar, and submarines. Without such effective preparation, the Navy would not have been able to meet the challenge presented in the Pacific so quickly after the loss of the battle line.

Carrier task forces became the new focus. Although the Navy's prewar experience with them was very different from that of the Japanese, in many respects the Navy's approach was more flexible. Coordination between multiple carriers was more limited, but air groups could be interchanged more easily, and when the test came at Midway, the broad spectrum of the Navy's approach integrated cryptology with aggressive tactics to obtain victory.

The attritional struggle off Guadalcanal pushed the prewar Navy to its limits. Without the time to develop task force doctrines or disseminate battle plans, commanders sent ships that had not maneuvered or fought as a unit into combat. The results were predictable, but it is worth remembering that despite the losses, the Navy met its strategic objective in all the battles off Guadalcanal except Savo Island, and even in that action, the sacrifice of the covering force helped prevent a Japanese strategic victory.

The initial phase of the Battle of the Atlantic, dominated by the German U-boats, provides a more negative picture of the Navy's preparation for war. There is little doubt that the Navy was not ready for the struggle. Insufficient attention had been given to the problem of commerce protection, and without the assistance of the Royal Navy, the situation would have been far worse. Despite these initial failures, the Allies had gained the upper hand by mid-1943. The Germans continued the campaign but at ever-increasing cost; without the ability to contest the movement of an army across the Atlantic, defeat became inevitable.

In the Pacific, Nimitz took advantage of the initiative won through the hard fighting at Guadalcanal to launch the Central Pacific offensive in late 1943. He integrated the step-by-step approach of the "Cautionaries" with the aggressive pace of the "Thrusters." The movement through the Japanese perimeter was methodical; each leap was made within range of land-based air. But it was also extremely rapid. Key strongholds between and among island groups were bypassed, thus conserving Nimitz's limited resources and avoiding Japanese concentrations of strength. The new carrier task forces, which incorporated the best lessons of prewar experiments and wartime battles, led the way. The Japanese Combined Fleet made ready to meet the Americans but was kept off balance by the fast pace of operations in the Central and South Pacific and was unable to force a fleet action until the result was a foregone conclusion.

Meanwhile, the Navy's submarines were sinking Japanese merchant vessels at an alarming rate; the Imperial Navy largely ignored commerce protection, and its efforts at rectifying the situation would prove to be "too little, too late"; American submarines sank nearly 5 million tons of Japanese merchant shipping. Success in the campaign strangled the Japanese war effort and forced its fleet to concentrate in the East Indies, close to the source of fuel, due to a shortage of tankers to supply it.

When the anticipated fleet action finally materialized in June 1944, it was anticlimactic. Japanese losses in carrier pilots had reduced the effectiveness of their strike forces. Coached on target by new fighter-direction techniques, the Navy's F6Fs decimated the Japanese attackers. The great "Turkey Shoot" of the Marianas signaled the inevitable end of the Pacific War, but more than a year of difficult fighting remained.

At Leyte Gulf in October 1944, the Navy had an opportunity to finish off the remaining elements of the Japanese surface fleet, but an emphasis on concentrated action prevented Admiral William F. Halsey from incorporating the necessary flexibility in his battle plans. The Japanese planned a diversion to draw his powerful forces northward, away from the battle area. He obliged them, but the success of this diversion only limited the extent of the Japanese defeat. The last of the decisive battles had been won, and the Imperial Navy was defeated.

But the Japanese would not surrender, and their last efforts were ones that caught the Navy off guard. The transition to suicide tactics in late 1944 had not been anticipated. The resulting kamikaze attacks were surprisingly effective, and the Japanese offensive against the fleet off Okinawa was devastating. The VT fuze, heavy antiaircraft batteries, and alert combat air patrols helped reduce the effectiveness of these attacks, but flaws in the Navy's air defense systems were exposed. In effect, the kamikazes were the first "smart bombs," and more advanced systems were required to deal with them. The war ended before they could be put into service.

On 6 August 1945, the B-29 *Enola Gay* took off from Tinian, one of the Marianas captured during the previous year's offensive. She released the world's first atomic bomb dropped in anger, over the city of Hiroshima, resulting in obliteration of the target and enormous loss of life. Soon thereafter, Japan capitulated.

The Navy's success in the Pacific War followed the strategies outlined long before during the interwar period. "The only surprise, as Fleet Admiral Nimitz observed years later, was the kamikaze."[24] That this was so, that the Navy could execute its plan with so few surprises in the face of numerous challenges, is a testament not only to the effectiveness of the prewar planning and preparation but also to the soundness of the strategic principles upon which it was based. Those principles rested on a firm foundation: the influential writings of Mahan, which the Navy had learned quite well.

chapter seven

USSR: The Voenno-morskoi Flot SSSR

I. BACKSTORY

A. HISTORY

Like Soviet Russia itself, the Red Navy was born amid the confusion and turmoil of revolution and civil war. Following the February Revolution of 1917, the Russian navy was subjected to a dizzying series of changes in nomenclature, organizational structure, and leading personalities. This process continued after the Bolsheviks seized power in November 1917 and culminated in July 1926 when the navy was reduced to the status of an "administration" within the army, becoming the "Naval Forces of the Workers' and Peasants' Red Army" (Voenno-morskie sily Raboche-krestianskoi Krasnoi Armii, VMS RKKA).

The new socialist nation worried about an attack by hostile capitalist powers, in which case the Red Navy would probably have to defend the country's Baltic coasts against a powerful maritime assault. The tsarist-trained officers who dominated the navy at this time—men later dubbed the "Old School"—believed that by using submarines and torpedo boats, the defenders could whittle down the enemy's battle fleet as it made its way through the Gulf of Finland. Then, at a carefully prepared "mine-artillery position" about thirty-five nautical miles west of Leningrad, the Baltic Fleet would make its stand, delivering a "concentrated blow" using battleships, light surface forces, submarines, aircraft, even coast artillery. This doctrine formed the basis for the annual Baltic Fleet maneuvers in the latter half of the 1920s. A broadly similar strategy was developed for the Black Sea, although here the fleet's cruisers, destroyers, torpedo boats, and submarines had to defend against enemy landings in southern Russia without the help of flanking coast artillery.

The Old School's approach to naval strategy was essentially defensive and was not well integrated with the Red Army's plans for offensive war, which called for deep and rapid penetrations into enemy territory. It was this strategic disconnect that helped to bring forth the "Young School," which began to emerge in the late 1920s. There was also a generational shift involved—whereas the Old School was composed of veterans of the tsarist navy, the Young School's leaders were all "Red Commanders"—men young enough to have thoroughly absorbed Marxist-Leninist theories. They argued that classic command-of-the-sea theory had been invalidated by "unblockad-able" weapons—submarines and aircraft. Having a superior surface fleet no longer guaranteed command of the sea, and decisive battle was a chimera. Future wars at sea would involve "successive" or "continuous" operations by light forces—submarines, torpedo boats, and aircraft—that would paralyze the enemy's surface forces and allow the weaker Red Navy to provide support to the army, which was the decisive arm. This outlook made the Young School popular with the Red Army, while its use of Marxist-Leninist arguments gave it a patina of political correctness.

The rise of the Young School coincided with that of Iosif Vissarionovich Stalin, who by the late 1920s had achieved a position of unquestioned author-ity within the Communist Party. In 1928 Stalin instigated a nation-wide purge of tsarist-educated men in all fields, and in 1930 this process swept through the Red Army and Navy. Almost at a stroke, the Old School was eliminated and the Young School took over command of the navy. For a while the navy's new masters seemed to be riding high; the curricula of the naval educational institutions were radically altered, the construction program of the second Five-Year Plan (1933–1937) was tailored to suit the Young School's ideas, and the defensive cast of the annual maneuvers was changed to emphasize landing operations on the enemy's seaward flank.

But the Young School's dominance of naval policy was short-lived, for in 1937–1938 they were decimated in the Great Purge. Stalin wanted a navy built around a fleet of giant battleships and fast battle cruisers, and those who failed to conform to the dictator's views quickly enough were arrested, imprisoned, or shot. In the space of two years, more than 3,000 naval officers out of a total of 19,500 (15.4 percent) were "repressed." The higher ranks were hit especially hard; among those executed were 4 navy chiefs, 6 fleet or flotilla commanders, 5 chiefs or deputy chiefs of fleet staff, and 22 commanders of major warships.

But building the battle fleet Stalin wanted would take time, as would the ongoing expansion and restructuring of the Red Army, and there was no guar-antee that the USSR's most likely enemies, Japan and Germany, would allow it that time. Stalin therefore sought an accommodation with Hitler's Germany, believing this would postpone a conflict the Soviet Union was not yet ready to face. The result was the Soviet-German Non-Aggression Pact, signed on the eve of Germany's attack on Poland. When, in response to that attack, Britain and France declared war on Germany, Stalin believed he had successfully diverted Hitler into a prolonged war in the west. Stalin now took advantage of the secret clauses of the nonaggression pact, taking a slice of eastern Poland in September 1939 and annexing the Baltic Republics in August 1940.

Despite the Red Army's embarrassing performance against the Finns in the Winter War (November 1939–March 1940), things seemed to be going well for Stalin. He had gained territory that would allow him to erect a deep system of defense, including new naval and air bases. Although the sudden collapse of France in May–June 1940 temporarily threw his calculations out, the dictator's arrogant self-confidence soon returned; against expectations, Britain continued to hold out, and Stalin believed that Hitler would not be foolish enough to start a two-front war. It was a belief he would maintain, in spite of mounting evidence to the contrary, until 22 June 1941.

B. MISSION

The Red Navy, more than any other, was constrained by geography. It had to maintain fleets in four separate theaters—the Baltic, Black Sea, Arctic, and Pacific—each with very different operational conditions. There was some degree of "intertheater maneuverability" thanks to the White Sea Canal (linking the Baltic to the Arctic Ocean) and the Northern Sea Route, which connected the Arctic and Pacific oceans along the Siberian coast. But the White Sea Canal, built by forced labor at a horrifying cost in human lives, could handle only destroyers, submarines, and smaller vessels while the Northern Sea Route was navigable only from about July to October. So despite these connections, the fleets could not provide mutual support, nor could their main forces be concentrated. Each fleet therefore had to operate in a different theater, confronting different potential enemies.

In 1941 an operational plan was drawn up that established the tasks each fleet was to fulfill in the event of war. The Baltic Fleet was to defend the gulfs of Finland and Riga against German naval forces, prevent amphibious landings by the enemy, interrupt the enemy's sea communications, and support the Red Army's maritime flank. The Black Sea Fleet was to secure control of the Black Sea, prevent enemy naval forces from entering through the Turkish Straits, destroy the Romanian navy if it entered the war, and support the Red Army. The Northern Fleet was to defend the Soviet Arctic coasts, cooperate with the Red Army, and attack the enemy's sea communications with submarines, the latter to operate as far south as the Skagerrak.

For the Pacific Fleet, the main enemy was Japan, which had a fleet that the USSR could not hope to match for many years to come. Moreover, the Soviet Pacific Fleet's main base was Vladivostok, which in the event of war would be vulnerable not only to attack by the Japanese fleet but also to land assault from Japanese-occupied Manchuria. Therefore, the Pacific Fleet was to prevent enemy amphibious landings on the Soviet coasts of the Sea of Japan, the Sea of Okhotsk, or the Kamchatka Peninsula; interrupt maritime communications between Japan and its forces on the Asian mainland; and conduct submarine warfare against commerce east of the Japanese archipelago.

II. ORGANIZATION

A. COMMAND STRUCTURE

1. Administration

After more than a decade as an integral part of the Red Army, an independent People's Commissariat of the Navy (Narodnyi komissariat Voenno-morskogo flota) was established on 30 December 1937. Unfortunately, this coincided with the height of the purges; as a result, the leadership of the navy was subjected to a deadly whirlwind of changes. Between August 1937 and April 1939, five heads or acting heads of the navy were arrested and shot. It was only with the appointment of Nikolai Gerasimovich Kuznetsov on 27 April 1939 that the deadly turnover in the naval leadership finally ended. Kuznetsov is highly regarded by all Russian writers, and there seems no reason to doubt that he was an able and energetic administrator who was not afraid to stand up to Stalin on some issues.

After the outbreak of war, Kuznetsov was briefly included in the Stavka, or high command, but in July 1941 it was reorganized as the Stavka of the Supreme Command (Stavka Verkhovnogo Glavnokomandovaniia), and Kuznetsov was not included. The various fleets and flotillas were subordinated to the local army commands—a theoretically sensible arrangement since the chief role of the navy was to support and protect the seaward flanks of the army. But the sheer scale of land operations meant that army command staffs could rarely take the time to understand naval operations or coordinate their planning with that of the local naval commanders. So despite formal subordination, naval forces often carried out operations independently of the army. A corollary to this situation was that the army often failed to take full advantage of the navy's capabilities. Kuznetsov clearly found the situation unsatisfactory, and as a result of his efforts, on 31 March 1944, the Stavka altered the command arrangements—while the Baltic and Pacific fleets remained subordinate to local army commands, the Northern and Black Sea fleets as well as the Caspian, Azov, and Volga flotillas were placed directly under Kuznetsov's control.

The role of the political officers—usually called military commissars—calls for a brief mention. Their basic function was to ensure the political reliability of military commanders and units. Their importance had been in decline since the mid-1920s, but in 1937 Stalin reintroduced the concept of "dual command" under which all orders had to be signed by both the commanding officer and the commissar in units at the level of regiments and above in the army, and squadrons and above in the navy. This situation persisted until 12 August 1940, when, in a move to restore military morale and efficiency following the disastrous Winter War with Finland, dual command was eliminated. On 16 July 1941, as the Red Army was reeling backward in the face of the German invasion, the system of political commissars was revived only to be abolished once again in October 1942. From this point on, military commissars became responsible for political education and morale and had no command functions.

2. Personnel

The Red Navy's enlisted personnel generally impressed foreign observers favorably; for example, a U.S. Navy intelligence report noted that they were "extremely well set up, well-disciplined and exceptionally tough. . . . Although the personal appearance of Red sailors is far below the standard of other western navies, it is much cleaner and neater than that of the soldiers of the Red Army."[1] The officers, on the other hand, were far less impressive. To a large degree, this was a result of the weaknesses of Soviet society as a whole. Despite rapidly rising school enrollment, in 1939–1940 there was still a relatively small pool of educated young men to fill the needs of government, industry, and the armed forces. In consequence, both the Red Army and Navy suffered from a chronic shortage of officers. Against this background, the combination of purges and expansion in the 1930s was devastating; as shown in table 7.1, the number of officer billets rose threefold between 1935 and 1941, at the same time that three thousand officers were purged. The upshot of all this was that inexperienced junior officers were promoted to senior positions, and in many cases they were replaced by promoting noncommissioned officers (NCOs) to junior officers, which exacerbated the chronic shortage of NCOs. Even with these measures, there was a large number of unfilled billets; on 1 January 1941, the seagoing and shore-support units of the navy had only 72 percent of the officers required by their establishment strength, and the situation was even worse in the navy's coast defense units, where there was a 40 percent shortage.

TABLE 7.1 Growth in Number of Officers, 1930–1941 (as of 1 January)

	1930	1935	1937	1938	1939	1941
Number of officers	3,040	9,580	13,562	19,455	28,753	30,189

Note: Figures are for establishment strength (*shtatnaia chislennost'*), not actual strength, which was lower due to vacancies.
Source: V. A. Zolotarev and V. S. Shlomin, *Kak sozdavalas' voenno-morskaia moshch' Sovetskogo Soiuza* (Moscow: AST, 2004), 1:36.

Under these circumstances, it is hardly surprising that Royal Navy observers characterized some Soviet officers as "pathetic" and incompetent.[2] U.S. Navy officers were inclined to be somewhat less harsh; a report by the Office of Naval Intelligence (ONI) concluded that "vessels are always well kept and, considering the inexperience of the officers, quite well handled. Organization and staff work are generally on a very low level."[3] Finding reliable figures for the personnel strength of the navy during the war is surprisingly difficult; the figures shown in table 7.2 should be of the right order.

TABLE 7.2 Soviet Naval Personnel Strength, 1941–1945

	1941	1942	1943	1944	1945
Personnel	344,000	526,000	505,000	483,000	564,325

Sources: Mark Harrison, Accounting for War: Soviet Production, Employment, and the Defence Burden, 1940–1945 (Cambridge: Cambridge University Press, 1996), 270; David M. Glantz, Stumbling Colossus: The Red Army on the Eve of World War (Lawrence: University Press of Kansas, 1998), 293; and Moskva i sud'by rossiiskogo flota (Moscow: Mosgorarkhiv, 1996), 317.

Apart from shipboard duties, naval personnel served in coastal batteries, shore establishments, and the naval air force, as well as in naval infantry units—there was only a single brigade of the latter in 1941, but by the end of the war more than 230,000 troops had served in the naval infantry. This figure does not include the large numbers of men transferred outright to the army—in 1941, 146,899 men; in 1942, 188,976 men; and in 1943, 54,100 men.

Training of Officers/Naval Academies. The Frunze Naval School in Leningrad was the equivalent of the U.S. Naval Academy. In 1937 the Black Sea Naval School was founded in Sevastopol, and the Pacific Naval School in Vladivostok, to train the increased number of officers required to command the "great oceanic fleet"; soon afterward yet another naval school was established at Baku for the Caspian Flotilla. The Frunze Naval School provided the nucleus of the faculties of the new institutions, which inevitably led to a dilution of instructors and a decline in the quality of instruction.

The postgraduate institution was the Voroshilov Naval Academy. It provided senior officer courses and often served as a think tank for the navy, helping to plan and evaluate the annual maneuvers and analyzing proposed ship designs through war-gaming.

Like so many other Soviet institutions of the Stalin era, the system of military and naval ranks underwent a number of nomenclature changes in the 1930s and early 1940s. After the revolution, "personal ranks" were abolished in the Soviet armed forces; that is to say, an officer's rank depended upon the post he held, and he did not retain that rank when he moved to a new post. Personal ranks were reintroduced by a decree of the Council of People's Commissars dated 22 September 1935. While the ranks below flag officers were similar to those of the old imperial navy, the politically sensitive terms "admiral" and "general" were not adopted; in the navy, the word "flagman" (literally, "flag officer") was used.

On 7 May 1940, following the Finnish war, the rank of admiral replaced flagman because of a perceived need to enhance the authority and prestige of senior officers. See appendix II for a listing of ranks and equivalents.

Training. In general, the Red Navy carried out its annual maneuvers in the autumn, after the summer program of training cruises and exercises. During the late 1920s the problems studied during the maneuvers grew increasingly complex, with the ultimate goal being a combined-arms form of naval tactics that would use mine barriers, aircraft, surface ships, submarines, and coast artillery to repulse enemy attacks. The most frequent problems noted in the postmortems were lapses in reconnaissance work and problems in the performance of command staff, but in general, the fleet's skills were improving.

The purges and the rapid expansion of the navy in the late 1930s seem to have drastically reduced the navy's tactical skills. In some years there were no annual maneuvers, and even training exercises seem to have been simplified. Accident rates increased, as did drunkenness and suicide rates, hinting at the pressures that inexperienced and poorly trained officers were being subjected to as new duties were thrust upon them. In 1939–1940 navy commissar N. G. Kuznetsov issued several circulars that noted the high accident rate and laid out a program to improve training. Kuznetsov's efforts came too late; only during the latter stages of the war does the Red Navy seem to have regained the skills necessary to mount combined air-surface and air-submarine attacks, and even then the efforts were generally unsuccessful.

3. Intelligence
Prior to the formation of an independent navy commissariat at the end of 1937, the navy had to rely on Red Army intelligence; only in early 1938 did the navy establish its own intelligence department. It was, however, very much the junior member of the Soviet Union's intelligence services and remained dependent to some degree upon both the army and the Narodnyi komissariat vnutrennikh del (NKVD, the forerunner of the Komitet gosudarstvennoi bezopastnosti, or KGB) for facilities and agent networks.

Although Soviet intelligence can boast of many notable successes in other areas, there is no evidence that Soviet agents significantly penetrated the Kriegsmarine or the Imperial Japanese Navy. Signal intelligence was a far more significant source of information, with a network of fifty radio-monitoring and direction-finding stations erected before the war. These proved valuable for traffic analysis, an area where there was considerable cooperation with the Royal Navy's "Y" service. British colleagues believed that the Soviet service was able and efficient. However, Soviet intelligence agencies did not have access to German Enigma-ciphered communications, nor did the British reveal this source of information.[4]

Despite Soviet expertise in radio intelligence, the Red Navy's own communications appear to have been far from secure. The German B-Dienst radio organization had penetrated Soviet naval codes in the 1930s, and there were several occasions during the war when the British learned through Enigma intercepts that Soviet military and naval communications were being deciphered by the Germans, information that they passed on to their allies without revealing the source.

B. DOCTRINE
1. Surface Warfare
The navy's major doctrinal works were the provisional BUMS-37 "Combat Manual of the Naval Forces," issued in March 1937, and the NMO-40 "Regulations for the Conduct of Naval Operations," promulgated in December 1940. BUMS-37 introduced the idea of "maneuver formations" consisting of a variety of ship types and assembled on an ad hoc basis for the task at hand. Battleships would provide "combat stability"—stiffening—for the light forces. In order to have support of shore-based aircraft, the Red Navy would not fight far from its own coasts, but it would nevertheless fight "deep-sea battles"— that is, it was no longer to be tied to fixed, defensive mine-artillery positions. The offensive trend was reinforced in a May 1939 revision of BUMS-37, which specified that the role of the Red Navy was to "defend the Soviet Union's sea borders in the course of an offensive action."

The NMO-40 regulations emphasized the need for a "decisive blow" against the target, since the best means for defending the USSR's maritime borders and sea lines of communication would be the "annihilation or paralysis of the enemy fleets." The enemy's seagoing forces might be attacked at sea or in his bases, with the aim of destroying or weakening them. As before, the goal was to deliver a "concentrated blow" using a combination of weapons— aircraft, submarines, and surface forces. Battleships, however, were singled out as the "backbone" of the fleet.

Operations to support and protect the Red Army's maritime flank were also stressed in both BUMS-37 and NMO-40. Providing fire support, conducting amphibious landings in the enemy's rear, and frustrating enemy attempts to accomplish similar missions were seen as vital tasks. The Red Army's doctrine was also increasingly oriented toward deep and rapid advances that would force the enemy to fight on his own territory, so the fleet would have to push forward alongside the army to provide flank support. But it was also noted that the navy might undertake "independent" operations—that is, operations with a strategic purpose beyond supporting the army.

The reorganization of the Baltic Fleet on 28 August 1939 reflected the developing prewar doctrine. The surface forces were divided into a squadron, consisting of the two battleships and the Third Destroyer Division (four older *Novik*-type ships), which could conduct "independent" operations and could range over the entire theater, and the Detachment of Light Forces (Otriad legkikh sil, or OLS), which included the cruisers *Kirov* and *Maksim Gorkii* and the First and Second Destroyer Divisions, composed of modern boats, which were intended to operate against the enemy's lines of communications. The OLS was therefore based at Ust-Dvinsk (now Daugavgriva), near Riga, where it could both defend the Gulf of Riga and operate on the flank of any enemy force attempting to penetrate into the Gulf of Finland.

2. Aviation
Naval aviation was not seen as having an independent role in Soviet doctrine; rather, it was an integral element in securing all Red Navy operations. The revised version of BUMS-37, issued in May 1939, noted that shore-based aircraft could carry out a wide range of tasks—attacking enemy sea-lanes, warships, and bases using bombs, torpedoes, or mines, as appropriate. Air cover was necessary for ships operating at sea, as was air reconnaissance. The general view seems to have been that land-based air cover could extend about ninety to one hundred miles from shore.

Cooperation of aircraft with surface vessels and submarines was stressed. The combination of aircraft and motor torpedo boats (MTBs) in coastal regions was seen as an especially useful tactic. The navy was also responsible for the air defense of its own bases, so land-based fighter squadrons were included in naval aviation.

3. Antisubmarine
On 15 January 1931 the naval command issued a directive, "On the Extraordinary Importance of Questions of Anti-Submarine Defense for the Naval Activities of the Navy," which noted that antisubmarine warfare (ASW) training was not receiving sufficient attention. The directive pointed out the need to study methods for protecting the fleet, both when under way and when anchored. Nevertheless, little work on ASW seems to have been done before the war; although by 1933 new models of depth charges had been adopted, the development of submarine detection gear was slow, and doctrine for escorting

surface ships and the tactics of attacking submerged submarines was apparently not addressed in either the BUMS-37 or NMO-40 regulations.

4. Submarine

The submarine warfare regulations issued in 1939 (NPL-39) specified a wide range of missions for submarines—reconnaissance, minelaying, attacks on enemy maritime communications, and special operations, such as inserting small landing parties in the enemy's rear. There were two basic tactics when operating against enemy warships or commerce: the "positional method," in which a submarine was stationed at a specific area and waited for targets to appear, and the "maneuver method," in which the boats would follow a patrol route. The regulations also envisioned submarine scouting lines composed of several boats for sweeping an area.

Under NMO-40, the chief role of submarines was stated to be attacks on the enemy's communications. It was indicated that, while international prize law would be observed when operating against the enemy's sea lanes, there might be occasions when the government would approve "unrestricted warfare." In such cases, zones of "restricted" and "unrestricted" warfare would be announced by the Soviet government. After the outbreak of war, however, the Soviet government never officially declared such zones.

In general, submarine doctrine moved from its initial defensive roles toward offensive use on the enemy's sea lanes, but the tactics necessary for such operations seem to have been inadequately considered. Despite the example set by the German U-boat campaign, no thought seems to have been given to "wolf pack" methods. And although it was noted in October 1940 that the positional method would probably be ineffective, this remained the chief operational mode for submarines after the outbreak of war.

5. Amphibious Operations

The Red Navy extensively studied landing operations in the 1920s; not only would they be useful in supporting the maritime flanks of the army but the navy also believed that a landing to seize the Finnish coast batteries at Björkö would be a vital mission in wartime because the six 10-inch guns there could hamper the movements of surface ships over a wide area. Therefore, landings became a regular part of maneuvers starting in the late 1920s.

NMO-40 divided landing operations into four types: strategic, which would open a new front on enemy territory; operational, which were intended to strike at the enemy's rear to seize important objectives; tactical, which would attack the enemy's flank or immediate rear to gain an advantage in a specific army operation; and diversionary, which might be mounted in conjunction with any of the other three types of landing to confuse the enemy and

PHOTO 7.1. Soviet S-class submarines. Harsh conditions could have a severe impact on both combat operations and training. (The Boris Lemachko Collection)

divert his forces. Airborne forces might be used in conjunction with a landing; indeed, the Russian word *desant* can refer to both amphibious and airborne operations. In any operation, the appointment of a single overall commander, usually an army officer, was considered vital.

Despite the emphasis on amphibious operations, however, the Red Navy devoted little attention to the development of specialized landing craft. Although specifications for such craft had been prepared in 1929, the issue languished until 1940, when four self-propelled landing barges were built for the Baltic Fleet. Given the lack of landing craft, opposed landings were not considered feasible, and the regulations specified out-of-the-way places as most suitable for landings—small commercial ports, bays with fishing villages where piers or jetties would be available, or gently sloping, unwooded beaches where troops could wade ashore.

The Red Navy carried out numerous landing operations during the war. The largest were the Kerch landings on the Crimean Peninsula, 25 December 1941–2 January 1942, in which 42,000 men took part.[5] Many types of vessels were used to transport the troops—everything from destroyers to subchasers, tugs, torpedo boats, minesweepers, and submarines. This sort of improvised transport was possible because the distances to be covered were short. Thirty American landing craft were transferred to the Pacific Fleet under Lend-Lease and used in landing operations during the USSR's brief participation in the war with Japan.

6. Trade Protection

Perhaps due to overconfidence in the Soviet Union's self-sufficiency after its rapid industrialization of the 1930s, the Red Navy paid little attention to the question of trade protection. Even in late 1940, with the example of the ongoing Battle of the Atlantic to study, ASW doctrine was concentrated on defending the fleet rather than commerce. Although convoy was discussed as a means of protecting transports at sea, equal weight was given to the method of patrolling the maritime sea routes with surface warships—an idea whose ineffectiveness had been amply demonstrated in the First World War, not to mention the first year of the Second World War. This failure is even more surprising, given the Red Navy's own emphasis on using submarines against the enemy's maritime communications.

7. Communications

The available sources do not suggest that the Red Navy's means or methods of communication were marked by any particular distinctions. Flags, signal lamps, and radio were all used, but it is not clear if any form of talk-between-ships gear was developed.

III. MATERIEL

A. SHIPS

Soviet shipbuilding was initially hampered by damage to many shipyards during the civil war; that conflict also scattered the talented pool of naval constructors assembled in the last decade of the tsarist regime. The Soviet-educated constructors were inexperienced and the qualities sought in new ship designs were frequently overambitious. As a result, Moscow sought foreign technical assistance, especially from Italy and Germany, in the design and construction of new ships. The warships available at the outbreak and end of the war are shown in tables 7.3 and 7.4.

At the outbreak of war there were three 59,000-ton *Sovetskii Soiuz*–class (Project 23) battleships and two 35,000-ton *Kronshtadt*-class (Project 69) battle cruisers under construction; none was ever completed. The Red Navy's only battleships were the three ships of the *Marat* class (formerly the *Sevastopol* class), which had been built in 1909–1915; they were armed with twelve 12-in/50 guns in four triple turrets disposed along the centerline, with all turrets on one level. The two Baltic Fleet ships, *Marat* (ex-*Petropavlovsk*) and *Oktiabrskaia revoliutsiia* (ex-*Gangut*), were modernized in 1928–1931 and 1931–1934, respectively, but the work was limited to converting the machinery from coal- to oil-burning, improving the fire-control systems (which

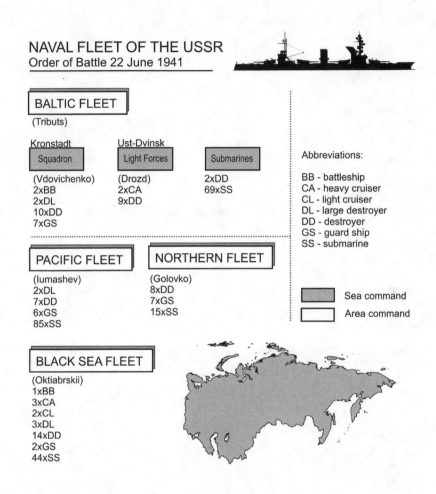

NAVAL FLEET OF THE USSR
Order of Battle 22 June 1941

BALTIC FLEET
(Tributs)

Kronstadt
Squadron

(Vdovichenko)
2xBB
2xDL
10xDD
7xGS

Ust-Dvinsk
Light Forces

(Drozd)
2xCA
9xDD

Submarines

2xDD
69xSS

Abbreviations:

BB - battleship
CA - heavy cruiser
CL - light cruiser
DL - large destroyer
DD - destroyer
GS - guard ship
SS - submarine

PACIFIC FLEET

(Iumashev)
2xDL
7xDD
6xGS
85xSS

NORTHERN FLEET

(Golovko)
8xDD
7xGS
15xSS

Sea command
Area command

BLACK SEA FLEET

(Oktiabrskii)
1xBB
3xCA
2xCL
3xDL
14xDD
2xGS
44xSS

required considerable elaboration of the superstructures), and adding some antiaircraft (AA) guns. The weak deck armor was not increased, and bulges were not fitted. The third ship, *Parizhskaia kommuna* (ex-*Sevastopol*), had been transferred from the Baltic to the Black Sea in 1929–1930 and was subjected to a more extensive modernization than her sisters in 1936–1939. She was fitted with bulges, and her deck protection was increased. The armor of all three ships remained weak, however, and they were ill-suited to modern war.

The Black Sea Fleet included three light cruisers originally laid down in 1913 by the tsarist regime: *Krasnyi Krym* (ex-*Svetlana*, ex-*Profintern*; entered service in 1928), *Chervona Ukraina* (ex–*Admiral Nakhimov*; entered service in 1927), and *Krasnyi Kavkaz* (ex–*Admiral Lazarev*; entered service 1932). The first two were little modified from the original design, armed with fifteen 130-mm guns in single shielded mounts and casemates for a broadside of eight

TABLE 7.3 Red Navy Strength and Distribution on 22 June 1941

	Baltic	Black Sea	Northern	Pacific	Total
Battleships	2	1	0	0	3
Cruisers	2	5	0	0	7
Destroyer leaders	2	3	2	0	7
Destroyers	21	14	8	7	50
Guard ships	7	2	7	6	22
Gunboats	2	4	0	0	6
Minelayers	4	2	1	5	12
Minesweepers	30	12	2	18	62
Submarines	71	44	15	85	215
Sub chasers	20	24	14	19	77
Motor torpedo boats	67	78	0	145	290
Guard cutters	15	0	0	0	15
Armored cutters	4	0	0	0	4
Motor minesweepers	2	0	0	0	2

Source: A.V. Basov, ed., Boevoi put' Sovetskogo Voenno-morskogo flota (Moscow: Voennoe izdatel'stvo, 1988), 540.

TABLE 7.4 Red Navy Strength and Distribution at the End of the War

	Baltic	Black Sea	Northern	Pacific & Amur	Total
Battleships	2[a]	1	1	0	4
Cruisers	2	4	1	2	9
Destroyer leaders	2	0	1	1	4
Destroyers	10	6	16	12	44
Guard ships	5	2	6	19	32
Gunboats	10	3	0	0	13
Minelayers	6	3	3	10	22
Minesweepers	69	24	26	52	171
Submarines	20	30	22	78	150
Large sub chasers	0	0	45	22	67
MTBs	68	53	56	204	381
Guard cutters	127	111	51	27	316
Armored cutters	45	0	0	0	45
Motor minesweepers	215	36	17	0	268
Landing craft	67	0	0	19	86

Note: Figures include Lend-Lease and transfers from the United States and Great Britain; figures are for 1 January 1945, except for Pacific Fleet, where numbers for 9 August 1945 are given.
[a] Including the heavily damaged battleship Petropavlovsk, ex-Marat, used as a floating battery.
Source: Zolotarev and Shlomin, Kak sozdavalas', 1:249.

guns, but *Krasnyi Kavkaz* was much altered, armed with four 180-mm single turrets on the centerline. These guns proved disappointing in service, with a very short barrel life.

The *Kirov* and *Maksim Gorkii* classes represented the modern generation of cruisers; one of each type had been laid down for the Baltic and Black Sea fleets, and these four ships had all entered service by the time of the German invasion; two more *Maksim Gorkii*–class vessels were built in the Far Eastern shipyard at Komsomolsk-na-Amure and entered service in 1943–1944. Based loosely on the Italian *Raimondo Montecuccoli* class, they featured a main battery of nine 180-mm guns of an improved type. They were fast, fitted for minelaying, and the Baltic and Black Sea ships did useful service in shore bombardment during the war; *Maksim Gorkii* and *Molotov* both survived considerable underwater damage.

Seventeen *Novik*-type destroyers of various subclasses had survived the war and revolution. These fine ships proved valuable during the First World War, having generally good seakeeping characteristics and strong hulls. The three 2,000-ton *Leningrad*-class (Project 1) destroyer leaders, the first large Soviet warship design, were built specifically to lead the *Noviks*; they were generally a satisfactory design, fast (they all managed better than forty knots on trial) and with adequate stability—something that would not be the case in later Soviet designs. The three *Minsk*-class (Project 38) ships were very similar to the *Leningrads*, but the Italian-built *Tashkent* was a new departure. Displacing 2,876 tons standard, she was intended to serve as the basis for a three similar Soviet-built ships, but the design proved difficult to convert to Soviet practices, so a completely new type was designed, the *Kiev* class (Project 48); two units were launched before the war but were never completed.

The Project 7- and Project 7U-class destroyers were the backbone of the Red Navy's surface forces during the war and suffered heavy losses accordingly. The Project 7 ships suffered from excess top weight, which necessitated the use of fixed ballast; they also had their boiler rooms grouped forward of the engine rooms, so a single torpedo or mine hit could immobilize a ship. The Project 7U ("U" for *uluchshennaia*, "improved") attempted to fix this defect by arranging the machinery on the unit system; the result, however, was a rather cramped ship. Both the Project 7 and 7U ships had a tendency to lose the bow or the stern when damaged; the worst case was *Sokrushitelnyi*, which lost her stern and sank in a severe storm. An American officer toured the Project 7 destroyer *Razumnyi* in early 1944 and commented that "the general impression gained was that this ship, built in 1937, was inferior in every respect to a contemporary American vessel; that her effectiveness in battle would be not greater than that of a World War I type U.S. destroyer."[6]

The British motor torpedo boat (MTB) attack on Kronshtadt harbor in August 1919 had impressed the Soviets, and the first generations of *torpednye katera* (torpedo cutters, that is, motor torpedo boats) closely followed the pattern of the British boats—small size, hulls of the stepped-planing type, and stern-launched torpedoes. The most numerous class in service at the start of the war was the G-5, which was originally adopted in 1934. The hull was made of duralumin, and the armament consisted of two 533-mm torpedoes and two machine guns. These boats displaced 15 tons, and their seagoing performance was poor; boats sent to Spain during the 1936–1939 civil war proved unsuited for the open sea. Their combat radius of ninety miles also imposed severe operational limitations. Recognition of these problems led to the development of the D-3 boat, a wooden-hulled, 31-ton craft with side-launched torpedoes generally similar to British and American MTBs.

Soviet submarine construction began with the "D" class of 1927; these were large (934/1,360 tons surface/submerged displacement) boats of double-hull construction. Although their performance was somewhat disappointing, they were a creditable start. While they were under construction, the British submarine L-55, sunk on a mine in the Baltic in 1919, was raised, studied, and eventually repaired and put into service. Many features of the British boat were adopted in subsequent Soviet submarines, including the single-hull construction with external ballast tanks (called "one-and-a-half-hull construction" by the Soviets).

From these beginnings, Soviet submarines developed along four general lines: small (the "M" types); medium (the "*shchuka*" and "S" types); minelaying (the "L" types); and "squadron" (the "P" and "K" types). The small boats warrant only a brief description because, as one Russian historian has noted, they "did not possess real combat significance."[7] Known as the *maliutki* (little ones), these boats were designed for overland transport by railroad and ranged from 157/197 tons displacement in the first series to 281/351 tons in the final batch. The latter group had four torpedo tubes while all the earlier boats had only two torpedo tubes; none carried reloads. Although built in large numbers, they scored few successes during the war, and were suited only to local defense.

The medium boats were a far more useful type. The "Shch" boats (*shchuki*) displaced 578/705 tons (increased slightly in later batches), used the single-hulled construction with external ballast tanks copied from the L-55, and had an armament of six 533-mm torpedo tubes and one 45-mm gun. The light gun armament and low surface speed (11.6 knots) were the chief flaws of this type, and it was to remedy these defects and to learn from foreign experience that in 1933 it was decided to purchase a design from the German-backed IvS firm in The Hague. The resulting "S" class (*srednaia*, "medium"; 840/1,070 tons)

PHOTO 7.2. In addition to the sea-going ships described in the text, the Red Navy also built numerous specialized craft for river and lake operations. Here are a Project 1125u "armored cutter" (*bronekater*) and a Project 1124 armored cutter in the background. (The Boris Lemachko Collection)

proved a success; one of their strong points was that they were much quieter than previous Soviet boats.

Minelaying submarines fell into the "L" series (1,040/1,340 tons, increased slightly in later batches), which usually carried twenty mines in two horizontal tubes aft. Early problems with poor-quality batteries were eventually solved, and the boats came to be one of the mainstays of the Red Navy's submarine force.

The "squadron" submarines were originally intended to work with surface ships and therefore required a high surface speed. The first attempt, the "P" class (1931; 955/1,690 tons), proved unsuccessful because the boats were slow to dive and overly complicated; all three were soon relegated to training duties. The "K"-class (*kreiser*, "cruiser") proved far more successful and saw considerable action during the war. They were large boats (1,500/2,117 tons) with a heavy armament (ten 533-mm torpedo tubes and two 100-mm guns).

B. AVIATION

1. Ship-based

The Red Navy possessed no dedicated aviation vessels before or during the war, so shipboard aviation was limited to the seaplanes carried by the battleships and cruisers. The roles envisioned for these aircraft were reconnaissance and spotting—the Baltic Fleet's battleships operated with spotter aircraft for the first time in May 1928. The standard seaplane in use was the KOR-1, which began entering service in 1937. It was a run-of-the-mill biplane with a speed of about 170 mph. In 1941 a more impressive shipboard aircraft, the KOR-2 (Be-4), a single-engine flying boat with a maximum speed of 220 mph, began entering service. It was built in limited numbers during the war.

2. Shore-based

The Red Navy had an extensive shore-based air force, as shown in tables 7.5 and 7.6. The preponderance of fighters was because the navy was responsible for the air defense of its own bases.

TABLE 7.5 Red Navy Aircraft Strength on 22 June 1941 (All Types) by Fleet

Type of Aircraft	Northern	Baltic	Black Sea	Pacific	Flotillas	Other	Total
Bombers/ Torpedo- bombers	11	183	143	186	14	76	613
Reconnaissance	56	159	167	307	89	81	859
Fighters	49	367	315	385	45	191	1,352

Trainers, transport, etc.	26	160	172	205	20	431	1,014
Total	142	869	797	1,083	168	779	3,838

Source: Zolotarev and Shlomin, *Kak sozdavalas'*, 1:30.

TABLE 7.6 **Red Navy Combat Air Strength, 1941–1945**

Fleet	22 June 1941	1 January 1943	1 January 1944	1945
Northern	116	284	298	400
Baltic	709	208	313	787
Black Sea	625	213	429	400
Pacific	878	n/a	n/a	1,495

Sources: Von Hardesty, *Red Phoenix: The Rise of Soviet Air Power, 1941–1945* (Washington, DC: Smithsonian Institution Press, 1982), 255; and Zolotarev and Shlomin, *Kak sozdavalas'*, 1:30.

The aircraft were the same types as those used by the army air force, with the exception of flying boats. Unfortunately, many naval aircraft at the start of the war were of obsolete types, such as the I-15bis and I-153 biplanes and the stubby I-16 monoplane fighter; only later would more advanced types such as the MiG-3, Yak-1, LaGG-3, and La-5 fighters join the fleet.

The naval air arm also lacked an effective dive-bomber until the twin-engined Pe-2 began entering service toward the end of 1941. The horizontal- and torpedo-bomber roles were filled by the DB-3 and DB-3T; when the war started, the more advanced DB-3F torpedo bomber was just entering service.

Horizontal bombing accuracy was poor; during the Winter War, sixty-three tons of bombs were expended in repeated attacks on the Finnish coast defense ships, without a single hit being scored. War with Germany would not see a marked improvement of the performance of the Red Fleet's air arm.

C. WEAPON SYSTEMS

1. Gunnery

Surface. In general, the Red Navy favored guns with high velocities and heavy shells. This was a reflection of the desire for long ranges; to some degree, it was also the result of Soviet technological overconfidence. These tendencies were especially evident in the first Soviet-designed major-caliber naval gun, the 180-mm (7.1-inch)/60 mounted in single turrets in the cruiser *Krasnyi Kavkaz*. This ambitious weapon was intended to have a rate of fire of six rounds per minute and muzzle velocity of no less than 1,000 m/s. It was soon clear, however, that both the gun and mounting were problematic; proving ground trials showed that the semiautomatic loading system did not work, and the muzzle velocity had to be reduced to 920 m/s. Moreover, the rate of bore erosion was so great that the barrel had a life of only fifty-five full-charge rounds.

An entirely new gun of the same caliber and ballistic performance was developed for the Kirov class cruisers; barrel life was increased by making the rifling deeper and accepting a greater loss in muzzle velocity before replacement was required. Despite such early problems, however, Soviet naval guns generally seem to have been reliable and accurate by the outbreak of war; their characteristics are shown in appendix I.

The Soviets had a variety of domestic and foreign fire-control equipment in service. The battleship *Marat* had a Pollen Argo V computer purchased before World War I, while her sister ships, *Parizhskaia kommuna* and *Oktiabrskaia revoliutsiia* as well as the cruiser *Krasnyi Kavkaz* were equipped with British Vickers computers bought in the late 1920s. In 1931 an Italian system from the firm of Galileo was purchased for the *Leningrad*-class destroyer leaders; it formed the basis for subsequent Soviet-made fire-control computers for the Project 7- and 7U-class destroyers, as well as the systems developed for the *Kirov*- and *Maksim Gorkii*–class cruisers. In all cases, the gear kept track of own-ship and target-ship courses and speeds and calculated the required data for aiming the guns. Stereoscopic rangefinders were used, 6-m instruments in the modernized battleships and new light cruisers, and 4-m instruments in the new destroyers.

Fire was corrected by three distinct methods: by observation of the fall of shot, that is, the observation of splashes as short or over; by measured ranges, where both the range to the target and the range to the splashes of one's own shells were measured (hence the multiple rangefinders in many Soviet director posts), and by measured divergence, where a device of Italian origin called a scartometer was attached to a rangefinder and was used to measure the distance between the target and one's own shell splashes.

Given the importance of supplying seaward support for the Red Army, the problems of shore bombardment received special attention. The computers of the *Kirov* and *Maksim Gorkii* classes allowed for firing at shore targets invisible from the ship by means of an auxiliary point of aim—a visible landmark ashore whose distance and direction from the target were known. These ships could fire at such unseen shore targets while under way.

Antiaircraft. The standard heavy AA guns were the 76 mm and 100 mm; the failure to develop a medium-caliber, dual-purpose mounting meant that even new destroyers carried a pair of 76-mm guns for AA defense.

The modernized battleship *Parizhskaia kommuna* was equipped with two SVP-1 manually stabilized AA directors on her tower mast; these proved too heavy for accurate stabilization when the ship was maneuvering, so a lighter director was developed for the *Kirov*-class cruisers, designated SPN-100. The effectiveness of this gear is unknown; as one Russian source notes, "during the entire war . . . the cruisers did not once use their 100-mm guns against aerial targets while rolling, and thus an objective evaluation of the high-angle fire control system from the point of view of stabilization is simply not possible."[8]

As for light AA guns, the older 45 mm's low rate of fire (30 rpm) made it minimally effective. The 37 mm was a much superior weapon, with a rate of fire of 180 rpm; single mountings were standard although a prototype quad mounting was fitted aboard the battleship *Oktiabrskaia revoliutsiia* during the war. Most ships also carried 12.7-mm machine guns.

Before the war, the navy showed little interest in the army's radar development program, and by the outbreak of war, only one warship was equipped with radar, the Black Sea Fleet cruiser *Molotov*, which had a Redut-K air-search radar. This set proved very reliable, but Soviet industry managed to manufacture only three more naval radar sets during the war, and these did not enter service until 1944. Designated Giuis-1, they were installed on the destroyers *Strogii*, *Gromkii*, and *Rianyi*. All other shipboard radar sets were of British or American manufacture, with the British Type 291 air-search set the most widespread type in Soviet use.

2. Torpedoes

Soviet torpedo development was generally unsuccessful until the purchase in 1932 of an Italian 533-mm torpedo, which formed the basis for the major types used during the war, the 53-38 21-inch torpedo and its successor, the 53-38U. A more advanced model, the 53-39, was delayed in entering service, due in part to industrial disruptions caused by the purges, and only a few were used during the war. The purges also delayed the development of magnetic noncontact detonators, which began reaching the fleet only in 1942.

Just before the war the Red Navy tested the electrically driven ET-80 torpedo, but production problems delayed the introduction of this weapon, and only sixteen ET-80s were used in attacks during the war. Some work had also been done before the war on acoustic guidance for torpedoes, but this reached fruition only after the war.

As for aviation torpedoes, there were two basic types. The parachute-equipped "TAV" series ("aviation torpedo of high-altitude torpedo-release") could be dropped from two thousand to three thousand meters and was set to run circular or spiral courses after hitting the water; apparently intended for mass attacks on large enemy formations, they proved completely ineffective during the war. The "TAN" series ("aviation torpedo of low-altitude torpedo-release") was a more conventional type. They could be dropped from a maximum height of 30 m, at a speed of approximately 320 kph while flying a strictly horizontal course. Any deviation could lead to the torpedo either breaking up when it hit the water, or diving too deeply. In 1944 the Soviets began receiving American aerial torpedoes (probably Mk 13), which were used by modified Shturmovik (IL-2T) aircraft. These had much more flexible drop characteristics than Soviet torpedoes. In general, the Soviets thought their torpedoes had performed reliably during the war, but German sources indicate that there were "numerous reports of torpedoes passing under ships or detonating without hitting anything," as well as surface-runners.[9]

3. Antisubmarine Warfare

Antisubmarine warfare was not a priority in the prewar years. The first hydrophone gear to enter service was the Poseidon set of 1937, followed by the slightly improved Tsefei-2 set in 1940, but neither could be used with the ship under way. Nevertheless, sets were supplied to subchasers and submarines. The first Soviet active sonar set, Tamir-1, entered service only in 1940, but due to lack of operator training, it was often used simply as a passive hydrophone. Moreover, to work at all the ship's speed had to be less than six knots—reduced to three knots when used passively.

By the outbreak of war, not a single Soviet destroyer or escort ship was fitted even with the limited sonar equipment available. It was only with the receipt of British Asdic sets, starting in the autumn of 1941, that the Red Navy acquired a real ASW capability, although the complexities of ASW equipment and methods initially proved baffling to many Soviet officers and crews. Great Britain sent 293 Asdic sets to the USSR by between 1 October 1941 and 31 March 1946.

The standard Soviet depth charges were the BB-1 (135-kg TNT, sink rate 2.3–2.5 m/sec) and BM-1 (25-kg TNT, sink rate 2.1–2.3 m/sec), which had both been adopted in 1933. During the war, Soviet ships were equipped with various British and American ASW weapons, including Hedgehog.

4. Mines

The most widely used anchored mine was the M-26, employed predominantly in defensive minefields. Its main defects were its short mooring cable (130 m) and tendency toward sympathetic detonation—that is, it could be detonated by the explosion of neighboring mines. The KB (*Korabelnaia bolshaia*, "large ship-laid [mine]"), introduced in 1940, had a 260-m mooring cable.

Antisubmarine mines included the AG type (antenna galvanic [mine]), which entered service in 1940. It had two antennae, an upper one suspended from a buoy 30 m above the mine, and a lower one, extending 30 m below the mine; an electrical charge created when the steel hull of a submarine came into contact with an antenna detonated the mine. However, the copper section of the mooring cable was not very strong; moreover, each mine required 30 kg of copper, a metal in great demand. A modified version was therefore developed, the AGS mine (antenna deep-water [mine] with steel antennae). Based on the AG, it used steel antennae coated with zinc. It turned out, however, that the zinc corroded rapidly in seawater, and mines with copper antennae continued in use.

There were a handful of air-laid noncontact MIRAB mines (induction river aviation mine for laying from low-level flight) on hand at the start of the war, but they proved too fragile for aircraft laying. As a result, the Soviets requested and received shipments of British A Mark IV and A Mark V mines. Eventually the Soviets produced the rugged AMD-500 and AMD-1000 aviation ground mines, which entered production in 1943.

Submarine-laid mines included the PLT (submarine tube [mine]), designed for use in the large-diameter (912-mm) mine tubes of the L-class submarines. During the war, the PLT-Z mine was developed to fit in conventional 533-mm torpedo tubes; it had a smaller charge than the PLT mine.

D. INFRASTRUCTURE

1. Logistics

For the most part, the prewar Red Navy did not expect to have to fight at great distances from its bases, so ships were short-ranged and no work was done on underway replenishment; some mobile support facilities, mostly floating workshops to support submarines and MTBs, were acquired.

The supply of fuel oil was recognized as a critical issue. The Soviet Union possessed immense reserves of oil, especially in the Caucasus, and during the war the navy usually had sufficient fuel for its needs. The great exception was the Baltic Fleet; fuel deliveries to Leningrad had to be halted on 3 September 1941 due to the German blockade, and it was only after the "Road of Life" was established over frozen Lake Ladoga in December that limited deliveries of food and fuel were possible. Many of the Baltic Fleet's surface ships had to be placed in conservation to limit fuel consumption, and ships providing artillery support to the defenders had only sufficient fuel to operate their gun mountings. The navy's overall consumption during the war is shown in table 7.7.

TABLE 7.7 Total Consumption of Fuel by the Red Navy, 1941–1945 (tons)

Form of Fuel	1941 (Jul–Dec)	1942	1943	1944	1945 (to 1 May)	Total
Liquid Fuels	379,700	765,800	613,300	703,700	~230,000	~2,692,500
Coal	~350,000	693,900	641,800	573,200	~190,000	~2,448,900

Source: Zolotarev and Shlomin, Kak sozdavalas', 1:405.

As the war went on, the major problem was not the productivity of the oil fields or of the refineries, but transportation. The increasingly mechanized Red Army needed almost all the available rolling stock to feed its tanks and Lend-Lease Studebaker trucks. The situation was eased in August 1944 when the Romanian oil fields and refineries were captured virtually intact.

2. Bases

The main naval base in the Baltic was Kronshtadt, on Kotlin Island, about fifteen miles west of Leningrad at the narrow eastern extremity of the Gulf of Finland. Kronshtadt had repair facilities and dry docks and was heavily fortified. The Gulf of Finland generally freezes from mid-December to April, so vessels based at Kronshtadt were immobilized for several months every year. Icebreakers extended the navigation season to some degree.

The absorption of the Baltic states opened up new possibilities; the fleet's main base was relocated to Tallinn, the Detachment of Light Forces was based at Ust-Dvinsk, the outer port of Riga, and the 1st Submarine Brigade moved to Libau in Latvia. After the Winter War with Finland, the Red Navy established a base at Hanko, at the northern flank of the entrance to the Gulf of Finland. However, Libau fell to the Germans on 26 June 1941, Tallinn was evacuated on 28 August, and Hanko was abandoned by 3 December. The fleet was once again restricted to Kronshtadt, where it remained until the siege of Leningrad was broken in January 1944.

Matters were even worse in the Black Sea. The main base here was Sevastopol, on the Crimean Peninsula. By October 1941 advancing German forces had cut off the Crimea from the mainland, and by the spring of 1942, the fleet had abandoned it as a base altogether, falling back on the Caucasian port of Novorossiisk. After stubborn resistance, supported by the fleet, Sevastopol fell to the Germans on 4 July 1942. Novorossiisk was a large and well-equipped harbor, but the German summer offensive of 1942 led to its capture in September. This forced the fleet to base itself at the unsuitable ports of Poti and Batumi, with Tuapse used as a forward base. Two floating dry docks had been towed from Novorossiisk to Poti, where they proved invaluable for ship repairs.

The Northern Fleet's principal base was the ice-free port of Polyarnoe (renamed Polyarny postwar) on the Kola Inlet near Murmansk, which served as the fleet's repair base. Facilities at these bases were limited, and there were only two dry docks available, located at Rosta, three miles north of Murmansk. Other dry docks were under construction at the new shipyard complex at Molotovsk (now Severodvinsk) but were not completed during the war.

In the Far East, the main naval base was Vladivostok, which included shipyards, dry docks and repair facilities. Although generally frozen two months

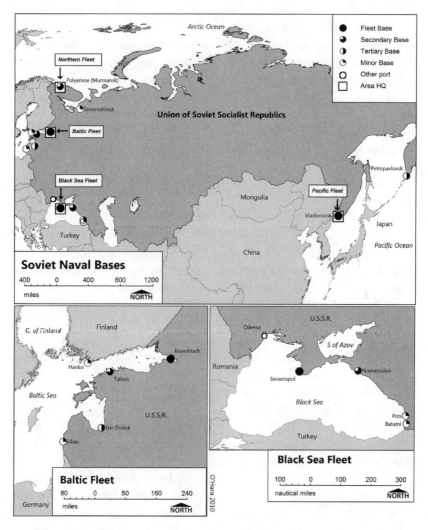

of the year, icebreakers kept it open year-round. Its chief disadvantage was its proximity to Japan, which made it vulnerable to attack. Before the start of the war, work was started to convert Petropavlovsk, on the Kamchatka Peninsula, into a major naval facility, and it served as the main operating base for the Soviet Pacific Fleet during its brief the war against Japan.

3. Industry
During the 1920s, Soviet shipbuilding, like the rest of the economy, recovered slowly from the devastation of the civil war. New construction centered on the merchant vessels necessary to restore trade; naval work was limited to the repair or completion of tsarist-era ships. Only in 1928 were the first halting steps taken

toward new warship construction—the Series I submarines, the *Uragan*-class guard ships (escorts), and the first MTBs. Foreign assistance was necessary for all these ships—German help with the turbines of the *Uragans*, drawings of the *Balilla*-class submarines purchased from the Italians for the Series I boats, and American-made Wright Typhoon and Italian Isotta-Fraschini engines for the MTBs. This trend continued with the next designs; the *Leningrad*-class destroyer leaders had an Italian fire-control system, the *Kirov*-class cruisers were based on an Italian design, and the lead ship was driven by Italian-made turbines.

Overoptimistic assessments of industrial growth during the first Five-Year Plan (1928–1932) led to unrealistic targets being set for the second Five-Year Plan (1933–1937)—8 cruisers, 47 destroyers or destroyer leaders, and 310 submarines, plus numerous smaller vessels. In fact, the tempo of construction was much slower than hoped, and most of the vessels had to be carried over into the third Five-Year Plan, by which time emphasis had shifted to capital ships. Building modern battleships and battle cruisers required an enormous expansion of the existing shipyards, not to mention armor-rolling mills and gun factories. Stalin's emphasis on unrealistic production targets led managers to sacrifice quality for quantity, a problem exacerbated by an inexperienced and poorly educated workforce. The purges of 1937–1938 also played into these problems, and many managers, technical specialists, and experienced workers were dismissed, arrested, or executed. The result was disorganization on a massive scale, and materials were almost always delivered late and often unusable. Thus the rivets supplied for the construction of the battleship *Sovetskaia Belorussiia* proved defective, and work on the ship had to be halted. Castings for various types of machinery sometimes had to be poured fifteen or twenty times to get a satisfactory unit, and the rejection rate of armor plate was 30–40 percent.

The outbreak of war disrupted and dislocated the entire shipbuilding industry—to begin with, about 50 percent of its industrial capacity was turned over to the production of materials for the army. But there were compensations. Efforts were concentrated on a few essential types—just the sort of program Soviet managers could handle—while submarines and light surface vessels did not require heavy armor plate or complex gun mountings. Specialists evacuated from Leningrad before the city was cut off were sent to other shipyards, boosting their level of expertise.

The Black Sea shipyards presented a special case. Whereas Leningrad remained in Soviet hands throughout the war, the Germans took both Nikolaev and Sevastopol. Had it not been for massive evacuations, the Black Sea Fleet would have been left without any shipbuilding or repair facilities at all (see tables 7.8 and 7.9). More than ten thousand specialists were evacuated from the Black Sea shipyards, along with a great deal of equipment, which allowed the Black Sea Fleet to continue fighting. Several incomplete warships,

Photo 7.3. A group of German officers inspecting the Nikolaev shipyard in 1941. (The Boris Lemachko Collection)

including a cruiser, several destroyers, and submarines, were also towed from Nikolaev to Caucasian ports to keep them out of German hands.

TABLE 7.8 Major Shipbuilding Yards, Showing Workforces at Start of War

Name	Location	Workforce, 22 June 1941
Krasnoe Sormovo	Gorkii	?
Baltic Works (S.Ordzhonikidze Works)	Leningrad	15,500
A. A. Zhadanov Works	Leningrad	11,500
A. Marti Works	Leningrad	11,300
Sudomekh Works	Leningrad	4,200
A. Marti Works	Nikolaev	22,500
Amurskaia Yard	Komsomolsk-na-Amure	?
61 Kommunara Works	Nikolaev	10,800
Sevmor Works named for S. Ordzhonikidze	Sevastopol	6,937
Dalzavod named for K.E. Voroshilov	Vladivostok	?
Severnyi Works	Molotovsk	?

Source: I. P. Spasskii, ed., *Istoriia otechestvennogo sudostroeniia*, 5 vols. (St. Petersburg: Sudostroenie, 1994–1996), 4:275, 4:450.

TABLE 7.9 Warships Delivered, 22 June 1941–9 May 1945

Type of Ship	1941	1942	1943	1944	1945	Total
Light cruisers	0	1	0	1	0	2
Destroyers	14	3	0	0	1	18
Guard ships	0	0	2	1	0	3
Minesweepers	1	1	1	1	8	12
Large subchasers	2	3	1	9	3	18
Submarines	23	13	11	5	3	55
Monitors	0	1	1	0	0	2
Motor cutters	97	62	177	216	39	591
Motor minesweepers	23	80	93	123	8	327

Source: Zolotarev and Shlomin, *Kak sodavalas'*, 1:234.

IV. RECAPITULATION

A. WARTIME EVOLUTION

Although the Winter War with Finland (30 November 1939–12 March 1940) proved less embarrassing for the Red Navy than it had for the Red Army, there was still little cause for satisfaction with its performance. Surface forces had bombarded the Finnish batteries at Björkö, submarines had carried out patrols, and naval aviation had mounted attacks, but little had actually been accomplished. The submarines sank only five merchant ships while aircraft sank another four. Despite numerous air attacks, no hits were scored on the two Finnish coast defense ships. In the end, the blundering Red Army overwhelmed Finnish resistance by virtue of its massive numerical superiority, and the peace treaty granted Moscow the border adjustments it desired as well as the naval base at Hanko at the mouth of the Gulf of Finland.

During the interlude of peace following the Winter War, both the Red Army and Navy undertook a series of reforms, but these steps were far from complete when the Germans invaded on 22 June 1941. For the Baltic Fleet, the opening phases of what the Russians call the Great Patriotic War were characterized by confusion and heavy losses. In rapid succession, the bases gained in 1939–1940 were lost, and eight destroyers as well as a variety of other surface craft were sunk during the evacuations of Tallinn and Hanko; as for the toll in human lives, estimates suggest that it was close to 20,000 seamen and soldiers. In other circumstances, these evacuations would have been considered fiascos, but the two operations delivered more than 30,000 soldiers to Leningrad—an important addition to the city's defenses.

Nevertheless, it was unclear if Leningrad itself could be held, and on 13 September 1941 the Stavka ordered preparations to destroy the Baltic Fleet and its shore facilities. A detailed plan was worked out to use torpedo warheads and depth charges to destroy the ships. Fortunately, it never had to be put into effect, and the guns of the warships played an important role in the city's long defense. The battleship *Marat*'s bow was blown apart when a bomb penetrated the forward main battery magazine on 23 September 1941, but she sank in shallow water. By the end of October, the surviving three-quarters of the ship had been refloated and her guns were back in action.

But shore bombardment of the besieging German troops would be the only contribution made by the big surface ships for the remainder of the war in the Baltic theater. Hemmed in by enemy minefields, subjected to sporadic attacks by the Luftwaffe, starved of fuel, and with many of the crew landed to serve ashore, the Baltic Fleet's war now became an affair of submarines and aircraft. The island of Lavansaari (Moshchnyy), sixty-five miles west of Kronshtadt, remained in Soviet hands and became "a stationary carrier from which planes supported the minesweepers when they worked at clearing passages for their submarines through the Finnish-German minefields."[10] These minefields were a formidable barrier, and the difficulties experienced by Soviet submarines in getting out into the Baltic were compounded in 1943 when the Germans installed a double row of antisubmarine nets at the mouth of the Gulf of Finland.

The Baltic situation changed radically in 1944. In January the Soviets raised the siege of Leningrad; by September Finland was forced to sign an armistice that granted base rights to Soviet submarines, which could now operate freely in the central Baltic. Nevertheless, the Baltic Fleet's submarines, MTBs, and aircraft were unable to stop German seaborne supplies from reaching the isolated Courland army. The fleet's most spectacular successes came in the first months of 1945, during the evacuation of East Prussia, when the submarine *S-13* sank *Wilhelm Gustloff* (30 January) and *General Steuben* (10 February); tragically, about nine thousand refugees were lost in these sinkings.

Events had followed a broadly similar course in the Black Sea, but at a slower pace. The fleet ably supported Odessa during its siege by German-Romanian forces (13 August–16 October 1941), but by the end of September the decision was made to evacuate Odessa and use the troops to assist in the defense of Sevastopol, now threatened by the German advance. The evacuation, carried out 1–16 October, was well executed; 86,000 soldiers, 15,000 civilians, more than 1,000 vehicles, and 462 guns were pulled out, mostly during the nights, so the process was completed almost before the enemy realized that it had started.

The battle for Sevastopol was a prolonged operation and again the Black Sea Fleet operating from Novorossiisk provided support. Large-scale landings, ultimately involving 42,000 men, were carried out at Kerch and Feodosiia on the Crimean Peninsula in the period 25 December 1941–2 January 1942 to divert German forces from the siege. Although these bridgeheads were eventually eliminated, they helped prolong Sevastopol's resistance until July 1942. However, the Black Sea Fleet lost Novorossiisk when the Germans captured it on 6 September 1942.

The German forces occupying the Crimea were supplied by sea, and the Black Sea Fleet's destroyers staged a number of raids on these coastal convoys; it was during one such operation on 6 October 1943 that the destroyer leader *Kharkov* and the destroyers *Sposobnyi* and *Besposhchadnyi* were lost to German air attacks. The ill-starred operation had far-reaching consequences because in its wake Stavka issued the following order: "Long-range operations of large surface forces of the fleet are to be carried out only with the permission of the Stavka of the Supreme Command."[11] Although directed specifically at the Black Sea Fleet, the principle that the surface ships should be used only with Stavka's approval was probably applied in the Baltic as well and explains in part the failure to use the surface forces to interfere with the many German maritime operations in support of their retreating forces in the war's latter stages.

Operations by submarines, MTBs, and aircraft continued, however, although with only limited success. The Black Sea Fleet did not seriously hinder the convoys supplying the German forces in the Crimea—or, in April–May 1944, the maritime evacuation of those forces. On 23 August 1944 the Red Army's advance forced Romania to capitulate, and Bulgaria followed suit on 8 September. These events ended the naval war in the Black Sea, although the Danube River Flotilla remained active until the end of hostilities.

The Northern Fleet played an important role in supporting Soviet troops on the Rybachii Peninsula, on the flank of the German forces operating in northern Norway. This was a critical factor in preventing the enemy from capturing Murmansk, a port vitally important for receiving war materiel from the Western allies. The fleet was reinforced by six submarines transferred from the Baltic via the White Sea Canal (ten incomplete boats were also sent to the north) and by destroyers and submarines sent from the Pacific (three destroyers via the Northern Sea Route, six submarines via the Panama Canal). The destroyers, minesweepers, and other surface vessels helped secure the passage of the Arctic convoys; but although the Northern Fleet undertook to escort the convoys east of Bear Island, the limited number of Soviet destroyers and their lack of effective antisubmarine equipment made it necessary for British escorts to accompany the convoys all the way to Murmansk and Arkhangelsk. Submarines, MTBs, and aircraft attacked German coastal convoys supplying troops in northern Norway and Finland. In October 1944 landings were made in the rear of the German defenders in conjunction with an offensive by the 14th Army. Despite these operations, however, the Germans were able to withdraw most of their northern forces with negligible losses.

Throughout the war with Germany, the Pacific Fleet had served primarily as a source of additional ships for the Northern Fleet. After the German capitulation, substantial military and air forces were sent to the Far East; the fleet's strength had in the meantime been bolstered by large numbers of Lend-Lease vessels, including landing craft. On 8 August 1945 the USSR declared war on Japan and landings were carried out on the east coast of Korea in support of the Red Army. Despite the Japanese surrender on 14 August, the Soviet offensive continued, with landings on the southern half of Sakhalin and in the Kurile Islands. The occupation of the Kuriles was complete by 3 September, and military operations came to an end.

B. SUMMARY AND ASSESSMENT

Despite Stalin's enormous investment in capital ship construction in the late 1930s, the Red Navy fought three wars—the Winter War with Finland, the Great Patriotic War against Germany, and a brief conflict with Japan in the Far East in August–September 1945—with what was in essence the "Young School" fleet conceived in the early 1930s. The tactics of such a fleet based on submarines, MTBs, and aircraft had been intensely studied between the wars, yet the Red Navy's performance in general was poor.

Most puzzling in this regard is the minimal impact of the vast submarine fleet. During the war the Red Navy thought its subs were doing well—in February 1943 Admiral Kuznetsov assessed enemy losses from submarine attacks as 189 transports, 5 destroyers, 10 escort vessels, and a variety of other ships—but postwar data show that claims of sinkings were enormously exaggerated. Certainly the rapid prewar growth of the submarine force meant that few Soviet commanders had much experience with their vessels, and their crews were equally raw. Submarine doctrine was also deeply flawed; in the early phases of the war, submarines tended to attack with single torpedoes, which led to a very low hit rate. The ineffectiveness of the Soviet attack methods was highlighted when the British submarines *Tigris*, *Trident*, *Seawolf*, and *Sealion* operated out of Murmansk for a few weeks in the autumn of 1941; while there, they sank 6 transports and 1 escort—more ships than the entire Northern Fleet submarine force for that year (3 transports and 2 warships).

The British submariners taught their Soviet hosts their techniques, including two methods for firing spreads of torpedoes—the "firing interval" in which the sub fired torpedoes with a timed interval between launches so the torpedoes would cross the target's track at different times, thereby allowing for errors in estimating the target's speed, course, or both, and "firing on the swing," in which the torpedoes were fired while the submarine was under helm. The Soviets adopted both methods. But while the Soviets copied the British methods, they seem to have overlooked the most important element:

the ability of a captain to estimate, from a few brief observations, the target's course and speed. This was a skill that the Royal Navy's infamous "perisher" course was designed to develop in submarine commanders, but there is no evidence that the Red Navy developed an equivalent course during the war.

Soviet submarines also tended to dive immediately after attacking, so they often could not see the effects of their attacks. As a result, any explosion heard after attacking was interpreted as a hit. This explains the most famous Soviet claim—that the submarine *K-21*, under the command of Captain Second Rank N. A. Lunin, torpedoed the German battleship *Tirpitz* on 5 July 1942. Lunin's report shows that the submarine fired a spread of four torpedoes at a distance of 3,400–4,000 yards—a very great range—after which he dived deep, heard several explosions at about the right time, and assumed that he had hit. In fact he had not. There were also occasions when torpedoes hit the submerged rocks so prevalent in Norwegian coastal waters, leading other submarines to claim successes. These claims became part of a feedback loop: submarine commanders thought they were attacking successfully, so they saw no reason to change or even question their tactics and continued using the same unsuccessful methods.

A final problem was the operational use of the boats. Early in the war the "positional" method was used, with the submarines assigned to fixed areas, where they would wait for enemy vessels to appear. Without reconnaissance to locate targets, this was a haphazard method of employment, and because naval aviation was often diverted to supporting operations ashore, the result of these operations was minimal. Only after 1943, when the Soviet air force was gaining command of the air, could aircraft regularly be spared for maritime reconnaissance.

Table 7.10 summarizes Soviet submarine successes in terms of tonnage sunk. A few points should be noted. In addition to merchant ships, the Red Navy's submarines also sank twenty-two warships, mostly small escort vessels. Mines laid by submarines sank an additional 38,291 tons of merchant shipping and fifteen warships. The failure of Baltic Fleet submarines to score any successes in 1943 was due to the German-Finnish net barrier at the exit from the Gulf of Finland, which stopped any subs that made it through the mine barriers from reaching the central Baltic, where the enemy shipping routes ran. In 1944 naval operations in the Black Sea and the northern theater were winding down as the Germans retreated, which accounts for the few sinkings scored in those areas.

The Red Navy had also invested heavily in motor torpedo boats, and a great deal of attention had been devoted to developing tactics for them before the war, including the use of smokescreens to provide cover during daylight attacks. Yet in action, they also proved a disappointment. Unlike the problems

TABLE 7.10 Soviet Submarine Successes by Fleet, 1941–1945

Year	Northern		Baltic		Black Sea		Totals	
	Merchant Ships Sunk	GRT	Merchant Ships Sunk	GRT	Merchant Ships Sunk	GRT	Merchant Ships Sunk	GRT
1941	3	6,442	1	3,724	5	15,643	9	25,809
1942	10	17,873	20	40,613	10	11,220	40	69,706
1943	7	26,586	0	0	10	27,325	17	53,911
1944	2	6,786	11	18,808	2	153	15	25,747
1945	0	0	10	55,885	0	0	10	55,885
Totals	22	57,687	42	119,030	27	54,341	91	231,058

Source: Adapted from data in Rolf Erikson, "Soviet Submarine Operations in World War II," in *Reevaluating Major Naval Combatants of World War II*, ed. James J. Sadkovich, 155–79 (New York: Greenwood Press, 1990).

besetting the submarine force, however, the failings of the MTBs were seen relatively early in the war; Admiral Kuznetsov noted in a memorandum dated 21 January 1942 that "seven month's experience of war against German fascism shows that, despite the large number of torpedo cutters in the Navy . . . the use of torpedo cutters has been inadequately skillful and purposeful."[12] Kuznetsov considered that the problems lay in poorly conceived operations, the subordination of the boats to officers who did not understand their use, and the use of the boats for other roles, such as high-speed transports. He also emphasized the need for thorough reconnaissance before sending torpedo boats on a mission "because of the small operational radius" of the boats. While not criticizing the MTB crews directly, Kuznetsov also noted that, in attacking ships, the boats should launch their torpedoes at ranges no greater than eight hundred to one thousand yards, which suggests that crews were often firing from too long a range.

Despite Kuznetsov's criticisms, the performance of the boats does not seem to have improved much during the war. For example, in an attack by eight MTBs on a German convoy of thirty vessels off the Norwegian coast on 15 July 1944, the boats claimed to have sunk three large transports, two destroyers, and two smaller escort vessels; in fact, they had hit nothing at all, and one MTB was lost. In their reports, all the boats indicated they had launched their torpedoes from less than a thousand yards—that is, from within the range limit prescribed by Kuznetsov—but the German escort commander reported that the attackers had actually fired from much greater ranges. This suggests that the MTB commanders were either very bad at estimating ranges or were fudging their reports to appear to have complied with Kuznetsov's directive.

Enemy losses of merchant ships due to Soviet MTB attacks are shown in table 7.11. In addition to these, the torpedo boats also sank one U-boat, an

Italian midget sub (in the Black Sea), and perhaps twenty small surface ships ranging from subchasers to lighters.

TABLE 7.11 Soviet MTB Successes by Fleet, 1941–1945

Fleet	Merchant Ships Sunk	GRT
Northern Fleet	10	10,071
Baltic Fleet	7	5,700
Black Sea Fleet	5	?
Totals	22	>15,771

Source: Platonov, "Sovetskie torpednye katera," 95–96.

Naval aviation was seen as another critical element of naval power before the war, necessary for reconnaissance, for protecting surface forces against the enemy's air attacks, and for carrying out offensive strikes against the enemy's ships and bases. Like the submarine force and the MTBs, it was plagued by poor training—a problem exacerbated by the view, held in high political circles, that the normal accidents attendant upon any aviation training program were the work of "wreckers." As a result, the army's air force was subjected to rigorous purging long after the terror had abated in other fields; although evidence is lacking, it seems likely that the naval air arm was also subjected to this deadly process.

Following the German invasion, naval air units were desperately thrown into the fighting ashore, and few aircraft could be spared for maritime roles. From the navy's perspective the situation was so bad that, as Admiral Sir Geoffrey Miles, head of the British Naval Mission in Moscow, noted, "the Russian Admiralty were delighted when political pressure resulted in the Army having to divert some of their fighter aircraft to the North" to support the Arctic convoys.[13]

It was not only fighters that were diverted to the army's use; during the first two years of the war, naval torpedo bombers were "as a rule, used as bombers to attack targets ashore. For example, in 1941 in all fleets only 24 aviation torpedoes were used, and those were generally used against shore targets. The intense use of torpedo aviation for their primary purpose began to increase only from the end of 1942."[14] By that time the Luftwaffe's command of the air was waning; this, combined with increased Soviet aircraft production and deliveries of Lend-Lease aircraft, allowed more aviation to be devoted to naval uses.

But the hiatus in air cooperation with other naval units had taken its toll; coordination of air and surface units remained poor, and proper reconnaissance was a rare phenomenon. Nevertheless, there were attempts at combined aviation-submarine or aviation-MTB attacks on German convoys. Another technique widely used was "free hunting," in which small groups of aircraft, usually one or two torpedo bombers, went out looking for targets of opportunity. This practice was greatly facilitated by the arrival of American A-20G Boston bombers, which had a considerably greater range than Soviet-built torpedo planes. The Boston became a mainstay of the Red Navy's air arm and was involved in some of its most successful attacks.

Another favorite technique was the topmast attack, in which the aircraft came in low and launched its bomb into a ship's side. In the spring of 1944 a new tactic was developed in which the topmast bombers attacked with bombs from an altitude of two hundred to three hundred meters at the same time as the torpedo bombers. This split the ships' defensive fire and greatly improved the survival rate of the attackers. In a similar fashion, topmast attacks could be combined with dive bombing, a method used in the sinking of the German floating AA battery *Niobe* in the Finnish port of Turku on 8 June 1944. Despite such occasional successes, however, the overall performance of the Red Navy's air arm was disappointing.

Many of the shortcomings displayed by the Red Navy's submarines, MTBs, and aviation were due to failures in reconnaissance and in coordinating attacks by different arms, problems that can be traced back to the prewar period. The purges and the rapid expansion of the navy had disrupted naval education and training, and their effects were felt throughout the war—staff officers and ship commanders were inexperienced and poorly educated, leading to fundamental mistakes even in such basic skills as navigation. A good example of this can be found in a revealing admission by Admiral Golovko, commander of the Northern Fleet, who told British Rear Admiral Philip Vian during a visit to Polyarnoe in the summer of 1941 that his submarine crews were not trained well enough to carry out operations against the Germans.[15] As one Russian historian has noted, "The lack of systematic, high-quality battle preparation [was] the chief scourge of our nation's navy during the entire war."[16]

Thus, while prewar theories had stressed the importance of intelligence, reconnaissance, and combined attack, the Red Navy's officers were often incapable of carrying out such complex tasks. Their generally poor education and training, and their lack of experience were all the result of faults inherent in Soviet society under Stalin's regime. These shortcomings, however, should not be allowed to obscure the Red Navy's successes. Evacuations, fire support, and amphibious operations were done very well, even though they were often improvised at short notice. And nothing can detract from the courage and dedication of the Red Navy's officers and men.

TABLE 7.12 The Butcher's Bill: Red Navy Losses, 1941–1945

	Baltic Fleet	Black Sea Fleet	Northern Fleet	Total
Cruisers	0	1	0	1
Destroyer Leaders	1	3	0	4
Destroyers	16	11	3	30
Submarines	47	28	23	98
Gunboats	6	18	0	24
Guard Ships	9	2	16	27
Minelayers	1	5	0	6
Minesweepers	61	19	13	93
MTBs	72	60	12	144
Sub chasers	102	167	19	288
Armored launches	10	38	0	48
Motor minesweepers	53	95	4	152
Killed in action	19,836	16,942	7,854	44,632[a]

[a] Another 3,067 men were killed serving with the Pacific Fleet and the various flotillas for a total of 47,699. These losses do not include casualties suffered by naval infantry units fighting as part of the Red Army.

Sources: Zolotarev and Shlomin, Kak sozdavalas', 1:245; G. F. Krivosheev, ed., Soviet Casualties and Combat Losses in the Twentieth Century (London: Greenhill Books, 1997), 211–218.

Appendixes

Appendix One

Guns and Torpedoes

France

Bore (in/mm)	Cal	Model	Shell (lbs)	MV (f/s)	Range (yds)	F/C (sec)	Ship or classes
15.0/380	45	Mle 1935	1,949	2,723	45,620	45	*Richelieu*
13.0/330	52	Mle 1931	1,235	2,789	45,620	30	*Dunkerque*
8.0/203	50	Mle 1924	295	2,690	32,820	15	heavy cruisers
6.0/152	55	Mle 1930	120	2,854	28,990	7–8	*La Galissonnière, Émile Bertin, Richelieu* (DP)
5.46/138	50	Mle 1929/34	90	2,625	21,880	6–10	*Le Fantasque, Mogador*
5.46/138	40	Mle 1923/27	90	2,297	18,160	8–12	*Bison/Valmy, Aigle, Vauquelin*
5.1/130	45	Mle 1935	71	2,625	22,755	4–6	*Le Hardi, Dunkerque* (DP)
5.1/130	40	Mle 1924	77	2,400	20,400	10–12	*Jaguar, Bourrasque, L'Adroit*
3.9/100	45	Mle 1930	33	2,477	10,940	6	*Algérie, Richelieu*
3.5/90	50	Mle 1926	21	2,789	11,595	5	Later *Suffrens*
3.0/76	50	Mle 1922/24/27	13	2,789	8,750	5–6	*Tourville, Suffren*

Germany

Bore (in/mm)	Cal	Model	Shell (lbs)	MV (f/s)	Range (yds)	F/C (sec)	Ship or classes
16.0/406	52	SK C/34	2,271	2,658	39,810		H class
15.0/380	48	SK C/34	1,764	2,690	38,890	26	*Bismarck*
11.1/280	51	SK C/34	728	2,920	44,780	17	*Scharnhorst*
11.1/280	49	SK C/28	662	2,986	39,900		*Deutschland*
8.0/203	57	SK C/34	269	3,035	36,700	12	heavy cruisers

Bore (in/mm)	Cal	Model	Shell (lbs)	MV (f/s)	Range (yds)	F/C (sec)	Ship or classes
5.9/150	57	SK C/25	100	3,150	28,115	7.5	light cruisers
5.9/150	52	SK C/28	100	2,871	25,160	7.5	battleships
5.9/150	46	TBK C/36	88	2,870	25,700	7	Type 36A destroyers
5.9/150	42	SK L/45	100	2,740	21,225	15	*Emden* and old battleships
5.0/127	42	SK C/34	62	2,723	19,035		destroyers
4.1/105	45	SK C/32	33	2,576	16,600		torpedo boats
Great Britain							
16.0/406	45	Mk I	2,048	2,614	39,780	30	*Nelson* class
15.0/381	42	Mk I	1,938	2,460	33,550[a]	30	*Queen Elizabeth, Hood,* R class
14.0/356	45	Mk VII	1,590	2,480	38,560	30	*King George V* class
8.0/203	50	Mk VIII	256	2,800	30,650	10–12	County class
7.5/190	45	Mk VI	200	2,770	21,110		*Hawkins* class
6.0/152	45	BL Mk XII	100	2,807	20,000[a]	12	battleships; C-, D-, and E-class light cruisers; and some AMCs
6.0/152	50	BL Mk XXIII	112	2,760	25,480	7.5–10	new light cruisers
6.0/152	50	BL Mk XXII	100	2,960	25,800	12	*Nelson*
5.5/140	50	BL Mk I	82	2,790	17,770	7.5–10	*Hood,* some AMCs
5.25/134	50	QF Mk I	80	2,670	24,070	7.5–10	*Dido* and *King George V* classes
4.7/120	45	QF Mk IX	50	2,650	16,970	5	destroyers and sloops
4.7/120	40	QF Mk VIII	50	2,450	16,160	4–5	*Nelson, Glorious* classes

Bore (in/mm)	Cal	Model	Shell (lbs)	MV (f/s)	Range (yds)	F/C (sec)	Ship or classes
4.7/120	50	QF Mk XI	62	2,540	21,240	6	L and M classes
4.5/114	45	QF Mk I	55	2,450	20,750	5	battleships, carriers, *Scylla*, new destroyers
4.0/102	40	QF MK IV	31	2,180	11,580	5	S-class destroyers; *Halcyon*, *Bangor*, *Hunt*-class minesweepers
4.0/102	45	QF MK V	31	2,390	16,430	4	*Repulse*, *Eagle*, *York*, *Sydney*, *Coventry*; P-, O-class destroyers
4.0/102	45	Mk XVI HA	35	2,660	19,850	5	capital ships and cruisers; *Abdiel*; M- and *Hunt*-class destroyers
4.0/102	40	QF Mk XIX	35	1,300	9,700	4–5	corvettes, River-class escorts, *Bathurst*-class minesweepers

a Ranges given are generally ideal maximum. Ranges for this gun vary from class to class, or within class, depending on variables including elevation, mount, shell, or charge.

Italy

Bore (in/mm)	Cal	Model	Shell (lbs)	MV (f/s)	Range (yds)	F/C (sec)	Ship or classes
15.0/381	50	A1934/36	1,951	2,854	46,800	45	*Littorio* class
12.6/320	43.75	M1934/36	1,157	2,723	31,280	30	*Cavour* and *Duilio* classes
8.0/203	53	A1927/29	276	3,084	33,400[a]	16	*Zara* class and *Bolzano*
8.0/203	50	A1924	276	2,969	34,255	18–40	*Trento* class
6.0/152	55	A1934/O36	110	2,986	28,150	13–15	*Garibaldi* and *Littorio*
6.0/152	53	A1926/O29	110	3,281	31,060	12	*Giussano*, *Attendolo*, *Aosta*, and *Diaz* classes

Bore (in/mm)	Cal	Model	Shell (lbs)	MV (f/s)	Range (yds)	F/C (sec)	Ship or classes
5.3/135	45	O1937/38/A38	72	2,707	21,430	8–10	Dulio class and Capitani Romani-class light cruisers
4.7/120	50	A1926/O31	52	3,117	21,430	10	destroyers and Cesare class
3.9/100	47	O1924/27/28	30	2,887	16,670	6–7.5	torpedo boats and Gabbiano-class corvettes
3.5/90	50	A1938/O39	22	2,822	17,500	5	Littorio and Dulio classes

[a] Ranges given are generally ideal maximum. Ranges for this gun vary from class to class, or within class, depending on variables including elevation, mount, shell, or charge.

Japan

Bore (in/mm)	Cal	Model	Shell (lbs)	MV (f/s)	Range (yds)	F/C (sec)	Ship or classes
18.1/460	44.5	Type 94 (1934)	3,219	2,559	45,960	30	Yamato class
16.1/410	44.6	3rd yr (1914)	2,249	2,559	42,000	21.5	Nagato class
14.0/356	45	41st yr (1908)	1,485	2,526	38,770	30–40	other battleships
8.0/203	49.2	3rd yr (1914)	278	2,756	31,600	12–15	heavy cruisers
6.1/155	60	3rd yr (1914)	123	3,018	29,960	12	Yamato class and Oyodo
6.0/152	50	41st yr (1908)	100	2,789	22,970[a]	10–15	Kongō, Fusō, and Agano classes
5.5/140	50	3rd yr (1914)	84	2,789	21,600[a]	10	Nagato and Ise classes and old light cruisers
5.0/127	49	3rd yr (1914)	51	2,986	20,100	6–12	destroyers
5.0/127	40	Type 80 (1928)	51	2,362	16,075	4–7	heavy cruisers
4.7/120	45	11th yr (1922)	45	2,707	17,500	12	old destroyers
3.9/100	65	Type 98 (1938)	29	3,314	21,300	3–4	Akizuki-class destroyers, Oyodo, Taiho

[a] Ranges given are generally ideal maximum. Ranges for this gun vary from class to class, or within class, depending on variables including elevation, mount, shell, or charge.

United States

Bore (in/mm)	Cal	Model	Shell (lbs)	MV (f/s)	Range (yds)	F/C (sec)	Ship or classes
16.0/406	45	Mk 1	2,240	2,520	35,000	40	Maryland class
16.0/406	44.7	Mk 6	2,700	2,300	36,900	30	North Carolina, South Dakota classes
16.0/406	49.7	Mk 7	2,700	2,500	42,345	30	Iowa class
14.0/356	44.6	Mk 8	1,500	2,600	34,300[a]	50	Texas, Nevada, Pennsylvania classes
14.0/356	49.7	Mk 7	1,500	2,700	36,300	45	New Mexico, California classes
8.0/203	54.7	Mk 9	260	2,800	31,860	18	CV2-3, CA24-36
8.0/203	55	Mk 12	355	2,500	30,050	15	CA37-39, 44-45 and Baltimore class
6.0/152	52.6	Mk 12	105	3,000	25,300[a]		Omaha class
6.0/152	47	Mk 16	130	2,500	26,120	6–8	Brooklyn, Cleveland classes
5.0/127	50.6	Mk 7	50	3,150	18,850	10	BB33-48, CV1, some CVEs, some AMCs, others
5.0/127	25	Mk 10	54	2,110	14,500	3–4	BB36-48, CV2-3, CA24-37, Brooklyn class
5.0/127	38	Mk 12	55	2,600	18,200	3–4	destroyers, new/rebuilt battleships, wartime heavy cruisers, Helena, St. Louis
4.0/102	52	Mk 9	33	2,900	15,920	5–6	old destroyers
3.0/76	53.2	Mk 10–22	14	2,700	14,590	4	destroyer-minesweepers, old destroyers, many others

[a] Ranges given are generally ideal maximum. Ranges for this gun vary from class to class, or within class, depending on variables including elevation, mount, shell, or charge.

SOVIET UNION

Bore (in/mm)	Cal	Model	Shell (lbs)	MV (f/s)	Range (yds)	F/C (sec)	Ship or classes
16.0/406	50	B-37	2,443	2,723	54,700	24–34	Sovetskii Soiuz
12.0/305	54	B-50	1,036	2,953	56,888	18.5	Kronshtadt class
12.0/305	52	P1907	1,038	2,500	34,133[a]	28–33	Marat class
7.1/180	57	B-27	215	3,019	43,760	10	Kirov, Maksim Gorkii
7.1/180	60	B-1-K	215	3,019	46,167	11	Krasnyi Kavkaz
6.0/152	57	B-38	121	3,117	35,883	8	Sovetskii Soiuz, Kronshtadt, and Chapaev
5.1/130	50	B-13	74	2,854	30,413	5	modern destroyers
5.1/130	55	Po1913	74	2,825	20,400	10	old cruisers and Krasnyi Krym,
4.7/127	50	P1905	58	2,707	16,629	9	Marat class
4.0/102	60	P1911	39	2,700	19,254	5	old destroyers and escorts
3.9/100	56	B-24M	34	2,953	24,320	5	submarines, small combatants
3.9/100	50		35	2,625	21,400	6	Krasnyi Krym

[a] Ranges given are generally ideal maximum. Ranges for this gun vary from class to class, or within class, depending on variables including elevation, mount, shell, or charge.

TORPEDOES

FRANCE

Mark	Size (in)	Weight (lbs)	Explosive (lbs)	Range/Speed (yds/knots)	Use
23DT	21.7	4,560	683	9,840/39–14,200/35	large surface warships
24V, 24M	21.7	2,760	683	3,300/45–7,650/35	submarines
26V, W, DA	15.75	1,486	317	2,200/44–3,300/35	MTBs, submarines, aircraft

GERMANY

Mark	Size (in)	Weight (lbs)	Explosive (lbs)	Range/Speed (yds/knots)	Use
G7a T1	21	3,369	661	6,560/44–15,300/30	large surface ships and submarines
G7e T2	21	3,534	661	5,470/30 (electric)	submarines and MTBs
T5	21	3,290	660	6,200/25 (homing)	submarines and MTBs
F5b	17.7	1,790	551	2,200/40–6,560/24	aircraft

GREAT BRITAIN

Mark	Size (in)	Weight (lbs)	Explosive (lbs)	Range/Speed (yds/knots)	Use
Mk I	24.5	5,700	743	15,000/35–20,000/30	Nelson class
Mk IV	21	3,206	515	8,000/35–10,000/29	MTBs, old cruisers and destroyers, submarines
MK VII	21	4,106	740	8,000/35–16,000/33	heavy cruisers London class and newer
Mk VIII	21	3,450	805	5,000/45.5–7,000/41	submarines O class and newer, some MTBs
Mk IX	21	2,732	810	11,000/41–15,000/35	Leander-class cruisers and newer, modern destroyers
Mk XII	17.7	1,548	388	1,500/40–3,500/29	MTBs, aircraft through 1942
Mk XV	17.7	1,800	545	2,500/40–3,500/33	MTBs, aircraft from 1942

ITALY

Mark	Size (in)	Weight (lbs)	Explosive (lbs)	Range/Speed (yds/knots)	Use
W 250	21	3,417	595	4,400/43–10,940/28	submarines
W 27of	21	3,740	595	4,400/48–10,940/38	destroyers, cruisers
W 27ov	21	3,740	595	4,400/50–13,000/30	submarines,
W 200	17.7	2,046	441	3,300/44–8,800/30	destroyers, cruisers torpedo boats, MAS

JAPAN

Mark	Size (in)	Weight (lbs)	Explosive (lbs)	Range/Speed (yds/knots)	Use
8th Y	24	5,207	761	10,900/38–21,900/28	old destroyers and light cruisers
T90	24	5,743	827	7,650/46–16,400/35	Fubuki class, some heavy cruisers
T91/2	17.7	1,841	452	2,200/41	aircraft
T92	21	3,792	661	7,650/28	submarines
T93/1	24	5,952	1,080	21,900/48–43,700/36	new destroyers, cruisers
T93/3	24	6,173	1,720	16,400/48–32,800/36	from 1943

UNITED STATES

Mark	Size (in)	Weight (lbs)	Explosive (lbs)	Range/Speed (yds/knots)	Use
Mk 8	21	3,050	466	16,000/26	old destroyers
Mk 10	21	2,215	497	3,500/36	S-class submarines
Mk 11	21	3,511	500	6,000/46–15,000/27	destroyers/cruisers
Mk 12	21	3,505	500	7,000/44–15,000/26.5	destroyers/cruisers

Mark	Size (in)	Weight (lbs)	Explosive (lbs)	Range/Speed (yds/knots)	Use
Mk 13	22.4	2,216	600	6,300/33.5	airborne, also PTs
Mk 14	21	3,280	643	4,500/46–9,000/31	modern submarines
Mk 15	21	3,841	825	6,000/45–15,000/26.5	new destroyers
Mk 27	19	720	95	5,000/12 (homing)	submarines

Soviet Union

Mark	Size (in)	Weight (lbs)	Explosive (lbs)	Range/Speed (yds/knots)	Use
45-36NU	17.7	2,266	284	3,280/41–6,560/32	*Novik*-class destroyers
53-27	21	3,770	584	4,045/45	surface warships, submarines
53-38	21	3,560	661	4,720/44.5–10,940/30.5	surface warships, submarines, MTBs
53-38U	21	3,803	881	4,370/44.5–10,940/30.5	replaced 53-38
45-36AN	17.7	2,061	441	4,370/39	aircraft low attitude
ET-80	21	3,968	882	4,370/29 (electric)	submarines

Appendix Two

France	Germany	Great Britain	Italy	Japan	USA	USSR
	Grossadmiral, Generaladmiral	Admiral of the Fleet		Gen-sui	Fleet Admiral	Admiral Flota
Vice Amiral d' Escadre	Admiral	Admiral	Ammiraglio d'Armata	Tai-sho	Admiral	Admiral
Vice Amiral	Vizeadmiral	Vice Admiral	Ammiraglio di Squadra	Chu-sho	Vice Admiral	Vitse-admiral
Contre Amiral	Konteradmiral, Kommodore	Rear Admiral, Commodore	Ammiraglio di Divisione, Contrammiraglio	Sho-sho	Rear Admiral, Commodore	Kontr-admiral, Kapitan pervogo ranga
Capitaine de Vaisseau	Kapitän zur See	Captain	Capitano di Vascello	Tai-sa	Captain	Kapitan vtorogo ranga
Capitaine de Frégate	Fregattenkapitän		Capitano di Fregata	Chu-sa	Commander	Kapitan tret'ego ranga
Capitaine de Corvette	Korvettenkapitän	Commander	Capitano di Corvetta	Sho-sa	Lieutenant Commander	Kapitan-leitenant
Lieutenant de Vaisseau	Kapitänleutnant	Lieutenant Commander	Tenente di Vascello	Tai-I	Lieutenant	Starshii leitenant
Enseigne de Vaisseau 1ère Classe	Oberleutnant zur See	Lieutenant		Chu-I	Lieutenant (jg)	Leitenant
Enseigne de Vaisseau 2ème Classe	Leutnant zur See, Oberfähnrich zur See, Fähnrich zur See	Sub-Lieutenant, Midshipman	Sottotenente di Vascello, Guardiamarina	Sho-I, Sho-I Ko Hosei	Ensign, Midshipman	Mladshii leitenant, Kursant

Appendix Three

Conversions
1 nautical mile = 2,025 yards, 1,852 meters, or 1.151 statute miles
1 knot = 1.852 km/hour or 1.151 statute mile/hour
1 meter = 1.094 yards
1 yard = 0.9144 meters
1 centimeter = 0.3937 inches
1 inch = 2.54 centimeters
1 kilogram = 2.205 pounds
1 pound = 0.4536 kilograms
1 tonne = 0.9842 long tons
1 long ton = 1.016 tonnes

Abbreviations
General

AA	antiair, antiaircraft
ABDA	American-British-Dutch-Australian
ACNS	assistant chiefs of the naval staff
AG	antenna galvanic
AP	armor-piercing
A/S	antisubmarine
ASV	air-surface vessel (radar)
ASW	antisubmarine warfare
BCRA	*bureau central de renseignements et d'action*
CEPSM	Comission d'Etudes Pratiques des Sous-Marins
CIG	*centre d'information gouvernemental*
CINCUS	Commander in Chief, U.S. Fleet
COMINCH	Commander in Chief, U.S. Fleet
CSDN	Conseil Supérieur de la Défense Nationale
DC	depth charge
DCT	depth-charge thrower
DEA	Deutsche Erdöl AG
DEM	*détecteur électro-magnétique*
EMG/2	Etat-Major/Deuxième Bureau
FAA	Fleet Air Arm (British)
FHM	Forces de Haute Mer
FMF	Fleet Marine Force
FMF/2	Forces Maritimes Françaises/Deuxième Bureau

FNEO	Forces Navales d'Extrême-Orient
FNFL	Free French Naval Forces
GDP	gross domestic product
GHG	*Gruppenhorchgerät*
GRT	gross registered tons
HA	high angle
HO	hostilities only
IGHQ	Imperial General Headquarters
KB	*Korabelnaia bolshaia*
KGB	Komitet gosudarstvennoy bezopasnosti
NCO	noncommissioned officer
NID	Naval Intelligence Division
NKVD	Narodny komissariat vnutrennih del
NGS	Naval General Staff
NROTC	Naval Reserve Officers Training Corps
OIC	Operational Intelligence Centre
OKH	Oberkommando des Heeres
OKL	Oberkommando der Luftwaffe
OKM	Oberkommando der Kriegsmarine
OKW	Oberbefehlshaber der Wehrmacht
OLS	Detachment of Light Forces
ONI	Office of Naval Intelligence
OPL	Optique de Précision Levallois-Perret
RAF	Royal Air Force
RDF	radio-direction finding
RN	Royal Navy
RNR	Royal Naval Reserve
RNVR	Royal Navy Volunteer Reserve
SAR	search and rescue
SG	Seeaufklärungsgruppe
SIS	Servizio Informazione Segreto (Italy)
SIS	Secret Intelligence Service (Britain)
SLC	*siluro a lenta corsa*
SOM	Société d'Optique et de Méchanique de Haute Précision
STCN	*Service Technique des Constructions Navales*
TBS	Talk Between Ships
TPA	*telefono per ammiragli*
UAS	U-Boot-Abwehr-Schule
USN	United States Navy
VHF	very high freqency

VMS RKKA	Voenno-morskie Sily Raboche-krestianskoi Krasnoi Armii
VT	variable time
WRNS	Women's Royal Naval Service ("Wrens")

Ship Types

BAMS	British and Allied Merchant Ship
BB	battleship
BC	battle cruiser
BM	monitor
CA	heavy cruiser
CAM	catapult-armed merchant ship
CL	light cruiser
CLA	antiaircraft light cruiser
CV	aircraft carrier
CVE	escort carrier
DC	corvette
DD	destroyer
DE	destroyer escort
DF	frigate
DMS	fast minelayer
DS	sloop/escort
FCS	fighter catapult ship
GS	guard ship (Soviet sloop)
LCT	landing craft, tank
LST	landing ship, tank
LVT	landing vehicle, tracked
MAC	merchant aircraft carrier
MAS	Italian motor torpedo boat (*motoscafi armati siluranti* or *motoscafi anti sommergibili*)
MFP	*marinefährprahm* (German armed barge or "F" lighter)
MGB	motor gunboat
ML	minelayer or motor launch
MTB	motor torpedo boat
PG	gunboat (USN)
PT	patrol torpedo boat (USN)
S-boat	*schnellboot* (German motor torpedo boat or "E" boat)
SS	submarine
TB	torpedo boat
U-boat	*unterseeboot* (German submarine)
UJ-boat	*unterseebootsjäger* (German submarine chaser)

Notes

CHAPTER ONE. FRANCE

1. The size and composition of an *escadre* was dependent on the theater of operations and its assigned tasks.
2. Earlier coastal submarines had been competitive designs by the private shipbuilders to meet specified staff requirements.
3. Squadron designation had a first letter denoting type: A = *Avion* (aircraft), H = *Hydravion* (seaplane/floatplane); and a second letter denoting primary mission: C = *Chasse* (fighter), B = *Bombardement* (bomber), S = *Surveillance* (reconnaissance).
4. Trunnion height was a consideration, the early models of the 138-mm gun carried by the *contre-torpilleurs* were only 40 calibers long.
5. The Italian *Zaras* were equally impressive, but their designed displacement was well above treaty limits.

CHAPTER THREE. GREAT BRITAIN

1. These figures should be regarded as approximate. The naval estimates are quoted from David K. Brown, *Nelson to Vanguard: Warship Design 1923–1945* (Annapolis, MD: Naval Institute Press, 2000), 18; total spending comes from Peter Howlett, "New Light through Old Windows: A New Perspective on the British Economy in the Second World War," *Journal of Contemporary History* 28, no. 2 (April 1993): 362. The 1939 figure of £254 million is approximately £60 billion in 2008 pounds, calculated as a share of gross domestic product, and not much higher than the United Kingdom's 2005 military expenditures of £42.8 billion.
2. John Campbell, *Naval Weapons of World War Two* (Annapolis, MD: Naval Institute Press, 2002), 81.
3. Stephen Roskill, *The War at Sea 1939–1945: The Offensive* (London: HMSO, 1961), 436.
4. I. C. B. Dear, *The Oxford Companion to World War II* (Oxford: Oxford University Press, 1995), 1060; and Michael M. Postan, *Britsh War Production* (London: HMSO, 1952), 292–302. Major ships exclude landing craft, torpedo boats, and smaller auxiliary vessels.
5. Mass Observation 1940 report on British attitudes to World War II. Mass Observation Archive, University of Sussex.
6. Joseph Schull, *Far Distant Ships* (Toronto: Stoddart Publishing, 1950), 429.

CHAPTER FOUR. ITALY

1. Erminio Bagnasco and Enrico Cernuschi, *Le navi da guerra italiane 1940–1945* (Parma: Albertelli, 2005), 350.
2. W. H. Beehler, *The History of the Italian-Turkish War* (Annapolis, MD: The Advertiser-Republican, 1913), 107.
3. John Gooch, *Mussolini and His Generals: The Armed Forces and Fascist Foreign Policy, 1922–1940* (Cambridge: Cambridge University Press, 2007), 42.
4. MacGregor Knox, *Hitler's Italian Allies* (Cambridge: Cambridge University Press, 2000), 88 and 94.
5. Ibid., 30.
6. Raymond de Belot, *The Struggle for the Mediterranean 1939–1945* (Princeton, NJ: Princeton University Press, 1951), 41.
7. Jack Greene and Alessandro Massignani, *The Naval War in the Mediterranean 1940–1943* (London: Chatham Publishing, 1998), 48.
8. Quoted in G. H. Bennett and R. Bennett, *Hitler's Admirals* (Annapolis, MD: Naval Institute Press, 2004), 111.
9. Ibid.
10. de Belot, *Struggle for the Mediterranean*, 271.
11. Archivio Centrale dello Stato, Rome, Ministero della Marina, Direttive e norme per l'impiego della squadra nel conflitto attuale, January 1942, Part 1, 15.
12. Knox, *Hitler's Italian Allies*, 63–64.
13. John Campbell, *Naval Weapons of World War Two* (Annapolis, MD: Naval Institute Press, 2002), 318.
14. Angelo Iachino, *Tramonto di una grande marina* (Verona: Alberto Mondadori, 1966), 62–63.
15. Giuliano Colliva. "Questioni di tiro . . . e altre. Le artiglierie navali italiane nella Guerra nel Mediterraneo." *Bollettino d'archivio dell'Ufficio Storico della Marina Militare*, Anno XVII, September 2003.
16. "Direttive e Norme," January 1942, Part 1, 10.
17. Brian Lavery, *Churchill's Navy* (London: Conway Maritime Press, 2006), 54.
18. Samuel Eliot Morison, *Operations in North African Wars October 1942–June 1943* (Boston: Little, Brown, 1984).
19. James Sadkovich, *The Italian Navy in World War II* (Westport, CT: Greenwood Press, 1994), xviii.

CHAPTER FIVE. JAPAN

1. Much of this essay draws upon a major work by David C. Evans and Mark R. Peattie, *Kaigun: Strategy, Tactics and Technology in the Imperial Japanese Navy, 1887–1941* (Annapolis, MD: Naval Institute Press, 1997).
2. The IGHQ established in 1937 was the third such institution in the history of the navy. The first had been established at the outset of the Sino-Japanese War of 1894–1895 and abolished after the war. The second IGHQ was constituted during the Russo-Japanese War, 1904–1905, but was also subsequently abolished.

3. Arthur Marder, *Old Friends, New Enemies: The Royal Navy and the Imperial Japanese Navy*, Vol. 1, *Strategic Illusions* (New York: Oxford University Press, 1981), 285–292.

4. Chihaya Masataka, *Nihon kaigun no senryaku hassō* [Strategic concepts of the Japanese navy] (Tokyo: Purejidentosha, 1990), 105–106.

5. The U.S. Navy was not able to solve JN-25 before 1941 but was reading some of one version by that year; by the spring of 1942, its progress on JN-25 was so dramatic that it was able to achieve one of the great intelligence coups of World War II: the decryption of Japanese messages in JN-25 that led to the ambush of the Japanese strike force heading toward Midway. See Stephen Budiansky, *Battle of Wits: The Complete Story of Codebreaking in World War II* (New York: Touchstone Press, Simon and Schuster, 2000), 16–17; Evans and Peattie, *Kaigun*, 422–423; and Michael Barnhart, "Japanese Intelligence before the Second World War: 'The Best Case Analysis,'" in *Knowing One's Enemies: Intelligence Assessment between the Two World Wars*, ed. Ernest A. May (Princeton, NJ: Princeton University Press, 1986), 447.

6. A brilliant approach to the problem of synthesizing and sharing of aviation technology among the various Japanese aircraft companies and with the government, the system is explained in Mark R. Peattie, *Sunburst: The Rise of Japanese Naval Air Power, 1909–1941* (Annapolis, MD: Naval Institute Press, 2001), 21–28.

7. The term *logistics* is used here in its twofold sense: first the concern for materiel—weapons, ordnance, equipment, fuel, stores, and provisions—and second, the procedures—planning, allocation, transport, construction, and transfer techniques—involved in providing all these things to a navy's warships at sea or to the navy's land bases overseas.

8. Jerome B. Cohen, *Japan's Economy in War and Reconstruction* (Minneapolis: University of Minnesota Press, 1949).

CHAPTER 6. USA

1. Edward S. Miller, *War Plan Orange: The U.S. Strategy to Defeat Japan, 1897–1945* (Annapolis, MD: Naval Institute Press, 1991), 77–149.

2. Julius Augustus Furer, *Administration of the Navy Department in World War Two* (Washington, DC: Department of the Navy, 1959), 54 and 65–66.

3. Ibid., 19.

4. John T. Kuehn, *Agents of Innovation: The General Board and the Design of the Fleet that Defeated the Japanese Navy* (Annapolis: Naval Institute Press, 2008), 8–22.

5. Furer, *Administration of the Navy Department*, 64.

6. Thomas B. Buell, *Master of Sea Power: A Biography of Fleet Admiral Ernest J. King* (Boston: Little, Brown, 1980), 493.

7. Samuel Eliot Morison, *History of the United States Naval Operations in World War II*, Vol. 1, *The Battle of the Atlantic, 1939–1945* (Boston: Little, Brown, 1947), 206–207.

8. Thomas C. Hone and Trent Hone, *Battle Line: The United States Navy: 1919–1939* (Annapolis, MD: Naval Institute Press, 2006), 66.

9. Donald Chisholm, *Waiting for Dead Men's Shoes* (Stanford, CA.: Stanford University Press, 2001), 697–698, 701.

10. Furer, *Administration of the Navy Department*, 276.

11. Ibid., 119.

12. F.T.P. *143*, *War Instructions, United States Navy*, 1934, p. 87, Naval Historical Center, World War 2 Command File, Box 108.

13. The phrase "attack effectively first" was introduced by Wayne Hughes, who called it the "tactical maxim of all naval battles." See Wayne P. Hughes, *Fleet Tactics: Theory and Practice* (Annapolis, MD: Naval Institute Press, 1986), 25.

14. Morison, *Battle of the Atlantic*, iiv.

15. I. C. B. Dear and Michael Richard Daniel Foot, *Oxford Companion to World War II* (New York: Oxford University Press, 1995), 66.

16. Timothy S. Wolters, *Managing a Sea of Information: Shipboard Command and Control in the United States Navy, 1899–1945* (PhD diss., Massachusetts Institute of Technology, 2003), 187.

17. Hone and Hone, *Battle Line*, 1.

18. *C.I.C. Bulletin*, February 1945, National Archives, Records of the Office of the Chief of Naval Operations, Record Group 38, Box 1694.

19. Buford Rowland and William B. Boyd, *U.S. Navy Bureau of Ordnance in World War II* (Washington, DC: U.S. Government Printing Office), 223.

20. Ibid., 168–171.

21. Samuel Eliot Morison, *History of the United States Naval Operations in World War II*, Vol. 7, *Aleutians, Gilberts and Marshalls, June 1942–April 1944* (Boston: Little, Brown, 1951), 106–107.

22. Thomas Wildenberg, *Gray Steel and Black Oil: Fast Tankers and Replenishment at Sea in the U.S. Navy, 1912–1992* (Annapolis, MD: Naval Institute Press, 1996), 181.

23. Robert H. Connery, *The Navy and the Industrial Mobilization in World War II* (Princeton NJ: Princeton University Press, 1951), v.

24. Thomas C. Hone with Trent C. Hone, "The Pacific Naval War as One Coherent Campaign, 1941–1945," *International Journal of Naval History* 2, no. 2 (August 2003), http://www.ijnhonline.org/volume2_number2_Aug03/wip_hone_pacwar_aug03.htm.

CHAPTER 7. USSR

1. "U.S.S.R. Navy," Division of Naval Intelligence Report OP-16, PA-5, Serial No. 40-43, Washington, DC: Department of the Navy, 30 November 1943; available online at the Combined Arms Research Library Digital Library, http://cgsc.cdmhost.com/cdm4/document.php?CISOROOT=/p4013coll8&CISOPTR=90, accessed 4 November 2008, 10.

2. Bradley F. Smith, *Sharing Secrets with Stalin: How the Allies Traded Intelligence, 1941–1945* (Lawrence: University Press of Kansas, 1996), 77; and R. C. S. Garwood, "The Russians as Naval Allies 1941–45," in *The Soviet Navy*, ed. M. G. Saunders (New York: Praeger, 1958), 81–82.

3. "U.S.S.R. Navy," 10–11.

4. Robert W. Stephan, *Stalin's Secret War: Soviet Counterintelligence against the Nazis, 1941–1945* (Lawrence: University Press of Kansas, 2004), 8; Jak P. Mallmann Showell, *German Naval Code Breakers* (Annapolis: Naval Institute Press, 2003), 24–25; and Smith, *Sharing Secrets with Stalin*, 62, 182.

5. There is a useful appendix listing landing operations and the forces involved in A.V. Basov, ed., *Boevoi put' Sovetskogo Voenno-Morskogo flota* (Moscow: Voennoe izdatel'stvo, 1988), 546–552.

6. Kemp Tolley, *Caviar and Commissars: The Experiences of a U.S. Naval Officer in Stalin's Russia* (Annapolis, MD: Naval Institute Press, 1983), 261, 264.

7. V. Iu. Gribovskii, writing in I. D. Spasskii, ed., *Istoriia otechestvennogo sudostroeniia* (St. Petersburg: Sudostroenie, 1996), 4:137.

8. Ibid.

9. Friedrich Ruge, *The Soviets as Naval Opponents 1941–1945* (Annapolis, MD: Naval Institute Press, 1979), 101, 107, 115. See also Jürgen Rohwer, *Allied Submarine Attacks of World War Two: European Theatre of Operations 1939–1945* (Annapolis, MD: Naval Institute Press, 1997).

10. Ruge, *Soviets as Naval Opponents*, 25.

11. *Russkii arkhiv/Velikaia Otechestvennaia* (Moscow: Terra, 1999), series 5, vol. 3: *Stavka Verkhovnogo Glavnokomandovaniia: Dokumenty i materialy 1943 god*, 221.

12. A. S. Kiselev, ed., *Admiral Kuznetsov: Moskva v zhizni i sud'be flotovodtsa: Sbornik dokumentov i materialov* (Moscow: Mosgorarkhiv, 2000), 175–177.

13. R. C. S. Garwood, "The Russians as Naval Allies 1941–45," 77.

14. Iu. L. Korshunov and A. A. Strokov, *Torpedy VMF SSSR* (St. Petersburg: Gangut, 1994), 18.

15. Philip Vian, *Action This Day: A War Memoir* (London: Frederick Muller Limited, 1960), 66.

16. A. V. Platonov, "Sovetskie torpednye katera v bor'be s morskimi pereboz- kami protivnika," *Gangut*, no. 47 (2008): 88.

Bibliography

CHAPTER 1: FRANCE

Principal references used in writing this chapter include Michel Bertrand, *La Marine Française 1939–40* (La Tour-du-Pin: Editions Portail, 1984); Espagnac du Ravay, *Vingt ans de politique navale* (Grenoble: B. Arthaud, 1941); John Jordan and Robert Dumas, *French Battleships 1922–56* (London: Seaforth, 2009); and Henri Le Masson, *Histoire du torpilleur en France 1872–1940* (Paris: Académie de la Marine, 1963).

Marines Edition of Bourg en Bresse/Nantes has published a series of excellent monographs that cover the design and operations of specific classes. These include Jean Moulin, Lucien Morareau, and Claude Picard, *Le Béarn et le Commandant Teste* (1997); Claude Huan, *Les Sous-Marins Français* (1995); Jean Guiglini and Albert Moreau, *Les croiseurs de 8000T* (1995); Jean Lassaque, *Les CT de 2400 tonnes du type Jaguar* (1994); Marc Saibène, *Les Torpilleurs de 1500 tonnes du type Bourrasque* (2001); and René Sarnet and Eric Le Vaillant, *Richelieu* (1997). Also useful are monographs published by Editions Lela Presse of Outreau, including Gérard Garier and Patrick du Cheyron, *Les Croiseurs Lourds Français de 10000TW* and *Duquesne & Tourville* (2003).

John Jordan has authored comprehensive articles on the technical aspects and design histories of the Marine Nationale's ships in the annual *Warship* (London: Conway Maritime Press) from 1991 through 2008. Titles cover battleships, cruisers, auxiliaries, *contre-torpilleurs*, destroyers, escorts, and submarines.

There are few English histories of the Marine Nationale. Basic works include Paul Auphan and Jacques Mordal, *The French Navy in World War II* (Westport, CT: Greenwood, 1976) and Anthony Heckstall-Smith, *The Fleet That Faced Both Ways* (London: Anthony Blond, 1963). Thomas Martin has written several good articles including, "After Mers-el-Kébir: The Armed Neutrality of the Vichy French Navy 1940–1943," *The English Historical Review* (June 1997): 643–670; and "At the Heart of Things:

French Imperial Defense Planning in the Late 1930s," *French Historical Studies* 21 (Spring 1998): 325–361.

CHAPTER 2: GERMANY

Archival sources used in drafting this chapter are located in the files of the Bundesarchiv Militärarchiv, Freiburg, and include: M 350/5 (E); M 338/24 (E); M 954 (E); and M 983 (E).

For general organization and leadership, see Fritz Otto Busch, *Das Buch von der Kriegsmarine* (Berlin: Bong & Co., 1939); Konrad Ehrensberger, *100 Jahre Organisation der deutschen Marine* (Bonn: Bernard U. Graefe Verlag, 1993); Helmuth Giessler, *Der Marine-Nachrichten- und-Ortungsdienst* (München: Lehmann, 1971); Hans H Hildebrand, *Die organisatorische Entwicklung der Marine nebst Stellenbesetzung 1848–1945* (Osnabrück: Biblio-Verlag, 2000); and Michael Salewski, *Die deutsche Seekriegsleitung 1935–1945*, vols. 1–3 (Frankfurt am Main: Bernard & Graefe, 1970–1975).

For operations, see Walter Lohmann and Hans H. Hildebrand, *Die deutsche Kriegsmarine 1939 bis 1945: Gliederung, Einsatz, Stellenbesetzung* (Bad Nauheim: Podzum, 1956); Werner Rahn et al., *Kriegstagebuch der Seekriegsleitung* (Herford: Mittler, 1988); and Peter Schenk, *Landung in England: Das geplante Unternehmen "Seelowe": Der Beginn der amphibischen Grossunternehmen* (Berlin: Oberbaum, 1987).

Submarines are covered by Rainer Busch and Joachim Röll, *Der U-Boot-Krieg 1939–1945: Der U-Boot-Bau auf deutschen Werften* (Hamburg: Mittler & Sohn, 1997); Axel Niestlé, *German U-boat Losses during World War II: Details of Destruction* (Annapolis, MD: Naval Institute Press, 1998); and Söhnke Neitzel, *Die deutschen U-Boot Bunker und Bunkerwerften* (Koblenz: Bernard & Graefe 1991).

Jürgen Rohwer and Eberhard Jäckel, *Die Funkaufklärung und ihre Rolle im 2. Weltkrieg* (Stuttgart: Motorbuch Verlag, 1979); and Fritz Trenkle, *Die deutschen Funkmessverfahren bis 1945* (Stuttgart: Motrobuch-Verlag, 1979) cover intelligence.

For information on warships, see Harald Fock, *Kampfschiffe: Marineschiffbau auf deutschen Werften 1870 bis heute* (Hamburg: Koehlers, 1995); and Gerhard Hümmelchen, *Die deutschen Schnellboote* (Hamburg: Mittler, 1996).

Principal works on logistics include Dieter Jung, Martin Maass, and Berndt Wenzel, *Tanker und Versorger der deutschen Flotte* (Stuttgart: Motorbuch-Verlag, 1981); Wilhelm Meier-Dörnberg, *Die Ölversorgung der Kriegsmarine 1935 bis 1945* (Freiburg: Rombach, 1973); Thomas Sarholz, *Die Auswirkungen der Kontingentierung von Eisen und Stahl auf die Aufrüstung der Wehrmacht von 1936 bis 1939* (Darmstadt: Technische

Hochschule, 1983); and Paul Zieb, *Logistische Probleme der Kriegsmarine* (Neckargemünd: Vowinckel, 1961).

For weapons, see Wilhelm von Harnier, *Artillerie im Küstenkampf* (München: Lehmann, 1969); Friedrich Lauck, *Der Lufttorpedo: Entwicklung und Technik in Deutschland 1915–1945*. (München: Bernard & Graefe, 1981); Gerhard Freiherr von Ledebur, *Die Seemine* (München, 1977); Eberhard Rössler, *Die Torpedos der deutschen Marine* (Hamburg: Mittler, 2005); Paul Schmalenbach, *Die Geschichte der deutschen Schiffsartillerie* (Herford: Mittler, 1968); and Guntram Schulze-Wegener, *Die deutsche Kriegsmarine-Rüstung 1942–1945* (Hamburg: Mittler, 1997).

Important works discussing aviation include Gerhard Hümmelchen, *Die deutschen Seeflieger* (München: Lehmann, 1976); Ulrich Israel, *Marineflieger einst und jetzt* (Berlin: Brandenburgisches Verlagshaus, 1991); Dieter Jung, Arno Abendroth, and Berndt Wenzel, *Die Schiffe und Boote der deutschen Seeflieger* (Stuttgart: Motorbuch-Verlag, 1977); Franz Kurowski, *Seekrieg aus der Luft: Die deutsche Seeluftwaffe im Zweiten Weltkrieg* (Herford: Mittler, 1979); and Sönke Neitzel, *Der Einsatz der deutschen Luftwaffe über dem Atlantik und der Nordsee 1939 1945* (Bonn: Bernard & Graefe, 1995).

English histories include *Fuehrer Conferences on Naval Affairs, 1939–1945* (London: Chatham, 2005); and Erich Raeder, *Struggle for the Sea.* (London: Kimber, 1959), which are good for policy. Jak Showell, *The German Navy in WWII* (Annapolis, MD: Naval Institute Press, 1979) provides an excellent general overview of the Kriegsmarine. General histories from the German perspective, although somewhat dated, include Cajus Bekker, *Hitler's Naval War* (New York: Doubleday, 1974); Friedrich Ruge, *Der Seekrieg: The German Navy's Story 1939–1945* (Annapolis, MD: Naval Institute Press, 1957); and Edward P. Von der Porten, *The German Navy in World War II* (New York: Thomas Y. Crowell, 1968). For surface operations see Vincent P. O'Hara, *The German Fleet at War 1939–1945* (Annapolis, MD: Naval Institute Press, 2004), and for U-boats, Kenneth Wynn, *U-Boat Operations of the Second World War: Career Histories* (Annapolis, MD: Naval Institute Press, 1997 and 1998).

CHAPTER 3: GREAT BRITAIN

A starting point for an overview of the Royal Navy's operations, planning, and organization is the United Kingdom Military Series (London: HMSO), especially Stephen W. Roskill, *The War at Sea 1939–1945*, which includes *The Defensive, The Period of Balance,* and *The Offensive: Part I* and *Part II* (1954–1960). Naval operations and administrative matters are also covered in I. F. O. Playfair's *The Mediterranean and Middle East* (1954–1988) and S. Kirby's *War against Japan* (1957–1969). Intelligence is treated by F. H. Hinsley, *British Intelligence in the Second World War* (1979–1990).

Many of the naval staff histories produced during and shortly after the war, which treat operational and administrative matters in great detail, have been reprinted. Available titles include *The Royal Navy and the Mediterranean; The Royal Navy and the Mediterranean Convoys; Naval Operations of the Campaign in Norway; German Capital Ships and Raiders in World War II; The Evacuation from Dunkirk, Operation Dynamo; The Royal Navy and the Malta and Russian Convoys, 1941–1942;* and *The Defeat of the Enemy Attack on Shipping, 1939–1945.*

The standard references for the Dominion navies consist of Hermon G. Gill, *Royal Australian Navy 1939–1942* and *Royal Australian Navy 1942–1945* (Adelaide: Griffin, 1957–1968); S. D. Waters, *The Royal New Zealand Navy* (Wellington: War History Branch, 1956); and A. German, *The Sea Is at Our Gates: The History of the Royal Canadian Navy* (Toronto, 1990).

The best work about British warships is D. K. Brown, ed., *The Design and Construction of British Warships 1939–1945* (London: Conway Maritime Press, 1995–1996). Brian Lavery's *Churchill's Navy: The Ships, Men and Organisation 1939–1945* (London: Conway, 2006) provides a good overview of the Royal Navy. Paul Kemp, *The Admiralty Regrets: British Warship Losses of the 20th Century* (Phoenix Mill, England: Sutton, 1999) is also useful.

Many officers and men of the Royal Navy have written their memoirs. The most famous is Cunningham of Hyndhope, Admiral of the Fleet Viscount, RN, *A Sailor's Odyssey* (London: Hutchinson, 1951), but more useful are the collections of papers, reports, and correspondence published by the Naval Records Society, particularly Michael Simpson, ed. *The Cunningham Papers* (Aldershot, England: Ashgate, 1999–2006) and *The Somerville Papers* (Aldershot, England: Scolar, 1996).

CHAPTER 4: ITALY

The most important series of books about the Regia Marina's participation in World War II is the Ufficio Storico della Marina Militare, *La Marina Italiana nella Seconda guerra mondiale* (Rome: 1950–1978). Based on the original documents now in the Historical Branch (Ufficio Storico della Marina Militare) archives, this series covers statistics and ships lost (three volumes); naval actions (two volumes); the defense of traffic (four volumes); general operations by area and date (four volumes); submarines (three volumes); and special topics such as commandos, organization, and mines (six volumes). The Ufficio Storico della Marina Militare has also published an excellent series on the navy's warships, *Le Navi d'Italia*

(1962–1974). Separate volumes cover battleships, cruisers, destroyers, submarines, and motor torpedo boats.

There is a rich literature on Italian warships in addition to the official histories. For warships and weapons, see Erminio Bagnasco and Augusto De Toro, *Le navi da battaglia classe "Littorio" 1937–1948* (Parma: Albertelli, 2008); Erminio Bagnasco and Enrico Cernuschi, *Le navi da guerra italiane* (Parma: Albertelli, 2003); and Erminio Bagnasco, *Le armi delle navi italiane nella seconda guerra mondiale* (Parma: Albertelli, 1978).

General histories include Marc'Antonio Bragadin, *Il dramma della marina italiana 1940–1945* (Verona: Mondatori, 1981); Enrico Cernuschi, *Fecero tutti il loro dovere*, Supplemento della Rivista Marittima (November 2006); Giorgio Giorgerini, *Da Matapan al Golfo Persico, la Marina Militare italiana dal fascismo alla repubblica* (Milan: Mondatori, 1989); and Angelo Iachino, *Tramonto di una grande marina* (Verona: Mondadori, 1959).

Specific campaigns are the subject of Giorgio Giorgerini, *La battaglia dei convogli* (Milan: Mursia, 1977); Riccardo Nassigh, *Guerra negli abissi* (Milan: Mursia, 1971); and Alberto Santoni and Francesco Mattesini, *La partecipazione aeronavale tedesca alla guerra nel Mediterraneo (1940–1945)* (Rome: Ateneo e Bizzarri, 1980).

Naval battles are detailed by Enrico Cernuschi, *I sette minuti di Punta Stilo*. Supplemento della Rivista Marittima (February 1998) and *La notte del Lupo*, Supplemento della Rivista Marittima (May 1997); Chirco Giuseppe, *Il sacrificio della Prima Divisione a Capo Matapan* (Naples: Laurenzana, 1995). Angelo Iachino, who commanded Italy's battlefleet for much of the war, penned *Il punto su Matapan* (Verona: Mondadori, 1969); *La sorpesa di Matapan* (Verona: Mondadori, 1957); *Le due Sirti* (Verona: Mondadori, 1953); *Operazione Mezzo Giugno* (Verona: Mondadori, 1955); and *Gaudo e Matapan* (Verona: Mondadori, 1946). Riccardo Nassigh's *Operazione Mezzo Agosto* (Milan: Mursia, 1976) is one of the best treatments of this important series of actions.

Among the English works, see Valerio J. Borghese, *Sea Devils: Italian Navy Commandos in World War II* (Annapolis, MD: Naval Institute Press, 1995) for coverage of special operations. For naval events surrounding the armistice, see Enrico Cernuschi and Vincent P. O'Hara, *Dark Navy: the Regia Marina and the Armistice of 8 September 1943* (Ann Arbor, MI: Nimble Books, 2009). General histories include Marc' Antonio Bragadin, *The Italian Navy in World War II* (Annapolis, MD: Naval Institute Press, 1957); Raymond de Belot, *The Struggle for the Mediterranean 1939–1945* (Princeton, NJ: Princeton University Press, 1951); Erminio Bagnasco and Mark Grossman, *Regia Marina: Italian Battleships of World War II* (Missoula, MT: Pictorial Histories Publishing, 1986); Jack Greene and Alessandro

Massignani, *The Naval War in the Mediterranean 1940–1943* (London: Chatham, 1998); Vincent P. O'Hara, *Struggle for the Middle Sea: The Great Navies at War in the Mediterranean Theater, 1940–1945* (Annapolis, MD: Naval Institute Press, 2009); and James J. Sadkovich, *The Italian Navy in World War II* (Westport, CT: Greenwood, 1994).

CHAPTER 5: JAPAN

The military history department of Japan's defense agency has produced the *Bōeichō Bōeikenshūjō Senshibu* (Tokyo: Asagumo Shimbunsha, 1966–1980), often referred to as the Senshi sōsho. It consists of 102 volumes, of which 21 treat naval operations and affairs in great detail.

A short list of important works includes John Bullen, "The Japanese 'Long Lance' Torpedo and Its Place in Naval History," *Imperial War Museum Review*, no. 3 (1988); Chihaya Masataka, *Nihon kaigun no senryaku hassō* [Strategic concepts of the Japanese navy] (Tokyo: Purejidentosha, 1990); Jerome B. Cohen, *Japan's Economy in War and Reconstruction* (Minneapolis: University of Minnesota Press, 1949); David C. Evans and Mark R. Peattie, *Kaigun: Strategy, Tactics, and Technology in the Imperial Japanese Navy, 1887–1941* (Annapolis, MD: Naval Institute Press, 1994); Fukui Shizuo, *Nihon no gunkan: waga zōkan gijutsu no hattatsu to kantei no hensen* [Japanese warships: Japan's development of ship construction technology and changes in warships over time] (Tokyo: Shuppan Kyōdōsha, 1959); Arthur Marder, *Old Friends, New Enemies: The Royal Navy and the Imperial Japanese Navy*, Vol. 1, *Strategic Illusions* (New York: Oxford University Press, 1981); and Mark R. Peattie, *Sunburst: The Rise of Japanese Naval Air Power* (Annapolis, MD: Naval Institute Press, 2002).

The best English-language studies on the failure of Japan's antisubmarine warfare effort in World War II are Oi Atsushi, "Why Japan's Anti-Submarine Warfare Failed" in *The Japanese Navy in World War II in the Words of Former Japanese Naval Officers*, 2nd edition, ed. David C. Evans (Annapolis, MD: Naval Institute Press, 1986); and Mark P. Parillo, *The Japanese Merchant Marine in World War II* (Annapolis, MD: Naval Institute Press, 1993).

The definitive work on Japanese cruisers is the monumental study by Eric Lacroix and Linton Wells, *Japanese Cruisers of the Pacific War* (Annapolis, MD: Naval Institute Press, 1997).

More has been written about the *Yamato*-class battleships than any other ships in the Japanese navy. Janusz Skuski's *The Battleship Yamato* (Annapolis, MD: Naval Institute Press, 1988) has the most detailed drawings of the ship but is short on text. The two most authoritative English-language studies are Chihaya Masataka, "IJN *Yamato* and *Musashi*," in *Warships in Profile*, vol. 3., ed. Antony Preston (Garden City, NY: Doubleday, 1974);

and Kitarō Matsumoto and Masataka Chihaya, "Design and Construction of the *Yamato* and *Musashi*," in U.S. Naval Institute *Proceedings* 79 (October 1953).

The most detailed and comprehensive study of the Zero in English is Robert Mikesh, *Zero: Combat and Development of Japan's Legendary Mitsubishi A6M Zero Fighter* (Osceola, WI: Motorbooks International, 1994).

A number of references produced by the U.S. military before and shortly after the war continue to have value. These include U.S. Armed Forces Far East History Division, Japanese Monographs Series (Washington, DC: U.S. Army). Produced by Japanese authors at the behest of U.S. authorities, mostly from memory, they address specific operations, planning, organization, and some administrative matters. For exhaustive coverage of technical matters, refer to the "Reports of the United States Technical Mission to Japan, 1945–1946." An overview of the campaign from the Japanese perspective is provided by the United States Strategic Bombing Survey (Pacific), *The Campaigns of the Pacific War* and *Interrogations of Japanese Officials* (Washington, DC: U.S. Government Printing Office, 1946).

CHAPTER 6: UNITED STATES

The most comprehensive treatment of the Navy's involvement in World War II remains Samuel Eliot Morison's fifteen volumes, *History of the United States Naval Operations in World War II* (Boston, MA: Little, Brown), although Morison's work is limited because he lacked access to records detailing the Navy's extensive use of code-breaking. More recent histories, such as Ronald H. Spector's *Eagle against the Sun: The American War with Japan* (New York: Vintage Books, 1985), have filled this gap.

The early carrier battles are covered in exhaustive detail by John Lundstrom's works (Annapolis, MD: Naval Institute Press): *The First Team* (1984); *The First Team and the Guadalcanal Campaign* (1994); and *Black Shoe Carrier Admiral: Frank Jack Fletcher at Coral Sea, Midway, and Guadalcanal* (2006). Clark G. Reynolds's *The Fast Carriers: The Forging of an Air Navy* (Annapolis, MD: Naval Institute Press, 1992) discusses the development and employment of carrier doctrine later in the war.

The Navy's surface actions are described by Vincent P. O'Hara in *The U.S. Navy against the Axis* (Annapolis, MD: Naval Institute Press, 2007). Many other works cover individual battles; James W. Grace's *The Naval Battle of Guadalcanal* (Annapolis, MD: Naval Institute Press, 1999) is particularly useful. The development of surface tactics is covered by Wayne P. Hughes in *Fleet Tactics and Coastal Combat* (Annapolis, MD: Naval Institute Press, 1999) as well as in the articles of Trent Hone, "The Evolution of Fleet Tactical Doctrine in the U.S. Navy, 1922–1941," *Journal of Military*

History 67, no. 4 (October 2003), and "Give Them Hell! The U.S. Navy's Night Combat Doctrine and the Campaign for Guadalcanal," *War in History* 13, no. 2 (April 2006).

The relationship of operational doctrine and tactics is discussed in Trent Hone's "U.S. Navy Surface Battle Doctrine and Victory in the Pacific," *Naval War College Review* 62, no. 1 (Winter 2009). It is complemented by Milan Vego's *The Battle for Leyte, 1944* (Annapolis, MD: Naval Institute Press, 2006), which provides an exhaustive analysis of the Leyte operation and the planning for it.

John Prados's *Combined Fleet Decoded: The Secret History of American Intelligence and the Japanese Navy in World War II* (New York: Random House, 1995) discusses the important part intelligence played in the Pacific war. *The Code-Breakers* (New York: Signet, 1973) by David Kahn examines both the Pacific and Atlantic theatres.

The Navy's approach to mobile logistics is discussed by Thomas Wildenberg's *Gray Steel and Black Oil: Fast Tankers and Replenishment at Sea in the U.S. Navy, 1912–1992* (Annapolis, MD: Naval Institute Press, 1996).

The Navy's own records are an invaluable source. Beyond the records of the Navy Department and its Bureaus in the National Archives, there are many secondary sources. Julius Augustus Furer's *Administration of the Navy Department in World War Two* (Washington, DC: Department of the Navy, 1959) remains unparalleled. The official history of the Bureau of Ordnance, *U.S. Navy Bureau of Ordnance in World War II* (Washington, DC: GPO) is a vital source for the development of new weapons systems and refinement of old ones. The Navy's relationship with industry is recorded in Robert H. Connery's *The Navy and the Industrial Mobilization in World War II* (Princeton, NJ: Princeton University Press, 1951). Although not an official publication, the Navy assisted in its production. A variety of sources describe the Navy's preparation for war and evolution in the interwar period. Donald Chisholm's *Waiting for Dead Men's Shoes* (Stanford, CA: Stanford University Press, 2001) is a comprehensive examination of the development of the Navy's officer personnel system. Edward S. Miller's *War Plan Orange: The U.S. Strategy to Defeat Japan, 1897–1945* (Annapolis, MD: Naval Institute Press, 1991) is the definitive source on the Navy's war planning. *Battle Line: The United States Navy, 1919–1939* (Annapolis, MD: Naval Institute Press, 2006) by Thomas C. Hone and Trent Hone charts the evolution of the Navy between the wars. John T. Kuehn's *Agents of Innovation: The General Board and the Design of the Fleet that Defeated the Japanese Navy* (Annapolis, MD: Naval Institute Press, 2008) focuses on innovation and how the Navy went about it. *American and British Aircraft Carrier Development, 1919–1941* (Annapolis, MD: Naval Institute Press,

1999) by Thomas C. Hone, Norman Friedman, and Mark D. Mandeles is vital for the details it provides concerning the development of aircraft carrier doctrine. Thomas Wildenberg provides a very human view of the same topic with his biography of Admiral Joseph Mason Reeves, *All the Factors of Victory* (Washington, DC: Brassey's, 2003).

Numerous technical histories describe the design and construction of the Navy's ships, weapons, and fire-control systems. Foremost among these are the design histories of Norman Friedman: *U.S. Battleships*; *U.S. Aircraft Carriers*; *U.S. Cruisers*; *U.S. Small Combatants*; *U.S. Submarines through 1945*; and *U.S. Amphibious Ships and Craft* (all Annapolis, MD: Naval Institute Press, 1983–2002). Friedman's *U.S. Naval Weapons* (London: Conway, 1983) builds upon the Bureau of Ordnance history and describes the Navy's weapons systems in detail.

CHAPTER 7: SOVIET UNION

The most comprehensive and accessible overview of the Red Navy in this period is provided by Jürgen Rohwer and Mikhail S. Monakov, *Stalin's Ocean-Going Fleet: Soviet Naval Strategy and Shipbuilding Programmes 1935–1953* (London: Frank Cass, 2001). The interwar period has recently benefited from several outstanding studies, including N. Iu. Berezovskii, S. S. Berezhnoi, and Z. V. Nikolaeva, *Boevaia letopis' voenno-morskogo flota 1917–1941* (Moscow: Voennoe izdatel'stvo, 1993), which provides an enormous amount of information in the form of an extended chronology. V. Iu. Gibovskii's excellent *Morskaia politika SSSR i razvitie flota v predvoennye gody 1925–1941 gg.* (Moscow: Voennaia Kniga, 2006) is a more analytical look at the same period, as is Gunnar Åselius, *The Rise and Fall of the Soviet Navy in the Baltic, 1921–1941* (London: Frank Cass, 2005).

The general trends in Soviet naval doctrine are described in Robert Waring Herrick's classic study, *Soviet Naval Theory and Policy: Gorshkov's Inheritance* (Annapolis, MD: Naval Institute Press, 1989), but the more recent work by V. D. Dotsenko, A. A. Dotsenko, and V. F. Mironov, *Voenno-morskaia strategiia Rossii* (Moscow: Eksmo, 2005) is more detailed and based on archival sources.

Soviet ships and the shipbuilding industry are well covered in volume IV of I. P. Spasskii, ed., *Istoriia otechestvennogo sudostroeniia* (St. Petersburg: Sudostroenie, 1994–1996). Technical and operational information on surface warships as well as extensive descriptions of weapons and sensors can be found in A. V. Platonov, *Entsiklopediia Sovetskikh nadvodnykh korabli 1941–1945* (St. Petersburg: Poligon, 2002).

The immense task of reassessing the Red Navy's wartime performance free
from Soviet-era biases has not yet been tackled, but V. D. Dotsenko provides a good overview in *Flot-Voina-Pobeda, 1941–1945* (St. Petersburg:
Sudostroenie, 1995). More specific studies include A. V. Platonov's illu-
minating investigations, "Sovetskie podvodnye lodki na morskikh kom-
munikatsiiak protivnika," *Gangut* 48 (2008): 66–95; and "Sovetskie
torpednye katera v bor'be s morskimi perevozkami protivnika," *Gangut* 47
(2008): 82–96. Rolf Erikson's "Soviet Submarine Operations in World War
II," in *Reevaluating Major Naval Combatants of World War II*, ed. James J.
Sadkovich, 155–179 (New York: Greenwood Press, 1990) provides a useful though critical analysis. Finally, Friedrich Ruge's *The Soviets as Naval
Opponents 1941–1945* (Annapolis, MD: Naval Institute Press, 1979) is
still valuable for providing the "view from the other side of the hill."

GENERAL REFERENCES

David Brown, *Warship Losses of WW Two* (Annapolis, MD: Naval
Institute Press, 1995) is a convenient list of warships sunk in combat.
John Campbell's *Naval Weapons of World War Two* (Annapolis, MD:
Naval Institute Press, 2002) is the most comprehensive work of its
kind. For details about the warships themselves, the works of Michael
Whitley, all published by Naval Institute Press, are good. These include,
Battleships of World War Two (1998); *Cruisers of World War Two* (1995);
and *Destroyers of World War Two* (1998). Richard Worth's *Fleets of World
War II* (Cambridge, MA: Da Capo, 2001) is both handy and iconoclas-
tic, while Robert Gardiner's *Conway's All the World's Fighting Ships 1922–
1946* (New York: Mayflower, 1980), and *Conway's All the World's Fighting
Ships 1906–1921* (Annapolis, MD: Naval Institute Press, 1986) deserve
a place in every library. There are many photographic books, but Stuart
Robertson and Stephen Dent's *Conway's the War at Sea in Photographs
1939–1945* (London: Conway Maritime Press, 2007) stands out for its
depth of coverage. Finally, Jürgen Rohwer's massive *Chronology of the War
at Sea 1939–1945* (Annapolis, MD: Naval Institute Press, 2006) is indis-
pensible for keeping track of the naval war's widespread events.

Index